Effective Justice

Ius, Lex et Res Publica
Studies in Law, Philosophy and Political Cultures

Edited by Barbara Janusz-Pohl

Volume 38

Daniele Vicoli

Effective Justice. International and Comparative Approaches

Volume 1

PETER LANG

Berlin · Bruxelles · Chennai · Lausanne · New York · Oxford

Library of Congress Cataloging-in-Publication Data

Names: Vicoli, Daniele, editor.
Title: Effective justice, international, and comparative approaches.
Volume 1 / Daniele Vicoli (ed.).
Description: Oxford ; New York : Peter Lang, 2025. | Series: Ius, lex et res publica, 2191-3250 ; volume 38 | Includes bibliographical references.
Identifiers: LCCN 2025000647 | ISBN 9783631902011 (hardback) | ISBN 9783631929414 (ebook)
Subjects: LCSH: Effectiveness and validity of law--European Union countries. | International and municipal law--European Union countries. | Conflict of laws--European Union countries. | Justice, Administration of--European Union countries. | Comparative law--European Union countries. | Convention for the Protection of Human Rights and Fundamental Freedoms (1950 November 5) | Law--European Union countries.
Classification: LCC KJE5087 .E34 2025 | DDC 341.242/24--dc23/eng/20250113
LC record available at https://lccn.loc.gov/2025000647

Bibliographic Information published by the Deutsche Nationalbibliothek
The Deutsche Nationalbibliothek lists this publication in the Deutsche Nationalbibliografie; detailed bibliographic data is available in the internet at http://dnb.d-nb.de.

Cover illustration: Courtesy of Benjamin Ben Chaim.

This publication was financially supported by the Departement of Legal Studies, Alma Mater Studiorum University of Bologna, Italy.

ISSN 2191-3250
ISBN 978-3-631-90201-1 (Print)
E-ISBN 978-3-631-92941-4 (E-PDF)
E-ISBN 978-3-631-93511-8 (E-PUB)
DOI 10.3726/b22743

Published by Peter Lang GmbH, Berlin (Germany)

info@peterlang.com

This publication has been peer reviewed.

www.peterlang.com

Table of Contents

Daniele Vicoli
Introduction 7

Daniele Vicoli
Editorial – Effective Justice: Between Efficiency and Guarantees 13

Part I Organisation of Judicial Systems 17

Barbara Janusz-Pohl
I. Perceptions of the Effectiveness and Its Interdisciplinary Approach – Keynotes 19

Benedetta Arrighini
II. Effectiveness Through Approximation in the EU Area of Freedom Security and Justice 51

Jacek Szkudlarek
III. The Impact of the Rule of Law Backslide on Revision of the Competences of the Court of Justice of the European Union on the Matter of Member States' Domestic Jurisprudence 69

Ana Beltrán Montoliu
IV. Organizational Efficiency in the Spanish Judicial Power: New Trends 93

Andrea Planchadell-Gargallo
V. Access to Justice and Proximity Justice in Spain: the Valencian Model 109

Justyna Głębocka
VI. Model of Pre-trial Proceedings and Its Influence on the Judicial Stage of Criminal Proceedings: A Comparative Analysis of European Legal Systems 121

Konrad Burdziak
VII. Applying the Achievements of 20th and 21st-Century Psychology to the Organisation of Justice: Remarks on the Improvement of Judicial Activity 139

Marcin Rau
VIII. Challenging Legal Education in Pursuit of Judicial Efficiency: A Comparative Analysis of Poland and Italy 173

Part II Digital Justice 193

Alejandro Hernández López
I. The European Union's Strategy on Digitalisation of Judicial Cooperation in Criminal Matters: Towards a More Effective Justice in Cross-Border Scenarios? 195

Marianna Biral
II. The Italian Route towards Digitalisation of Criminal Proceedings – The Latest Developments in the Field of Remote Justice 217

Ewa Aleksandra Płocha
III. The Impact of AI-based Recidivism Risk Assessment Instruments on Human Decision-Making in Criminal Justice: COMPAS Case Study in the Context of Polish and European Union Law 235

Kristjan Kask, Annegrete Palu, Mari-Liis Tohvelmann, Pekka Santtila
IV. Systematic Literature Review of Associations Between Question Type and Adult Witnesses' Accuracy: A Step in Creating a Digital Solution to Train Law Enforcement Personnel's Investigative Interviewing Skills 259

Daniele Vicoli

Introduction

The following book is the culmination of the collaborative efforts of dedicated researchers within the Effective Justice International and Comparative Approaches Platform, which officially launched its activities in December 2021. This platform was led by Prof. UAM Dr. hab. Barbara Janusz-Pohl from the Faculty of Law and Administration at Adam Mickiewicz University and Prof. Daniele Vicoli from the Department of Legal Sciences at the University of Bologna.

The platform was dedicated to advancing scientific knowledge through a wide range of activities, including hosting international seminars and spearheading initiatives aimed at consolidating research efforts in the field of effectiveness, particularly in criminal proceedings at large. With an emphasis on comparative and international analysis, the platform attracted a diverse and global community of researchers. This resulted in a robust network of over 40 individuals representing more than 20 scientific centers, fostering both permanent and periodic cooperation. The platform's activities can be followed at www.effective-justice.com.

This book is divided into two parts. The first focuses on organisation of judicial systems, while the second on digital justice. The topics discussed in both parts are related to the effectiveness of criminal proceedings, procedural actions, and selected legal institutions. The chapters address a range of issues, including national and international themes, particularly those relevant to the links with the European Convention on Human Rights and the European Union law.

The first part is introduced by Barbara Janusz-Pohl's chapter *Perceptions of the Effectiveness and Its Interdisciplinary Approach – Keynotes*. The author explores the concept of effectiveness from various perspectives. Starting from a semantic point of view, the essay provides a comprehensive examination of how effectiveness is perceived in economic sciences and psychology, drawing on selected philosophical concepts such as the praxeological perception of action by Tadeusz Kotarbiński and the frame of constitutive rules as elaborated by John Searle and Stanisław Czepita. Against this background it is outlined that effectiveness is perceived as a complex notion in legal sciences, especially in the field of procedural law. Regarding criminal proceedings, it is suggested that the concept of effectiveness must be analyzed on the basis of the goals set for the given activities.

In the two chapters that follow the crucial role of European institutions in the pursuit of effectiveness in the field of criminal proceedings is highlighted.

Based on the assumption that approximation (i.e, harmonization) represents an instrument for effective cooperation between EU Member States, *Effectiveness through Approximation in the EU Area of Freedom Security and Justice* by Benedetta Arrighini analyses the degree of harmonization of national criminal procedures in the light of selected relevant Directives. The author concludes that, at this stage, the process of achieving full effectiveness through approximation still needs to be completed, as challenges persist in balancing national sovereignty with EU-wide integration and (especially) with the rights of the accused.

The Impact of The Rule of Law Backslide on Revision of the Competences of The Court of Justice of the European Union on the Matter of Member States' Domestic Jurisprudence by Jacek Szkudlarek explores the European Court of Justice's case-law regarding the organization of the judiciary in the Member States. Firstly, the attention is focused on the guarantees of independence and impartiality that, according to the European Court of Justice, must inspire the rules concerning the appointment and composition of judicial bodies, the length of service, and the grounds for abstention, rejection, and dismissal of its members. Then, looking in particular at the Polish system, three fields are taken into consideration: the disciplinary measures upon judges, the appointment of judges, and judicial cooperation in criminal matters. The paper aims to highlight some degree of incoherence and inconsistency of the European Court of Justice's approach when it comes to the protection of fundamental rights and the rule of law.

The two following chapters are focused on the Spanish judicial system.

Organizational Efficiency in the Spanish Judicial Power: New Trends by Ana Beltrán Montoliu examines the reforms enacted within the Justice 2030 framework, and in particular the laws on Organizational Efficiency (LOE), Procedural Efficiency (LPE), and Digital Efficiency (LDE). The author emphasizes the aims pursued by the legislator: to restructure court models, enhance specialization, and increase the use of technology in order to improve access and communication within the judiciary.

In *Access to Justice and Proximity Justice in Spain: The Valencian Model* by Andrea Planchadell-Gargallo the efficiency of the judicial system is considered from the perspective of the right to access to justice. From this point of view, there is a need to adapt the territorial organization of the courts with a closer approach to citizens. In this regard, the author mentions the *Justiprop* service, i.e., a legal aid service set up in the Valencian Community, whose aim is to ensure citizens' access to justice, both in terms of knowing their rights and effectively exercising them.

Within the chapter entitled *Model of Pre-Trial Proceedings and Its Influence on the Judicial Stage of Criminal Proceedings: A Comparative Analysis of European Legal Systems* the analysis of the relationship between organizational aspects (understood in a broad sense) and effectiveness of criminal proceedings is carried out on the basis of a comparative approach. In particular, Justyna Glebocka gives an overview of four European systems: French, German, Italian, and Polish. The starting point is that although they share the same or similar values, European legislations uphold different pre-trial proceedings models, which fundamentally affect the shape of the overall judicial proceedings. In particular, the choice impacts the effectiveness of the entire criminal procedure, understood as the demand for a quick, efficient, but also fair (truthful and respectful of the guarantee rights of the parties and participants) adjudication of the criminal case. On the basis of this assumption, the author discusses the most important features of the pre-trial investigation models in force in the considered countries, indicating their objectives, the scope of evidentiary activities, and, consequently, their impact on the stage of court proceedings.

The chapter by Konrad Burdziak *Applying the Achievements of 20th and 21st-Century Psychology to the Organisation of Justice. Remarks on the Improvement of Judicial Activity* deals with the influence of fields of knowledge other than law – in this case, psychology – on evaluating and redesigning a given legislation to make it work better and more effectively. The case study is represented by the regulation of pre-trial detention in the Polish system. The author analyses the relationship between the rationality of decisions and the provisions regulating them. According to the results of a legal-dogmatic method, the work gives a negative answer to whether the Polish legislator has created conditions for courts to make rational decisions regarding the possibility and justification of applying the institution of pre-trial detention in a given case. Consequently, several solutions – based on the achievements of modern psychology – are proposed to improve the degree of rationality of judicial decisions in the field of pre-trial detention.

In the last chapter of the first part *Challenging Legal Education in Pursuit of Judicial Efficiency: A Comparative Analysis of Poland and Italy* the value of effectiveness is considered from the perspective of legal education. As the value of legal education has a direct impact on the level of efficiency of the justice system, it is crucial that teaching methods keep pace with the contemporary legal landscape. Based on this assumption, Marcin Rau carries out a comparative analysis of legal education systems in Poland and Italy against the innovative model at Berkeley Law School in the United States and points to a significant disconnect between the traditional academic approach and the evolving needs of the legal profession, particularly in the digital age. Considering the successful experience of Berkeley's integrated teaching approach, reforms are proposed to adapt legal education to the expectations of new generations, incorporating interactive and technologically advanced methods.

The second part of the book is dedicated to digital justice. The topic is explored from different perspectives.

In the chapter *The European Union's Strategy on Digitalisation of Judicial Cooperation in Criminal Matters: Towards a More Effective Justice in Cross-Border Scenarios?* by Alejandro Hernández López, the focus is on European policies on new technologies applied to judicial cooperation between EU Member States. The author analyses the content of the Proposal for a Regulation COM (2021) 759 and the Proposal for a Directive COM (2021) 760, which have subsequently led to the adoption of Regulation 2023/2844/EU. Among the issues addressed, communication by digital means and the use of videoconferencing in cross-border criminal proceedings are outlined as of paramount importance.

The topic of videoconferencing is also addressed in the following chapter. *The Italian Route towards Digitalisation of Criminal Proceedings. The Latest Developments in the Field of Remote Justice* by Marianna Biral analyzes the significant increase in the use of video links for participation in procedural acts and hearings provided by the Italian legislator in 2022. After an overview of the milestones in the evolution of the meaning and scope of remote justice within the realm of the Italian criminal procedure, the author highlights potentialities and drawbacks of the recent legislative developments. She also offers some insights on making the regulation of the waiver of physical participation of parties and witnesses more guarantee-oriented.

The chapter by Ewa Aleksandra Płocha (*The Impact of AI-based Recidivism Risk Assessment Instruments on Human Decision-Making in Criminal Justice: COMPAS Case Study in the Context of Polish and European Union Law*) addresses a topic of paramount importance: the use of Artificial Intelligence systems as an assistive tool on human decision-making in criminal cases and, in the most radical scenario, as a substitute for the judge. In this regard, a significant development is represented by the COMPAS (Correctional Offender Management Profiling for Alternative Sanctions) software, which has been used as a recidivism risk assessment instrument in the United States. After describing COMPAS and the approach of American jurisprudence and scholars towards it, the author examines the possibility of using such an algorithm under Polish and EU legal regulations. The analysis shows that COMPAS does not meet the constitutional and EU standards regarding human rights ('AI Act'). In the author's view, such a conclusion does not lead to an outright and irrefutable rejection of AI systems. Algorithmic tools for assessing the risk of recidivism are still being improved, and perhaps in the future, they will become trustworthy (legal, ethical, and robust), and the EU will change its attitude toward them. However, in the author's opinion, using such tools is not recommended at the moment: the risk of violating fundamental human rights and freedoms is too high.

In the last chapter, entitled *Systematic Literature Review of Associations Between Question Type and Adult Witnesses' Accuracy: A Step in Creating a Digital Solution to Train Law Enforcement Personnel's Investigative Interviewing Skills* Kristjan Kask, Annegrete Palu, Mari-Liis Tohvelmann, and Pekka Santtila address the topic of witness interviewing skills on the part of the law enforcement personnel. The essay moves from the recognition of a lack. While the issue of interviewing techniques is broadly acknowledged and discussed both in literature and among legal practitioners, attention is paid almost exclusively to challenges arising when child witnesses are to be examined. The authors' proposition is to contribute both theoretical and practical to the debate on interviewing techniques for adult witnesses. In this regard, they illustrate the results of an extensive review of the relevant literature and provide valuable insights and suggestions to develop solutions – also in the form of dedicated software and other digital systems – to train law enforcement agencies.

Daniele Vicoli*

Editorial – Effective Justice: Between Efficiency and Guarantees

In the context of analyses that outline the foundations on which a procedural system must be built, one of the most controversial and debated issues concerns balancing the various interests deserving protection.

The approach to the problem must start from a premise that cannot be doubted: the criminal trial must be attributed the function of guaranteeing the defendant. Recognition of the right to personal liberty implies that means of protection are provided with respect to the activities of the public authorities aimed at ascertaining crimes. This perspective highlights the relationship that links the inviolable nature of personal liberty to the necessary provision of adequate guarantees. In this sense, the right to judicial protection must be included among the individual's fundamental rights.

At the same time, trial is the means by which the provisions of criminal law are implemented. Consequently the legislator must also consider the need to ascertain crimes when laying down procedural rules.

In this respect, there is a widespread tendency to consider that the State's interest in punishing the perpetrators of criminal conducts finds expression in the value of efficiency, which thus assumes the role of an essential component of the procedural system.

Such an idea is further developed in a logical scheme that opposes guarantees and efficiency. In particular, this way of reasoning, with a view to ensuring a reasonable balance between the different interests involved, assigns to efficiency the function of limiting the expansion of guarantees, which might otherwise grow to the point that the process cannot go ahead.

It has been suggested however that this approach should be superseded by a different idea of efficiency, i.e., as a value to be related not only to the public interest in combating crime but, more generally, to all the objectives underlying criminal justice.

---

* Associate Professor of Criminal Procedure, Department of Legal Sciences, Alma Mater Studiorum University of Bologna, Italy.

According to this view, the criminal process can be considered efficient when it recognizes and achieves the plurality of purposes it is built upon, among which protecting the defendant's fundamental rights plays a prominent role. From this perspective, efficiency must be translated into a 'balanced' procedural system, i.e., one capable of functioning as a whole with a reasonable cost-benefit scheme.

The advantages of this approach are easy to understand. If efficiency is related to the overall purposes of criminal justice, its implementation is also instrumental in strengthening guarantees according to a pattern under which implementing efficiency would mean implementing guarantees.

This approach reflects the idea that efficiency is necessary to make the criminal justice system effective by considering all the interests and needs that qualify the criminal procedure.

Of course the concept of effectiveness is not easy to define. In legal philosophy effectiveness refers to norms: a norm is effective if observed or applied. This definition is helpful because it highlights that effectiveness is a gradable concept according to the degree of compliance. This is a good starting point; however, further steps must be taken for the purposes here. The concept of effectiveness must be considered in relation to another criterion: efficacy.

The reference is not to the technical-legal notion of efficacy (i.e., the attitude of a rule to produce legal effects) but to the philosophical one, according to which a rule is efficacious if it fulfills its intended purposes.

Traces of this approach can be found in the jurisprudence of the European Court of Justice (ECJ), which, over the years, has developed the principle of effectiveness as a cornerstone of European Union law. In particular, with regard to individual rights and their protection, the principle of effectiveness has been intended and conceptualized in these words: "This philosophy is very simple indeed. It means that legal rules, by their very nature, have a practical purpose. Any legal rule is devised to operate effectively (…). If it is not operative, it is not a rule of law (…). Effectiveness is the very soul of legal rules and therefore (…) it is not excessive to say that any legal rule must be at first sight presumed to be operative in view of its object and purpose" (P. Pescatore, 'The Doctrine of Direct Effect: An Infant Disease of Community Law', 8 *European Law Review* 1983, p. 155).

A similar perspective has been developed within the European Convention on Human Rights (ECHR) system. On many occasions, the importance of the principle of effectiveness as an interpretative criterion has been stressed: conventional provisions must be interpreted in such a way that the affirmed rights are of "practical and effective" use to the complaints.

Understood in this way, effectiveness can also be examined according to reasoning models based on the economic analysis of law. Studies of this kind consider efficiency as the critical parameter of evaluation and selection among different regulations of a particular phenomenon the one that produces the most efficient results. In this sense, rules are conceived as mechanisms for allocating limited resources.

In particular, when discussing justice systems, efficiency concerns the relationship between the aims pursued and the means employed to achieve them. From this point of view, a rule can be said to be efficient if there is no way of fulfilling the aim with less expensive means or if there is no way of fulfilling the objective to a higher degree using the same means.

In evaluations following schemes of this kind, efficacy also comes into play. Indeed, a rule can be able to reach the intended goal but excessively costly, as it achieves its purpose but at an excessive cost. Therefore, under the economic analysis of law, an efficient rule is also efficacious, meaning that it achieves its purpose in the most advantageous and resource-saving way, i.e., without wasting resources, whereas an efficacious rule is not always efficient.

The economic theory must be cautiously considered when applied to criminal proceedings: there is the risk of weakening the protection of fundamental rights, first and foremost, the right to personal liberty.

However, also in this field, the economic theory based approach is relevant and helpful as it enlightens an other aspect of the concept of effectiveness. It has been said that, in general terms, effectiveness is a trait of the rules as applied. More specifically, effectiveness must be combined with the parameter of efficacy, understood as the suitability of a rule to achieve the purpose given which it is set; in addition, effectiveness must be pursued efficiently, i.e., on the basis of a balanced relationship with the means employed.

The outcome of the reasoning is that effectiveness must be considered in close connection with the means chosen to achieve the procedural system's underlying purposes. Those means must be both efficacious and efficient.

In this regard, the direction to be taken is very clear: the means must be found in the 'due process' clause as it is outlined by supranational sources, particularly Art. 6 ECHR and Arts. 47 and 48 Charter of Fundamental Rights of the European Union (CFR).

'Due process' guarantees represent, in fact, the ultimate chain ring in the sequence that starts from the inviolable nature of personal liberty and develops through the recognition of the right to lawful judgment.

The adversarial process, the impartial role of the judge, the equality of arms, and the reasonable length are fundamental traits of criminal proceedings, meaning that a criminal proceedings is to be deemed 'fair' provided that these requirements are met.

The mentioned guarantees constitute the means for adjudicating the case which are capable of ensuring the effectiveness of the interests involved in criminal proceedings. In this sense, the 'due process' clause traces the path to the judgment, which finds justification based on the route covered to get there.

Each of those principles and guarantees represents a necessary condition in the absence of which it is not permissible or is prohibited to punish.

It is in light of this idea that effectiveness shall be acknowledged. In other words, effectiveness cannot be interpreted in bare economic terms: it must be considered as the expression of the optimal relationship between the aims pursued and the means (i.e., the 'due process' clause) to be employed.

Part I
Organisation of Judicial Systems

Barbara Janusz-Pohl*

I. Perceptions of the Effectiveness and Its Interdisciplinary Approach – Keynotes

Abstract: In this paper, the author explores the concept of effectiveness from various perspectives. The author delves into the etymology of the term 'effectiveness', tracing it back to the Latin word 'effectivus'. From a semantic standpoint, the paper analyzes three synonymous terms: effectiveness, efficacy and efficiency. Furthermore, the chapter provides a comprehensive examination of how effectiveness is perceived in economic sciences and psychology, drawing on selected philosophical concepts such as the praxeological perception of action by Tadeusz Kotarbiński and the frame of constitutive rules as elaborated by Searle and Czepita. It is said that in legal sciences, especially procedures, effectiveness is perceived as a complex notion. More often used somehow intuitively, those intuitions align with the linguistic perception of notions at hand (based on the dictionary). However, the adjective effective is a part of legal language, as, for example, in reference to Art. 13 ECHR or Art. 19 TEU (effective remedy). Lawey's perception of effectiveness refers to the particular actions, tools, or par/whole of the proceedings. Regarding the effectiveness of proceedings, this notion is analysed through its goals.

Keywords: Effectiveness, efficacy, efficiency, constitutive rules, praxeology

1. Introduction

The analysis of effectiveness addressed to the law can cover many aspects, among them the effectiveness of the law itself (taken phenomenologically), law-making and implementation of legal policies, as well as such topics as the efficacy of legal norms coupled with the issue of validity and observance to the law, or even the effectiveness of the legal system from the perspective

* Professor UAM Dr. hab., Adam Mickiewicz University, Poznan, Poland.

of the implementation of its selected functions, such as social participation in the justice system[1].

Crucially for these considerations, the study of effectiveness (this term in general discussion will be interchangeably explored with the terms effectivity and efficacy)[2] from the point of view of legal sciences may also concern legal proceedings, taken both *in abstracto* (as established procedures) and *in concreto* (as a set of participants in legal proceedings' actions). The examination of the concrete legal proceedings based on the rules of a given system shall, in turn, includes the study of the realisation of the goals and functions assigned to the types of proceedings, effectiveness of the actions of individual participants in these proceedings due to the chosen tactics of action (this prism of analysis is relevant, especially in the case of the so-called private non-institutional participants in legal proceedings). In addition, inquiries into the effectiveness may concern selected institutions and their functioning efficacy, or, finally, it may include individual acts, i.e. the specific actions of the participants in the proceedings ('effectiveness of procedural actions'). Moreover, in law research, effectivity can have praxeological connotations, consistent with the perception of the concept at hand in general (standard) language and within other sciences: psychology, management sciences or philosophy. Nonetheless, in the study of effectiveness

---

1 Efficacy has different meanings within legal discourse. It may, e.g., refer to the capacity of legal norms to produce legal effects (e.g., rights, duties, liabilities, etc.) or to their capacity to realise the goals for which they were produced or to the fact that the addressees of legal norms actually behave as they require of them: see Z. Ziembiński, 'The Typology of Legal Norms' in: P. Kwiatkowski, M. Smolak (eds.), *Poznań School of Legal Theory*, Leiden: Brill 2021, pp. 77–90; Z. Ziembiński, 'Legal Provisions and Legal Norms' in: P. Kwiatkowski, M. Smolak (eds.) *Poznań School of Legal Theory*, Leiden: Brill 2021, pp. 63–76. See also on basics L. Burazin, 'The Concept of Law and Efficacy' in: M. Sellers, S. Kirste, S. (eds.) *Encyclopaedia of the Philosophy of Law and Social Philosophy*, Dordrecht: Springer 2017. The conducted research indicates that the effectiveness of legal norms, which indirectly can be combined with the principle of general prevention in criminal cases when the efficacy of legal norms refers to the fact that the addressees of legal norms observe to them, as well as the perception of effectiveness and the other categories, are proportional to the participation in criminal proceedings - both active and fair participation of private participants in the proceedings, as well as the so-called social participation.

2 The example of the use of the term effectivity, see J. d'Aspremont, *'Effectivity' in international law: self-empowerment against epistemological claustrophobia*, available at: effectivity_in_international_law_selfempowerment_against_epistemological_claustrophobia.pdf [accessed on: July 1st, 2024].

as a category referred to the law, one shall point to an issue (that is distinct to this area of knowledge) purely in the normative connotation of the effectiveness perceived as a sanction for violating the rules for performing certain legal actions. In the present discussion, we will focus on these two variants, the effectiveness conceived praxeologically and perceived normatively. Moreover, in further analysis, the mixt category will also be explained.

At the outset, it should be noted that the study of the meaning of effectiveness is carried out on the grounds of the English language. At the same time – undoubtedly- this term and its synonyms occur in all other languages and, for each country, appear in standard and legal (statutory) or juridical languages. Since analyses referring to effectiveness are often originally written in national languages and only secondarily translated into English, the fine semiotic differences between effectiveness and its synonyms might be lost in the translation process. Consequently, such a state of affairs does not help when exploring linguistic approaches to effectiveness in legal sciences.

Thus, the purpose of this paper is primarily to carry out an attempt to define the perceptions of effectiveness (effectivity) in the legal sciences and to indicate the coherent methodological basis for this concept. In pursuit of the goal, the following steps are to taken: a) dictionary definitions will be traced (linguistic approach) b) then the use of the concepts of effectiveness (effectivity), efficacy and efficiency use in various fields of knowledge and scientific disciplines, including psychology, management sciences, philosophy (especially praxeology) will be explored (interdisciplinary approach), and finally c) selected contexts of the functioning of the concept of effectiveness in legal systems will be examined (application oriented approach). Due to the limited scope of this study, the discussion referred strictly to legal sciences will be given through the example of criminal proceedings, with particular regard to the regulations on Polish criminal procedure.

2. Description of the Relevant Notions – Linguistic Approach

The foundational step in our exploration is an in-depth semantic analysis. As a preliminary framework, do note that the starting term is the adjective 'effective', that finds its roots in the Latin word *effectivus*. Based on the derivation of the etymons 'effective' and the suffix '-ness' or '-ity', the nouns effectiveness and effectivity are created[3]. In our consideration, the assumption has

3 '*Effective*' in: *Merriam-Webster Dictionary*, available at: https://www.merriam-webster.com/dictionary/effective [accessed on: September 11th, 2024].

been taken that the term effectiveness is the principal version to be explored. However, both terms are defined by English language dictionaries based on the definition of the same adjective effective. Consequently, based on linguistic approaches, any differentiation between the terms effectiveness and effectivity cannot be made.

Assumedly, when analysing the notion of effectiveness in legal sciences, so in statutory and legal (jurisprudential) language, first, we must refer to its meaning as general (standard) language, namely notions by the dictionaries (by exploring the linguistic approach), thus when it comes to the topic at hand, one may distinguish three relevant terms that refer to three adjectives: effective, efficacious and efficient and the nouns derived from them: so about adjective effective, the nouns effectiveness and effectivity; in relation the adjective efficacious the noun efficacy; and regarding the adjective efficient the noun efficiency. One may add to this additional adjective effectual that has similar phraseological ground but a different meaning, as effectual specifically implies the production of the desired effect or result[4].

Let's commence our investigation with a comprehensive approach be based on several different sources: *Cambridge Dictionary*, *Oxford Dictionary*, *Collins Dictionary*, *Merriam-Webster Dictionary* and *Britannica Dictionary*.

The *Cambridge Dictionary* emphasises that effectiveness and the noun effectivity are derived from the adjective "effective", which is defined as the degree to which something successfully produces the intended results[5].

Moreover, this definition is very typical for other English language dictionaries as well. It must be mentioned that recognition of its crucial element, which is centred on the formula of "intended results", is also typical in legal analysis (these perceptions are based on the observation of the legal proceedings (as a whole) through the lens of the realisation of goals attributed to such proceedings. On the other hand, the term efficacy is characterised as the ability of something to produce the intended effect; the quality of being effective; and as synonymous with the term effectiveness (effectivity)[6]. In the same dictionary, among the definitions of the term efficiency, the most characteristic are those stipulating that it is the quality of achieving the largest amount of useful work using as little energy, fuel,

4 'Effectual' in: *Collins Dictionary*, available at: https://www.collinsdictionary.com/dictionary/english/effectual [accessed on: July 1st, 2024].

5 'Effectiveness' in: *Cambridge Dictionary*, available at: https://dictionary.cambridge.org/dictionary/english/effectiveness [accessed on: July 1st, 2024].

6 'Efficacy' in: *Cambridge Dictionary*, available at: https://dictionary.cambridge.org/dictionary/english/efficacy [accessed on: July 1st, 2024].

effort, or the quality of working well in an organised way, without wasting time or energy; or something that is done to avoid wasting time, energy, or money[7].

In another source, namely in the *Collins Dictionary* the term efficacy is defined as the quality of being successful in producing an intended result; the closest synonymous of effectiveness (effectivity)[8]. In the *Merriam-Webster Dictionary*, efficacy is the power to produce effects or intended results (also effectiveness)[9]. Moreover, in both dictionaries, effectiveness is defined as the ability to produce intended results[10]. Notably, there is no difference in these definitions of efficacy and effectiveness. In turn, the *Collins Dictionary* defines efficiency as the quality or state of being efficient and as the *ratio* of the useful work done by a machine, engine, device, etc, to the energy supplied to it, often expressed as a percentage[11]. Additionally, efficiency in American English, based on *Merriam-Webster Dictionary*, is defined as the ability to produce a desired effect, product, etc., with a minimum of effort, expense, or waste; quality or fact of being efficient; the *ratio* of effective work to the energy expended in producing it, as of a machine; output divided by input[12].

So far, the dictionary definitions presented by various sources are quite uniform. So, let's examine some more examples. Thus, based on the *Britannica Dictionary*, efficacy is proposed as the closest synonymous with effectiveness and characterises as the power to produce a desired result or effect[13]. Effectiveness (and effectivity) is defined by the adjective effective, which means producing

---

7 'Efficiency' in: *Cambridge Dictionary*, available at: https://dictionary.cambridge.org/dictionary/english/efficiency [accessed on: July 1st, 2024].

8 'Efficacy' in: *Collins Dictionary*, available at: https://www.collinsdictionary.com/dictionary/english/efficacy [accessed on: July 1st, 2024].

9 'Efficacy' in: *Merriam-Webster Dictionary*, available at: https://www.merriam-webster.com/dictionary/efficacy [accessed on: July 1st, 2024].

10 'Effectiveness' in: *Collins Dictionary*, available at: https://www.collinsdictionary.com/dictionary/english/effective [accessed on: July 1st, 2024]; 'Effectiveness' in: *Merriam-Webster Dictionary*, available at: https://www.merriam-webster.com/dictionary/effectiveness [accessed on: July 1st, 2024].

11 'Efficiency' in: *Collins Dictionary*, available at: https://www.collinsdictionary.com/dictionary/english/efficiency [accessed on: July 1st, 2024].

12 'Efficiency' in: *Merriam-Webster Dictionary* https://www.merriam-webster.com/dictionary/efficiency [accessed on: July 1st, 2024].

13 'Efficacy' in: *Britannica Dictionary*, available at: https://www.britannica.com/dictionary/efficacy [accessed on: July 1st, 2024].

a result that is wanted: having an intended effect[14]. This dictionary offers a very typical definition of efficiency as the ability to do something or produce something without wasting materials, time, or energy: the quality or degree of being efficient[15].

At the end, have a look at the definitions given by the *Oxford Dictionary*. This collection explores the term efficacy as the ability to create (the expected) effect, and yet, based on the examples of its use, seems to be broader than effectiveness[16]. On the contrary, effectiveness is understood as the quality of being effective[17], and effective means producing the result that is wanted or intended or producing a successful result[18]. This collection presents several definitions of efficiency (adjective efficient). The first one is very general, "The state or quality of being efficient". The second one – the technical definition – is much more interesting. It defines efficiency as the *ratio* of the valuable work performed by a machine or in a process to the total energy expended or heat taken in[19]. Consequently, efficiency is about doing things most economically regarding time, energy, or money.

When analysing the definitions indicated above, several conclusions may be drawn.

First, on the one hand, the definitions presented are very similar, but on the other hand, closer inspection allows for the conclusion that they differ slightly in some aspects, especially when one explores the phraseological constructions, being the examples of the use of relevant notions.

Secondly, it can indeed be pointed out that the dictionary definitions enable one to indicate that connotations of the terms effectiveness and efficacy shall be distinguished from the meaning of the word efficiency. At the same time, against the background of some dictionary definitions, the meanings of effectiveness

---

14 'Effectiveness' in: *Britannica Dictionary*, available at: https://www.britannica.com/dictionary/effective [accessed on: July 1st, 2024].

15 'Efficiency' in: *Britannica Dictionary*, available at: https://www.britannica.com/dictionary/efficiency [accessed on: July 1st, 2024].

16 'Efficacy' in: *Oxford Dictionary*, available at: https://www.oed.com/search/dictionary/?scope=Entries&q=efficacy [accessed on: July 1st, 2024].

17 'Effectiveness' in: *Oxford Dictionary*, available at: https://www.oed.com/search/dictionary/?scope=Entries&q=effectiveness [accessed on: July 1st, 2024].

18 'Effective' in: *Oxford Dictionary*, available at: https://www.oed.com/search/dictionary/?scope=Entries&q=effective [accessed on: July 1st, 2024].

19 'Efficiency' in: *Oxford Dictionary*, available at: https://www.oed.com/search/dictionary/?scope=Entries&q=efficiency [accessed on: July 1st, 2024].

and efficacy are identical or very similar, as these notions are the closest synonyms to each other. Nevertheless, according to some definitions of effectiveness and efficacy, it can be pointed out that the concept of efficacy is somewhat broader than effectiveness. Regarding definitions of efficacy, the elements in the form of "intended results", and "obtaining result that is wanted" are less significant. Moreover, it should be added that the term "intended results" explored in the definitions of effectiveness should be equated with the term: "objectives or goals". Yet, when it comes to efficacy, it is often sufficient that the condition of "ability to create the effect" is met, and there is no requirement of "achieving intended results".

Thirdly, unfortunately, these dictionary definitions do not provide for an ultimate and unambiguous understanding of the differences between efficacy and effectiveness, and what is worse, all these terms are treated as synonyms, with the proviso that effectiveness and efficacy are the closest synonyms for each other, and (both) they are further synonyms for efficiency. All this makes it hard to explore these terms precisely in legal and juridical language.

Nevertheless, anticipatively using the knowledge about these three terms' definitions on the grounds of various sciences (especially management sciences and philosophy), and only If one would try to grasp the semantic differences between these notions, the following description shall be proposed.

- Efficacy means getting things done.
- Effectiveness (effectivity) shall mean getting the right things done (focusing on the purposes of a given act)
- Efficiency means doing things right—comparing a solution's input to its output.

Consequently, it is not feasible to place a sign of equality between, on the one hand, effectiveness and efficacy and, on the other hand, efficiency; precisely, one shall effectively get (the right, intended) things done, but in an inefficient manner. As a result, the notion of effectiveness (effectivity) covers the ability to achieve intended goals, while efficiency is the level of performance that uses the least amount of inputs, such as resources. Consequently, effectiveness produces an improved result (the result is perceived as preferable based on the given system of accepted values). In contrast, efficiency produces a result that utilises the fewest number of resources or the least amount of time. In this 'triada' of notions, efficacy seems to be more generic than effectiveness.

At this point of the inquiry, it is essential to note that the concept of effectiveness is more specialised in numerous scientific disciplines; some of these meanings will be discussed below.

3. Effectiveness Based on Interdisciplinary Approaches: Economic Sciences, Psychology, Philosophy

Noticeably, the concepts of effectiveness, efficacy and efficiency function differently in the various sciences. Further analysis will show certain rules. Yet, in the framework of sciences in which the objectives of activities being evaluated in the plane of effectiveness are measurable in objective reality (material realm) then, the notions of effectiveness, efficacy and efficiency appear almost as interchangeable, and indeed, the perception of efficiency becomes very close to the effectiveness (effectivity) or efficacy. On the other hand, effectiveness becomes much broader than efficacy in areas where the objectives of the activities to be evaluated are – diversified or non-measurable, difficult to assess, not quantified, or mixed (i.e. combining measurable and non-measurable objectives) as well as purely axiological (being subject to advanced relativisation - if only because of who is evaluating the activity). The economic sciences undoubtedly are examples of the former category, i.e. areas in which the achievement of the goals programmed for the given activities is objectively measurable.

Nevertheless, in the area of economic sciences, one can point to at least a few examples of differentiation of effectiveness and efficiency. Similarly, a psychology that is based on quantified evaluation and empirical studies. Different examples are set by philosophy or legal sciences, especially in the latter, where effectiveness evaluation is multilayered.

A) Economic and psychological theories: goals-oriented and systemic perception of the effectiveness and optimal efficiency and 'self-efficacy beliefs' ideas

As mentioned in the introduction, to gain a profound understanding closely tied to the study of effectiveness, we must refer to its interpretation in the economic sciences, especially in management sciences. Yet, in the realm of economic perception, the distinction between being 'effective' and 'efficient' is subtle[20]. Generally, when studying economic concepts, we do not focus on the terminological framework but on developing the concept of efficacy.

---

20 R. Poskart, 'A definition of the concept of economic effectiveness', 2(3) *Central Eastern European Journal of Management and Economics* 2014, pp. 179–187. The Author presents an overview of the Polish literature on the subject i.e. works: M. Bielski, *Organizacje: istota, struktury, procesy*, 3rd ed., Łódź: University of Łódź Publishing 2001; L. Czechowski, *Wielowymiarowa ocena efektywności ekonomicznej przedsiębiorstwa przemysłowego*, Gdańsk: University of Gdańsk Publishing 1997.

Hence, in the economic dimension, effectiveness is most commonly understood as a firm acting in such a way as to maximise the output given certain (constant) inputs – this is the so-called productivity formulation. In this field, it is also important to differentiate and compare concepts of effectiveness in resource utilisation, production, and labour[21]. For our discussion, the distinction between the goal-based and systemic interpretations of effectiveness seems to be valid. The first accentuates the goal of the actions carried out (utilisation of resources) within a firm/organisation, whereas the second treats the organisation as a system with similar properties to a living organism (effectiveness is understood as the ability of such an organism to obtain resources from the environment and utilise them to function and develop)[22]. As it is explained, the goal-oriented perception means that achieving goals is the starting point of the activities of a given entity, and the management should make decisions to achieve the stated goals at the lowest possible cost[23]. In this perception, effectiveness is measured by the efficacy of a firm (in achieving its goals) and efficiency in using resources (achieving a given ratio of outputs to inputs). As observed in the literature, the essence of effectiveness is understood based on three elements: goals, effects, and inputs[24].

In turn, it is said that in the systemic approach, the effectiveness is understood from the point of view of three elements: inputs, the transformation process and effects[25]. Consequently, one element differs between the goal-oriented and systemic approaches, and an estimation point is pushed from the goals to the transformation process. Shortly, instead of the assessment versus the realisation of goals, the whole transformation process of the given unit creates the prism for the evaluation[26]. In a systemic approach, effectiveness is measured by the ability of a firm to overcome difficulties resulting from variability in the firm's situation

21 R. Poskart, 'A definition…', p. 180; R. C. Sickles, V. Zelenyuk, *Measurement of Productivity and Efficiency: Theory and Practice*, Cambridge University Press 2019, *passim*.

22 R. Poskart, 'A definition…', pp. 180–181 and the literature cited therein.

23 R. Poskart, 'A definition…', p. 181. The criterion for assessing effectiveness is the efficacy of a firm's activities in the sense of maximising the level of agreement between the effects and the firm's goals and the rationality of the utilisation of resources according to two measures: profit and profitability.

24 R. Poskart, 'A definition…', p. 182.

25 R. Poskart, 'A definition…', pp. 181–182.

26 See R. Poskart, 'A definition…', p. 182, and the literature cited therein. When researching the systemic approach, scholars assume that the resources (broadly taken) required by a firm to survive and develop are limited and that firms optimise the processes for obtaining and using resources to gain and maintain a competitive position in the market.

and to shape characteristics of the market to both favour the organisation and improve its ability to gain and utilise the necessary resources. In the systemic approach, the entity under evaluation is perceived as a system with properties similar to those of a living organism[27]. Under the systemic approach, the criterion for assessing effectiveness is assessed externally (when it comes to the ability of a system (organisation) to obtain the maximum level of resources about the industrial sector as a whole or to the most prominent competitors), as well internally (as the internal efficiency of the organisation, interpreted as the inverse of the transformation costs)[28].

To collect the core elements of the interpretations at hand, one shall say that according to the goal-based interpretation, effectiveness is understood from the point of view of achieving goals (efficacy) and how resources are used (efficiency). In this perception, considering previous terminological assumptions, one shall say that the notion of effectiveness is used in *sensu largo* formula (effectiveness *sensu largo*). It is not the closest synonym of efficacy, but it is a broader term that encompasses two different layers: efficacy and efficiency. Hence, it isn't easy to describe the effectiveness of a society, justice systems, etc. From this point of view, the effectiveness of a firm can be measured objectively, and the efficacy of a society can only be measured subjectively.

Turning briefly to selected psychological captures, let us mention that an apprehensive psychological approach to effectiveness covers the theory of optimisation, which explains the underlying process of optimal best or "optimal efficiency"[29]. *Optimal efficiency* focuses on utilising resources as well as the amount of time and effort a person would have to expend during intellectual activities[30]. Based on this theory, scientists present a pattern referring to how the effectiveness of intellectual processes is measured. Among the psychological theories, one shall also point to the "Self-efficacy beliefs" idea by Alber Bandura[31]. This concept is

27 R. Poskart, 'A definition…', p. 182. Effectiveness understood in this way is related to the realisation of the (long-term) goals of a firm, namely survival and development.

28 R. Poskart, 'A definition…', p. 183 - pointing to the stance of M. Bielski, *Organizacje: istota, struktury, procesy*, 3rd ed., Łódź: University of Łódź Publishing 2001, *passim*.

29 H. P. Phan, B. H. Ngu, K. McQueen, 'Future time perspective and the achievement of optimal best', 11 *Front. Psychology* 2020, p. 1037.

30 H. P. Phan, B. H. Ngu, *Perceived 'optimal efficiency': theorization and conceptualization for development and implementation*. doi: 10.1016/j.heliyon.2021.e06042.

31 A. Bandura, 'Self-efficacy: Toward a unifying theory of behavioral change', 84(2) *Psychological Review* 1977, pp. 191 ff.; A. Bandura, 'Cultivate Self-efficacy for Personal and Organizational Effectiveness', in: E. A. Locke (ed.), *Handbook of Principles of Organizational Behavior*. doi.org/10.1002/9781119206422.ch10.

defined as people's domain-specific perceptions of their ability to perform the actions necessary to achieve valued goals. The self-efficacy beliefs theory has been proven as a crucial mechanism of change in psychological treatments of mental illness[32]. It is said that: "[T]he higher the people's perceived efficacy to fulfill educational requirements and occupational roles, the wider the career options they seriously consider pursuing, the greater the interest they have in them, the better they prepare themselves educationally for different occupational careers, and the greater their staying power in challenging career pursuits"[33]. As mentioned before, the psychological concept exploring the effectiveness assessment is based on empirical research; data gathered in this research often provides grounds to present general patterns, and many of them may be grasped numerically and as mathematic equations.

For apparent reasons, the concepts of effectiveness (efficacy, efficiency) presented in economics and psychology are hardly likely to be directly applicable in legal sciences, as law, being a much more abstract phenomenon, is a much more complex substance to measure. However, certain institutional aspects of the law can be based on economic and psychological approaches to effectiveness. Specifically, the goal-oriented approach in economic perception allows for even terminological distinction in the frame to the effectiveness *sensu largo* among the efficacy (category-oriented to the measurement of achieving the goal) and efficiency (category-oriented to the measurement of the use of resources). It seems that the analysis that covers the realisation of the goals and function of criminal proceedings (or any other legal procedure) might explore the concept of effectiveness *sensu largo* in the given elaboration. When applying the economic view of efficiency in the goal-oriented variant to legal sciences, the assumption that effectiveness might be measured internally and externally is applicable. However, with the caveat that the effectiveness of the concrete criminal proceeding shall be examined internally in terms of whether the goals of such a proceeding have been achieved. While examining externally means testing the effectiveness of the criminal process (or processes) in terms of the effectiveness of the whole penal justice system.

B) Philosophical theories: praxeology and constitutive rules

Philosophical concepts, especially those based on the praxeological theory of actions, are of particular importance for conceptualising effectiveness in the legal sciences. A specific theory was formulated in the 1950s by T. Kotarbiński as

32 M. W. Gallagher, 'Self-Efficacy' in: V. S. Ramachandran (ed.), *Encyclopaedia of Human Behavior*, 2nd ed., Academic Press 2012, pp. 314–320.

33 A. Bandura, 'Cultivate Self-efficacy...', p.

"The Theory of Efficient Action"[34], also called 'praxiology'[35], and elaborated mainly in his Treatise on A Good Job[36]. It is said that the definition of praxiology highlights that it is a philosophy of action-oriented towards human effectiveness[37]. Following Kotarbiński's thinking, if your actions – especially the ones whose results are inter-subjectively important – are effective and bring desired changes in the world, you do a 'good job'[38]. According to Kotarbiński: "All work, all activity, and in general all active behaviour is fully built of simple acts (…)"[39]. In the concept at

---

34 However, later on, it was pointed out that the translation from Polish to English was not accurate, and the name of this theory should be Theory of Efficacious Action. See footnote no. 43.

35 The term praxiology is used for this conception instead of the term praxeology: see M. W. Bukała, W. W. Gasparski, 'The Polish School of Praxiology: Historical Background, Essential Features, the Founder and Main Representatives', 74 *Edukacja Filozoficzna* 2022, pp. 183 ff. Polish school of praxiology is opposed to American school elaboration on praxeology.

36 T. Kotarbiński, *Traktat o dobrej robocie*, Wrocław: Ossolineum 1955. See P. T. Makowski, *Tadeusz Kotarbiński's Action Theory. Reinterpretive study*, Springer Nature 2017, *passim*. See also M. W. Bukała, W. W. Gasparski, 'The Polish School of Praxiology…', pp. 183 ff.; W. W. Gasparski, 'A Philosophy of Practicality: A Treatise on the Philosophy of Tadeusz Kotarbiński', 53 *Philosophical Society of Finland - Acta Philosophica Fennica* 1993; W. W. Gasparski, 'Tadeusz Kotarbiński and His Philosophical Transitions' in: W. W. Gasparski, B. Rok (eds.), *Transition Redesigned: A Practical Philosophy Perspective*, New York: Routledge, 2013, pp. 3–13; T. Kotarbiński, *Praxiology: An introduction to the sciences of efficient action* (trans.: O. Wojtasiewicz), Oxford: Pergamon Press/Warszawa: PWN 1965.

37 P. T. Makowski, 'Kotarbiński's Praxiology and the Analytic Action Theory' in: Wojciech W. Gasparski (ed.), *Praxiological Essays: Texts and Contexts*, New York: Routledge 2017, pp. 101–113.

38 Interpretation of P. T. Makowski, 'Kotarbiński's Praxiology…', p. 103. The principles of good work by Kotarbiński consist of encouraging to take effective action, fostering innovation, enabling disclosure of task forces' knowledge, eliminating the randomness of effects, mobilising the achievement of clearly established goals, determining the repeatability and regularity of actions, allowing for maintaining a sense of confidence even in situations where working conditions are disturbed; – enabling perceiving new and untypical situations, which can inspire change; – eliminating the freedom of choice of how to perform work; – allowing for verification of action results; – enhancing new teamwork skills; – integrating the employee group; – fostering the economisation of actions; – distinguishing important events from unimportant ones; rationalising activities; – allowing for seeing things realistically; – allowing for respecting reasonably established borders; – allowing for the adoption of the proper hierarchy of values; – triggering the willingness to act.

39 T. Kotarbiński, *Praxiology*…, p. 14.

hand causality of action is of pivotal importance. It is described by the concept of agenthood, which captures the relation between the agent and the result of his action. Doing so, Kotarbiński explores the idea of 'optional impulse'. As this Author says: "The agent of an event is he whose optional impulse is a cause of that event. Shifting a lever, pushing a button, striking a piano key – all these are examples of optional impulses – in those particular cases, we may also say optional pressures. But I prefer the term 'impulse' since it better covers those simple acts in which the behaviour of the agent … does not principally consist of any muscular exertion, such as when one makes an effort to recollect a forgotten name or to concentrate when carrying out a mental arithmetical operation. (…) Every impulse is directional and intentional; it is an impulse aimed at something (…)"[40].

As mentioned at the outset, based on natural (standard) language, terms such as effectiveness, efficacy, and efficiency are sometimes used as semantically interchangeable. The main question in this study that needs to be resolved is: Are we justified in treating them equivalently? Undoubtedly, efficiency is not the same as effectiveness—the latter usually involves economic solutions, while the former may be devoid of them. Nevertheless, the reasons to differentiate them seem to be stronger[41]. The path of searching for analytic clarity has been chosen by Kotarbiński.

As Makowski elaborated: "Having noted that efficiency is nonetheless an ambiguous term, the author of the Treatise distinguished between three forms of efficiency; let me describe them as follows. Efficacy: the universal value of action; 'a generic name for every practical value, so that it covers precision, productivity, simplicity, etc.'[42]. Efficiency: the technical (operational or 'manipulative') value of action roughly equivalent in meaning with skill Efficiency: the synthetic value of action, the more efficient an action is, the more it approaches the ideal embodying all the values of a good job, and that in the maximum degree"[43].

---

40 T. Kotarbiński, *Praxiology…*, pp. 14–15.

41 P. T. Makowski, *Tadeusz Kotarbiński's Action Theory. Reinterpretive study…*, pp. 47 ff.

42 T. Kotarbiński, *Praxiology…*, p. 84

43 As Makowski emphasises: "Translations of the quoted sentences are slightly changed. The Kotarbińskian three-fold division makes more sense in the Polish language since all these three dimensions can be reasonably subsumed under the efficiency heading (in Polish *sprawność*). This manoeuvre is problematic in English. Following Professor Gasparski […], in the first case, I changed the translation and used the term efficacy. Wojtasiewicz's translation of the Treatise uses, unifyingly, efficiency. This translational problem confirms my remarks about the worries related to interpreting the Treatise". P. T. Makowski, *Tadeusz Kotarbiński's Action Theory. Reinterpretive study…*, p. 60, reference no. 6.

Without entering into the intricacies of the concept at hand, it should be pointed out that the most critical aspect of our discussions is clarifying the mere essence of praxiology. Consequently, the task of praxiology is to investigate the conditions on which the maximisation of efficiency depends. Moreover, praxiology highlights that the value of human action often cannot be cashed out, measured, and expressed precisely in monetary quotas because too many individual and vague factors are at stake.

For our investigation, the terminological assumptions are of great importance. In Kotarbiński's works, effectiveness is a part of a more generic property of actions, namely efficacy, which covers every praxiological value of action[44]. In this sense, effectiveness is an essential feature of properly executed actions. It is explained that: "We call an action effective which leads to the intended effect as its objective"[45]. Any action that is usually thought to be subject to the constraints of instrumental rationality can be evaluated as effective, ineffective, counter-effective, or indifferent concerning its intended goal[46].

In Kotarbiński's concept, efficiency is something different[47]. In turn, as Makowski observes efficiency belongs to a whole catalogue of the evaluative properties of actions and agents[48]. This catalogue serves as a methodological listing of praxiological evaluation. The interpretation distinguishes effectiveness from efficiency with the use of the concept of 'the economy of action'.

It is *expressis verbis* said by Makowski when interpreting Kotarbiński's concept that: "In fact, efficacy, in a somewhat essentialistic manner, is meant to capture any praxiological value by which an action may be characterised. In this sense, it does not matter if a given action is not economic if it still brings something about, then it instantiates the generic property of efficacy. To call an action efficacious, it is sufficient merely that it instantiates one of the praxiological properties (values) …. Let us check this claim. Except for these values which have been introduced so far, the list Kotarbiński gave embraces usefulness, precision, carefulness, elegance, purity, simplicity, sureness, rationality, caution, importance, boldness, vigorousness and correctness (there also are other values which are resultant of some of

---

44 T. Kotarbiński, *Praxiology…*, p. 75.

45 T. Kotarbiński, *Praxiology…*, pp. 75–76.

46 P. T. Makowski, *Tadeusz Kotarbiński's Action Theory…*, p. 20; P. T. Makowski, 'Kotarbiński's Praxiology and the Analytic Action Theory…', pp. 101–113.

47 T. Kotarbiński, *Praxiology…*, p. 84.

48 T. Kotarbiński, *Praxiology…*, pp. 81 ff.

the above, as maturity, reliability, or mastery)"[49]. In this sense, efficacy may be taken as a general praxiological 'super-value'.

Additionally, we must point to operational and synthetic efficacy. The former is semantically equivalent to skill, and the latter embraces all the practical values that can be reasonably ascribed to an action (such as precision, economy, simplicity, correctness, sureness, reliability, etc.). In its synthetic sense, it means all those values taken as a whole; in this interpretation, the more efficient an action is, the more it approaches the ideal embodying all the values of a good job, and that to the maximum degree[50]. Moreover, the concept of synthetic efficacy shows that action/activities must be measured separately based on this formula. The question still remains whether, if we take two different but synthetically efficacious actions, how can we tell which of them is more synthetically efficient—the one which instantiates more praxiological values but to a low degree or the one which instantiates a small number of them but to a very high degree[51].

Applying Kotarbiński's concept to the study over legal problems, it should be seen that it is the observation of synthetic efficacy referring to the multi-level dimension of assessing the 'practical values' of given action/activities that has potential. Nevertheless, we should keep in mind that the emphasised difference between effectiveness and efficiency is a philosophical distinction; that is, it cannot be drawn solely on the basis of the standards of natural language. However, a further consequence of this is the distinction between efficacy in the (legally) normative sense and strictly praxeological efficacy [this issue will be clarified in subsequent discussion].

For an analysis aimed at analysing the efficiency of the criminal process, as well as the efficiency of the actions of participants in the criminal process, it may also be inspiring to use Kotarbiński's idea of a dichotomous division of principles of praxeology, based on the distinction between 1) fighting principles; 2) cooperation principles[52]. At the same time, one should make a reservation that in this approach

49 P. T. Makowski, *Tadeusz Kotarbiński's Action Theory. Reinterpretive study...*, p. 51. According to Kotarbiński, the list is complete (T. Kotarbiński, *Praxiology...*, p. 92).

50 T. Kotarbiński, *Praxiology...*, p. 84.

51 P. T. Makowski, *Tadeusz Kotarbiński's Action Theory. Reinterpretive study...*, pp. 71 ff.

52 In the consideration of the principles of cooperation, the central concepts are: "integration" and "synthesis of actions", which means that "While acting, one must be able to integrate all component activities into the most efficient whole for achieving a goal, and integration of actions is precisely this merging. The term could be used here accurately". It is argued when interpreting Kotarbiński concept that discussion of the specific rules of negative cooperation concerning attack, defence, prevention or threat is pioneery in philosophy and in the social sciences. See P. T. Makowski, *Tadeusz Kotarbiński's Action Theory ...*, p. 22.

fight is perceived as: "[...] any action of at least two actors (assuming that a team can be an actor), where at least one of actor disturbs another. In a particular, most ordinary and perhaps most interesting case, both actors not only strive objectively for incompatible goals, but they also know about it and take into account actions of the opposite side while developing their own plans of action"[53]. What is crucial, neither does T. Kotarbiński value positively nor does he encourage using methods contrary to morality. In Treaty about good work, he does not consider "the emotional side of fighting each other, but he is interested only in the efficiency of fighting techniques"[54]. Fighting methods are analysed in order to show how deviousness and flair can ensure gaining an advantage in a real clash. He indicates effective, although not always moral, modes of action, including also those that mislead an enemy and are effective at his or her expense. T. Kotarbiński himself admits that one should look at conflicts and ways to solve them not only from the perspective of praxeology but also ethics. He accepts this point of view as superior in works in practical philosophy by showing how vital ethical, fair action.

Summarising, Kotarbiński's praxeology allows for the examination of both individual action and their aggregates and sequences. This concept is founded on the assumption of the rationality of the acting subject[55], which determines the question of the realisation of specific goals (strategies) by the given subject. The idea of rationality at hand also means targeting the action being performed for interpretation, including its recognition by other participants in social interaction. As a side note, it must be said that the component of the rationality of action is also part of another crucial philosophical concept for the interpretation of legal actions, which we will discuss a little further, namely the idea of conventional acts (conventionalisation and formalisation) and constitutive rules.

Yet, the praxeological approach to legal actions (their aggregates and sequences and the whole proceedings) permits us to grasp normative goals (defined by law) and extra-normative goals (such as behaviour tactics) for the given action (aggregate or sequence). From this distinction, we can derive the basis for the effectiveness in a purely normative sense. In my other works, to distinguish effectiveness on the one hand in praxeological and, on the other hand, in a purely normative sense, the concept of futility (in negation – non-futility) has been explored. Effectiveness in a purely normative sense refers to the production of the effects described for a given legal (procedural) act in the law (e.g., the submission of

53 T. Kotarbiński, *Praxiology...*, p. 73.

54 T. Kotarbiński, *Praxiology...*, pp. 74 ff.

55 See L. Nowak, 'Juristic Interpretation' in: P. Kwiatkowski, M. Smolak, (eds.), *Poznań School of Legal Theory*, Leiden: Brill 2021, pp. 140–162.

an evidentiary motion by a party will have the effect of the consideration of this motion by the procedural body), or in the case of a violation of the rules for the performance of a legal (procedural) act; it can combine with the sanction of ineffectiveness (non-futility)[56].

To be more precise, it must be explained that the concept of normative effectiveness shall be characterised based on the idea of constitutive rules as well as conventionalisation and formalisation. The most significant contribution to conceptualising these conceptions was made by the language philosopher J. Searle[57]. At the same time, it should not be forgotten that the idea of constitutive rules originally referred to the interpretations of speech acts. Therefore, from the perspective of its further application in legal sciences, works of scholars from the so-called Poznan School of General Theory of Law[58] became of core significance.

Clearly, though, let us at the same time point out that the concept that we can describe as operative from a jurisprudential (law application) standpoint is the result of a complex evolution[59]. The idea that the 'legal universe' is based on certain artificial and formalised rules, 'conventions' – and that it is a realm of conventional concepts that is materialised within the framework of concrete social relations – cannot be attributed to a single author. Thus, supposedly, the inquiries on the concept of constitutive rules have started with the works that characterise in more detail the actions of participants in conventional discourse, including the processes of social communication and the application of law. From this perspective, the works of Austin and especially Searle are worth noting. So let us remember that in formulating the concept of constitutive rules, Searle refers to the conception of performative utterances developed by Austin, specifically to locutionary, illocutionary and perlocutionary acts[60]. These categories were referred to as speech acts, which are much simpler conventional creations compared to legal acts. At the same time, the regularities observed in the framework of their

---

56 See B. Janusz-Pohl, *Definitions ad typologies of legal acts in criminal proceedings. Perspective of conventionalisation and formalisation*, Poznań 2017, pp. 23–24 and the literature referred therein. In Polish language also broader study: B. Janusz-Pohl, *Formalizacja i konwencjonalizacja jako instrumenty analizy czynności karnoporcesowych w prawie polskim*, Poznan 2017, *passim*.

57 J. R. Searle, *Speech Acts: An Essay in the Philosophy of Language*, London 1967, *passim*.

58 P. Kwiatkowski, M. Smolak (eds.), *Poznań School of Legal Theory*, Leiden: Brill, 2021, *passim*.

59 Description based on my previous work: B. Janusz-Pohl, *Definitions…*, pp. 23–24 and the literature referred therein.

60 J. L. Austin, *How to Do Things with Words*, Oxford: Clarendon Press 1962, pp. 311 ff.

study have implications for the study of law. Just drafting these assumptions (as they are being auxiliary to the consideration of the concept of effectiveness), let us emphasise that an illocutionary act is an intentional act performed by an individual uttering a performative sentence (locutionary act), the purpose of which is to create a new state of affairs unattainable in any other way[61].

In this definition, several elements such as "intentionality of action", "purpose of", and "create a new state of affairs" attract attention. All these elements are essential, as legal actions are an example of illocutionary acts. Thus, the essence of Searle's achievements was to display the rules for the performance of illocutionary acts and to clarify the nature of these rules. The assumption was taken into account that these actions have a rational character, the subject of the action pursues certain goals, and one such goal (primary goal) is the valid and effective performance of such an action. From the beginning, the assumption was included that the rules for the performance of illocutionary acts – later viewed rather as formalised conventional acts are connected with a set of specific rules attached to the given type of action. As further discussion will clarify, this set of rules is divided by scholars into two groups: Searle's concept includes a) constitutive rules and b) regulative rules, and Czepita's concept covers a) rules of conventionalisation and b) rules of formalisation[62].

Searle's conception distinguishes speech acts as uttering (muscle movements), propositional, and illocutionary acts. Its crux is the distinction of the so-called elementary illocutionary act[63].

Searle stressed that: "In our analysis of illocutionary acts, we must capture both the intentional and the conventional aspects, especially the relationship between them. In the performance of an illocutionary act in the literal utterance of a sentence, the speaker intends to produce a certain effect by means of getting the hearer to recognise his intention to produce that effect"[64]. Furthermore, component acts can be distinguished in any act, not only intentional. A component of a given act is held to mean an act, the performance of which is a necessary albeit

61 See more B. Janusz-Pohl, *Definitions…*, p. 25. See also J. R. Searle, *Speech Acts: An Essay in the Philosophy of Language*, London 1967, *passim*; J. R. Searle, *Czynności mowy. Rozważania z filozofii języka*, Warsaw 1987, *passim*.

62 Cf. C. Czepita, 'O koncepcji czynności konwencjonalnych w prawie', in: M. Smolak (ed.), *Wykładnia konstytucji. Aktualne problemy i tendencje*, Warsaw 2016, pp. 138–139; S. Czepita, *Reguły konstytutywne a zagadnienia prawoznawstwa*, Uniwersytet Szczeciński, Studia i Rozprawy, Szczecin 1996, pp. 146 ff.

63 J. R. Searle, *Speech Acts…*, *passim*.

64 J. R. Searle, *Speech Acts…*, p. 45.

insufficient condition of performing a given act. A component of a given act is renowned based on another theoretical conception as the material substrate of a conventional act. In Searle's conception, it is crucial to observe that illocutionary acts are interpreted by opposing constitutive rules for given speech acts to regulative rules. As the latter, Searle considered such rules regulate antecedently or independently existing forms of behaviour. In turn, constitutive rules not merely regulate but, above all, create or define new forms of actions (we could say conventional forms); they thus create new beings. Searle introduced a pattern of the constitutive rule. The pattern ran as follows: X counts as Y in context C. He emphasised that constitutive rules were thus rules of conventionalisation. It is worth mentioning that Searle analysed regulative rules, such as the rules of etiquette, finding that their observation did not undermine the existence of specific acts but determined their form[65].

When it comes to relevance to our inquiries, it is important to emphasise that in Searle's opinion, two goals of an intentional act, as they were, can be distinguished: a direct goal and a final goal. The final goal is the one the person performing an illocutionary act aims at consciously and with intent. The direct goal is the one achieved at the moment of completing the performance of an intentional act appropriate or suitable for achieving the final goal. The achievement of the direct goal is a necessary, but not always sufficient, condition for achieving the final goal. The achievement of the final goal always means the achievement of the direct goal. However, the reverse is not always true. Thus, the direct goal is, as a rule, a means for achieving the final goal, but not guaranteeing its achievement[66].

Let us note that it was drafted in very general terms without going into detail about all the complexities of Searle's conception. Regardless, the latter has inspired many scholars.

One of them was the Polish legal philosopher Stanisław Czepita. This Author has developed the concept of constitutive and regulative rules by denominating them as constitutive rules (rules of conventionalisation) and formalisation rules. Both types have been divided into two other groups: constructive rules and

65 J. R. Searle, *Speech Acts…*, p. 36. It appears that disavowing the approach to regulative rules as second types of rules helped Searle discern a new approach to illocutionary acts. It inspired scholars to search for such conventional act rules whose breaking would not undermine the validity (existence) of a given act. In this sense, it appears that regulative rules inspired Czepita to distinguish the formalisation rules of conventional acts and devise a related mechanism of formalisation See B. Janusz-Pohl, *Definitions…*, pp. 25 ff.

66 J. R. Searle, *Speech Acts…*, p. 24 ff.

consequential rules. The constructive rules (rules of construction) indicate how to perform a conventional act validly (constitutive rules) and effectively (formalisation rules). Nevertheless, effectiveness here is linked with the typical purpose (result) for the given legal action. So, from this perspective, effective legal action is valid action performed in accordance with formalisation rules for the given type of action, and its effect is described by law[67].

To simplify this concept, one shall say that consequential rules of legal action indicate the legal consequences of, on the one hand, conventional rules and, on the other hand, formalisation rules. Through this approach, this Author has analysed the issue of the defectiveness of legal actions, starting with the sanction of 'non-existent legal action' and nullity *ex tunc* (in case of breach of constitutive rules) through inadmissibility (in case of breach of some constitutive rules) to nullity *ex nunc* and the non-futility (in case of breach of formalisation rules)[68]. Besides, he observed that many formalisation rules remain only the rules of construction and are not linked with consequential rules, the so-called *lex imperfecta*. It means that any legal consequence is not connected with the breach of formalisation rules of this type. As we may observe, when it comes to the issue of effectiveness, based on the constitutive rules and the ideas of conventionalisation and formalisation, one shall distinguish the category of ineffectiveness in the legal sense perceived as a sanction for variolation of formalisation rules. This sanction shall be stipulated by law *expressis verbis*, when the law says that the legal action is ineffective. Based on this concept, it was decided to call the sanction of infectivity non-futility just to make a terminological distinction between the legally-oriented category and the praxiological category of effectiveness.

4. Features of the Effectiveness in Criminal Justice: Standard of Effective Remedy

In legal sciences, effectiveness is perceived as a complex notion, especially when researching procedural law. More often used somehow intuitively by the authors; however, these intuitions align with the linguistic perception of notions at hand. Yet, the adjective 'effective' is a part of statutory language, for example, in Art. 13 ECHR or Art. 19 TEU or Art. 47 Charter of Fundamental Rights of the European Union (CFR). These three Articles are the core legal sources for an institution of effective remedy.

67 B. Janusz-Pohl, *Definitions…*, p. 25 ff.

68 The notion of non-futility was proposed by B. Janusz-Pohl, *Definitions…*, pp. 20 ff.

According to Art. 13 ECHR: "Everyone whose rights and freedoms as set forth in this Convention are violated shall have an effective remedy before a national authority, notwithstanding that the violation has been committed by persons acting in an official capacity".

Due to the limited scope of this study, we must refer to numerous papers on the interpretation of Art. 13 ECHR[69] as well as to the jurisprudence of the ECtHR, which has developed the concept of an effective remedy, clarifying its essence[70].

Summarising this exhausted discussion, it must be said that to be effective, the remedy must meet several conditions. First is directness, as the remedy shall be capable of directly remedying the impugned situation[71]. The states do have some margin of appreciation when it comes to constructing the national system of remedies. So, the contracting states are given some discretion regarding how they provide the requisite remedy and conform to their obligations under Art. 13 ECHR[72].

The next condition is *in concreto* evaluation. Thus, the effectiveness of the remedy is assessed in relation to each complaint (*in concreto*)[73].

The next element is linked with the guarantee-oriented prism of evaluation. The ECtHR emphasises that the requirements of Art. 6 ECHR (fairness of procedure) may be relevant for the assessment of the effectiveness of a remedy for the purposes of Art. 13 ECHR, and for example, the fundamental criterion of fairness, which encompasses the equality of arms, is a constitutive element of an effective remedy. A remedy cannot be considered effective unless the minimum conditions enabling an applicant to challenge a decision that restricts his or her

---

69 See also chapters on *Effective remedies*, in: B. Janusz-Pohl (ed.), *Effective Justice. International and Comparative Approaches*, vol. 2, Peter Lang (in print), especially inquiries by Dr. Bernardini and Prof. Pawelec and the literature cited therein.

70 See the collection of judgments included in *Guide on Article 13 of the European Convention on Human Rights Right to an Effective Remedy*, pp. 14–20, available at https://ks.echr.coe.int/documents/d/echr-ks/guide_art_13_eng# [accessed on: June 1st, 2024].

71 See ECtHR, *Pine Valley Developments Ltd and Others v. Ireland*, November 29th, 1991.

72 See ECtHR, *Kaya v. Turkey*, September 2nd, 1998, § 106; ECtHR, *Silver and Others v. the United Kingdom*, March 25th, 1983, § 113; ECtHR, *Council of Civil Service Unions and Others v. the United Kingdom*, January 20th, 1987; ECtHR, *Smith and Grady v. the United Kingdom*, September 27th, 1999, § 138; ECtHR, *Peck v. the United Kingdom*, January 28th, 2003, §§ 105–106; ECtHR, *Hasan and Chaush v. Bulgaria*, October 26th, 2000, § 100; ECtHR, GC, *Hatton and Others v. the United Kingdom*, July 8th, 2003, § 141; ECtHR, *Glaș Nadezhda EOOD and Elenkov v. Bulgaria*, October 11th, 2007, § 69; ECtHR, *Boychev and Others v. Bulgaria*, January 27th, 2011, § 56.

73 See ECtHR, *Glas Nadezhda EOOD and Elenkov v. Bulgaria*, October 11th, 2007, §§ 68–70; ECtHR, Grand Chamber, *Hatton and Others v. the United Kingdom*, July 8th, 2003, § 141; ECtHR, *Colozza and Rubinat v. Italy*, February 12th, 1985.

rights under the Convention are provided[74]. The remedy must be potential; on the one the effective remedy is the tool available in theory and in practice[75]; on the other hand, the 'effectiveness' of a remedy for the purposes of Art. 13 ECHR does not depend on the certainty of a favourable outcome for the applicant[76]. Moreover, it is expressly said that the term 'effective' means that the remedy must be sufficient and accessible, as well as fulfilling the obligation of promptness[77]. Accessibility of remedy means that the excessively restrictive requirements may render the remedy ineffective. In addition, the aggregate of remedies provided for under domestic law may meet the requirements of Art. 13 ECHR, even where no single remedy may itself entirely satisfy them[78]. This concept generally refers to several remedies which can be taken up one after the other or in parallel and which cater for different aspects of redress, such as a civil remedy providing for compensation and criminal action for the purposes of satisfying the procedural aspect of Arts. 2 and 3 ECHR. The Court will consider whether a given remedy has acquired a sufficient degree of certainty in its implementation[79]. Additionally, under the court jurisprudence 'effective remedy' requirement means a remedy that is as effective as can be having regard to the restricted scope for recourse inherent in the context[80]. Nevertheless, a domestic court's scope of judicial scrutiny must be sufficient to guarantee protection under Art. 13 ECHR. Insufficient powers of judicial review exercised by the courts may entail a violation of Art. 13 ECHR[81]. Finally, the government must demonstrate the effectiveness of all the remedies

---

74 See ECtHR, *Csüllög v. Hungary*, June 7th, 2011, § 46.

75 See ECtHR, GC, *Sürmeli v. Germany*, June 8th, 2006, § 113; ECtHR, *Abramiuc v. Romania*, February 24th, 2009, § 128.

76 See ECtHR, *Swedish Engine Drivers' Union v. Sweden*, February 6th, 1976, § 50; ECtHR, GC, *Kudła v. Poland*, October 26th, 2000, § 157; ECtHR, *Costello-Roberts v. the United Kingdom*, March 1993, § 40; ECtHR, *Hilal v. the United Kingdom*, March 6th, 2001, § 78.

77 See ECtHR, *Paulino Tomás v. Portugal*, May 22nd, 2003; ECtHR, *Çelik and İmret v. Turkey*, October 26th, 2004, § 59.

78 ECtHR, *Silver and Others v. the United Kingdom*, March 25th, 1983, § 113; ECtHR, *Leander v. Sweden*, March 26th, 1987, § 77; ECtHR, GC, Chahal v. the United Kingdom, November 15th, 1996, § 145; ECtHR, GC, *Kudła v. Poland*, October 26th, 2000, § 157; ECtHR, *De Souza Ribeiro v. France*, December 13th, 2012, § 79; ECtHR, *Brincat and Others v. Malta*, July 24th, 2014, § 64.

79 ECtHR, *Čonka v. Belgium*, February 5th, 2002, § 83; ECtHR, *Krasuski v. Poland*, December 11th, 2007, § 68.

80 See ECtHR, GC, *Klass and Others v. Germany*, September 6th, 1978 § 68–78.

81 See ECtHR, *Smith and Grady v. the United Kingdom*, September 27th, 1999, §§ 136–139; ECtHR, *Hatton and Others v. the United Kingdom*, July 8th, 2003, §§ 141–142; ECtHR, GC, *Soering v. the United Kingdom*, July 7th, 1989, §§ 121–124.

on which they rely, failing which the Court may find a violation of Art. 13 ECHR or decline to rule on the matter[82].

On the other hand, Art. 19 point 1 TEU states that Member States shall provide remedies sufficient to ensure effective legal protection in the fields covered by Union law[83]. This provision must be read in conjunction with Art. 47 CFR: "Everyone whose rights and freedoms guaranteed by the law of the Union are violated has the right to an effective remedy before a tribunal in compliance with the conditions laid down in this Article. Everyone is entitled to a fair and public hearing within a reasonable time by an independent and impartial tribunal previously established by law. Everyone shall have the possibility of being advised, defended, and represented. Legal aid shall be made available to those who lack sufficient resources in so far as such aid is necessary to ensure effective access to justice".

As a side note, it must be added that the notion of 'effective remedy' has been explored also by secondary law, namely by directives. It is said that the directives grant building common standards for the protection of fundamental rights and values. It is particularly a right to effective remedy that ensures the common denominator for creating the guarantee-oriented model of criminal proceedings in member states[84].

Given the prism of the present analysis, let us point out that based on the given regulations defining the European (Strasbourg and Luxembourg) standards of effective remedy, one shall unambiguously claim that the meaning of the adjective

---

82 See ECtHR, GC, *Wille v. Liechtenstein*, Ocotober 28th, 1999, §§ 74–78; ECtHR, *Yarashonen v. Turkey*, June 24th, 2014, §§ 64–66.

83 See C. H. H. Hofmann, *A Commentary on the Right to an Effective Remedy in the Case Law of the CJEU*, University of Luxembourg Law, Working Paper no. 2019-016, available at: https://ssrn.com/abstract=3503540 or http://dx.doi.org/10.2139/ssrn.3503540 [accessed on: July 1st, 2024]; C. H. H. Hofmann, 'The Right to an Effective Remedy and to a Fair Trial – Article 47 of the Charter and the Member States' in: S. Peers T. Harvey (eds.), *The Charter of Fundamental Rights of the European Union*, Oxford: Hart Bloomsberg, 2019, pp. 30–34; K. Gutman, 'The Essence of the Fundamental Right to an Effective Remedy and to a Fair Trial in the Case-Law of the Court of Justice of the European Union: The Best Is Yet to Come?', 20(6) *German Law Journal* 2019, pp. 884–903.

84 Noted by P. Wiliński, K. Kiejnich-Kruk, 'Right to Effective Legal Remedy in Criminal Proceedings in the EU. Implementation and Need for Standards', 54(3) *Review of European and Comparative Law* 2023. See also M. Caianiello, G. Lasagni, 'Comparative Remarks' in: G. Contissa, G. Lasagni, M. Caianiello, G. Sartor (eds.), *Effective Protection of the Rights of the Accused in the EU Directives*, Leiden: Brill, 2022, pp. 229 ff; P. Wiliński (ed.), *Effective Legal Remedies in Criminal Justice System. European Perspective*, Peter Lang 2024, *passim*.

"effective" in the expression "right to effective remedy" is determined by a set guarantees indicated in the cited legal regulations. Yet, these guarantees are specifically related to the protection of the fundamental rights of the individual and constitute the fair trial standard. Consequently, the effectiveness based on the interpreted provisions is therefore linked to the realisation of the objectives (goals) fulfilling the standard of fairness, that is, i.e. access to a fair and public hearing within a reasonable time by an independent and impartial tribunal previously established by law. An effective remedy in the general sense, namely thus, within the framework of a general scope presented above, is subject to clarification within the framework of specific standards, such as those described in the particular directives (*in concreto* approach).

As was said before, the ECtHR interprets Art. 13 ECHR, emphasising this from a *concreto* perspective of evaluation. It means that the essence of the right to effective remedy consists of examining the particular institutions. However, sometimes it can concern entire proceedings, primarily when an element of the right to an effective remedy under verification is related to the legitimacy of the enforcement authorities in a given procedure or guarantees related to principles of the court independence.

Initially, it was acknowledged that the effectiveness in legal deliberations must be viewed once as a praxeological or legal-praxeological category and once as a strict normative category (in the latter as a sanction for violation of the rules set for the effective performance of a procedural act).

Based on the considerations so far, it follows that the lawyer's perception of the effectiveness in praxeological or legally-praxeological dimension refers to a) the selected institutions (as based on the concept of the right of effective remedy), b) the entire procedure (which examines whether the goals set for the procedure of a given type have been achieved), or even c) the individual actions as long as they are assessed from the point of view of the entire procedure (e.g., in the context of the analysis of the examination of the violation of the rules for individual actions and the impact of this violation on the entire process, and thus the fulfillment of the standard of due process). Admittedly, a purely normative perception of effectiveness refers to the sanction for violation of the rules for the performance of a given action.

5. Purposes of Criminal Procedure: Effective Criminal Procedure versus Effective Action in Criminal Proceedings

The effectiveness of proceedings is analysed through its goals. Proceedings, perceived as a chain of legal actions being the rational activities, must refer to the particular goal of selected action in the given sequence and to the overall purposes of the given proceedings. As long as the proceedings consist of legal actions of all participants (who perform activities in a rational way, so in a purposeful manner), the goals of the entire procedure shall not be realised by all participants in the same manner. The involvement of the participants in the proceedings depends on their position in the given model and other features, i.e. the distribution of procedural burdens.

Nevertheless, the discussion of the proceedings' effectiveness must meet several standards. The goals of such proceedings should first be defined, and they have to be clear and at least at some point measurable (i.e. when it comes to the length of proceedings). Referring to the theory of efficacy in the economic sciences, however, let us point out that in legal sciences, a concept of the goal-oriented perception of effectiveness is applicable; however, in this field effectiveness can be measured only subjectively. Effectiveness in the criminal process, therefore, refers to the overall goals that the legislator[85] has assigned to the criminal process (it includes both the sphere of measurable assets, time, and costs, as well as unmeasurable assets). Meanwhile, efficiency is a category that refers to only measurable (in terms of time and costs) parameters.

As an example of a codification that expresses the goals of the criminal process, one can point to Art. 2 § 1 CPP-Poland. Thus, according to this provision: "Goals of regulations of this Code is to establish such course of criminal procedure that:

1. the perpetrator of a criminal offence shall be detected and called to penal responsibility, and that no innocent person shall be so called;
2. by a correct application of measures provided for by criminal law, and by the disclosure of the circumstances which favoured the commission of the offence, the tasks of criminal procedure shall be fulfilled not only in combating the offences, but also in preventing them as well as in consolidating the rule of law and the principles of community life;
3. legally protected interests of the injured party shall be secured, at the same time, the dignity of the injured be preserved, and
4. determination of the case shall be achieved within a reasonable time".

According to § 2 of Art. 2 CPP-Poland, on the other hand: "The foundation of any decision should be based on true factual findings".

85 'Legislator' in continental law systems, but also jurisprudence and legal doctrine.

It should be observed that the quoted provision contains several procedural principles: the principle of appropriate criminal response (1), the principle of general and individual prevention (2), the principle of protection of the victim (3), the principle of promptness (4), and moreover, the principle of material truth (5) is codified in paragraph two[86].

These principles protect different values; in particular, in some cases a collision between these values may occur, and consequently also a contradiction between principles[87]. Thus, even if we assume that effective proceedings (under this provision) is the one that fulfills the objectives (set forth in the analysed Art. 2 CPP-Poland), at the same time, we do not know how to resolve the collision between these principles, the exploration of the effectiveness is rather illusory[88].

One shall ask: will an effective proceedings be only prompt and not expensive regardless of the protection of victims, or will an effective proceedings prioritises the protection of victims over the realisation of the principle of an appropriate criminal response, or will a given proceeding be effective if the realisation of individual prevention occurs in violation of the principle of material truth? We can proliferate similar questions all over again. Let us, therefore, ask more abstractly whether it can be considered that the hierarchy of the principles might be assessed based on their location in progressively further editorial sections of the analysed Art. 2 CCP-Poland, and thus the realisation of the directive of an appropriate criminal response is more important than the realisation of the principles codified below (in further sections or Art. 2 § 1 CCP-Poland), that the former is, therefore, more important than the principle of promptness contained in the last section (4) of § 1 of Art. 2 CPP-Poland? It would seem that such an interpretation could be accepted. Yet it also encounters the most significant problem, namely how to read the principle of appropriate criminal response. More

86 B. Janusz-Pohl, 'The model of the Polish criminal procedure. An analysis from the perspective of its structure and the form of process functions and procedural guarantees' in: B. Janusz-Pohl, Ł. Pohl, W. Achrem (eds.), *Forensic Identification Based on Biological Testing in Cross-Border Criminal Proceedings: Legal, Methodological and Praxeological Aspects*, vol, 1, Szczecin 2022, pp. 31–47.

87 M. Kordela, 'Axiological Law Interpretation' in: P. Kwiatkowski, M. Smolak (eds.), *Poznań School of Legal Theory*. Leiden: Brill 2021, pp. 339–349.

88 About the possibility of resolving the collisions among principles, see M. Kordela, 'Principles of Law' in: P. Kwiatkowski, M. Smolak (eds.), *Poznań School of Legal Theory*, Leiden, Brill 2021, pp. 327–338.

precisely, whether to reconstruct it in the spirit of so-called 'substantive justice', in the realisation of the principle of material truth is prioritised, or so-called formal (procedural) justice, under which the fairness of the trial is determined not by its final outcome, i.e. whether the decision reached is based on true facts findings, but whether the application of procedural law was flawless, proportional and guarantee-oriented[89]. Undoubtedly, resolving this exceeds the framework of this article essay. Nonetheless, when analysing the relationship between substantive justice and formal justice, it is essential to highlight the relevance of supranational bodies' jurisprudence. The ECHR is of such importance in the context of counties under the Council of Europe umbrella and the ECJ within the EU. However, the relationship between values determining the goals of criminal proceedings in national regulations and values reproduced based on the ECHR and European Treaties and the CFR is vital. The most impressive thing in this regard seems to be the question of the influence of conventional regulations on the perception of the hierarchy of these goals.

6. Instead of Conclusions

The thoughts given is this essay clearly show that the perception of effectiveness or efficacy in the legal sciences (with particular reference to procedural criminal law) slips through the usual linguistic conventionalities, which give the terms effectiveness, effectivity, efficacy and even the notion of efficiency the status of equivalent expressions. In terms of the natural language background, it is legitimate to use them almost interchangeably. However, we see that on the grounds of the examples of their use in various sciences, the connotation of these names becomes much more specific. Therefore, we can ask whether this is just a meaningless name juggling. Or rather, is it an attempt to describe a specific fragment of reality in the meticulous way possible? The analysis carried out gives an argument that it is the second case. The conducted examinations allow us to concretise methodological assumptions about the perception of effectiveness in legal sciences. An attempt has been made to organise the meanings of effectiveness according to the context of its use. However, it is not only the terminological issues that are at stake here but first of all, the specification of what is most vital for lawyers, i.e. how to measure effectiveness. To answer this question, it is necessary to meticulously analyse the area to be studied in the framework of said effectiveness measurement. It is also

---

89 J. Raz, 'The rule of law and its virtue' in: *The authority of law: Essays on law and morality*, Oxford 1979, pp. 25 ff.

necessary to distinguish whether effectiveness is to be researched in a praxeological, legal-praxeological oriented or purely normative sense. This is only the first step; further on, the determinants of effectiveness regarding the goals set for the given activities should be carefully examined. However, we touch on axiological problems, often beyond solution.

7. Bibliography

Literature

Austin J. L., *How to Do Things with Words*, Oxford Clarendon Press 1962.

Bandura A., 'Cultivate Self-efficacy for Personal and Organizational Effectiveness', in: E. A. Locke (ed.), *Handbook of Principles of Organizational Behavior*. doi.org/10.1002/9781119206422.ch10 [accessed on: July 1st, 2024].

Bandura A., 'Self-efficacy: Toward a unifying theory of behavioral change', 84(2) *Psychological Review* 1977.

Bielski M., *Organizacje: istota, struktury, procesy*, 3rd edition, University of Łódź Publishing, Łódź 2001.

Bukała M. W., Gasparski W. W., '*The Polish School of Praxiology: Historical Background, Essential Features, the Founder and Main Representatives*', 74 *Edukacja Filozoficzna*, 2022.

Burazin L., 'The Concept of Law and Efficacy' in: M. Sellers, S. Kirste (eds.) *Encyclopaedia of the Philosophy of Law and Social Philosophy*, Dordrecht: Springer 2017.

Caianiello M., G. Lasagni, 'Comparative Remarks', in: G. Contissa, G. Lasagni, M. Caianiello, G. Sartor (eds.), *Effective Protection of the Rights of the Accused in the EU Directives*, Leiden: Brill 2022.

Czechowski L., *Wielowymiarowa ocena efektywności ekonomicznej przedsiębiorstwa przemysłowego*, Gdańsk: University of Gdańsk Publishing 1997.

Czepita S., ‚O koncepcji czynności konwencjonalnych w prawie' in: M. Smolak (ed.), *Wykładnia konstytucji. Aktualne problemy i tendencje*, Warsaw 2016.

Czepita S., *Reguły konstytutywne a zagadnienia prawoznawstwa*, Uniwersytet Szczeciński, Studia i Rozprawy, Szczecin 1996.

d'Aspremont J., '"*Effectivity" in international law: self-empowerment against epistemological claustrophobia*', available at: effectivity_in_international_law_selfempowerment_against_epistemological_claustrophobia.pdf [accessed on: July 1st, 2024].

Gallagher M. W., 'Self-Efficacy' in: V. S. Ramachandran (ed.), *Encyclopaedia of Human Behavior*, Academic Press 2012.

Gasparski W. W., 'Tadeusz Kotarbiński and His Philosophical Transitions' in: W. W. Gasparski, B. Rok (eds.), *Transition Redesigned: A Practical Philosophy Perspective*, New York: Routledge 2013.

Gasparski W. W., 'A Philosophy of Practicality: A Treatise on the Philosophy of Tadeusz Kotarbiński', 53 *Philosophical Society of Finland - Acta Philosophica Fennica*, 1993.

Gutman K., 'The Essence of the Fundamental Right to an Effective Remedy and to a Fair Trial in the Case-Law of the Court of Justice of the European Union: The Best Is Yet to Come?', 20(6) *German Law Journal* 2019.

Hofmann C. H. H., 'The Right to an Effective Remedy and to a Fair Trial – Article 47 of the Charter and the Member States' in: S. Peers T. Harvey (eds.), *The Charter of Fundamental Rights of the European Union*, Oxford: Hart Bloomsberg 2019.

Hofmann C. H. H., *A Commentary on the Right to an Effective Remedy in the Case Law of the CJEU* (December 13th, 2019), University of Luxembourg Law, Working Paper no. 2019-016, available at: https://ssrn.com/abstract=3503540 or http://dx.doi.org/10.2139/ssrn.3503540 [accessed on: July 1st, 2024].

J. Raz J., *The rule of law and its virtue*, in: *The authority of law: Essays on law and morality*, Oxford 1979.

Janusz-Pohl B. (ed.), *Effective Justice International and Comparative Approaches*, vol. 2, Peter Lang (in print).

Janusz-Pohl B., 'The model of the Polish criminal procedure. An analysis from the perspective of its structure and the form of process functions and procedural guarantees' in: B. Janusz-Pohl, Ł. Pohl, W. Achrem (eds.), *Forensic Identification Based on Biological Testing in Cross-Border Criminal Proceedings: Legal, Methodological and Praxeological Aspects*, vol. 1, Szczecin 2022.

Janusz-Pohl B., *Definitions ad typologies of legal acts in criminal proceedings. Perspective of conventionalisation and formalisation*, Poznań 2017.

Janusz-Pohl B., *Formalizacja i konwencjonalizacja jako instrumenty analizy czynności karnoporcesowych w prawie polskim*, Poznań 2017.

Kordela M., 'Axiological Law Interpretation', in: P. Kwiatkowski, M. Smolak (eds.), *Poznań School of Legal Theory*, Leiden: Brill 2021.

Kordela M., 'Principles of Law' in: P. Kwiatkowski, M. Smolak (eds.), *Poznań School of Legal Theory*, Leiden: Brill 2021.

Kotarbiński T., *Traktat o dobrej robocie*, Wrocław: Ossolineum, 1955.

Kotarbiński, T., *Praxiology: An introduction to the sciences of efficient action* (trans: O. Wojtasiewicz), Oxford: Pergamon Press/Warszawa: PWN [*Traktat o dobrej robocie*, Ossolineum, Wrocław 1955], 1965.

Kwiatkowski P., Smolak M. (eds.), *Poznań School of Legal Theory*, Leiden: Brill 2021.

Makowski P. T., 'Kotarbiński's Praxiology and the Analytic Action Theory' in: W. W. Gasparski (ed.), *Praxiological Essays: Texts and Contexts*, New York: Routledge 2017.

Makowski P. T., *Tadeusz Kotarbiński's Action Theory. Reinterpretive study*, Springer Nature 2017.

Nowak L., 'Juristic Interpretation' in: P. Kwiatkowski, M. Smolak, (eds.), *Poznań School of Legal Theory*, Leiden: Brill 2021.

Phan H. P., Ngu B. H., McQueen K., 'Future time perspective and the achievement of optimal best', 11 *Front. Psychology* 2020.

Phan H. P., Ngu B. H., *Perceived 'optimal efficiency': theorisation and conceptualisation for development and implementation*, Heliyon. doi: 10.1016/j.heliyon.2021.e06042.

Poskart R., 'A definition of the concept of economic effectiveness', 2(3) *Central Eastern European Journal of Management and Economics* 2014.

Raz J., 'The rule of law and its virtue' in: *The authority of law: Essays on law and morality*, Oxford 1979.

Searle J. R., *Czynności mowy. Rozważania z filozofii języka*, Warsaw 1987.

Searle J. R., *Speech Acts: An Essay in the Philosophy of Language*, London 1967.

Sickles R. C., Zelenyuk V., *Measurement of Productivity and Efficiency: Theory and Practice*, Cambridge University Press 2019.

Wiliński P. (ed.), *Effective Legal Remedies in Criminal Justice System. European Perspective*, Peter Lang 2024.

Wiliński P., Kiejnich-Kruk K., 'Right to Effective Legal Remedy in Criminal Proceedings in the EU Implementation and Need for Standards', 54(3) *Review of European and Comparative Law* 2023.

Ziembiński Z., 'Legal Provisions and Legal Norms' in: P. Kwiatkowski, M. Smolak (eds.), *Poznań School of Legal Theory*, Leiden: Brill 2021.

Ziembiński Z., 'The Typology of Legal Norms' in: P. Kwiatkowski, M. Smolak (eds.), *Poznań School of Legal Theory*, Leiden: Brill 2021.

Collection of jurisprudence

Guide on Article 13 of the European Convention on Human Rights Right to an Effective Remedy, available at https://ks.echr.coe.int/documents/d/echr-ks/guide_art_13_eng# [accessed on: June 1st, 2024].

English Language Dictionaries

Britannica Dictionary, available at: https://www.britannica.com/dictionary [accessed on: July 1st, 2024].

Cambridge Dictionary, available at: https://dictionary.cambridge.org/ [accessed on: July 1st, 2024].

Collins Dictionary, available at: https://www.collinsdictionary.com/ [accessed on: July 1st, 2024].

Merriam-Webster Dictionary, available at: https://www.merriam-webster.com/ [accessed on: July 1st, 2024].

Oxford Dictionary, available at: https://www.oed.com/ [accessed on: July 1st, 2024].

Benedetta Arrighini*

II. Effectiveness Through Approximation in the EU Area of Freedom Security and Justice

Abstract: Guaranteeing effective criminal justice at the EU level has never been simple due to its inherently national character. After many discussions and legal changes, such as the implementation of the Internal Market and the establishment of Schengen, criminal justice became an EU law issue. The Treaty of Lisbon defined the Judicial Cooperation in Criminal Matters: Arts. 82–86 TFEU providing for mutual recognition and approximation as two complementary instruments for effective cooperation. This chapter explores the relationship between effectiveness and approximation in the context of the European Union's Area of Freedom, Security, and Justice (AFSJ). The effectiveness of approximation is analysed through the lens of key criminal procedural directives, which aim to harmonise rights during criminal proceedings across the EU. Despite these advances, the paper argues that the process of achieving full effectiveness through approximation remains incomplete, as challenges persist in balancing national sovereignty with EU-wide integration and (especially) with the rights (too often forgotten) of the suspect and the accused.

Keywords: Approximation, effectiveness, criminal justice, Area of Freedom Security and Justice, procedural rights

1. Introduction: Connecting Effectiveness and Approximation

At the end of June 2023, I had the opportunity to attend, as a participant, the Conference on 'EU Directives on Procedural Rights in Criminal Matters: 15 years after the Roadmap, where do we stand, where do we go?', celebrating, as written, the roadmap provided by the Council, which gives guidelines to establish minimum rules in criminal procedure at the EU level[1]. On this occasion, there was an interesting metaphor for the almost-15-year-Roadmap, because this age represents the age of an advanced teenager who has matured and is

* MSCA PhD Candidate in Law at the ULB Bruxelles, Fundaçao Getullio Vargas Direito Rio, Luiss University.

1 The programme of the conference is available at: https://www.law.kuleuven.be/eur/en/events-eu-law/closing-academic-year-event-2023.

approaching adulthood. However, it still has room to grow and find its place[2]. This is exactly where the Procedural Directives are: they grew up, but there is a margin for improvement.

The Procedural Rights Directives are the products of a vital instrument for the construction of the EU Area of Freedom Security and Justice (hereinafter AFSJ): approximation, meaning the competence of the EU to establish minimum rules for the Member States[3]. This instrument has been discussed in the years by criminal scholars and it is intriguing to explore the intricate nexus between the efficacy of criminal justice systems and approximation. In this regard, approximation can be a useful tool to build a more effective EU criminal law system[4]. This contribution aims at understanding approximation, framed in the EU AFSJ, to then grasp its role in enhancing effectiveness in the region. Approximation will be the instrument analysed to discuss effectiveness in the EU AFSJ. The discussion will be related to the following question: is approximation ensuring effectiveness? Is it enough? The discussion will be driven in the light of the EU Directives on Procedural Rights[5]. First one must define effectiveness and approximation to understand the main issue.

---

2 I. Gambardella, V. Davio, 'Introduction' in: I. Gambardella, V. Davio (eds.), *EU Directives On Procedural Rights In Criminal Matters: 15 Years After The Roadmap, Where Do We Stand, Where Do We Go?*, 156 *Eu Law Live* 2023, Special Issue, p. 3.

3 A. Weyembergh, 'The Functions of Approximation of Penal Legislation within the European Union,' 12(2) *Maastricht Journal of European and Comparative Law* 2005, p. 150.

4 A. Weyembergh, 'The Functions of Approximation...', p. 150. Despite the utility of approximation, on the other side one should read Weyembergh opinion on approximation, stating: 'On the one hand, approximation constitutes a stronger model of legal integration than coordination and cooperation, in the sense that, in principle, the first implies adjustments of the internal laws to meet specific objectives whereas the latter do not aim at modifying national legislation, do not concern the norms themselves or their contents but rather the effects of the norms. On the other hand, approximation constitutes a weaker means of legal integration than unification'.

5 Directive 2010/64/EU on the right to interpretation and translation in criminal proceedings; Directive 2012/13/EU on the right to information in criminal proceedings; Directive 2013/48/EU on the right of access to a lawyer in criminal proceedings; Directive 2016/343/EU on the strengthening of certain aspects of the presumption of innocence and of the right to be present at the trial in criminal proceedings; Directive 2016/800/EU on procedural safeguards for children who are suspects or accused persons in criminal proceedings; Directive 2016/1919/EU on legal aid for suspects and accused persons in criminal proceedings.

1.1. What's the best way to capture the idea of effectiveness in the EU Area of Freedom, Security and Justice?

Effectiveness is "a key principle aimed to ensure the enforcement of European Union law in national legal orders"[6]. In the realm of European Criminal Law, the primary concept of effectiveness is predominantly centred around the restraint of state authority, a *facet* that holds significant importance within this legal domain[7]. In this context, it is essential to establish an initial premise that outlines the trajectory of the EU collaboration in criminal affairs. Criminal law primarily hinges on the concepts of territoriality, and national territoriality. Consequently, Member States have not always been eager to relinquish their sovereignty in criminal matters[8].

As will be explained in the following paragraphs, the evolution of the AFSJ was gradual; after several tries, the Treaty of Lisbon managed to extend the EU's competence to achieve more effective cooperation in criminal matters. In this context, according to Arts. 82 §2 and 83 TFEU, the EU shall approve Directives to "establish minimum rules' (1) to improve mutual recognition among Member States; in addition, the EU can act through these 'minimum rules' in '(2) the areas of grave crime with a cross-border dimension".

1.2. What is approximation?

Approximation or harmonisation involves the adaptations of national laws according to European objectives; they differ from unification (through Regulation, for example), which is a more advanced form of integration[9]. However, Approximation and unification have something in common because they both pass through the acceptance of the EU's sovereignty. The core of the two is the same, but the degree

6 V. Mitsilegas, 'From Overcriminalisation to Decriminalisation: The Many Faces of Effectiveness in European Criminal Law', 5(3) *New Journal of European Criminal Law* 2014, p. 417: 'Effectiveness is a fundamental constitutional principle of EU law, deemed to be inextricably linked with other fundamental principles of EU law including primacy and direct effect, but also the autonomy of EU law and state liability for damages. It is a key principle aimed to ensure the enforcement of European Union law in national legal orders.'

7 V. Mitsilegas, 'From Overcriminalisation...', p. 418.

8 A. Weyembergh, 'La coopération pénale dans l'Union européenne: de mécanismes classiques marqués par le principe de la territorialité nationale à la mise sur pied d'un territoire pénal européen?' in: L. P. Solis (ed.), *L'Union européenne et les territoires*, Bruylant 2022, p. 300.

9 A. Weyembergh, 'The Functions of Approximation...', p. 150.

of sovereignty is different because, with approximation, Member States maintain a certain degree of autonomy in domestic legislation. The ultimate idea is to create a common EU legal language to deal with criminal matters[10].

The following paragraphs will introduce the development of the EU criminal law and the birth of approximation in this field (2); secondly, (3) it will discuss approximation under the Treaty of Lisbon, focusing on the approximation and the Directives on Procedural Rights. The conclusion (4) will combine the concepts of effectiveness and approximation.

2. The Path of Approximation in the Evolution of the AFSJ: From Scepticism and Course Changes (A)

"The EU's institutional framework for the adoption of Justice and Home Affairs law has gone through several phases"[11]. It is not possible to explain in detail the inclusion and implementation of approximation in the EU criminal law's evolution, however, the Section will try to draw an overview of the problems encountered by the EU in the discussion on this subject. In this spirit, the section will start with the first steps made by the European Commission to harmonize penalties and the first reluctance of the Member States (1). Then, it will go through the formal introduction of EU criminal law with the Treaty of Maastricht (2). To the last, there is a need to talk about the Treaty of Amsterdam and its importance in the affirmation of the EU Area of Freedom, Security and Justice (3). Traversing the history of the harmonization of criminal law is crucial to understanding how and why we are where we reached, to better understand the meaning of the Procedural Rights Directives.

---

10 K. Zoumpoulakis, 'From the Ground up: The Use of Minimum Rules in EU Procedural Criminal Law and the Question of Member States' Discretion', 5 *European Papers – A Journal on Law and Integration* 2020, p. 1290.

11 S. Peers, 'The Rise and Fall of EU Justice and Home Affairs Law', in *The European Union as an Area of Freedom, Security and Justice*, Routledge 2016, pp. 11–33.

2.1. The beginning of approximation and the obstacles in building a community in criminal law

Due to the strong national territorial character of criminal law, the birth of EU criminal law passed through the intergovernmental system[12]. The European Community Treaty did not provide for clear legal bases concerning criminal law, apart from the obligation of the Member States to criminalize possible violations of Euratom confidentiality or perjury in front of the European Court of Justice[13]. This had a central role in the limitation of Member States' autonomy in the field of criminal law. Interpreting Art. 10 ECC, duty of cooperation, "the Court has established that the Member States must enforce Community law, whereby they must provide for procedures and penalties that are effective, proportionate, and dissuasive and that offer a degree of protection that is analogous to that offered in the enforcement of provisions of national law of a similar nature and importance (the assimilation principle)"[14].

Between 1975 and 1990 the Commission proposed the harmonization of sanctions for EU competences crimes[15]. The Member States did not appreciate this move, and they asked the Court of Justice if the Commission had the competence to harmonize penalties. The CJEU stated that "the EC was competent to adopt the measures including the punitive sanctions which without a doubt fall within the scope of application of the criminal law guarantees of Art. 6 ECHR"[16]. This was a first, decisive, step ahead, but many others might have been made[17].

---

12 The first appearance of EU cooperation in criminal matters was made through Conventions related to specific issues implying transnational interest, for example the TREVI Group funded to build a coherent and united fight against terrorism. The group's work was based on intergovernmental cooperation between the 12 states, a process which excludes the main European Community institutions - the European Commission and the European Parliament. In addition, another vital document is the Convention on Implementing the Schengen Agreement (hereinafter CISA) in which there was the creation of transborder cooperation due to the abolition of the EU borders.

13 J. A. E. Vervaele, 'The European Community and Harmonization of the Criminal Law Enforcement of Community Policy' 3–4 *EUCRIM Br* 2006, p. 3.

14 J. A. E. Vervaele, 'The European Community...', p. 3.

15 J. A. E. 'The European Community...', p. 4.

16 J. A. E. Vervaele, 'The European Community...', p. 4. ECJ, *Germany v. Council and Commission*, C-240/90, October 27th, 1992.

17 It is not possible to discuss in depth what happened between the Commission and the EU Member States in these years. For a more detailed explanation see J. A. E. Vervaele, 'The European Community...', *passim*.

Nonetheless, upon recognizing a more effective collaboration facilitated by this instrument, subsequent treaties transformed the EU's approach to criminal law.

2.2. Maastricht and the europeanization of criminal law (also in criminal matters)

"The Europeanisation of criminal law has developed steadily since the entry into force of the Maastricht Treaty"[18]. In this respect, the Treaty of Maastricht introduced the Pillars' structure[19]: the justice and home affairs pillar followed the intergovernmental process[20] and the Council had the competence to vote unanimously on conventions or other acts covering criminal law. Parliament had still no role[21]. The inclusion of criminal law in the third pillar was considered a conquest. On the other side, this automatically excluded any community competence[22].

The Treaty of Maastricht legally introduced "the criminal harmonization of policy areas that are not part of the EC Treaty, but that are nevertheless necessary for the objectives of the Area for Freedom, Security and Justice are placed within the third pillar"[23]. The EU Member States achieved the Convention on the protection of the European Community's financial interest, different actions were taken against the participation in a criminal organization, and many others[24]. However, there was still reluctance, and the Commission and the Council did not find a common ground to start thinking effectively about

18 J. A. E. Vervaele, 'The European Community...', p. 2.
19 EU Community (1st), the Common Foreign Security Policy (2nd) and Justice and Home Affairs (3rd).
20 J. A. E. Vervaele, 'Harmonised Union policies and the harmonisation of substantive criminal law' in: F. Galli, A. Weyembergh (eds.), *Approximation of substantive criminal law in the EU. The way forward*, Éd. de l'Université de Bruxelles 2013, pp. 43–72.
21 S. Peers, 'The Rise and Fall of EU Justice and Home Affairs Law...', p. 12.
22 J. A. E. Vervaele, 'Harmonised Union policies...', p. 47.
23 J. A. E. Vervaele, 'The European Community and Harmonization...', p. 14.
24 Examples of this are the 1995 Convention on the protection of the European Community's financial interests, about the 1997 Convention on the fight against corruption or about the different joint actions adopted at the time in the field of participation in a criminal organisation, trafficking in human beings, racism and xenophobia, corruption in the private sector. See F. Galli, 'Approximation of substantive criminal law: The new institutional and decision-making framework and new types of interaction between EU actors' in: F. Galli, A. Weyembergh (eds.), *Approximation of substantive criminal law...*, p. 10.

approximation[25]. Furthermore, there was an initial need for common definitions, but it involved more the explanation of transnational crimes and not (yet) the criminal procedure. Nevertheless, appreciating the glass as half full and not half empty, despite the steps behind the Treaty of Lisbon, Maastricht went one step ahead. Not only that it opened the way to successive implementation. In this wake, the treaty of Amsterdam continued and improved *approximation.*

2.3. The Treaty of Amsterdam and the Council's turn for enhanced cooperation, also through approximation

Art. 31 of the Treaty of Amsterdam[26] provided for the progressive adoption of measures *establishing minimum rules* relating to the constituent elements of criminal acts and penalties in organized crime. While Maastricht introduced EU criminal law and *approximation* of criminal laws, the Treaty of Amsterdam gave an explicit role to EU cooperation in criminal matters, keeping the Council as the main legislator. In this context, more than ten framework decisions were adopted[27]. The common denominator of these legal acts is the transnationality and

---

25 J. A. E. Vervaele, 'Harmonised Union policies...', p. 47–48. The author talks about three different type of conflicts: 1) Warding off: The Commission submits proposals for criminal law harmonization of Community law which the Council subsequently rejects. At best the proposal is neutralized and stripped of its criminal law packaging. The Council here applies an old legislative tactic that was used in the period before the entry into force of the Treaty on European Union. 2) Hijacking: whereby the content of a proposal for a regulation or directive is copied into a proposal for a framework decision or vice versa. The Commission and the Member States take turns to hijack the content of each other's proposals and subsequently package it in a different legal instrument. 3) Cohabitation force: whereby two proposals are elaborated alongside each other and in harmony with each other. The substantive provisions and, as the case may be, provisions concerning administrative harmonization are included in a proposal for a directive or a regulation, while the criminal law harmonization aspects are incorporated in a framework decision.

26 Art. 31: (a) facilitating and accelerating cooperation between competent ministries and judicial or equivalent authorities of the Member States in relation to proceedings and the enforcement of decisions; (b) facilitating extradition between Member States; (c) ensuring compatibility in rules applicable in the Member States, as may be necessary to improve such cooperation; (d) preventing conflicts of jurisdiction between Member States; (e) progressively adopting measures establishing minimum rules relating to the constituent elements of criminal acts and to penalties in the fields of organised crime, terrorism and illicit drug trafficking.

27 F. Galli, 'Approximation of substantive criminal law...', p. 10.

the gravity of the offences. Indeed, these crimes show more clearly the impellent need for cooperation in the EU.

The European Council adopted 5-years-program defining the policy orientations and priorities for the AFSJ: the Vienna Action Plan of 1998[28] and the Tampere Council of October 1999[29] to arrive at the Hague Programme 2004[30]. All these had a role in the birth and development of the AFSJ, and, in this, of approximation of legislation[31]. These are all signs of the need to strengthen cooperation, and approximation is seen to this end[32].

---

28 Action Plan of the Council and the Commission on how best to implement the provisions of the Treaty of Amsterdam on an area of freedom, security and justice, Text adopted by the Justice and Home Affairs Council, December 3rd, 1998.

29 Tampere European Council, October 15th–16th, 1999, Presidency Conclusions, Preamble and §§ 29–37.

30 The Hague Programme, Strengthening Freedom, security and justice in the European Union, adopted by the Brussels European Council, November 4th–5th, 2004, Presidency Conclusions.

31 For a clear understanding of the historical development of approximation see A. Weyembergh, 'The Functions of Approximation…', pp. 150–155.

32 Tampere European Council, Presidency Conclusions, Preamble and §§ 29 and 33 ("Enhanced mutual recognition of judicial decisions and judgements and the necessary approximation of legislation would facilitate cooperation between authorities and the judicial protection of individual rights. The European Council therefore endorses the principle of mutual recognition which, in its view, should become the cornerstone of judicial cooperation in civil and criminal matters within the Union. The principle should apply both to judgements and to other decisions of judicial authorities"); and § 48 ("Without prejudice to the broader areas envisaged in the Treaty of Amsterdam and in the Vienna Action Plan, the European Council considers that, about national criminal law, efforts to agree on common definitions, incriminations and sanctions should be focused in the first instance on a limited number of sectors of particular relevance, such as financial crime (money laundering, corruption, Euro counterfeiting), drugs trafficking, trafficking in human beings, particularly exploitation of women, sexual exploitation of children, high tech crime and environmental crime"). In addition, see the Hague Programme, Strengthening Freedom, security and justice in the European Union, adopted by the Brussels European Council, November 4th–5th, 2004,' § 3.3.2 ("Approximation of law The European Council recalls that the establishment of minimum rules concerning aspects of procedural law is envisaged by the treaties in order to facilitate mutual recognition of judgments and judicial decisions and police and judicial cooperation in criminal matters having a cross-border dimension. The approximation of substantive criminal law serves the same purposes and concerns areas of particular serious crime with cross border dimensions. Priority should be given to areas of crime that are specifically mentioned in the treaties. To ensure more effective implementation within national systems, JHA Ministers should be responsible within the Council for defining criminal offences and determining penalties in general").

The discussion on EU criminal law leads the Member States to interrogate themselves on possible effective approaches to cooperation: approximation will serve to boost mutual recognition between Member States: "approximation is a condition for smooth judicial cooperation"[33].

3. Change of Paradigm in the Area of Freedom Security and Justice: the Lisbon 'Revolution' (B)

The Treaty of Lisbon outlines judicial cooperation in criminal matters in Title V, Chapter 4, which concerns the Area of Freedom Security and Justice, specifically in Arts. 82 to 86 TFEU. Art. 82 § 1 TFEU[34] outlines the two instruments of EU cooperation in criminal matters[35]: mutual recognition and approximation. The two instruments are complementary and not alternative because they serve to improve each other[36]. The following pages will focus on the role of approximation, giving the right attention to the link with mutual recognition.

The paragraph will introduce Arts. 82 § 2 and 83 TFEU concerning the role of approximation within the EU AFSJ (1). Then it will analyse the approximation of criminal procedural rights, starting with the Council's Resolution on a Roadmap for strengthening the procedural rights of suspected or accused persons

---

33 A. Weyembergh, 'The Functions of Approximation...', p. 155 ("According to its first auxiliary function, approximation is a condition for smooth judicial cooperation. This is true despite a certain trend at present that tends to deny or reduce approximation's role since the process of mutual recognition was launched. This process is based on mutual confidence, which plays a more important role here than in the context of classical mechanisms of cooperation").

34 "1. Judicial cooperation in criminal matters in the Union shall be based on the principle of mutual recognition of judgments and judicial decisions and shall include the approximation of the laws and regulations of the Member States in the areas referred to in paragraph 2 and in Article 83. The European Parliament and the Council, acting in accordance with the ordinary legislative procedure, shall adopt measures to: (a) lay down rules and procedures for ensuring recognition throughout the Union of all forms of judgments and judicial decisions; (b) prevent and settle conflicts of jurisdiction between Member States; (c) support the training of the judiciary and judicial staff; (d) facilitate cooperation between judicial or equivalent authorities of the Member States in relation to proceedings in criminal matters and the enforcement of decisions".

35 P. De Pasquale, C. Pesce, 'Article 82 – Principle of Mutual Recognition' in H.-J. Blanke, S. Mangiameli (eds.), *Treaty on the Functioning of the European Union – A Commentary*, Cham: Springer International Publishing 2021, p. 1563.

36 P. De Pasquale, C. Pesce, 'Article 82...', p. 1563.

in criminal proceedings[37] (2). To that end, the Procedural Directives protecting the rights of the suspect and the accused and the right to a fair trial are established based on Art. 82 § 2 TFEU and they will be analysed to identify the function of approximation in the EU AFSJ (3). From here, the paragraphs will proceed to understand the relationship between approximation and effectiveness.

3.1. Arts. 82 § 2 and 83 TFEU: why 'establishing minimum rules'?

Why does the EU AFSJ need approximation? Two functions were identified: the ancillary/auxiliary function and the autonomous function[38]. In the first case, approximation is applied to facilitate mutual recognition: it is not an instrument of cooperation *per se*, but 'an instrument for the instrument' of mutual recognition. In the second case, approximation is alone a tool for cooperation and "one can distinguish approximation's function as regards the fight against crime on the one hand and its other autonomous functions, concerning individual rights, free movement and equality of treatment before the law on the other hand"[39].

The ancillary function is evident[40] in Art. 82 § 2 TFEU:

> "To the extent necessary to facilitate mutual recognition of judgments and judicial decisions and police and judicial cooperation in criminal matters having a cross-border dimension, the European Parliament and the Council may, employing directives adopted following the ordinary legislative procedure, establish minimum rules. Such rules shall consider the differences between the legal traditions and systems of the Member States.
>
> They shall concern:
>
> (a) mutual admissibility of evidence between Member States;
> (b) the rights of individuals in criminal procedure;
> (c) the rights of victims of crime;
> (d) any other specific aspects of criminal procedure which the Council has identified in advance by a decision; for the adoption of such a decision, the Council shall act unanimously after obtaining the consent of the European Parliament.
>
> Adoption of the minimum rules referred to in this paragraph shall not prevent Member States from maintaining or introducing a higher level of protection for individuals".

37 Resolution on a Roadmap for strengthening procedural rights of suspected or accused persons in criminal proceedings, November 30th, 2009.
38 F. Galli, 'Approximation of substantive criminal law...', p. 20.
39 A. Weyembergh, 'The Functions of Approximation...', p. 163.
40 A. Weyembergh, 'The Functions of Approximation...', p. 155.

Approximation facilitates mutual recognition because establishing common general principles in the EU Member States enhances mutual trust. This should increase mutual recognition and consequently the effectiveness of cooperation[41]. In addition, the EU judicial actors also need approximation: the work of the European Judicial Network, of Eurojust, of the joint investigation teams, and the European Public Prosecutor can act more effectively with an approximation of substantive and procedural criminal law of the Member States.

Secondly, approximation has autonomous functions because it is considered an instrument to fight crimes. It aims to harmonize the definitions, sanctions and procedural rules across Member States, ensuring a cohesive approach to combating serious crimes that transcend national borders. This independent role of approximation facilitates a more effective and unified response to criminal activities that affect multiple jurisdictions within the EU. Art. 83 § 1 TFEU expresses the autonomous function[42], stating:

> "The European Parliament and the Council may, by means of directives adopted in accordance with the ordinary legislative procedure, establish minimum rules concerning the definition of criminal offences and sanctions in the areas of particularly serious crime with a cross-border dimension resulting from the nature or impact of such offences or from a special need to combat them on a common basis.
>
> These areas of crime are the following: terrorism, trafficking in human beings and sexual exploitation of women and children, illicit drug trafficking, illicit arms trafficking, money laundering, corruption, counterfeiting of means of payment, computer crime and organized crime.
>
> On the basis of developments in crime, the Council may adopt a decision identifying other areas of crime that meet the criteria specified in this paragraph. It shall act unanimously after obtaining the consent of the European Parliament".

---

41 'Given the wording of Article 82 TFEU, harmonization of criminal law and criminal procedure is also a necessary tool for strengthening judicial cooperation in criminal matters based on mutual recognition and mutual trust'. See J. A. E. Vervaele, 'Harmonised Union policies…', p. 61.

42 F. Galli, 'Approximation of substantive criminal law…', p. 20 ("We would like to point out that approximation's autonomous functions include the development of the so-called 'sword function' of EU substantive criminal law which aims at enhancing the fight against crime and at preventing criminals from benefitting directly or indirectly from the existing disparities in substantive criminal law between the EU Member States. The importance of such an autonomous function already resulted from Art. 29 TEU since it mentioned approximation among the measures to ensure a high level of security").

The rationale behind these areas is related to their cross-border dimension resulting from the crime *per se*, or from the impact of the crime[43]. The effectiveness of approximation is, again, guaranteeing more security once there is more freedom for the EU citizens. Furthermore, Art. 83 § 2 TFEU expands the competence of the EU in areas of crime that are not provided in the previous paragraph affirming that:

> "If the approximation of criminal laws and regulations of the Member States proves essential to ensure the effective implementation of a Union policy in an area which has been subject to harmonization measures, directives may establish minimum rules regarding the definition of criminal offences and sanctions in the area concerned. Such directives shall be adopted by the same ordinary or special legislative procedure as was followed for the adoption of the harmonization measures in question, without prejudice to Article 76".

In this paragraph, the need for the EU to 'ensure effective implementation' of a coherent EU policy is more evident than in the others. This is the biggest novelty of the Treaty; in this case, the EU designates criminal law as an instrument to protect a wide range of interests[44]. Art. 83 §§ 1 and 2 do not define an exhaustive list[45]. This may allow the EU to expand its competence in legislating in criminal matters. If on one side this could be a way to guarantee more effectiveness in the fight against crime, on the other there is always the risk of an over-expansion of a criminal action which is not only triggering the EU competence according to the TFEU but also the principle of criminal law as *extrema ratio*[46]: criminal law shall not be the immediate answer to every offence and the fact that the EU can

43 I. Wieczorek, 'The Emerging Role of the EU as a Primary Normative Actor in the EU Area of Criminal Justice', 27(4–6) *European Law Journal* 2023, p. 388. 'The first paragraph of Art. 83 TFEU includes a specific reference to legal cross-borderness when limiting EU harmonisation only to serious and cross-border crimes as resulting from the nature or impact of such offences or from a special need to combat them on a common basis'.

44 A. Weyembergh, 'The Functions of Approximation…', p. 21.

45 P. De Pasquale and C. Pesce, 'Article 83 – Minimum Harmonisation' in: H.-J. Blanke, S. Mangiameli (eds.), *Treaty on the Functioning of the European Union – A Commentary*, Cham: Springer International Publishing 2021, p. 1584. But also see the text of Art. 83 § 1 TFEU concerning the possibility for the Council to expand its legislative competence 'on the basis of the development of crime'.

46 For example, there is a lot to say about the EU directive on counter-terrorism 541/2017 in which there is an expansion of the offence. See B. Arrighini, 'The EU Directive 2017/541 from a Fundamental Rights' Perspective', 24(1) *ERA Forum* 2023, p. 24. And also I. Wieczorek, 'The Emerging Role…', p. 398.

insert new offences according to the 'effective implementation of a Union policy' allows the EU to introduce other offences. Additionally, the EU Member States already have their definition of crimes and insisting on new EU crimes could unnecessarily expand the criminal law action.

In this, it is suggested that approximation should serve an autonomous function not only in defining criminal offences but also in affirming the rights of individuals. Since the EU is a Union of values, Member States should adopt minimum standards protecting fundamental rights to facilitate mutual recognition and as principles of the EU[47]. The EU is not there yet. Indeed, the EU Criminal Procedural Directives outlining the rights of the suspects and the accused serve to facilitate mutual recognition, as I will illustrate in the following paragraph.

3.2. Effectiveness through approximation: the criminal procedural directives

On the wave of the Lisbon Revolution within the AFSJ, in November 2009 the Council published a Resolution recognizing the importance of approximation to implement mutual recognition between Member States[48]. In this spirit, it invited the EU's institutions to provide for general standards to be followed by the Member States in criminal proceedings[49]. The Annex of the Resolution indicated six different measures: A) Translation and interpretation; B) Information on Rights and information about the Charges; C) Legal Advice and Legal Aid; D) Communication with Relatives, Employers and Consular Authorities; E) Special Safeguards for Suspected or Accused Vulnerable Persons; F) A Green Paper on Pre-Trial Detention[50].

---

47 J. Öberg, *The Normative Foundations for EU Criminal Justice: Powers, Limits and Justifications*, 1st ed., Hart Publishing 2024, p. 61. The Author explains how there is an interest in protecting fundamental rights in cross-border situations but there is not the same need for a domestic dimension. The problem is that the protection of the rights of the suspect and the accused should be the central part of the functioning of a rule-of-law region.

48 Resolution on a Roadmap for strengthening procedural rights of suspected or accused persons in criminal proceedings, November 30th, 2009.

49 Resolution on a Roadmap for strengthening procedural rights of suspected or accused persons in criminal proceedings, November 30th, 2009, §§ 1–2.

50 Resolution on a Roadmap for strengthening procedural rights of suspected or accused persons in criminal proceedings, November 30th, 2009, Annex.

From this ambitious Resolution, the Directives on Procedural Rights were proposed, discussed, and then approved. They were presented and published gradually over time, trying to maintain a general consistency between the different legal provisions. These cover the following domains: right to interpretation and translation in criminal proceedings[51]; right to information[52]; right of access to a lawyer[53]; strengthening the presumption of innocence[54]; safeguards for children who are suspects or accused[55]; legal aid for suspects and accused persons[56]. While practitioners have generally welcomed these legal acts[57], it is essential to acknowledge and address the criticisms highlighted by scholars. The following paragraphs will delve into the introduction of a critical analysis of this 'package', being aware that the Directives have diverse content, but the same legal basis and the same ambitious purpose.

At first glance, the Directives are a signal of an EU increasing power to legislate criminal law. In this regard, if we reflect on the path of EU criminal law, twenty years ago there was no space for the EU to legislate in certain areas of criminal matters. In addition, the beginnings of approximation focused on substantive criminal law, since the Commission started from the harmonization of penalties, and then of offences. Criminal procedure, and especially criminal procedural guarantees, have always been subjected to the power of the Member States. Yet, approximation of criminal procedural guarantees appears necessary to facilitate mutual recognition in EU cross-border cases[58]. In this context, "it is abundantly clear that criminal (procedural) law belongs to the sphere of competence of the Member States, but that Community law may impose requirements as to the

51 Directive 2010/64/EU on the right to interpretation and translation in criminal proceedings.
52 Directive 2012/13/EU on the right to information in criminal proceedings.
53 Directive 2013/48/EU on the right of access to a lawyer in criminal proceedings.
54 Directive 2016/343/EU on the strengthening of certain aspects of the presumption of innocence.
55 Directive 2016/800/EU on procedural safeguards for children who are suspects or accused.
56 Directive 2016/1919/EU on legal aid for suspects and accused persons in criminal proceedings.
57 G. Jansen, 'The Need for a New Roadmap of Procedural Safeguards: A Lawyer's Perspective', 22(2) *ERA Forum* 2021, p. 280.
58 M. Panzavolta, 'Some critical reflections on the Procedural Rights Directives' in I. Gambardella, V. Davio (eds.), *EU Directives On Procedural Rights In Criminal Matters: 15 Years After The Roadmap, Where Do We Stand, Where Do We Go?*, 156 *EU Law Liv*, 2023, pp. 9–14.

fulfilment and interpretation of this competence within the framework of the enforcement of Community law"[59].

Due to the abovementioned reasons[60], the Procedural rights Directives guarantee more effectiveness in the EU criminal justice[61]. In this regard, "harmonization of procedural laws facilitates mutual recognition not only because it can reduce the cases of refusals but also because it can allow judicial cooperation to function smoothly while ensuring the fair and just treatment of suspects and accused"[62]. Indeed, on one side EU judicial cooperation in criminal matters will assure more security in the realm of transborder crime, on the other side, there must be attention on the individual. To that end, there is a positive outcome in the protection of individual rights as well as the desire for all Member States to fulfil these conditions. However, every development, however positive, has flaws, and directives are not an endpoint but a starting point. That is why it is essential to look at them with a critical eye and thus point out their weaknesses.

First, one must start from their legal basis: Art. 82 § 2 TFEU. This provision is "too confined to respond to the demand for a self-standing EU policy on procedural safeguards for defendants in criminal proceedings and, hence, recommend a broader mandate in this area, allowing both functional and self-standing powers"[63]. In this regard, the competence of 'establishing minimum rules' – as said above – is part of the *ancillary* function of approximation[64]. Öberg affirmed that "One of the central limits [of harmonisation] is the requirement that harmonisation of procedural standards must facilitate 'mutual recognition' of judgments or decisions and 'judicial cooperation'"[65]. In this, the author suggests framing criminal procedural guarantees as the minimum standards for a rule-of-law region (the EU) and not only as a tool to facilitate mutual recognition.

Secondly, Panzavolta analysed the weakness of the Directives concerning the application of fundamental rights[66]. In this, the Directives define fundamental

---

59 J. A. E. Vervaele, 'Harmonised Union policies...', p. 47.

60 See § 3.1.

61 J. Ouwerkerk, 'EU Competence in the Area of Procedural Criminal Law: Functional vs. Self-Standing Approximation of Procedural Rights and Their Progressive Effect on the Charter's Scope of Application', 27(2) *European Journal of Crime, Criminal Law and Criminal Justice* 2019, p. 90.

62 M. Panzavolta, 'Some critical reflections...', p. 11.

63 J. Ouwerkerk, 'EU Competence ...', p. 90.

64 J. Ouwerkerk, 'EU Competence ...', p. 90.

65 J. Öberg, *The Normative Foundations for EU Criminal Justice...*, p. 39.

66 M. Panzavolta, 'Some critical reflections...', pp. 9–14.

rights as enshrined in Art. 6 ECHR, Arts. 47 and 48 Charter of Fundamental Rights of the European Union (CFR). "Fundamental rights are normally conceived to be applicable in all areas where their safeguarding nature is needed. (…) It is not the case of directives"[67]. The author has analysed the Directives pointing out the necessity for the secondary Act to be more precise and specific, and this may lead to limitations. In this regard, the European legislator must proceed with caution because there is the risk that embedding a fundamental right in a Directive will limit the right[68].

As said, the Directives are an advanced attempt to enhance cooperation within Member States; yet, after 15 years, the EU must project their 'adulthood'[69] by being more ambitious in pursuing greater regional integration, while also guaranteeing stronger respect for fundamental rights.

4. Shaping Effectiveness and Approximation: It Is Not Over Yet (C)

Approximation is one of the essential tools to build a genuine Area of Freedom Security and Justice[70]. To build an effective AFSJ, one could add. In this spirit, the paper had the aim to analyse approximation considering the effectiveness of criminal justice at the EU level. It has illustrated the history of EU criminal law, to then focus on one of the instruments utilised to implement the AFSJ. The EU made significant steps towards integration, even in criminal justice. In this regard, the idea of this chapter was to underline the role of approximation as an instrument of effectiveness that could be implemented more by the EU. As affirmed in the introduction to this article, the effectiveness of EU law is the possibility for the EU to expand its powers, since Member States alone cannot coordinate as they can through the Community method. However, I would add that effectiveness in EU criminal law also expresses a higher grade of trust and, consequently, smoother cooperation. And as we saw, approximation is an essential instrument to improve both.

Concluding this overview and this synthetic analysis, the EU Directives on Procedural Rights can be a good example of enhancing effectiveness in EU criminal justice. Still, the way forward is long. Indeed, the approximation of procedural

67 M. Panzavolta, 'Some critical reflections…', p. 10.
68 M. Panzavolta, 'Some critical reflections…', p. 11.
69 See § 1: they are like a teenager approaching adulthood.
70 A. Weyembergh, 'La coopération pénale dans l'Union européenne'…, p. 300.

rights is pivotal to reaching an effective implementation of EU criminal justice, as well as being aware of the respect of fundamental rights.

Some suggestions must be made. Approximation of legislation as provided in the EU Treaties and the Directives is not enough; there is a need to enhance approximation to implement mutual recognition, but especially to build an EU of values, more specifically, of criminal guarantees. First, this needs to be done not only among Member States but also in the field of the EU judicial actors' collaboration. Second, the approximation of procedural criminal law must always remember the rights of the suspect and the victim, being aware of the sensitiveness of criminal trial. Thirdly, the legislator willing to use approximation needs to acknowledge the *extrema ratio* of criminal law and the guarantees of criminal procedure: cooperation is extremely useful and should attire, in the opinion of the author, more attention from the EU legislator; however, it must not forget the tension with fundamental rights. In this, approximation through the EU law can be a useful tool for effectiveness.

5. Bibliography

Literature

Arrighini B., 'The EU Directive 2017/541 from a Fundamental Rights' Perspective', 24(1) *ERA Forum*, 2023.

De Pasquale P., Pesce C., 'Article 83 – Minimum Harmonisation' in: H.-J. Blanke, S. Mangiameli (eds.), *Treaty on the Functioning of the European Union – A Commentary*, Cham: Springer International Publishing, 2021.

De Pasquale P., Pesce C., 'Article 82 Principle of Mutual Recognition' in: H.-J. Blanke, S. Mangiameli (eds.), *Treaty on the Functioning of the European Union – A Commentary*, Cham: Springer International Publishing, 2021.

Galli F., 'Approximation of substantive criminal law: The new institutional and decision-making framework and new types of interaction between EU actors' in: F. Galli F., A. Weyembergh (eds.), *Approximation of substantive criminal law in the EU: The way forward*, Éd. de l'Université de Bruxelles 2013.

Gambardella I., Davio V., 'Introduction' in: I. Gambardella, V. Davio (eds.), *EU Directives On Procedural Rights In Criminal Matters: 15 Years After The Roadmap, Where Do We Stand, Where Do We Go?*, 156 *Eu Law Live* 2023, Special Issue.

Gless S., Vervaele J. A. E., 'Law Should Govern: Aspiring General Principles for Transnational Criminal Justice', 9(4) *Utrecht Law Review*, 2013.

Jansen G., 'The Need for a New Roadmap of Procedural Safeguards: A Lawyer's Perspective', 22(2) *ERA Forum* 2021.

Mitsilegas V., 'From Overcriminalisation to Decriminalisation: The Many Faces of Effectiveness in European Criminal Law', 5(3) *New Journal of European Criminal Law*, 2014.

Öberg G., *The Normative Foundations for EU Criminal Justice: Powers, Limits and Justifications*, 1st ed., Hart Publishing 2024.

Ouwerkerk J., 'EU Competence in the Area of Procedural Criminal Law: Functional vs. Self-Standing Approximation of Procedural Rights and Their Progressive Effect on the Charter's Scope of Application', 27(2), *European Journal of Crime, Criminal Law and Criminal Justice* 2019.

Panzavolta M., 'Some critical reflections on the Procedural Rights Directives' in: I. Gambardella V. Davio (eds.), *EU Directives On Procedural Rights In Criminal Matters: 15 Years After The Roadmap, Where Do We Stand, Where Do We Go?*, 156 *Eu Law Live* 2023, Special Issue.

Peers S., 'The Rise and Fall of EU Justice and Home Affairs Law' in: *The European Union as an Area of Freedom, Security and Justice*, Routledge 2016.

Peršak N., 'Principles of EU Criminalisation and Their Varied Normative Strength: Harm and Effectiveness', 27 (4–6), *European Law Journal* 2021.

Vervaele J. A. E., 'The European Community and Harmonization of the Criminal Law Enforcement of Community Policy', 3–4 *EUCRIM Br* 2006.

Vervaele J. A. E., 'Harmonised Union policies and the harmonisation of substantive criminal law' in: F. Galli, A. Weyembergh (eds.), *Approximation of substantive criminal law in the EU: The way forward*, Éd. de l'Université de Bruxelles 2013.

Vervaele J. A. E., 'Closing Remarks', 14(1) *New Journal of European Criminal Law* 2023.

Weyembergh A., 'La coopération pénale dans l'Union européenne: de mécanismes classiques marqués par le principe de la territorialité nationale à la mise sur pied d'un territoire pénal européen?' in: L. P. Solis (ed.), *L'Union européenne et les territoires*, Bruylant 2022.

Weyembergh A., 'The Functions of Approximation of Penal Legislation within the European Union', 12(2) *Maastricht Journal of European and Comparative Law* 2005.

Wieczorek, I., 'The Emerging Role of the EU as a Primary Normative Actor in the EU Area of Criminal Justice', 27(4–6) *European Law Journal* 2023.

Zoumpoulakis K., 'From the Ground up: The Use of Minimum Rules in EU Procedural Criminal Law and the Question of Member States' Discretion,' 5 *European Papers – A Journal on Law and Integration* 2020.

Zoumpoulakis K., 'Approximation of Criminal Sanctions in the European Union: A Wild Goose Chase?', 13(3) *New Journal of European Criminal Law* 2022.

Jacek Szkudlarek*

III. The Impact of the Rule of Law Backslide on Revision of the Competences of the Court of Justice of the European Union on the Matter of Member States' Domestic Jurisprudence

Abstract: This paper analyses the judgments of the European Court of Justice (ECJ) that interfere with the organisation of constitutional matters, which fall within the exclusive competence of the national authorities of the Member States. The strengths of the judicial activity of the ECJ, focused on the protection of fundamental rights and the rule of law, are both contested, as well as negative aspects resulting from inconsistencies, incoherence, and Court's political involvement in the dispute. The scholarly disclosure cited in this paper relates to the manifestations of judicial activism by the ECJ, and it attempts to evaluate them through the prism of a specific criterion, usually a particular legal principle.

Keywords: European Court of Justice, constitutional matters, fundamental rights, rule of law

1. Establishing a Robust Position by the ECJ Through the Broadening of Its Jurisdictional Competence

1.1. The core of the Court's intervention in the legal order of Member States

The acknowledgement of the ECJ and the Commission exercising the function of being the "guardians of rights"[1] through their respective competencies in scrutinising the legality of acts enacted by national authorities gives rise to the

---

* Master of Law, Prosecutor's Assistant at the Military Department, District Prosecutor's Office in Warsaw, delegated to the National Public Prosecutor's Office, Poland.

1 The ECJ makes such observation in a pivotal context for the further development of jurisprudence in this field, as stated in the case *Les Verts*, C-294/83, April 23rd, 1986, § 23. On the other hand, the identification of the Commission's own competences can be found in the published communications, such as the Communication from the Commission to the European Parliament, the European Council, the Council, the European Economic and Social Committee and the Committee of the Regions, 'Strengthening the Rule of Law within the Union: A Blueprint for Action', July 17th, 2019, COM/2019/343 final.

impression of convergence of roles between these two institutions in the realm of ensuring compliance with EU law. Therefore, in the international discourse, bolder propositions are being formulated regarding the part of the ECJ in the political dynamics within the community, manifested in its often polemical decisions[2]. This perspective stems from the assumption that the law is generally an incomplete and imprecise agreement, thus requiring interpretation[3]. Considering the above, the Court's interference in legislative actions, such as setting aside measures deemed incompatible with the law, represents a strong manifestation of its intervention in the political crucible of influences within the European community.

The consolidation of the Court's influence is in the expansion of its competencies and resources to monopolise the areas under its jurisdiction, as well as the increasing autonomy of decision-making by including new elements that form an extensive judicial network[4]. In other words, the euro-centric activity of the ECJ can be categorised into two main areas depending on the overall assessment: codification and 'jurisdictionalisation', or adopting the view that the ECJ participates in the political game, 'jurisditionalisation' and 'politicisation' of various areas of member state's functioning.

These assumptions correlate with the concept developed by Carolyn Moser and Berthold Rittberger, which deserves attention as its adoption will have significant implications for further consideration.

The elevation of the integration method between states to the level of supernational public debate strongly impacts the polarising society and, consequently, the political elites, replacing dialogue and consensus-seeking with the limitation of the effects of existing disagreements[5].

Given the existence of conflicts in the political sphere, which are subjected to limited legal control, a court adjudicating in this area can, in a more operative manner, intensify its law-making effort due to a broader scope of interpretation[6].

2 E. Muir, M. Dawson, B. De Witte, 'Introduction: The European Court of Justice as a Political Actor' in: M. Dawson, B. De Witte, E. Muir (eds.), *Judicial Activism at the European Court of Justice*, 2013, pp. 4–5.

3 S. Schmidt, 'The European Court of Justice as a Political Actor', *The European Court of Justice and the Policy Process: The Shadow of Case Law*, Oxford 2018.

4 S. Schmidt, 'The European Court...'

5 C. Moser, B. Rittberger, 'The CJEU and EU (de-)constitutionalization: Unpacking jurisprudential responses', 20(3) *International Journal of Constitutional Law* 2022, p. 1046.

6 C. Moser, B. Rittberger, 'The CJEU...', p. 1047.

The low level of jurisprudence and intense 'politicisation' (or inadequate codification) allow for assuming the role of a moderator who, by employing a set of unquestionable interpretative mechanisms, goes beyond their scope, thereby regulating a specific matter.

There exists no ambiguity regarding the assertion that the realisation of the notion of the rule of law, which constitutes a shared axiom within all European legal frameworks integrated into the triad of EU values, decisively shapes the trajectory of establishing a supranational legal order. In this regard, it ought to should be constructed as a potent constitutionalising force, transcending mere conceptual contours. This is particularly discernible in relation to the procedural safeguards associated with the impartial administration of justice. Consistent with the adopted conceptual framework, the impact of these principles *vis-à-vis* sociopolitical tensions assumes heightened significance, given their vulnerability to erosion under such circumstances. In such a distorted system, the normative outcomes, despite their formal alignment with the legal framework, relinquish the characteristics inherent o the prescribed paradigm.

The ECJ has embraced the view that Art. 19 (1) § 2 of the Treaty on European Union (TEU): "requires Member States to provide remedies that are sufficient to ensure effective legal protection, within the meaning in particular of Art. 47 of the Charter, in the fields covered by EU law"[7] with the attainment of the outcome being unconditional[8]. The assertiveness of this assertion is derived from the close nexus between the provision and the overarching treaty principle. Art. 19 TEU, which specifies the principle enunciated in Art. 2 TEU: "entrusts the responsibility for ensuring the full application of EU law in all Member States and judicial protection of the rights of individuals under that law to national courts and tribunals"[9], while noting that although "the organisation of justice in the Member States falls within the competence of those Member States [...] when exercising that competence, the Member States are required to comply with their obligations deriving from EU law"[10]. Simultaneously, with regard to the scope of application in relation to Art. 47 of the Charter of Fundamental Rights of the European Union (CFR), it defines it as narrower than that of Art. 19 § 2 TEU, owing to its limited subject matter – only individuals may invoke it, provided that their rights have

7 ECJ, *Commission v. Republic of Poland*, C-619/18, June 24th, 2019, § 54.
8 ECJ, *Krajowa Rada Sądownictwa*, C-824/18, March 2nd, 2021, § 146.
9 ECJ, *Commission v. Republic of Poland*, C-619/18, June 24th, 2019, § 47.
10 ECJ, *Commission v. Republic of Poland*, C-619/18, June 24th, 2019, § 52.

been infringed[11]. The ECJ firmly intervenes in the relationship between treaty law and the national judicial system with such a stance, solidifying the interplay between them[12].

The complete legitimacy of the competence to examine constitutional issues in a particular Member State has allowed the ECJ to assess the legislative acts adopted by national authorities that do not fulfil the aforementioned obligation.

The Disciplinary Chamber of the Polish Supreme Court, due to its specific context and objective circumstances of its establishment, as well as the judges serving in it, may: "give rise to reasonable doubts in the minds of individuals as to the imperviousness of that body to external factors, in particular the direct or indirect influence of the Polish legislature and executive, and its neutrality with respect to the interests before it and, thus, are likely to lead to that body's not being seen to be independent or impartial, which is likely to prejudice the trust which justice in a democratic society governed by the rule of law must inspire in those individuals"[13]. In this regard, the measure of compliance with the obligation to establish effective judicial remedies necessary for effective judicial remedy lies in the justified doubts individuals have regarding the subordination of the decision-making body to political authorities. The politicisation of Romania's Section to Investigate Offenses in the Judiciary (SIIJ) is manifested in the possibility of filing "complaints to be lodged unreasonably, inter alia for the purposes of to interfere in ongoing sensitive cases, in particular complex and high-profile cases linked to high-level corruption or organised crime, since if such a complaint were lodged, the matter would automatically fall within the competence of the SIIJ"[14]. According to this stance, effective judicial protection is therefore excluded because there is a body whose exercise of competence aims to avoid criminal proceedings.

The expenditure of funds from the EU budget allocated to the remuneration of a ECJ adjudicating on the application of Union law constituted a sufficient basis for substantive control of the judiciary. Despite not recognizing its competence

---

11 L. Pech, *The European Court of Justice's jurisdiction over national judiciary-related measures*, Brussels 2023, p. 73.

12 See ECJ, *Krajowa Rada Sądownictwa*, C-824/18, March 2nd, 2021, § 68, and ECJ, *Repubblika v. Il-Prim Ministru*, C-896/19, April 20th, 2021, § 48.

13 ECJ, *Commission v. Republic of Poland*, C-791/19, July 15th, 2021, § 112.

14 ECJ, *Asociația 'Forumul Judecătorilor din România'*, Joined Cases C-83/19, C-127/19, C-195/19, C-291/19, C-355/19 and C-397/19, May 18th, 2021, § 218.

in salary matters[15], ECJ formulated several overarching principles defining its position within the hierarchical structure in relation to national courts[16].

However, in not every case did the ECJ allow itself such bold interference in the moderation of the structures of the judiciary by other branches of power. For instance, it stated that the intervention of the executive authority of the German state of Hessen falls within its competent powers, which should not raise doubts regarding the independence of the judges concerned from external factors and their neutrality[17]. In another case, it acknowledged that the Prime Minister's competencies in appointing judges are limited by the requirements that candidates must meet, and a recommendation to the President for a candidate not proposed by the aforementioned commission requires justification. Applying this procedure as an exception does not raise justified doubts regarding the independence of the selected candidates[18]. In the Hungarian case concerning the OBH, the ECJ also found no room for itself to intervene in the regulations concerning the constitutional issues of the national system[19].

The ECJ doesn't indiscriminately seek to expand its powers. Not all inquiries pertaining to constitutional matters result in the ECJ engaging in legislative activities; instead, some seek to reinforce the ECJ's already established position with regarding constitutional issues. Consequently, the ECJ imposes self-imposed limitations beyond which it refrains from venturing. It appears to be guided by moral considerations that define the essence of intervening in the constitutional frameworks of Member States.

Concurrently, these boundaries demarcate the definitional scope within which the court establishes the observance of fundamental rights, including the principle of the rule of law.

1.2. Systematic and functional interpretation as the primary tools of the ECJ's activity

Having delineated the trajectory embraced by the Tribunal, it is necessary to discuss the tools it employs to achieve the intended outcome. Laurent Pech highlighted that in summarizing the Tribunal's achievements thus far, six constitutional

---

15 ECJ, *Associação Sindical dos Juízes Portugueses*, C-64/16, February 27th, 2018, § 52.

16 ECJ, *Associação Sindical dos Juízes Portugueses*, C-64/16, February 27th, 2018, §§ 37–38.

17 ECJ, *Land Hessen*, C-272/19, July 9th, 2020, § 59.

18 ECJ, *Repubblika v. Il-Prim Ministru*, C-896/19, April 20th, 2021, §§ 70–71.

19 ECJ, *IS*, C-564/19, November 23rd, 2021, § 143.

signposts could be identified, delineating the directions for further development of the rule of law[20]. Such transmission of the rule of law from the conceptual sphere to the realm of procedural norms has given rise to new competencies vested in the enforcement bodies for assessing legal orders through the prism of this modified criterion.

Such an endeavour would not be feasible within the scope of a linguistic interpretation of treaty law, as its textual formulation rather reflects the distinctiveness of the member states' legal system and facilitates the integration issue to a general notion.

Therefore, the ECJ exercises its competence by resorting to "non-linguistic methods of interpretation, namely systemic (including systematic) and teleological interpretation"[21]. A transparent reflection of the first-mentioned approach is considering primary law as the foundation for the norms discussed in secondary law. In this regard, particular importance is attributed to the fundamental rights and general principles of law contained therein. The vertical relationship between provisions of different normative acts serves as the basis for applying proper systemic interpretation. At the same time the context in which they are placed is relevant for apparent systemic (contextual) interpretation[22].

Furthermore, for the ECJ, the treaties also determine the scope of application of the specified cooperation mechanisms. They constitute an essential criterion for their evaluation, as they establish principles capable of a direct application when determining the meaning of a legal situation arising from secondary law. In this way, they form o specific normative chain that serves as the basis for functional and purposive interpretation. General principles ensure the effectiveness of the law, as the "principle of effect utile aims to achieve the objectives of EU law by

---

20 Firstly, Art. 2 TEU possesses substantive rather than merely declaratory dimensions; secondly, Art. 2 TEU constitutes a solid core of community law; thirdly, Art. 2 TEU, in addition to its political character, imposes legal obligations enforceable by the Tribunal under Art. 19 TEU; fourthly, Art. 19 TEU carries a jurisdictional condition strongly linked to Art. 2 TEU; fifthly, within the general framework of statehood, member states must ensure the independence of their courts; lastly, the duty to guarantee judicial independence derives directly from Art. 2 TEU as a justification and Art. 19 TEU as a jurisdictional condition. See L. Pech, J. Grogan, *Meaning and Scope of the EU Rule of Law*, London 2020, p. 19.

21 M. Rams, 'Pytanie o model wykładni prawa unijnego w orzecznictwie Trybunału Sprawiedliwości' in: *Specyfika wykładni prawa karnego w kontekście brzmienia i celu prawa Unii Europejskiej*, Warsaw 2016, p ….

22 J. Helios, W. Jedlecka, *Wykładnia prawa Unii Europejskiej ze stanowiska teorii prawa*, Warsaw 2018, p. 160.

emphasising the element of ensuring the proper fulfilment of obligations arising from the provisions of the EU legal system by all entities obligated to comply with them"[23].

By utilizing such tools, the ECJ was able to establish, as early as the 1980s, that since the Member States constitute a community based on the rule of law, both the states themselves and their institutions are subject to scrutiny regarding the compatibility of their adopted measures with the fundamental constitutional charter, namely the Treaty[24]. Less than 20 years later, the scope of review also extended to compliance with "the general principles of law which include fundamental rights"[25].

Expanding the scope of EU law application should be considered as a process that, along with the creation of new cooperation mechanisms, requires an appropriate legal response. Jurisdiction over a state's constitutional issues, which impact judicial cooperation in criminal matters through the level of politicization of the judiciary, influences the increasing perception of the form of governance in a given Member State as an element of EU's supranational policy[26].

The systematic and functional interpretation of EU treaty law does not fully exhaust the issue of the mechanisms by which the ECJ entered the realm of constitutional law. The ECJ's mandate did not solely originate from its judgments. The foundations of its competence were shaped by the Commission and the Council, which conferred the right to enforce primacy of the application and protection of Union Law on the Member States, establishing the standards on which the principle of mutual recognition is based[27]. This view finds strong support in the history of European Union cooperation, where each step forward implied the attribution of competencies by international bodies in various areas of law.

Taking into account the viewpoint, assuming a gradual federalisation of the European Union will imply a gradual departure of its institutions from a linguistic interpretation of provisions in order to expand their competencies. Since European cooperation in criminal matters, including issues related to the

---

23 J. Helios, W. Jedlecka, *Wykładnia…*, p. 183.

24 EJC, *Les Verts*, C-294/83, April 23rd, 1986, § 23.

25 ECJ, *Unión de Pequeños Agricultores*, C-50/00, July 25th, 2002, § 38.

26 S. Jagdhuber, 'Unexplored Variation in European Integration Research: Mapping and Discussing Vertical Differentiation in the EU's Area of Freedom, Security and Justice', 67/68 *Politique Européenne* 2020, p. 64.

27 A. Willems, 'The Court of Justice of the European Union's Mutual Trust Journey in EU Criminal Law: From a Presumption to (Room for) Rebuttal', 20(4) *German Law Journal* 2019, p. 493.

protection of fundamental rights, has developed significantly beyond the scope defined in Art. 82 (2) of the Treaty on the Functioning of the European Union (TFEU), not only through case law but also through legislative acts, it is necessary to reformulate the established framework of cooperation, taking into account the unique nature of the values enshrined in the CFR and Art. 2 TFEU[28]. With the adoption of successive acts standardising Union law in criminal procedure, the community is entering into a sphere previously regulated by national law. Further directives referring to the protection of fundamental rights contribute to expanding their scope of application, continuously strengthening their impact.

On the other hand, this trend may give rise to increasingly contentious jurisdictional disputes between the institutions, which contradicts the concept of the rule of law that emphasises the separation of powers.

It is inconsistent for two organs from different branches to perform equivalent functions within the system. The demarcation line of competencies between them should be much more delineated. Thus, a paradox emerges where, on the one hand, inevitable processes of deepening cooperation lead to the delegation of powers to supernational organs. On the other hand, these organs fail to adhere to the principles they ardently defend. Establishing more specific provisions that curtail excessive judicial activism while also delineating the scope of the Court's capacity to formulate law-making principles appear to be an unavoidable necessity in this regard.

2. Interpretation of the Requirements Imposed on the Judiciary

2.1. The essence of judicial independence and the autonomy of judges

Establishing a coherent concept characterising the position of the judicial power in relation to other authorities is present in the case law of the ECJ prior to the Lisbon Treaty. The relevant literature references the groundbreaking case of *Graham J. Wilson v. Ordre des avocats du bureau de Luxembourg*, which defined independence through the prism of its constituent principles. The ECJ stated that: "Those guarantees of independence and impartiality require rules, particularly as

---

28 J. Ouwerkerk, 'EU Competence in the Area of Procedural Criminal Law: Functional vs. Self-standing Approximation of Procedural Rights and Their Progressive Effect on the Charter's Scope of Application', 27(2) *European Journal of Crime, Criminal Law and Criminal Justice* 2019, pp. 93–94.

regards the composition of the body and the appointment, length of service and the grounds for abstention, rejection and dismissal of its members, in order to dismiss any reasonable doubt in the minds of individuals as to the imperviousness of that body to external factors and its neutrality concerning the interests before it"[29].

At the same time, this judgment encompassed both external and internal aspects of independence. The former entails the protection of the body from external interference and pressures that may jeopardise the independence of the judgments rendered in the considered disputes[30]. The latter is linked to the notion of impartiality and concerns an equal distance from the parties to the conflict and their interests in relation to its subject matter (relating to objectivity)[31]. These statements are highly significant and currently serve as a starting point for further considerations by the ECJ regarding the cases it adjudicates[32].

Subsequent concerns will refer to the established premises, highlighting violations of the legal order primarily resulting from the so-called justice system reforms in Poland and other cases in which the ECJ has identified capacity for judicial intervention. The assumption that needs to be taken into account considering the fact that the category of effective judicial control serves as a bridge for the ECJ between judicial independence and the observance of the rule of law. Member States are obliged to fulfil the requirement of effective judicial protection through the designated bodies referred to as "court" within the meaning of Union law, which are part of its system of remedies[33]. In the event of non-compliance with aforementioned standard, a "court is not in a position to ensure the effective judicial protection required by the second part of Art. 19 § 1 TEU"[34].

The ECJ clearly distinguishes between the separation of powers and the independence of the judiciary. As in the previously mentioned case of Land Hessen,

---

29 ECJ, *Graham J. Wilson v. Ordre des avocats du barreau de Luxembourg*, C-506/04, September 19th, 2006, § 53.

30 ECJ, *Graham J. Wilson v. Ordre des avocats du barreau de Luxembourg*, C-506/04, September 19th, 2006, § 51.

31 ECJ, *Graham J. Wilson v. Ordre des avocats du barreau de Luxembourg*, C-506/04, September 19th, 2006, § 52.

32 See ECJ, *Krajowa Rada Sądownictwa*, C-824/18, March 2nd, 2021, § 117; ECJ, *Repubblika v. Il-Prim Ministru*, C-896/19, April 20th, 2021, § 53; ECJ, *WB and Others*, Joined Cases C-748/19 to C-754/19, November 16th, 2021, § 71.

33 B. Janusz-Pohl, 'Mutual Recognition of Judicial Decisions in Criminal Matters in Relation to the Rule of Law Concepts – example of the EAW execution refusal' in: G. Pastuszko (ed.), *Rule of Law*, Warsaw: Wydawnictwo IWS 2023, p. 82.

34 ECJ, *Euro Box Promotion and Others*, Joined Cases C-357/19, C-379/19, C-547/19, C-811/19 and C-840/19, December 21st, 2021, § 230.

the competence of the executive authority does not automatically imply dependence on it or compromise impartiality. However, in order to establish a violation, when considering a case against the personnel changes in the National Council of the Judiciary, the ECJ further specifies this criterion, adapting it to the specific factual circumstances. It states that it is essential that, after assuming the position of a judge, they are not exposed to any form of pressure and do not receive instructions concerning their duties[35]. On the other hand, Csaba Cservák cites the example of the German system, in which the body appointing federal judges (*Richerwahlusschus*) consists exclusively of politicians, proportional to the representation of each party in the parliament[36]. Personal connections can play a significant role in the appointment process, which makes it difficult to speak of organizational independence. The researcher points out that established systems in Western and Northern Europe position judicial assemblies not as separate judicial power structures but rather closely aligned with the executive branch, which is primarily reflected in their administrative system[37].

The principles governing the functioning of a regarded independent and impartial court must be built on legal norms. The ECJ refers to the jurisprudence of the ECtHR, which in the case of Savino[38] ruled that the expression "established by law" in Art. 6 § 1 of the European Convention on Human Rights (ECHR) applies "not only the legal basis for the very existence of the tribunal but also the composition of the bench in each case"[39].

Following the line developed by the Strasbourg court and referring to the Miracle Europe kft[40], it also held that the requirement for the existence of a court by operation of law precludes the possibility of assigning a particular case to a court in a different jurisdiction at the discretion of a specific institution[41]. In practice, this judgment invalidates the exercise of powers granted to The President of the Supreme Court directing the work of the Disciplinary Chamber. The mere inclusion of principles allowing for the disciplinary control of judges is, therefore, insufficient for their validity. According to the ECJ, these regulations, in reference

35 ECJ, *Krajowa Rada Sądownictwa*, C-824/18, March 2nd, 2021, § 122.

36 C. Cservák, 'Rule of Law and Constitutional Law' in: G. Pastuszko (ed.), *Rule of Law*, Warsaw: Wydawnictwo IWS 2023, pp. 254–255.

37 C. Cservák, 'Rule of Law...', pp. 256–258.

38 ECtHR, *Savino v. Italy*, April 28th, 2009, §§ 94–95.

39 ECJ, *Commission v. Republic of Poland*, C-791/19, July 15th, 2021, § 168.

40 ECtHR, *Miracle Europe kft v. Hungary*, January 12th, 2015, §§ 58, 63, 67.

41 ECJ, *Commission v. Republic of Poland*, C-791/19, July 15th, 2021, § 171.

to the SIIJ in Romania, should not have a deterrent effect on judges[42] but, in line with the requirement of independence, must "provide the necessary guarantees ensuring that those criminal proceedings cannot be used as a system of political control over the activity of those judges and prosecutors"[43]. The failure to comply with the standard of judicial independence has also been acknowledged by the ECJ in the principles relating to the delegation of judges because "those rules are liable to affect both the composition of the body which is called upon to hear and determine a case and the length of service of the judges thus seconded. They also provide for the possibility of terminating the secondment of one or more of the members of that body"[44]. It is necessary to point out the inconsistency arising from conditions adopted into Polish legal order before the contested so-called reforms of Polish judiciary were launched, regarding, for example, the formulation of the criteria for qualifying judges for disciplinary responsibility or the competence of the Minister of Justice in the temporary delegation of judges, there are concerns[45]. This implies that the law did not comply with the established standards from the beginning of its implementation. The inconsistency is exacerbated by the fact that the ECJ, at the same time, the Member States a competence to establish "a system according to which judges may, in the interests of the service, be temporarily seconded from one court to another"[46]. These same regulations, which previously did not raise doubts before the ECJ, have now taken on an entirely different character in light of the new political situation.

The stringency associated with the reasons for disqualification and removal of judges has also been intensified due to the shortened tenure of Supreme Court judges. The ECJ seems to have rightly adopted the assumption that retirement under the so-called judicial reforms should be treated as a termination of tenure. The ECJ has specified the principle of irremovability, indicating that its limits are determined by the mandatory retirement age or the expiration of the term of office. Exceptions to this should stem from major and legally justified reasons[47]. The fact of "extending by six years the period for which the judge carries out his or her duties at the same time as the lowering by 5 years of the retirement age of

42 ECJ, *Asociația 'Forumul Judecătorilor din România'*, Joined Cases C-83/19, C-127/19, C-195/19, C-291/19, C-355/19 and C-397/19, May 18th, 2021, § 237.

43 ECJ, *Asociația 'Forumul Judecătorilor din România'*, Joined Cases C-83/19, C-127/19, C-195/19, C-291/19, C-355/19 and C-397/19, May 18th, 2021, § 213.

44 ECJ, *WB and Others*, Joined Cases C-748/19 to C-754/19, November 16th, 2021, § 71.

45 For example Art. 77 § 1 Act of July 27th, 2001 Law on Common Courts Organisation.

46 ECJ, *WB and Others*, Joined Cases C-748/19 to C-754/19, November 16th, 2021, § 72.

47 ECJ, *Commission v. Republic of Poland*, C-619/18, June 24th, 2019, § 76.

judges of the Sąd Najwyższy"[48] indicates, according to the ECJ, that the reform does not aim to standardise the retirement age. Furthermore, the discussed prerogative has a discretionary character "inasmuch as its adoption is not, as such, governed by any objective and verifiable criterion and for which reasons need not be stated"[49]. The reduction of the retirement age, combined with the establishment of an unchallengeable competence as a whole, constitutes a significant violation of independence, an inherent element of the right to effective judicial protection and the fundamental right to a fair trial[50].

In line with the aforementioned assumption made at the outset of the subsection, this characterization positions it as a value inherent to the principle of the rule of law, upon which the Union is founded in accordance with Art. 2 TEU. Furthermore, it assumes particular significance within the framework of Art. 19 TEU, which delineates this value and confers the responsibility of ensuring legal oversight within this framework to national courts[51].

By acknowledging that the issue of establishing judicial organs within member states constitutes a pivotal component of the right to an efficacious appellate remedy, the ECJ has expanded its jurisdiction, thereby delimiting the realm of state sovereignty and the exclusive national competencies enshrined in treaties[52]. The establishment of an international judiciary standard, as seen in the case of Graham J. Wilson v. Ordre des avocats du bureau de Luxembourg, is a significant step toward realising the ideals of protecting fundamental rights and the rule of law beyond national borders. To ensure this system works effectively, all community members must equally adhere to the prescribed standard. However, this obligation should apply uniformly to all without discrimination. Any variations would go against the principles of standardisation, leading to categorising states based on their obligation to uphold a higher standard and creating disparities in evaluating systems.

2.2. The prohibition of regression as a safeguard for upholding judicial standards

To establish a basis for assessing violations of judicial independence standards, it was essential to define a reference point for evaluating deviations from the

48 ECJ, *Commission v. Republic of Poland*, C-619/18, June 24th, 2019, § 84.
49 ECJ, *Commission v. Republic of Poland*, C-619/18, June 24th, 2019, § 114.
50 ECJ, *Erik Simpson*, Joined Cases C-542/18 and C-543/18, March 26th, 2020, § 71.
51 ECJ, *Land Hessen*, C-272/19, July 9th, 2020, § 45.
52 B. Janusz-Pohl, *Mutual Recognition…*, p. 85.

constitutional order. The ECJ autonomously formulated a fundamental principle for judicial deliberations. When a Member State joined the community, it committed to upholding the rule of law standards. The current factual state aligns with both propriety and desirability in shaping the Member State's judicial framework. This standard extends beyond the internal community and affects the Union's engagement with its geopolitical surroundings. By emphasising the duty to ensure effective judicial remedy, the ECJ gradually gains influence over constitutional matters, particularly during significant judicial reforms.

"The principle of non-regression of the independence of the judiciary" resonated strongly in the case law of the ECJ in relation to Poland and Romania. Still, it was also alluded to in reference to Maltese judges[53].

In the first instance, the change in the method of appointment of judges to the National Council of the Judiciary and the expanded role of the Sejm[54] in the decision-making process, according to the Court, leads to the nullification of the effectiveness of existing legal measures by overwriting them with new rules[55]. The ECJ did not limit the principle of non-regression solely to situations where one of the authorities, contrary to a clear interpretation of constitutional law, operates using methods that essentially stem from an axiological gap on its side.

This also applies to the primary activity of the legislative power - the enactment of legal provisions. The ECJ indicated that: "The Member States are thus required to ensure that, in the light of that value, any regression of their laws on the organisation of justice is prevented, by refraining from adopting rules which would undermine the independence of judges"[56].

In the case of Romania, the ECJ adopted a similar scope of application of the principle. In this instance, it emphasised a systemic inconsistency aimed at circumventing the law. The amendment caused an unreasonable "need for the case to be examined twice at first instance and, potentially, a third time on appeal"[57]. According to the ECJ, the judgments issued by the Romanian judicial authority leading to the reopening of proceedings "may have the effect of prolonging the duration of the corresponding criminal proceedings beyond the applicable limitation periods, thus meaning that the risk of that category of persons going

53 ECJ, *Repubblika v. Il-Prim Ministru*, C-896/19, April 20th, 2021, § 63.

54 Lower House of the Polish Parliament.

55 ECJ, *Krajowa Rada Sądownictwa*, C-824/18, March 2nd, 2021, § 156.

56 ECJ, *Commission v. Republic of Poland*, C-791/19, July 15th, 2021, § 51.

57 ECJ, *Euro Box Promotion and Others*, Joined Cases C-357/19, C-379/19, C-547/19, C-811/19 and C-840/19, December 21st, 2021, § 196.

unpunished becomes systemic"[58]. As the cited cases involve crimes of financial misconduct and corruption committed by political decision-makers and exposing EU finances to harm, the ECJ observes that exempting them from criminal liability would be "incompatible with Art. 325 § 1 TFEU, read in conjunction with Art. 2 of the PFI Convention and with Decision 2006/928"[59].

The escalating divergence in the policies of states contravening the rule of law principle *vis-à-vis* the ECJ's jurisprudence may engender adjudicatory pronouncements that are incongruous with the stance proffered by the Luxembourg court and EU legal corpus. Such infringement - if deemed sufficiently serious and if the loss or damage incurred by individuals is adequately justified through the perspective of casual link - may engender state liability[60]. The "sufficient seriousness" criterion is likewise satisfied by the ECJ when its jurisprudence[61] or EU legal norms[62] are infringed by a judicial decision. Nevertheless, a query arises as to whether domestic courts, as organs that breach these standards, will independently adjudicate in a scenario wherein they apply domestic law that has been ascribed as unsuitable by the Court. The enforcement of the ECJ's decisions *vis-à-vis* Member States arises from treaty law[63].

3. The Main Defects of the Polish Legal System as Identified by the ECJ

The discourse with the ECJ concerning compliance with the rule of law by Member States comes down to specific pillars intrinsic to the construct of a democratic constitutional state. The evaluation encompasses matters of power division, judicial independence, as well as constitutional remedies and civil liberties. With regard to legal institutions, it pertains to the structuring of the judicial disciplinary system.

---

58 ECJ, *Euro Box Promotion and Others*, Joined Cases C-357/19, C-379/19, C-547/19, C-811/19 and C-840/19, December 21st, 2021, § 201.

59 ECJ, *Euro Box Promotion and Others*, Joined Cases C-357/19, C-379/19, C-547/19, C-811/19 and C-840/19, December 21st, 2021, § 203.

60 ECJ, *Gerhard Köbler v. Republik Österreich*, C-224/01, September 30th, 2003, § 51.

61 ECJ, *Gerhard Köbler v. Republik Österreich*, C-224/01, September 30th, 2003, § 56.

62 ECJ, *Gerhard Köbler v. Republik Österreich*, C-224/01, September 30th, 2003, § 59.

63 See Arts. 267 and 288 TFEU; Art. 4 (3) TEU.

3.1. Defects in the disciplinary measures upon judges

Based on the judgments against Poland and Romania, the ECJ has established a framework for the disciplinary system for judges that confirms and realizes the concept of judicial independence.

From the perspective of organizing the system, the ECJ has established requirements for the body responsible for conducting disciplinary proceedings against judges and prosecutors. In determining its relationship with other political entities, the ECJ acknowledged the opinion of the Advocate General, indicating that the "body in charge of initiating disciplinary procedures such as the Judicial Inspection should demonstrate at least some degree of operational and investigative independence"[64]. This standard would not be violated by executive authorities' appointment of its management[65]. However, the decisions issued by this body must be subject to judicial review. The ECJ imposes higher requirements on the entity conducting the assessment of the challenged decision, as it should demonstrate a higher degree of resistance to political pressure and "must offer all the necessary guarantees as regards its independence and impartiality"[66].

Subsequently, the ECJ established standards that provisions concerning disciplinary proceedings should meet, referring to the designing provisions[67] as well as substantive conditions[68].

One must agree with the ECJ on the following issues. Firstly, the disciplinary system for judges, as described in both the law on the ordinary courts and the new Law on the Supreme Court, in the form of general criteria, not only failed to provide a clear and precise delineation of disciplinary liability[69] but also allowed for disciplinary action related to the application of the law by the courts.

Therefore, initiating such proceedings on the grounds of a court's referral to the ECJ "for a preliminary ruling"[70] is unacceptable. Secondly, the organization of the Disciplinary Chamber of the Supreme Court, as a second-instance body in disciplinary proceedings, must ensure its independence. However, the ECJ has

---

64 Opinion of Advocate General of September 23rd, 2020, *Asociația 'Forumul Judecătorilor din România'*, Joined Cases C-83/19, C-127/19 and C-195/19, § 269.

65 ECJ, *Asociația 'Forumul Judecătorilor din România'*, Joined Cases C-83/19, C-127/19, C-195/19, C-291/19, C-355/19 and C-397/19, May 18th, 2021, § 202.

66 ECJ, *Commission v. Republic of Poland*, C-791/19, July 15th, 2021, § 80.

67 ECJ, *Commission v. Republic of Poland*, C-791/19, July 15th, 2021, § 98.

68 ECJ, *Commission v. Republic of Poland*, C-791/19, July 15th, 2021, § 137.

69 ECJ, *Commission v. Republic of Poland*, C-791/19, July 15th, 2021, § 141.

70 ECJ, *IS*, C-564/19, November 23rd, 2021, § 93.

expanded its concept of independence[71], and thus all the elements described in the previous subsections of this paper should be considered. Thirdly, the transfer of judges between chambers without their consent should not be treated as a sanction by the organising disciplinary body[72]. Fourthly, bodies such as the Disciplinary Officer of the Judges of the Common Courts or the Disciplinary Officer of the Minister of Justice may accurately raise concerns about the requirements imposed by the ECJ on the initiating and conducting authorities of disciplinary proceedings. Fifthly, the concept that allowed for at least rudimentary independence of prosecutors has been eliminated from the Polish legal system in favour of complete subordination to the executive authority.

On the other hand, the opposing view to the ECJ's narrative argues that the condition for suspending the operation of the Disciplinary Chamber of the Supreme Court is unattainable in the Polish legal system due to the lack of means enabling such a result. According to this position, the obligation imposed by the ECJ has a disintegrating and destabilizing effect on the functioning of the legal system due to its non-normativity – the ECJ's judgment would acquire a law-making character, constituting a source of law unknown in the national legal system[73]. The principle of sovereignty stands against the obedient application of EU law, preventing external interference in the organization of the state. The problem is that the national authority, i.e., the Sejm, violates the Polish Constitution, but the EU body is not competent to establish this violation[74]. The ECJ's actions, interpreted through the prism of protecting the values expressed in EU law, allow for a partial resolution of the above doubts. It can be observed that "the ECJ does not assess the compatibility of adopted solutions with the standards of the Polish Constitution, including constitutional case law, but refers to those elements of the national system that potentially threaten the effectiveness of judicial protection from the perspective of EU law treaties and the Charter of Fundamental Rights"[75].

71 ECJ, *Commission v. Republic of Poland*, C-791/19, July 15th, 2021, § 81.

72 ECJ, *W.Ż.*, C-487/19, October 6th, 2021, § 114.

73 G. Pastuszko, 'Influence of the EU institutions on the Polish constitutional order in the context of the dispute over the rule of law' in: G. Pastuszko (ed.), *Rule of Law*, Warsaw: Wydawnictwo IWS 2023, p. 48.

74 J. Zaleśny, 'Aktualny ustrój Izby Dyscyplinarnej SN nie ma racji bytu, ale TSUE nie ma kompetencji, aby to stwierdzić', available at: https://serwisy.gazetaprawna.pl/orzeczenia/artykuly/8209593,tk-tsue-wyrok-izba-dyscyplinarna-jacek-zalesny.html [accessed on: June 17th, 2023].

75 M. Safjan, 'Prawo do skutecznej ochrony sądowej – refleksje dotyczące wyroku TSUE z November 19th, 2019 r. W sprawach połączonych C-585/18, C-624/18, C-625/18', 5 *Palestra* 2020, p. 13.

3.2. Defects in the appointment of judges

The ECJ has addressed the judicial review of judgments not only within the context of disciplinary proceedings but also in relation to the functioning of the National Council of the Judiciary under new rules and, therefore, in the process of judicial appointments.

Regarding to the new method of appointing members of the National Council of the Judiciary itself, the ECJ has adopted the established interpretation that appointing members of the judges' selection committee by the legislative authority should not raise doubts about the independence of judges[76]. In the context of the organization of Malta's judiciary, the ECJ has observed that the creation of a body responsible for appointing judges "may, in principle, be such as to contribute to rendering that process more objective"[77], than if another branch of power carried it out.

In the context of judicial appointments, the aforementioned principle also applies, for instance, to the Romanian Constitutional Court[78]. However, it is subject to narrowing down by additional factors, which may lead to a different conclusion when combined with the discussed principle, may lead to a different conclusion[79]. For example, the modification required the formulation of material conditions and procedural regulations related to appointments so that they would not give rise to: "reasonable doubts with respect to the judges appointed"[80]. In assessing the violation of European standards by Polish legislative bodies, a limiting factor is the violation of impartiality through exerting pressure or receiving instructions in performing their duties[81]. Therefore, the ECJ focuses on the judge's independence regarding their influence on adjudication. It does not implement all elements comprising its developed concept of judicial independence in the context of the appointment process. The discussed context of the rule of law implies a systemic perspective. At the same time, the approach presented by the ECJ allows for the subordination of judicial power to executive or legislative power. According to this line of reasoning, only subsequent forms of pressure applied to individual judges are considered violations of independence. The ECJ seems

---

76 See ECJ, *Land Hessen*, C-272/19, July 9th, 2020, § 55–56.

77 ECJ, *Repubblika v. Il-Prim Ministru*, C-896/19, April 20th, 2021, § 66.

78 ECJ, *Euro Box Promotion and Others*, Joined Cases C-357/19, C-379/19, C-547/19, C-811/19 and C-840/19, December 21st, 2021, § 233.

79 ECJ, *Commission v. Republic of Poland*, C-791/19, July 15th, 2021, § 103.

80 ECJ, *Erik Simpson*, Joined Cases C-542/18 and C-543/18, March 26th, 2020, § 71.

81 ECJ, *Land Hessen*, C-272/19, July 9th, 2020, § 45.

to not comprehend the prohibition of interference in the independence of the judiciary as a dynamic element within the structure of independence, limiting the independence of the judiciary in the name of defending the independence of the judge. Therefore, the ECJ asserts that judges can be independent in a dependent judicial system. Otherwise, even in the appointment process of members of the appointing authority, attributes of independence would be sought.

The reform of the method of controlling the resolutions of the organ to judicial review was assessed by the ECJ as implemented, "preventing any possibility of exercising judicial review of the appointments made on the based on those resolutions of the KRS and likewise, moreover, of all other appointments made in the Sąd Najwyższy (Supreme Court) since the establishment of the KRS in its new composition"[82]. Hence, the ECJ proposes non-recognise and non-apply the adopted provisions and to continue using control mechanisms under the current conditions[83]. However, it should be emphasized once again that the provisions referred to by the ECJ are not related to the functioning of member states' judicial systems[84]. This position is argued by the view that the ECJ acts without explicit legal authorization thereby legitimising the possibility of examining the independence of judges appointed in accordance with the law[85]. Consonance with this line of reasoning, an external body to the national legal system dictates the conditions that the judiciary should meet and recommends that the national court engage in activities that contradict national law. However, this argument should be confronted with the reasoning regarding the essence and manner of the ECJ's intervention. Through its claims, the ECJ defines the framework and limits "within which the freedom of member states in relation to the organization of the judiciary and procedural autonomy is contained"[86].

In none of the aforementioned rulings does the ECJ negate the significance of appointing judges. Instead, it identifies breaches of the established standards and points out specific provisions that, in its opinion, should not be enforced. However, the ECJ refrains from declaring the nullity of resolutions pertaining to appointing new members within the judiciary.

82 ECJ, *Krajowa Rada Sądownictwa*, C-824/18, March 2nd, 2021, § 138.
83 ECJ, *Krajowa Rada Sądownictwa*, C-824/18, March 2nd, 2021, § 149.
84 G. Pastuszko, *Influence of…*, Warszawa 2023, p. 43.
85 G. Pastuszko, *Influence…*, p. 46.
86 M. Safjan, *Prawo do…*, p. 8.

3.3. Defects of judicial cooperation in the criminal matters

The deepening of judicial cooperation in criminal matters required the creation of increasingly higher standards to realise cooperation based on the principle of mutuality. The transposition from an international to a supranational level needed states to sacrifice a portion of their sovereignty to effectively manage criminal policy. However, in a reality where state borders no longer serve as barriers to the actions of judicial authorities, the Polish judicial system has come to be marked by a violation of the rule of law. The transfer of the dispute related to judicial reforms onto the arena of criminal proceedings directly undermines the effectiveness of cross-border investigations. Judicial authorities in other member states have expressed doubts regarding applying instruments within the new legal framework in cooperation with Poland. The European Arrest Warrant (EAW) has become a focal point of discontent with the current political situation. Paradoxically, it is the first instrument that realizes the principle of mutual trust but has also become the first one in which the principle of mutual trust has been shaken. Further considerations will revolve around this mechanism of cooperation.

By entering an intra-community discussion on this matter, the ECJ assumed a very active role as a moderator, categorising Poland as a member of a particular category with whom cooperation should occur based on the newly established method set by the ECJ itself. The foundations for this chosen direction had already been developed earlier. In the context of the *ne bis in idem* principle enshrined in the EAW, despite the inclusion of judicial cooperation in the third pillar, the ECJ deemed it necessary to strengthen it by interpreting the provisions applicable in each legal order "as far as possible in the light of the wording and purpose of the framework decision"[87]. This opens the way for applying a functional interpretation based on the formulation of the EU law. In this aspect, the assessment applies not only to the provisions but also to the authorities. According to the ECJ, their opportunistic approach hinders the functioning of mutual recognition. Proper implementation of the ENA can only occur when member states strive for convergence "of the laws and regulations of the Member States with regard to judicial cooperation in criminal matters and, more specifically, of the rules relating to the conditions, procedures and effects of surrender as between national authorities"[88]. The ECJ associates the principle of mutual recognition with ensuring the functioning of minimum standards in each legal system. Afterwards, in the judgment of NS of December 21st, 2011, on the one hand, it recognised that the principle of

87 ECJ, *Pupino*, C-105/03, June 16th, 2005, § 43.

88 ECJ, *Advocaten voor de Wereld VZW*, C-303/05, May 3rd, 2007, § 29.

mutual recognition imposes an obligation to apply regulations enabling free cooperation in criminal matters. On the other hand, in the face of serious concerns regarding systemic irregularities in the application of the cooperation instrument, which are associated with inhuman or degrading treatment, the implementation of cooperation should be blocked[89]. The defined margins of cooperation also establish criteria related to individual rights, such as Art. 4 (3) TEU, which states that member states shall "ensure judicial protection of an individual's rights under EU law" which also applies "to ensure effective legal protection in the fields covered by EU law"[90].

An elaboration of this principle is found in Art. 47 CFR[91]. In this field, even regarding the application of the extradition instrument, states "are required to exercise that power following EU law"[92].

A turning point in the application of the principle of mutual recognition in the context of executing the EAW was the Aranyosi and Căldăraru case, in which the ECJ departed from its previous stance, indicating that refusal to execute a warrant is only possible in the presence of a condition specified in the framework decision[93], using the category of the "exceptional circumstances"[94]. In such cases, the initiative rests with the judicial authority of the executing state, which, through the application of a two-stage test, assesses the system of the issuing state.

The ECJ has adapted the key aspect of the mutual recognition principle test to the legal issue presented by judicial authorities concerning doubts about Poland's compliance with the rule of law[95]. Assessing guidelines, Theodore Konstadinides identified four essential aspects of the judgment: "(A) the application of the Aranyosi and Căldăraru test in LM. The test relied upon principles of mutual trust and mutual recognition and was designed to guide the control exercised by national courts on the execution of EAWs; (B) striking a balance between the effectiveness of mutual recognition (a structural principle) and fundamental rights protection (a substantive principle); (C) establishing rules regarding the protection afforded to individuals in accordance with the principles of judicial

---

89 ECJ, *N.S.*, Joined Cases C-411/10 and C-493/10, December 21st, 2011, §§ 79–86.

90 ECJ, *The Queen*, C-404/13, November 19th, 2014, § 52.

91 ECJ, *PJSC Rosneft Oil Company v. Her Majesty's Treasury and Others*, Case C-72/15, March 28th, 2017, § 73.

92 ECJ, *Raugevicius*, C-247/17, November 13th, 2018, § 45.

93 See ECJ, *Wolzenburg*, C-123/08, October 6th, 2009, § 57.

94 ECJ, *Aranyosi and Căldăraru*, Joined Cases C-404/15 and C-659/15, April 5th, 2016, § 82.

95 ECJ, *Celmer (LM)*, C-216/18, July 25th, 2018, § 61.

independence and impartiality as general principles of EU law; and (D) protecting the rule of law in the EU as a foundational and overarching principle that encompasses general principles of EU law"[96]. Satisfying the second level of the test, as defined by Dimitry Kochenov, has been deemed an undue burden on the individual, who must demonstrate that the systemic violation will have an individual impact on their case, so it has been suggested that the burden of proof in this part of the test should rest on the stronger party, namely the state issuing the warrant[97]. Subsequent judgments have confirmed that concerns[98].

The ECJ has decided to continue along the established path by recommending that competent courts conduct a two-stage examination[99]. At the same time, the ECJ has stated that adopting the notion that systemic or general deficiencies in the independence of the judiciary of the issuing Member State automatically result in the refusal to execute an EAW would effectively suspend its functioning[100]. The ECJ notes that such a situation would lead to consequences comparable to the sanctions provided for in Art. 7 §§ 2 and 3 TEU against a Member State whose breach has been determined under Art. 7 § 1 TEU[101].

3.3.1. Summary

In the context of mutual trust, Member States with a strong record of fundamental rights protection are presumed to comply with EU law. However, if doubts arise regarding their commitment to fundamental rights[102], this can impact mutual recognition. Clear evidence of violations is needed to challenge this presumption. Hence, only when the European Council, as outlined in Art. 7 § 2 TEU, determines a severe and persistent breach of Art. 2 TEU principles, like the rule of law, in the issuing Member State and the Council suspends Framework Decision 2002/584

96 T. Konstadinides, 'Judicial Independence and the Rule of Law in the context of non-execution of a European Arrest Warrant', 56(3) *Common Market Law Review* 2019, p. 742.

97 D. Kochenov, P. Bard, 'The Last Soldier Standing? Courts vs. Politicians and the Rule of Law Crisis in the New Member States of the EU', *Social Science Research Network Electronic Paper Collection* 2019, p. 28.

98 ECJ, *X and Y*, Joined Cases C-562/21 and C-563/21, February 22nd, 2022, §§ 83–85.

99 ECJ, *L and P*, Joined Cases C-354/20 and C-412/20, December 17th, 2020, § 54–55.

100 ECJ, *L and P*, Joined Cases C-354/20 and C-412/20, December 17th, 2020, § 59.

101 ECJ, *X and Y*, Joined Cases C-562/21 and C-563/21, February 22nd, 2022, §§ 64–65.

102 W. Czapliński,'Zasady prawa Unii Europejskiej' in: W. Czapliński, *Znaczenie Orzecznictwa Trybunału Sprawiedliwości Unii Europejskiej w procesie rozwoju prawa europejskiego*, Warsaw 2021, pp. 137 ff.

for that state, would the executing judicial authority be obligated to automatically reject any European Arrest Warrant from that Member State. This would not require a specific assessment of the actual risk to the individual's fundamental right to a fair trial[103].

On the other hand, this factor, and others relating to the arbitrary determination of the validity of measures adopted in a given legal system, should be interpreted as negative aspects of the so-called pragmatic harmonization[104] of EU law.

Departing from the pursuit of automating the execution of instruments based on mutual trust loosens cooperation and potentially opens possibilities to avoid the justice system. Just as attempts to improve prison conditions through additional inquiries in each proceeding lead to formalities[105], linking their execution to the proper outcome of a two-stage rule of law test partially deviates from the purpose for which such a cooperation instrument was established, namely, to enhance the effectiveness of cooperation in criminal matters. Even though the high requirements for undermining the credibility of the justice system imposed by the two-stage test have not yet been met[106], the German Constitutional Court has questioned the legality of actions taken by Polish judicial authorities and has twice refused to execute the warrants[107].

---

103 W. Czapliński, 'Zasady…', pp. 137 ff.

104 Pragmatic harmonisation is defined as the Member States' aim to penalize crimes committed against their national legal order and within the territorial jurisdiction of their law enforcement authorities – J. Spencer, 'Why is the harmonisation of penal law necessary' in: A. Klip, H. van der Wilt, *Harmonisation and harmonising measures in criminal law*, Amsterdam 2002, p. 47.

105 A. Klip, 'Eroding Mutual Trust in an European Criminal Justice Area without Added Value', 28(2) *European Journal of Crime, Criminal Law and Criminal Justice* 2020, available at: https://doi.org/10.1163/15718174-02802001 [accessed on: June 17th, 2023].

106 T. Wahl, 'Refusal of European Arrest Warrants Due to Fair Trial Infringements', *Focus: The Reception of European Legislation and Case Law in the Member States* 4/2020, available at: https://doi.org/10.30709/eucrim-2020-026 [accessed on: June 17th, 2023].

107 OLG Karlsruhe, January 7th, 2019 - Ausl 301 AR 95/18; OLG Karlsruhe, November 27th, 2020 - Ausl 301 AR 104/19.

4. Bibliography

Literature

Cservák C., 'Rule of Law and Constitutional Law' in: Pastuszko G. (ed.), *Rule of Law*, Warsaw: Wydawnictwo IWS 2023.

Czapliński W., 2.6. 'Zasady prawa Unii Europejskiej' in: W. Czapliński, *Znaczenie Orzecznictwa Trybunału Sprawiedliwości Unii Europejskiej w procesie rozwoju prawa europejskiego*, Warsaw 2021.

Helios J., Jedlecka W., *Wykładnia prawa Unii Europejskiej ze stanowiska teorii prawa*, Warsaw 2018.

Jagdhuber S., 'Unexplored Variation in European Integration Research: Mapping and Discussing Vertical Differentiation in the EU's Area of Freedom, Security and Justice', 67/68 *Politique Européenne* 2020.

Janusz-Pohl B., 'Mutual Recognition of Judicial Decisions in Criminal Matters in Relation to the Rule of Law Concepts – example of the EAW execution refusal' in: Pastuszko G. (ed.), *Rule of Law*, Warsaw: Wydawnictwo IWS 2023.

Klip A., 'Eroding Mutual Trust in an European Criminal Justice Area without Added Value', 28(2) *European Journal of Crime, Criminal Law and Criminal Justice* 2020, available at: https://doi.org/10.1163/15718174-02802001 [accessed on: June 17th, 2023].

Kochenov D., Bard P., 'The Last Soldier Standing? Courts vs. Politicians and the Rule of Law Crisis in the New Member States of the EU', *Social Science Research Network Electronic Paper Collection* 2019.

Konstadinides T., 'Judicial Independence and the Rule of Law in the context of non-execution of a European Arrest Warrant', 56(3) *Common Market Law Review* 2019.

Moser C., Rittberger B., 'The CJEU and EU (de-)constitutionalization: Unpacking jurisprudential responses', 20(3) *International Journal of Constitutional Law* 2022.

Muir E., Dawson M., De Witte B., 'Introduction: The European Court of Justice as a Political Actor' in: Dawson M., De Witte B., Muir E. (eds.), *Judicial Activism at the European Court of Justice* 2013.

Ouwerkerk J., 'EU Competence in the Area of Procedural Criminal Law: Functional vs. Self-standing Approximation of Procedural Rights and Their Progressive Effect on the Charter's Scope of Application', 27(2) *European Journal of Crime, Criminal Law and Criminal Justice* 2019.

Pastuszko G., 'Influence of the EU institutions on the Polish constitutional order in the context of the dispute over the rule of law' in: Pastuszko G. (ed.), *Rule of Law*, Warsaw: Wydawnictwo IWS 2023.

Pech L., Grogan J., *Meaning and Scope of the EU Rule of Law*, London 2020.

Pech L., *The European Court of Justice's jurisdiction over national judiciary-related measures*, Brussels 2023.

Rams M., '2.2.7. Pytanie o model wykładni prawa unijnego w orzecznictwie Trybunału Sprawiedliwości' in: *Specyfika wykładni prawa karnego w kontekście brzmienia i celu prawa Unii Europejskiej*, Warsaw 2016.

Safjan M., 'Prawo do skutecznej ochrony sądowej – refleksje dotyczące wyroku TSUE z November 19th, 2019 r. W sprawach połączonych C-585/18, C-624/18, C-625/18', 5 *Palestra* 2020.

Schmidt S., 'The European Court of Justice as a Political Actor', *The European Court of Justice and the Policy Process: The Shadow of Case Law*, Oxford 2018.

Spencer J., 'Why is the harmonisation of penal law necessary' in: Klip A., van der Wilt H., *Harmonisation and harmonising measures in criminal law*, Amsterdam 2002.

Wahl T., 'Refusal of European Arrest Warrants Due to Fair Trial Infringements', *Focus: The Reception of European Legislation and Case Law in the Member States* 4/2020, available at: https://doi.org/10.30709/eucrim-2020-026 [accessed on: June 17th, 2023].

Willems A., 'The Court of Justice of the European Union's Mutual Trust Journey in EU Criminal Law: From a Presumption to (Room for) Rebuttal', 20(4) *German Law Journal* 2019.

Zaleśny J., 'Aktualny ustrój Izby Dyscyplinarnej SN nie ma racji bytu, ale TSUE nie ma kompetencji, aby to stwierdzić', available at: https://serwisy.gazetaprawna.pl/orzeczenia/artykuly/8209593,tk-tsue-wyrok-izba-dyscyplinarna-jacek-zalesny.html [accessed on: June 17th, 2023].

Ana Beltrán Montoliu*

IV. Organizational Efficiency in the Spanish Judicial Power: New Trends

Abstract: This chapter explores reforms aimed at improving the efficiency of the Spanish judicial system, focusing on the Justice 2030 framework. It highlights three key laws: on Organizational Efficiency (LOE), Procedural Efficiency (LPE), and Digital Efficiency (LDE). These laws aim to restructure court models, enhance specialization, and digitize judicial processes. The paper discusses the creation of Trial Courts and Justice Offices in municipalities to streamline operations. Additionally, it emphasizes the role of technology in improving access and communication within the judiciary, including initiatives like e-CODEX and telematic procedures.

Keywords: Judicial power, efficiency, judicial organization, digitalization of justice, judicial office, trial court

1. Introduction

In order to understand the scope of what the reforms affecting judicial organisation and procedural efficiency in the Spanish legal system will mean and imply, we must first explain the regulatory framework in which they are framed, which is the Justice 2030[1]. In this legal framework there are several programmes. It is important to highlight three legal initiatives regarding efficiency and the Public Justice Service that are Draft Laws: Law on the Organizational Efficiency of the Public Justice Service[2] (hereinafter LOE); Law on Procedural Efficiency of

---

* Lecturer of Procedural Law, University Jaume I, Castellón, Spain. The chapter is a contribution of the Research Project '*La mejora del acceso a la Justicia de la ciudadanía a través de una judicatura más cercana* (JusProx)' (Código: AICO 2021/272), financed by Generalitat Valenciana, Consellería de Educación, Investigación y Cultura. *Convocatoria 2021 de subvencions del Programa per a la Promoció de la Investigació científica, el desenvolupament tecnològic i la innovació en la Comunitat Valenciana Grupos consolidables*, being lead researcher Andrea Planchadell-Gargallo.

1 Further details on all the projects planned in the field of justice available at: https://www.justicia2030.es/proyectos [accessed on: October 3rd, 2023].

2 Proposal of *Ley Orgánica de eficiencia organizativa del servicio público de Justicia* (BOCG Congreso de los Diputados, Serie A, núm. 98-1, April 22nd, 2022). A complete dossier from a comparative perspective is available at: https://www.congreso.es/docu/docum/ddocum/dosieres/sleg/legislatura_14/spl_48/dosier_sl_48_eficiencia_organizativa_justicia_transparencia.pdf [accessed on: September 11th, 2023].

the Public Justice Service[3] (hereinafter LPE); Law on the Digital Efficiency of the Public Justice Service[4] (hereinafter LDE).

2. Organizational Efficiency

The LOE aims to restructure the organizational model of the Spanish judiciary. The traditional judicial organization provided for in Organic Law no. 6/1985[5], after more than thirthy five years of experience, has caused over time a series of dysfunctions in the Administration of Justice, such as, among others, the lack of specialization of the courts, the proliferation of bodies with identical jurisdiction in each judicial district, the favoring of interim and non-professional justice and inequalities in the workload and in the time to resolve cases. In order to adapt the judicial model to the new needs demanded by today's society, the regulation on organizational efficiency focuses on three fundamental aspects: specialization, homogeneity and organizational capacity. It also seeks to establish a model more in line with that of our European counterparts, where efficiency dictates that the first level of judicial organization should operate in a collegiate manner. This reform is based on three different levels of action: 1) Trial Court (*Tribunales de Instancia*); 2) Judicial Office; and 3) Justice Offices in Municipalities.

1) Trial Court

The justification for implementing this initiative is based on the fact that the mode of judicial organization based on the traditional one-person court is currently limiting the possibilities of achieving a more efficient public service of Justice. For all these reasons, the LOE faces a real transformation of the Courts into Trial Courts, with the support of redefined and restructured Judicial Offices.

---

3 Proposal of *Ley de medidas de eficiencia procesal del servicio público de Justicia* (BOCG Congreso de los Diputados, Serie A, núm. 97-1, April 22nd, 2022). A complete dossier from a comparative perspective is available at: https://www.congreso.es/docu/docum/ddocum/dosieres/sleg/legislatura_14/spl_49/dosier_sl_49_eficiencia_procesal_servicio_publico_justicia_transparencia.pdf [accessed on: September 11th, 2023].

4 Proposal of *Ley de Medidas de Eficiencia Digital del Servicio Público de Justicia*, (BOCG Congreso de los Diputados, Serie A, núm. 116-1, September 12th, 2022). A complete dossier from a comparative perspective is available at: https://www.congreso.es/docu/docum/ddocum/dosieres/sleg/legislatura_14/spl_63/dosier_sl_63_eficiencia_digital_justicia_transparencia.pdf [accessed on: September 11th, 2023].

5 *Ley Orgánica* no. 6/1985, available at: https://www.boe.es/buscar/act.php?id=BOE-A-1985-12666 [accessed on: September 19th, 2023].

Thus, in each judicial district there will be a Trial Court, which will be composed either of a single section (the equivalent of the courts of first instance and instruction) or, where provided for in the Law of Demarcation and Plan[6], of a civil section (courts of first instance) and an instruction section (courts of instruction). In addition, in the judicial districts where the law so provides, there may be Family Sections and Sections for Violence against Women; and, in the provincial capitals, Commercial, Criminal Trial (equivalent to the Criminal Courts), Juvenile, Penitentiary Surveillance, Contentious-Administrative and Social Sections.

2) Judicial Office
This new design establishes that the activity of the Judicial Office will be developed through the procedural processing units and the common procedural services to be determined (Art. 436 LOE).

With respect to the procedural processing units, it should be noted that they will perform procedural management functions and will directly assist judges and magistrates in the exercise of their functions. It will be directed by the Judicial Counsellors (*Letrado de la Administración de Justicia*), who will be responsible for the technical-procedural management and coordination of the lawyers that comprise it and it is important to note that, in order to facilitate its functionality, it may be subdivided into areas to facilitate the exercise of the jurisdictional function.

The functions of the common procedural services include those related to the provision of judicial assistance in the framework of international legal cooperation and those related to appropriate means of dispute resolution.

3) Justice Offices in Municipalities
In order to offer a closer and more sustainable justice, and to be able to make the most of the opportunities offered by new technologies, the evolution of the Justice of the Peace that will transform the Justice Offices in the municipalities is addressed.

According to Art. 439.1 LOE:

1. The Justice Offices in the municipalities are those units which, without being integrated into the structure of the judicial office, are set up within the organization of the Administration of Justice to provide services to the citizens for the provision of services to the citizens of the respective municipalities.

---

6 Law no. 38/1988, available at: https://www.boe.es/buscar/act.php?id=BOE-A-1988-29622 [accessed on: September 19th, 2023].

2. In each municipality in which a Trial Court does not have its seat, there shall be a Justice Office.
3. Justice Offices which shall serve the locality in which it is located. The premises and equipment of these offices shall be the responsibility of the respective municipalities the respective Local Council, except where it is appropriate for them to be managed in whole or in part by the Ministry of Justice or by the autonomous community with jurisdiction in matters of justice. Computer systems and equipment of the offices shall be provided by the Ministry of Justice or by the respective Autonomous where powers in the field of justice have been devolved to them.

Services to be provided in the municipalities by the Justice Offices are the following (Art. 439 *ter* LOE):

1. Practice of procedural communication acts for addressees residing in the municipality or municipalities for which it provides its services, provided that they could not have been practiced by electronic means;
2. Functions of the Civil Registry (those established by law or regulation);
3. Free legal aid (receipt of applications for recognition of the right to free legal aid and their referral to the Bar Associations responsible for processing them)[7];
4. Requests or management of citizens' petitions, addressed to the Territorial Departments of the Ministry of Justice or equivalent bodies in those communities that have assumed powers in matters of justice;
5. Collaboration with the units of appropriate means of dispute resolution existing in their territorial area, in coordination with the competent service administration;
6. Collaboration with the competent public administrations so that, as soon as the development of computer tools allows it, judges and magistrates, prosecutors, judicial counsellors who are not included in the lists of posts in these offices, may occasionally carry out their work activities in these facilities, communicating telematically with their respective offices in order to facilitate their work;
7. Other services included in collaboration agreements between different Public Administrations.

---

7 As reminded by J. L. Gómez Colomer, it should not be forgotten that the right of action would be of little use if it were not guaranteed that everyone could have access to the courts of justice, regardless of their economic status. In this sense, establishing a good system in the Justice Offices to facilitate this right as much as possible will be an essential aspect. J. L. Gómez Colomer, 'La asistencia jurídica gratuita' in: J. L. Gómez Colomer (ed.), *Introducción al derecho procesal: Derecho procesal I*, Tirant Lo Blanch 2021, pp. 221–235; J. L. Gómez Colomer, *El beneficio de pobreza (la solución española al problema del acceso gratuito a la justicia)*, Bosch 1982.

Another aspect to be considered is precisely what level of training will be required of the personnel working in these Justice Offices. In this regard, Art. 439 *quinquies* LOE establishes that the jobs in the Justice Offices, which will be determined by the Ministry of Justice and the Autonomous Communities with powers assumed, in their respective areas, will be filled by staff from the corps of civil servants in the service of the Justice Administration. However, the Secretariat of these offices is conditioned by establishing that it will be made up of personnel from the Corps of Procedural and Administrative Management. On the other hand, the City Council will also appoint suitable personnel in each of these offices to assist in the services entrusted to them, unless their execution is legally attributed to personnel from the Judicial Counselors Corp.

3. Digital Efficiency as a Trigger Mechanism in Judicial Organization

In order to understand the scope and significance of the introduction of measures that have a direct impact on procedural efficiency in the digital sphere, it is necessary to know how technologies have evolved in the Spanish legal system and in the European environment, by means of a brief reference to the legislative background, which will allow us to know where we have come from and where we are heading.

In the Spanish judicial system, we can mention the Royal Order of May 28th, 1904[8], which allowed the presentation in the courts and tribunals of the Kingdom of the written documents and their copies made with typewriters, as the first reference to the use of technical means in the administration of justice. It took ninety years for Organic Law no. 16/1994, which introduced the possibility of using technical, electronic and computerised means for the development of the activity and the exercise of the functions of the courts and tribunals, to appear. Later, Art. 147 Law no. 1/2000 on Civil Procedure[9] established that "oral proceedings in hearings and appearances shall be recorded on a medium suitable for the recording and reproduction of sound and image", with the legal counsel of the Administration of Justice being responsible for attesting to the recording and taking custody of the "tapes, discs or devices".

8 Available at: https://www.boe.es/gazeta/dias/1904/08/27/pdfs/GMD-1904-240.pdf [accessed on: September 19th, 2023].

9 Law no. 1/2000, available at: https://www.boe.es/buscar/act.php?id=BOE-A-2000-323 [accessed on: September 19th, 2023].

However, the key law in this area was Law no. 18/2011 regulating the use of information and communication technologies in the administration of justice[10], which established a real technological framework for the public service of Justice. The main new features introduced were concepts such as the General Access Point for the Administration of Justice and the Electronic Judicial Headquarters. This law brought about a substantial change in the way of accessing justice, moving from a completely paper-based process to the creation of an electronic judicial file, which was easier to consult and store and which already contemplated electronic signatures, as well as the practice of communication acts by electronic means. Since then, several regulations have led to considerable progress in this area, including Law no. 42/2015, which introduced electronic judicial auctions and the general obligation to communicate with the administration of justice by electronic means[11], except for certain exceptions such as natural persons, and Royal Decree no. 1065/2015 on electronic communications in the administration of justice in the territorial scope of the Ministry of Justice[12] and which regulates the LexNET system[13] which is an information system for the practice of acts of communication with professionals.

It is noteworthy that the pandemic caused by COVID-19 led to the approval of Law no. 3/2020 on procedural and organizational measures to deal with COVID-19 in the field of the administration of justice[14] and led to significant improvements in the field of holding hearings and procedural acts by telematic presence, which are now part of everyday life in our courts.

In the field of comparative law, we can highlight that there is a generalized trend towards digital efficiency and the essential adaptation of judicial systems to new technologies that is present at a global level. Thus, at European level, there are

10 Law no. 18/2011, available at: https://www.boe.es/buscar/act.php?id=BOE-A-2011-11605 [accessed on: September 19th, 2023].

11 Law no. 42/2015, available at: https://www.boe.es/buscar/doc.php?id=BOE-A-2015-10727 [accessed on: September 19th, 2023].

12 Royal Decree no. 1065/2015, available at: https://www.boe.es/buscar/act.php?id=BOE-A-2015-12999 [accessed on: September 19th, 2023].

13 More information available at: https://sedejudicial.justicia.es/-/lexnet [accessed on: September 19th, 2023].

14 Available at: https://www.boe.es/buscar/act.php?id=BOE-A-2020-10923. See European Comission, *Modernising EU justice systems: New package to speed up digitalisation of justice systems and boost training of justice professionals*, available at: https://ec.europa.eu/commission/presscorner/detail/en/ip_20_2246 [accessed on: September 19th, 2023].

numerous initiatives[15] that place special emphasis on the importance of digitalization to promote the efficiency and accessibility of judicial systems[16]. In 2021, progress was made in this direction by adopting a package of initiatives in the form of the Proposal for a Directive on the digitization of judicial cooperation[17], which involves amending various directives and framework decisions, and the Proposal for a Regulation on the digitisation of judicial cooperation[18].

On the other hand, as the European Parliament's 2022 report on Computerised system for communication in cross-border judicial proceedings (e-CODEX)[19] points out, the e-CODEX project will be the essential technological structure for the digitization of EU judicial cooperation in civil and criminal matters, as it includes a package of software products that enables reliable digital communication between the different actors: courts and citizens, and therefore allows for the secure exchange

---

15 The European Commission has published several very relevant studies on the digitisation of justice and its cross-border implications. European Commission, Directorate-General for Justice and Consumers, *Study on the use of innovative technologies in the justice field: final report*, Publications Office 2020, available at: https://data.europa.eu/doi/10.2838/585101 [accessed on: September 19th, 2023]; European Commission, Directorate-General for Justice and Consumers, *Cross-border digital criminal justice: final report*, Publications Office 2020, available at: https://data.europa.eu/doi/10.2838/118529 [accessed on: September 19th, 2023]; European Commission, Directorate-General for Justice and Consumers, *Study on the digitalisation of cross-border judicial cooperation in the EU: final report*, Publications Office of the European Union 2022, available at: https://data.europa.eu/doi/10.2838/174474 [accessed on: September 19th, 2023].

16 "Access to justice and facilitating cooperation between Member States are among the main objectives of the EU's area of freedom, security and justice enshrined in the Treaty on the Functioning of the European Union. The Charter of Fundamental Rights in its Article 47 guarantees right to an effective remedy and to a fair trial. Effective justice systems are also essential for the functioning of the internal market and a prerequisite for economic growth. Access to justice needs to be maintained and to keep pace with change, including the digital transformation affecting all aspects of our lives" (European Commission, *Communication from the Commission to the European Parliament, the Council, the European Economic and Social Committee and the Committee of the Regions, Digitalisation of justice in the European Union A toolbox of opportunities*, available at: https://eur-lex.europa.eu/legal-content/EN/ALL/?uri=CELEX%3A52020DC0710 [accessed on: September 19th, 2023].

17 Available at: https://eur-lex.europa.eu/legal-content/EN/TXT/?uri=COM%3A2021%3A760%3AFIN [accessed on: September 21st, 2023].

18 Available at: https://eur-lex.europa.eu/legal-content/ES/TXT/?uri=CELEX%3A52021PC0759&qid=1395839332065 [accessed on: September 19th, 2023].

19 Available at: https://www.europarl.europa.eu/RegData/etudes/BRIE/2021/690667/EPRS_BRI(2021)690667_EN.pdf [accessed on: September 19th, 2023].

of judicial documents. Being aware of the advantages of digitisation, but also of the difficulties faced by the European Union, the Parliament adopted a report in the same year analysing all the controversial issues in this context[20].

With regard to the current situation in European countries, it should be taken into consideration that countries such as Austria[21], France[22], Italy[23],

---

20 European Parliament, *Briefing Initial Appraisal of a European Commission Impact Assessment Digitalisation of cross-border judicial cooperation*, April 2022, available at: https://www.congreso.es/docu/docum/ddocum/dosieres/sleg/legislatura_14/spl_63/pdfs/22.pdf [accessed on: September 19th, 2023].

21 In Austria, the digital evolution has had its greatest exponent through *Strategische Initiative Justize 3.0*, available at: https://www.bmj.gv.at/themen/Justizverwaltung/justiz-3.0.html [accessed on: September 21st, 2023]. From mid-2023, digital criminal proceedings will be in full use by both courts and prosecutors. This means that the entire new generation will be handled exclusively digitally. In digital civil administrative and court proceedings, all new cases will be handled exclusively digitally by the end of 2023. The full nationwide conversion of all categories is planned for the end of 2025. In detail on the measures to be implemented see Bundesministerium für Justiz (BMJ) Abteilung Rechtsinformatik, Informationsund Kommunikationstechnologie, *IT Anwendungen in der österreichischen Justiz*, 2020, available at: https://www.congreso.es/docu/docum/ddocum/dosieres/sleg/legislatura_14/spl_63/pdfs/24.pdf [accessed on: September 21st, 2023].

22 In France, the justice transformation plan is part of the *chantiers de la justice* that were presented in 2017, the first being the digital transformation around the *justice.fr portal*, which will in particular facilitate online procedures for litigants, available at: https://www.gouvernement.fr/argumentaire/lancement-des-grands-chantiers-de-la-justice [accessed on: September 23rd, 2023]. Subsequently, thw *Loi* no. 222/2019 *de programmation 2018–2022 et de réforme pour la justice* has been the main legislation in this area (available at: https://www.legifrance.gouv.fr/dossierlegislatif/JORFDOLE000036830320/ [accessed on: September 21st, 2023]). As regards the concrete development of the objectives, aims, scope and concrete measures see Cour des Comptes, *Améliorer le fonctionnement de la justice – Point d'étape du plan de transformation numérique du ministère de la justice, Communication à la commission des finances du Sénat Janvier 2022*, available at: https://www.ccomptes.fr/sites/default/files/2022-01/20220126-plan-transformation-numerique-justice%C2%A0.pdf [accessed on: September 21st, 2023].

23 Italy has launched a series of initiatives on *Giustizia digitale*, (https://www.giustizia.it/giustizia/it/mg_2_20.page# [accessed on: September 21st, 2023]), within the framework of the *Strategia digitale del Ministero della Giustizia (2014–2020)*. See *Ricognizione della digitalizzazione del processo civile e penale e della transizione digitale del Ministero della giustizia* (febbraio 2021), available at: https://www.giustizia.it/cmsresources/cms/documents/studio_dgsia_ricognizione_digitalizzazione_febbraio2021.pdf [accessed on: September 21st, 2023], which explains the different measures to be implemented and how the digital transformation of procedures will be put into practice, through 'Cloud first' justice and the creation of a single document management platform.

Portugal[24] and the United Kingdom[25] are also adapting their legislation to the new implications of digital justice. In this way, they are making progress in this area with the aim of evolving in the digital framework, but at the same time, with full respect for the rights of the citizens concerned.

Within international organisations, it is undeniable that the Council of Europe is playing an essential role in relation to the different initiatives and action plans linked to new technologies and digital justice. We highlight as a relevant measure the CEPEJ Action Plan 'Digitalisation for a better justice'[26], adopted in December 2021. In addition, various guidelines[27] and supporting documents

---

24 In Portugal, within the innovation pillar of the Justiça + Proxima 2020–2023 programme (https://mais.justica.gov.pt/ [accessed on: September 21st, 2023]), a series of measures are proposed to provide access to a more modern and technologically advanced justice system. A number of measures are also envisaged in el *Plano de Recuperação e Resiliência*, available at: https://recuperarportugal.gov.pt/ [accessed on: September 21st, 2023]. On the other hand, the report on Transformação Digital da Justiça includes and sets out in detail future projects (see https://justica.gov.pt/Transformacao-Digital-da-Justica-2015–2022 [accessed on: September 21st, 2023]). For more information, please watch the video *Transformação digital dos Tribunais: Projetar o futuro*, available at: https://www.youtube.com/watch?v=RfeCVuKa3wA [accessed on: September 21st, 2023].

25 In the United Kingdom, it is worth highlighting His Majesty's Courts and Tribunal Service reform programme, which began in 2016 and continues today, which provides for different measures for digital transformation in all judicial orders (https://www.gov.uk/guidance/the-hmcts-reform-programme [accessed on: September 23rd, 2023]). It is also interesting to consult the action policy to be implemented by the Ministry of Justice 2025. See Ministry of Justice, *Policy paper Ministry of Justice Digital Strategy 2025*, available at: https://www.gov.uk/government/publications/ministry-of-justice-digital-strategy-2025/ministry-of-justice-digital-strategy-2025 [accessed on: September 21st, 2023].

26 Adopted at the 37th CEPEJ plenary meeting, available at: https://rm.coe.int/cepej-2021-12-en-cepej-action-plan-2022-2025-digitalisation-justice/1680a4cf2c [accessed on: September 21st, 2023].

27 European Commission for the Efficiency of Justice (CEPEJ), *Guidelines on how to drive change towards cyberjustice, Stock-taking of tools deployed and summary of good practices*, available at: https://edoc.coe.int/en/efficiency-of-justice/7501-guidelines-on-how-to-drive-change-towards-cyberjustice-stock-taking-of-tools-deployed-and-summary-of-good-practices.html# [accessed on: September 21st, 2023].

should be taken into consideration to develop e-justice[28], electronic filing and archiving and video-conferencing in judicial proceedings[29].

4. Law on the Digital Efficiency of the Public Justice Service

The LDE[30] deserves special attention, as it represents a substantial advance in the Spanish legal system in the field of new technologies and the digitalisation of justice. The aim of the regulation, as mentioned above, is to respect and guarantee the right to effective judicial protection in a digital justice environment that is secure and which fully respects all procedural rights.

Among the objectives pursued by this draft law, we can highlight the following:

1. The citizen as the main priority: to guarantee the provision of a quality public justice service by digital means throughout the territory;
2. Digital transformation: an instrument that serves to bring justice closer to the citizens;
3. Accessibility: to facilitate access to justice for all people through the use of technology;
4. Efficiency in procedural processing by digital means.

---

28 European Commission for the Efficiency of Justice (CEPEJ), *Toolkit for supporting the implementation of the Guidelines on how to drive change towards Cyberjustice*, adopted at the 32th plenary meeting of the CEPEJ 13 and 14 June, 2019, available at: https://rm.coe.int/cepej-toolkit-cyberjustice-en-cepej-2019-7/168094ef3e [accessed on: September 25th, 2023].

29 European Commission for the Efficiency of Justice (CEPEJ), *Guidelines on videoconferencing in judicial proceedings (2021)*, adopted by the CEPEJ at the 36th plenary meeting, available at: https://edoc.coe.int/en/efficiency-of-justice/10706-guidelines-on-videoconferencing-in-judicial-proceedings.html [accessed on: September 25th, 2023]; European Commission for the Efficiency of Justice (CEPEJ), *Guidelines on electronic court filing (e-filing) and digitalisation of courts*, adopted by the CEPAJ at the 37th plenary meeting, available at: https://rm.coe.int/cepej-2021-15-en-e-filing-guidelines-digitalisation-courts/1680a4cf87 [accessed on: September 25th, 2023].

30 The Law is structured in an Explanatory Memorandum, a Preliminary Title, seven titles, eight additional provisions, two transitional provisions, one derogatory provision, ten final provisions and an Annex of definitions.

As main novelties appearing in this digital panorama, it seems relevant to us to point out:

1. Digital disconnection and reconciliation of work, personal and family life;
2. Electronic identification and digital signature systems for legal proceedings by video conference (new regulation);
3. Compulsory submission of documents, consultation of files and services provided by the Administration by electronic means[31];
4. Notary and registry procedures: simplification and enhancement of the obtaining of information by means of telematic intervention;
5. Data orientation: massive exchange of information and new information and communication systems;
6. Cybersecurity: strengthening the process of digitisation of justice;
7. Directive on the digitisation of companies[32].

In terms of the specific aspects to be developed by this Law, the following areas can be identified:

1. Digital governance: the aim will be to regulate, promote and adjust administrative collaboration and the State Technical Committee for e-Judicial Administration (CTEAJE) will play a special role in the development of digital transformation. The creation of an Advisory Council for the Digital Transformation of the Administration of Justice is envisaged, which aims to encourage the initiative, design, development and production of systems to be carried out in coordination with the private sector[33].

---

31 It should be clarified that, although this generalisation can be considered for public administration operators, we understand that this possibility will not be automatically applicable to users or citizens. We consider it advisable and even necessary to promote existing electronic means to generate greater efficiency, but we maintain the position that the option of communicating and submitting documents in person should persist and be maintained, taking into account the circumstances of the case. It is one thing to recognise the right to use these electronic means and quite another to make it an obligation.

32 Also known as the Digital Tools Directive (Directive 2019/1151/EU amending Directive 2017/1132/EU as regards the use of digital tools and processes in the area of company law).

33 See in detail Title VII 'Cooperation between the administrations with powers in matters of Administration of Justice. The Judicial Interoperability and Security Scheme' (Arts. 88–103 PLED).

2. Digital services[34] for citizens, businesses and professionals: It details the rights of citizens, professionals and businesses. It reviews the rights and obligations recognised in Law 18/2011 and allows for mass exchanges.
3. Delocalised work: remote environments are regulated. It is essential that judicial immediacy is preserved in all proceedings by means of videoconferencing. To this end, the so-called 'secure access points' and 'secure locations' have been regulated by means of technical requirements and guarantees, from which telematic interventions can be carried out with full procedural effects, in the terms provided for in the amendments to the procedural laws. Art. 63 LDE is devoted to defining the difference between secure access points and secure locations, with the establishment of minimum requirements to be met.
4. Automatic processing: Automated proceedings, already defined in Law no. 18/2011, are encouraged and regulated. It also introduces, regulates and limits assisted and proactive actions.
5. Regulatory coverage, where appropriate, of country projects for the digital transformation of justice: Provisions on open data, digital services, gap mitigation.
6. Data-driven justice[35]: One of the fundamental pillars will be data-driven processing. In this sense, the information systems of the Administration of Justice will ensure the possibility, entry, incorporation, processing and exploitation of metadata information[36].

   Currently, the Spanish legal system already has instruments that follow or use this new methodology. Particularly interesting is https://datos.justicia.es/ where very useful information can be obtained on various aspects that affect justice at the functional, technological and political-territorial levels.

---

34 Art. 4 LDE.

35 Although traditionally, and in line with current procedural laws, the administration of justice has traditionally based its working model on the document, the aim is to update this model, basing it on data. The orientation towards data as a public good and the need to preserve it, as it enables trends to be detected and highly reliable predictions to be made. Therefore, a data-based information architecture is created for the function of generating information and knowledge for management, as well as a metadata-oriented information architecture for the function of application interoperability. See in detail Dirección General de Transformación Digital de la Justicia (DGTDAJ), *Justicia orientada al dato*, June 3rd, 2022, available at: https://www.mjusticia.gob.es/es/JusticiaEspana/ProyectosTransformacionJusticia/Documents/20220603_-_Justicia_Orientada_al_Dato.pdf [accessed on: September 21st, 2023].

36 Art. 35 LDE.

7. Digital immediacy and non-face-to-face services[37]. Regulates the identification and digital signature of professionals and citizens[38] in a delocalised manner and by videoconference[39].
8. Sustainable judicial record: general provisions on the electronic judicial record and its archiving are addressed. A definition of the electronic court file is provided as "the ordered set of electronic data, documents, formalities and proceedings, as well as audiovisual recordings, pertaining to a judicial proceeding, whatever the type of information they contain and whatever the format in which they have been generated" (Art. 47 LDE).
9. Cybersecurity and data protection: governance of cybersecurity; guaranteeing data protection in the digital sphere of justice. Another of the key aspects is undoubtedly cybersecurity. The State Technical Committee for e-Judicial Administration will be responsible for drawing up and updating the information security policy of the Administration of Justice, in its organisational, technical, physical and regulatory compliance aspects (Art. 96 LDE). Other operators responsible for ensuring security in this context also appear, such as the Security Subcommittee, a specialised and permanent body for judicial cybersecurity of the State Technical Committee for e-Judicial Administration (Art. 97 LDE) and the Cybersecurity Operations Centre of the Administration of Justice, which will strengthen the capacities for surveillance, prevention, protection, detection, response to cybersecurity incidents, advice and support for the management of cybersecurity in a centralised manner, allowing for greater effectiveness and efficiency (Art. 98 LDE).

In relation to digital efficiency, we must highlight the recent approval of Royal Decree-Law no. 6/2023, which approves urgent measures for the execution of the Recovery, Transformation and Resilience Plan in the areas of public service of justice, civil service, local regime and patronage[40]. On March 20th, 2024, the legislative reforms operated by Royal Decree-Law no. 6/2023, aimed at improving the digital efficiency of the Administration of Justice and streamlining judicial processes, came into force. The optimization of the efficiency of the Administration

---

37 Art. 60 LDE.

38 This is an extremely important aspect and one to which the legislator has paid particular attention, given the serious procedural consequences that a lack of identification and signature could have on the proceedings. See Art. 61 LDE.

39 It will be essential to ensure a secure identification system in video conferences (Art. 23 LDE).

40 Royal Decree-Law no. 6/2023.

of Justice is one of the objectives of the Royal Decree-Law no. 6/2023, which introduces legislative amendments related to the digitalization of Justice and to the streamlining of judicial processes.

The Royal Decree-Law no. 6/2023 introduces important changes in civil and criminal proceedings. On the one hand, in the Civil Procedure Law (*Ley de Enjuiciamiento Civil*, hereinafter LEC) are significant novelties regarding the following aspects: amendments aimed at guaranteeing accessibility for the elderly (Arts. 7 *bis* and 183 LEC); the accumulation of proceedings is promoted (Arts. 73.1, 73.2, 77 and 85.2 LEC); preference is given to telematic presence in procedural acts (Art. 129 *bis* LEC), providing for communication by videoconference (Art. 137 *bis* LEC) in certain cases; new features are introduced in relation to judicial assistance (Art. 169 LEC) and to the judicial request (Art. 171 LEC); the holding of certain procedural acts by electronic means is regulated (Arts. 152, 155, 160, 162 and 164 LEC); amendments are introduced in the presentation of documents (Arts. 152, 155, 160, 162 and 164 LEC); the presentation of documents by electronic means is regulated (Arts. 152, 155, 160, 162 and 164 LEC); it regulates the holding of certain procedural acts by electronic means (Arts. 152, 155, 160, 162 and 164 LEC); it introduces changes in the presentation of documents (Arts. 264, 268 bis, 270, 276 and 279 LEC), in the taking of evidence (Arts. 311, 312, 313, 320, 331, 337, 342, 346, 358, 359, 364, 374, 383, 445 and 446 LEC) and in the determination of procedural costs in appeals and cassation (art. 398 LEC).

It should also be noted that important changes are made in relation to the requirements for submission of lawsuits to ordinary (Art. 249 LEC) and verbal (Art. 250 LEC) proceedings, with the maximum amount of the verbal trial being set at 15,000 euros, instead of the previous limit of 6,000 euros and, within each of the aforementioned proceedings, it implements, among other new features, changes related to the pleadings and defence (Arts. 399, 405.1, 437 and 438 LEC); in verbal proceedings, it regulates the appearance by electronic means or videoconference in the preliminary hearing and oral trial (Arts. 414 and 438 LEC); in the verbal trial, the appearance by electronic means or videoconference in the preliminary hearing and the oral trial is regulated (Arts. 414 and 432 LEC) and the reference to the period of twenty days to issue a sentence after the practice of final proceedings is eliminated.

The new preferential witness procedure (*procedimiento testigo*) is incorporated in order to expedite proceedings in which identical claims have been filed previously (Art. 438 *bis* LEC) and changes are introduced in relation to appeals (Arts. 455, 458, 461, 463, 464, 465, 465 and 466 LEC), cassation (Art. 450 LEC) and review (Art. 457 LEC), highlighting, in the case of the appeal, that it must now be lodged with the body competent to hear the appeal and no longer with the body that issued the decision appealed against; in relation to the complaint appeal, the references to the appeal and the extraordinary appeal for procedural infringement (Arts. 494 and 495 LEC) are eliminated. It also introduces changes to the enforcement procedure and special family proceedings.

On the other hand, in the Criminal Procedure Law (*Ley de Enjuiciamiento Criminal*, hereinafter LECRIM) preference is given to telematic presence in procedural acts (Art. 258 *bis* LECRIM) and adaptations are introduced to guarantee communication, understanding and interaction with the environment of persons with disabilities (Art. 109 LECRIM). Electronic procedures are also introduced to facilitate referrals to various registers, such as the Central Register of Convicted Persons and other registers relevant to the protection of victims of violence (Art. 252 LECRIM). The amendment defines the content of the reports and distinguishes between the face-to-face signature and the telematic signature by means of an electronic signature (Arts. 265 and 266 LECRIM).

Moreover, it provides for the sending of requisitions to the System of Administrative Records to Support the Administration of Justice (*Sistema de Registros Administrativos de Apoyo a la Administración de Justicia*, SIRAJ) and their publication on the Single Judicial Notice Board (*Tablón Edictal Judicial Único*), ensuring interoperability between both platforms (Art. 512 LECRIM); it establishes the incorporation into the case of proof of sending and referral (Art. 514 LECRIM); it regulates the publication of edicts on the Single Judicial Notice Board in the event that the whereabouts of those interested in exercising the criminal action in relation to the dismissal of the case are unknown (Art. 643 LECRIM) and regulates the electronic documentation of the oral trial sessions and other oral proceedings (Art. 743 LECRIM).

5. Bibliography

Literature

Gómez Colomer J. L., *El beneficio de pobreza: (la solución española al problema del acceso gratuito a la justicia)*, Bosch 1982.

Gómez Colomer J. L., 'La asistencia jurídica gratuita' in: J. L. Gómez Colomer (ed.), *Introducción al derecho procesal: Derecho procesal I*, Tirant Lo Blanch 2021.

Andrea Planchadell-Gargallo*

V. Access to Justice and Proximity Justice in Spain: the Valencian Model

Abstract: The chapter describes the judicial system in Spain, highlighting access to justice and the reforms expected to make it more efficient. It mentions the need to adapt the territorial organisation of the courts and the evolution of Magistrates' Courts to Justice Offices, with a closer approach to citizens. The proposed reforms include the creation of Courts of First Instance to simplify access to justice and the implementation of municipal offices to avoid travel. In the Valencian Community, the Justiprop service offers local legal advice as part of this proximity effort.

Keywords: Spanish judicial system, proximity justice, access to justice, Justriprop

1. Access to a More Effective Justice: Expected Reforms in Spain

The main objective of these pages is to publicise a legislative proposal that has been recently passed in Spain[1], which aims to improve the efficiency of the Spanish justice system and make it more accessible to citizens by making important changes to the organisation of the judiciary. Irrespective of the outcome of this proposal, the Valencian Community has launched a project that pursues the same objectives without changing the organisation of the judiciary, which is not possible.

The right of access to justice, recognized in Art. 24 of Spanish Constitution (hereinafter SC) is the most important of the rights that give meaning to the right of action, since it is not difficult to deduce that the fulfilment of each and all fundamental procedural rights depends on the real possibility of approaching the courts to request the protection of our legitimate rights and interests. It is obvious that it would be meaningless to speak of a day in the Court, the right to defense

* Full Professor of Procedural Law, University Jaume I, Castellón, Spain.

1 Organic Law no. 1/2025 on measures for the efficiency of Public Service Justice, entered into force from January 2nd, 2025.

or of the right to appeals, if the mechanism that allows access to the courts is not previously articulated and guaranteed. In other words, it is not possible to raise claims and stand for our rights before the Courts if access to the process in which they should or can be asserted is unduly hindered[2].

This right of access to justice must now be interpreted in a broader sense. In other words, it should be more than just a right to be a party to proceedings. This something more, as we try to explain in these pages, is a justice that must be effective. But it must also be more human and closer to the people.

Since the approval of the Spanish Organic Law of the Judiciary of 1985 (LOPJ), and even though it has been object of quite a few reforms, the fact is that the organization of the Spanish courts has not changed substantially in terms of their territorial location (*planta and demarcación*), nor has it proposed an organizational structure which is not based on the municipality as a basic element. What's more, in this organization, the unipersonal bodies (judges) have always been considered the first link of access to justice for the citizens, the first judicial authority they have contact to.

In Spain, at the present time, the basic judicial organization is the following one:

- Magistrate Courts (*Juzgados de Paz*, JPaz)
- Courts of First Instance (*Juzgados de Primera Insancia*, JPI)
- Courts of preliminary investigation (*Juzgados de Instrucción*, JI)
- Courts of Violence against Women (*Juzgados de Violencia sobre la Mujer*, JVM)
- Family Courts (*Juzgados de Familia*)
- Commercial Courts (*Juzgados de lo Mercantil*)
- Juvenile Courts (*Juzgados de Menores*, JM)
- Penitentiary Surveillance Courts (*Juzgados de Vigilancia Penitenciaria*, JVP)
- Central Courts of Penitentiary Surveillance (in National Hight Court)
- Central Preliminary investigation Courts (in National Hight Court)
- Criminal Courts (*Juzgados de lo Penal*, JPe)
- Central Criminal Courts (in National Hight Court)
- Social Courts (*Juzgados de los Social*)

2 Constitutional Court, Judgement no. 2/2022; Judgement no. 189/2021; Judgement no. 142/2021.

- Contentious-Administrative Courts (*Juzgados de lo contencioso-administrativo*)
- Central Contentious-Administrative Court (in National Hight Court)
- Provincial Courts (*Audiencia Provincial*, AP)
- Superior Courts of Justice (*Tribunales Superiores de Justicia*, TSJ)
- National High Court (*Audiencia Nacional*, AN)
- Supreme Court (*Tribunal Supremo*, TS).

The question we must ask ourselves is whether this model is still valid today. Let us not forget that the current model, despite its modifications – we insist – is based on a nineteenth-century society very different from today's one (a society, that of the nineteenth century, essentially agrarian, dispersed, poorly communicated and with great mobility limitations). Today's society is undoubtedly very different, faced with more complex social and economic relations in which litigiousness has increased exponentially and, in this sense, the Administration of Justice must be required to adapt to it, as it has clearly become obsolete, that's way a change is needed.

The dysfunctions that this model has generated, as the legislator recognizes in the Act on measures for the efficiency of Public Service Justice, refer to the lack of specialization of the courts; the proliferation of organs with identical competence in each judicial district, which has led to a dispersion of means and efforts; favouring an interim and unprofessional justice; with unequal workloads and resolution times of the cases, being long, very disparate. In view of this situation, it is necessary to look for a model that responds more efficiently to the needs of society[3].

3 The new Act on measures for the efficiency of Public Service Justice understands that organisational efficiency is found in that structure which, by optimizing the available resources, is suitable for achieving its objectives. Of all the qualities that add value to an efficient organization, the law concentrates on three of them: Specialization, homogeneity and organizational capacity. See, also, A. Perea González et al., 'Diálogos para el futuro judicial. LXXV -Medidas de eficiencia Digital del Servicio Público Justicia', 104440 *Diario La Ley* 2024; F. de Asis González Campo, 'Justicia 2030 y la ley de medidas de eficiencia procesal y digital: una Justicia accesible, inclusiva y sostenible en el contexto del objetivo de desarrollo sostenible' in: J. Martínez Calvo (coord.), *El derecho privado ante los retos de la agenda 2030*, Pamplona: Thomson Reuter Aranzadi 2022, p. 345.

The Spanish pre-legislator has understood that one of the ways to achieve it is to transform the first step or level of judicial organization (individual judge – unipersonal trial bodies) into a collegiate body, aligning with other European countries. Thus, we have opted for a model based on the Courts of First Instance (*Tribunales de Instancia*), without altering the exercise of the jurisdictional function or the competencies of the unipersonal trial bodies.

Arts. 117 and 122 SC apply to all jurisdictional bodies regardless of whether they are single-member or collegiate in nature and configuration; what is more, it cannot be understood that the Constitution is providing for this first step to be single-member. Our Constitution chose that organization as the legislator thought it to be the most appropriate at the time; then, if it is not the most appropriate now, we will have to change it.

Therefore, the focus of this reform lies in the creation and constitution of the Courts of First Instance and the evolution of the Justice of the Peace (Magistrate Courts) into modern Justice Offices in the municipalities.

2. The Courts of First Instance

It is important to point out that the current one has not been the first attempt to establish these Courts of First Instance. Two of the most recent attempts, the one in 2008 and in 2012, clearly failed. The one in 2008 because the Houses of Parliament were dissolved and general elections called; the one in 2012 due to the inability to join an agreement on this point.

The model of judicial organisation based on the traditional one-person court has been identified as one of the aspects that determines the possibilities of achieving a more efficient public service of Justice. So far, the high number of litigious matters and the resulting increased workload of courts have been faced with the creation of new judicial bodies, mostly temporary, and reinforcement measures. However, and to be honest, these solutions do not seem to have solved the problem, mainly because no organisational decision was taken as an alternative to this increase. Moreover, this has been done through the laudable figures of substitute judges and substitute magistrates who wander from one court to another and from one jurisdictional order to another, with the consequent lack of professionalisation and specialisation.

The establishment of the Courts of First Instance is also supposed to simplify access to justice, insofar as it provides for the existence of a single court assisted by a single organisation that will provide it with support, the Judicial Office. In this way, the aim is to boost citizens' accessibility and confidence in the justice system.

Art. 26 LOPJ establishes that jurisdictional power is attributed to the Courts of First Instance and the corresponding Central Courts of First Instance, together with the others indicated in that Article (AP, TSJ, AN and TS). Meanwhile, Art. 84 of the law develops these Courts of First Instance establishing that there will be a Court of First Instance in each judicial district, with its place in the capital city from which it takes its name. From an organisational point of view, except in the cases where Law no. 38/1998 allows for the division of both jurisdictions into two separate sections, these Courts consist of a Single Section, with jurisdiction in civil matters and criminal investigation together in the same Section.

In addition to these, the Courts of First Instance may also be organized with sections regarding family matters, commercial matters, violence against women cases, criminal proceedings, juvenile matters, prison supervision, contentious matters, and social ones.

In each Court of First Instance there will be a Presidency, as there will also be one in each one of the Sections that may be formed therein, when the number of seats in the Court is equal to or greater than twelve or when there are eight or more judicial seats in the Section.

As an example of the types of cases these Courts can hear, in civil matters they have jurisdiction, among others, in the first instance of trials that are not attributed by law to other judicial bodies, they solve the applications for the recognition and enforcement of foreign judgments and other foreign judicial decisions and of the enforcement of foreign awards or arbitration decisions. In criminal matters they are responsible, among others cases, for investigating criminal cases that fall within the jurisdiction of Provincial Courts and the Criminal Prosecution Sections of the Courts of First Instance, with the exception of the investigation of those cases that fall within the jurisdiction of the Sections for Violence against Women, habeas corpus proceedings, to issue protection orders for victims of violence against women while on duty provided that they can't be adopted by the Section for Violence against Women or of the corresponding Section that assumes the knowledge of these matters, the autonomous procedure of confiscation for offences for which they are competent.

3. Justices of the Peace

The question of what to do with the Justices of the Peace and what their role should be in this new organisation has also been addressed by the legislator[4]. From our point of view, this is a very important decision, because Justices of the Peace have always had the function of extending the Administration of Justice to all territories. They are therefore particularly important in rural areas or those farthest from the capitals or large cities. In short, it might seem, from an organisational perspective, Justices of the Peace seem to be the closest and most accessible judicial bodies to the citizen.

Without denying what we have just said, the truth is, however, that Justices of the Peace have suffered an involution as a series of legal reforms have led to a progressive 'disempowerment' or 'loss' of their competences. This development has resulted in a curious paradox: while being true that they are the closest judicial body to the citizen, they can 'assist' them in fewer and fewer matters, which does not prevent the citizen to from having recourse to other further judicial bodies for the resolution of many of her or his dispute.

According to Art. 100 LOPJ its jurisdiction in civil matters focuses on the substantiation in the first instance, ruling and execution of cases involving sums of less than ninty euros, which according to the statistics are the remaining cases; and on the execution of rogatory letters to carry out acts of communication, which will be considerably reduced by digitisation. Their participation in the Civil Registry office has also been profoundly affected by legal reforms. Together with this matter, in criminal proceedings the disappearance of misdemeanours has all but emptied its powers in criminal matters.

The trend reflected in the statistics is significant. The number of cases they know has fallen significantly:

---

4 The Justices of the peace were created in the year 855, being conceived in the first Civil Procedure Code with the aim of taking over the jurisdictional competences previously exercised by the Mayors. About these courts, see I. Esparza Leibar, 'Sobre el potencial de la Justicia de Paz en España, en relación con el reforzamiento de la eficiencia y la correlativa legitimación del Poder Judicial' in: I. Ordeñana Gezuraga, K. Etxebarria Estankona (eds.), *Presente y futuro de la Justicia de Paz en el ordenamiento español*, Universidad del País Vasco 2013, p. 38; I. Ordeñana Guzuruga, 'Propuesta de futuro para la justicia de paz en España', 4 *Revista General de Derecho Procesal*, 2018; I. Ordeñana Guzuruga, *La justicia de paz: nuevos tiempos, ¿nuevas (infra)estructuras?. Disquisiciones ante la creación de las Oficinas de Justicia en los municipios en lugar de los Juzgados de Paz*, Bosch 2023, *passim*.

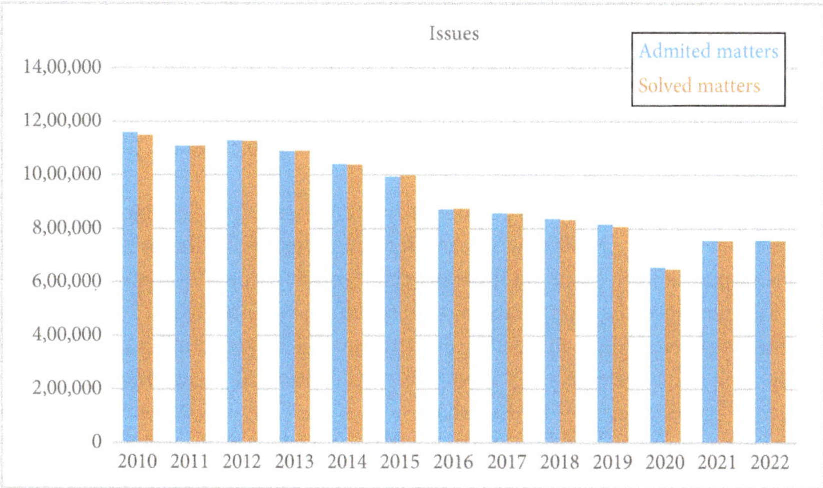

Justice data by date, General Council of the Judiciary, 2022

As a result, its original function, in which it could be said that it had the capacity the capacity to resolve the affairs of the citizens of its locality, has been very limited. However, this does not mean that it is not important that we, as citizens, have no place to go and ask for judicial protection. We still need a point of reference to go to that allows us access to the Administration of Justice near 'home', without having to travel far away. Then, if Justices of the Peace are to disappear, it is important to think about an alternative so that this proximity in not lost. That 'something' is another of the pillars of the planned reform, Offices of Justice in municipalities (*Oficinas de Justicia de los municipios*)[5].

4. Justice Offices

It is precisely for this reason that the creation of the Justice Offices in the municipality are envisaged as another key point in the legal reform and the new judicial organization (Arts. 439 *ter* to 439 *quinquies* of the law).

It should not be forgotten that the current secretariats of the magistrates' courts correspond to this structure. These Offices will add to their current services a catalogue of procedures within the administration of justice, bringing this public

5 I. Ordeñana Guruga, *La justicia de paz…*, *passim*.

service closer to all municipalities. In this way, these Offices will also fulfil the social function that the Justice of the Peace has performed for a long time, adapting the service, and replacing the Justice of the Peace.

The main idea is that the Justice Offices will respond to the same purposes, but in a way that is more in line with current social demands, and the provision of a public justice service of quality.

In this sense, the element of proximity and territory plays a fundamental role. It is intended that the people who live in these municipalities will not have to travel to the capital cities to carry out these procedures before the administration of justice. Furthermore, the digitalisation of these Offices will increase its functionality.

The Draf law defines these Offices as those which, without being integrated in the judicial structure, are part of the organization of the administration of justice to provide services to the inhabitants of their municipalities. They are to be found in those municipalities where there is no Court of First Instance, and the management of the installations and instrumental means corresponds to the Town Council, unless it corresponds partially or totally to the Ministry of Justice.

These offices will provide the following services:

- Acts of procedural communication, unless the same can be carried out by electronic means, with persons residing in the municipality or municipalities for which it provides its services, provided that the same have not been able to be practised by electronic means.
- Collaboration with the Civil Registry office in the way established by law or by regulation.
- Receiving applications for recognition of the right to free legal aid and their transmission to the Bar Associations responsible for their processing, as well as any other actions that may help to manage these applications and communicate them to the interested parties.
- Submitting or dealing with requests from citizens addressed to the Territorial Management Offices of the Ministry of Justice or equivalent bodies the municipalities that have taken under jurisdiction.
- Cooperation, in coordination with the competent Administration, with the Units in charge of the Appropriate Means of Dispute Resolution (ADR) existing in their territorial area.
- Collaboration with the competent Public Administrations so that judges, magistrates, public prosecutors, legal advisors in the Administration of Justice and staff working for this Administration may occasionally carry out their work telematically, insofar as the development of IT tools makes it possible.
- Those other services that appear in collaboration agreements between different Public Administrations.

The positions will be filled by members of the Corps of Civil Servants working for the administration of justice; the Secretary belongs to the staff of the Procedural and Administrative Management Corps.

5. The Valencian Proposal: *Justiprop* Service

5.1. Justification

In the Valencian Community[6] a local legal aid service called *Justiprop* has been set up. There are several reasons for creating this service, over and above which the Autonomous Communities will be obliged to adapt if the package of laws aimed at improving efficiency, which discussion has been stocked in the Parliament, is approved. It is worth mentioning the need to adapt the news content of the right to legal aid including advice and counselling prior to initiating judicial procedures, which can help avoiding artificial or unnecessary litigation.

Although the Justice of the Peace Courts have always been considered to be the service closest to the citizen, it should be noted that these courts have not traditionally had legal advice services and that the competencies of the Justice of the Peace Courts have been gradually reduced, to the point that, as we have already pointed out, they will disappear with the adoption of the Law on organizational efficiency.

This project is therefore perfectly in line with the Ministry of Justice's Justice 2030 Plan, and more specifically, with the clear priority of ensuring citizens' access to justice, both in terms of knowing their rights and effectively exercise them. It is obvious that there is no point in recognising or proclaiming certain rights to citizens if we do not have at our disposal the instruments to demand their fulfilment when they are threatened or violated. It is therefore necessary to create mechanisms and measures that ensure that the public service of justice is accessible to all, the creation of structural conditions of access to it that reach all citizens, without excluding anyone. Facilitating access to Justice to the most vulnerable groups and ensuring its ongoing adaptation to social realities must be, from this point of view, a priority.

Thus, in 2021, and to bring Justice closer to the citizens this local legal advice service (*Justiprop*) was introduced in municipalities with a population of more than 7,000 inhabitants. These are the municipalities than currently have Justices

6 The Valencian Community is divided into 3 provinces, with 34 counties and 542 municipalities. Its population reached a total of 5,090,839 inhabitants in 2022 (4th place in Spain), with a density of 217.47 inhabitants/km^2. More than 125 municipalities have fewer than 5,000 inhabitants. The least populated municipality is Castell de Cabres with 17 inhabitants.

of the Peace, suported by justice administration staff and which have expressed an interest in having this service. In 2022, the service has been extended to the cities head of the judicial district. It is being further extended in 2023.

The service is organized by the Bar Associations, with receive subsidies *by Generalitat de Justicia e Interior (before, Conselleria de Justicia, Interior i Administració Pùblica de la Generalitat Valencian)*, to compensate the legal professionals providing services in those offices[7].

5.2. Scope of action

What services does *Justiprop* provide? The services carried out by legal professionals in these offices refer to[8]:

1. Informing citizens about the services provided by the administration of the *Generalitat* and other administrations and public bodies in terms of access to justice, mediation, assistance to victims of crime, protection of rights and second chance mechanism and reducing financial burden; the location and contact details of the Judicial Offices, Assistance Offices for Victims of Crime, Complaints and Assistance Offices for Victims of Gender Violence, Counselling and Mediation Services (SOM); Bar associations and other legal professional associations; social centres; Civil Registry offices and any other entity that provides services related to aforementioned matters.
2. Informing citizens of the public or private resources to which they can turn for the protection and defence of their rights and legitimate interests.
3. Legal advice and pre-litigation counselling for persons who intend to claim judicial protection of their rights and interests, when their purpose is the avoiding of judicial conflict or the analysis the feasibility of the claim.
4. Information on administrative procedures before the Civil Registry offices, the Commercial Registry and the Real State Registry.
5. Assistance to citizens in the electronic consultation on judicial or administrative proceedings in matters of justice and/or administration of justice, particularly in matters of free justice, in collaboration with the Legal Advice Services (facilitating requests to interested parties, helping them to fill them in and send them to the relevant services together with the remaining documents presented, etc.), access the files in which they have the status of interested party, with prior authorization.
6. Information, advice, and legal assistance on social and energy emergencies.

---

7 In 2023, social and energy emergency matters have also been added.

8 Resolutions of the *Conselleria de Justicia, Interior i Administració Pùblica*, March 9th, 2022 and February 24th, 2023.

The service will be provided at offices dependent on local authorities or public bodies that express an interest, as well as at the offices of the *Generalitat* Administration. Since it is a 'pilot' project, they will be based on their interest in participating.

5.3 Organisation of the Justiprop Service

Once the institution has expressed its interest, the regional ministry will the professional association with the contact person of the respective entity concerned. A visit will be arranged and arranged with the person designated by the corresponding professional association to determine the implementation of the service. The professional association will nominate the professional(s) who will provide the service in this office.

In principle, the service is provided one day a week for four hours at a time (in the morning from 10am to 14pm; in the afternoon from 16pm to 20pm). This can be modified according to the workload.

The project will be financed, as we have said before, with subsidies. The money will come from the general budget of the *Generalitat*. The service will be evaluated periodically.

5.4 Some data

At the time of reviewing this chapter (July 2024), these offices can be found in the three provinces that are part of the Valencian Community[9]: 26 in Alicante; 12 in Castellón (two of them in the capital, one in the maritime district and the other on in the outskirts of the city) and 27 in Valencia.

The following conclusions can be drawn from the analysis of the results of the surveys carried out in these offices: it is worth noting the high level of satisfaction with the coordination, supervision and support functions carried out by the *Generalitat*, being the average score 8.5 out of 19; the level of satisfaction of local councils is generally high with regard to the function performed by the Bar and its legal professionals.

---

9 Generalitat Valenciana, *Oficinas Justiprop de la Comunitat Valenciana*, available at: https://cjusticia.gva.es/documents/162330279/174133635/2024-06-25++Relación+Justiprop+cast.pdf/0bc0b580-dcfd-abde-8e29-33952795aca0?t=1719390540163 [accessed on: August 1st, 2024].

6. Bibliography

Literature

Esparza Leibar I., 'Sobre el potencial de la Justicia de Paz en España, en relación con el reforzamiento de la eficiencia y la correlativa legitimación del Poder Judicial' in: Ordeñana Guzuruga I., Etxebarria Estankona K. (eds.), *Presente y futuro de la Justicia de Paz en el ordenamiento español*, Universidad del País Vasco 2013.

González Campo, F. de Asís, 'Justicia 2030 y la ley de medidas de eficiencia procesal y digital: Una Justicia accesible, inclusiva y sostenible en el contexto del objetivo de desarrollo sostenible 16' in: J. Martínez Calvo (coord.), *El derecho privado ante los retos de la agenda 2030*, Pamplona: Thomson Reuter Aranzadi 2022.

Ordeñana Guzuruga I., *La justicia de paz: nuevos tiempos, ¿nuevas (infra)estructuras?. Disquisiciones ante la creación de las Oficinas de Justicia en los municipios en lugar de los Juzgados de Paz*, Bosch 2023.

Ordeñana Guzuruga I., 'Propuesta de futuro para la justicia de paz en España', 4 *Revista General de Derecho Procesal* 2018.

Perea González, A et al., Diálogos para el futuro judicial. LXXV. Medidas de eficiencia Digital del Servicio Público Justicia, 104440 *Diario La Ley* 2024.

Justyna Głębocka*

VI. Model of Pre-trial Proceedings and Its Influence on the Judicial Stage of Criminal Proceedings: A Comparative Analysis of European Legal Systems

Abstract: There are several different constructions of models of preparatory proceedings, in both abstract and concrete terms, within which the goals and functions of this pre-trial stage of criminal proceedings can be defined in different ways. Clear differences are noticeable concerning continental and common law systems. However, even within continental solutions, different constructions can be distinguished. This chapter describes the relationship between different models of preparatory proceedings and the effectiveness of the judicial stage of criminal proceedings, taking the German, Polish, French and Italian systems as the assertive model. It attempts to evaluate different constructions by indicating the advantages and disadvantages of individual model solutions.

Keywords: Pre-trial proceedings, models of pre-trial proceedings, judicial phase, comparative approach

1. Introduction

A modern European criminal trial consists of two phases – the pre-trial phase and the main judicial phase. These two stages are governed by separate rules with significant differences between them, regarding both the applicable procedural rules, the leading authorities and the procedural guarantees of the parties. On the other hand, there are several links and connections between these phases of the process, and it must be emphasised that the interaction that occurs is always bilateral. The chosen model of pre-trial proceedings influences the model of judicial proceedings; a particular shaping of the jurisdictional proceedings is relevant from the point of view of the course of pre-trial proceedings.

Nowadays, there is no doubt that the pre-trial phase is an essential stage in criminal proceedings. Even in common law-based legislations, the pre-trial proceedings are distinguishable and based on specific statutory regulations[1].

---

* PhD, University of Warsaw, Poland.

1 J. R. Spencer, 'The English System' in: M. Delmas-Marty, J. R. Spencer (eds.), *European Criminal Procedures*, New York 2005, p. 151.

Also, in France, where for a long time, the activities performed during the *enquête de police* were not considered to be investigative acts *sensu stricte*, the entire pre-trial stage and all activities in their course now constitute an integral part of the criminal proceedings[2]. Nowadays, given the functions and objectives of this stage of the process, it is hard to imagine criminal proceedings existing without it. Moreover, there is a tendency to notice an apparent increase in the role of the pre-trial stage, especially concerning the evidentiary process, and the introduction of an increasing number of consensual solutions in typically continental legislation[3]. With regard to the interaction with each other, the literature points out that the construction of the criminal process in the preparatory phase is often of paramount importance. As H. Gross pointed out on the basis of the German proceedings, what has been well done by the investigating judge is conducive to a smooth and correct resolution of the case, whereas if there has been a wrong or faulty execution of the investigative steps, even the best conducted judicial proceedings cannot cure them[4]. Therefore, the choice of pre-trial model is of major importance in terms of the efficiency of the overall process.

Suppose we understand the model of pre-trial proceedings as a set of essential structural components and links occurring between the components co-creating this stage of the process, allowing it to be distinguished from other systems in terms of the normative shaping of a specific legal phenomenon[5]. Then, we may notice that it is related to the specific regulations of such aspects as the objectives and functions of this stage of the process, its authorities, the structure, the set of procedural guarantees of the parties or the forms of control over the activities of the preparatory proceedings[6]. All of these factors are or

---

2 H. Conchon, *L'évolution des nullités de l'instruction préparatoire*, Paris 2002, pp. 46–48.

3 More extensively on the development of consensualism in continental European countries see M. Wawrzyńczak, B. Janusz-Pohl, 'Study on general characteristics of consensual procedures and reform trends' in: S. Pawelec (ed.), *Consensual Mechanisms in Criminal Proceedings. Integrative and Comparative Perspective*, Peter Lang 2023, pp. 63 ff.

4 H. Gross, 'Die Ausbildung des praktischen juristen', 14 *Zeitschrift für die Gesamte Strafrechtswissenschaft* 1894, p. 2, cited by J. Zagrodnik, *Model interakcji postępowania przygotowawczego oraz postępowania głównego w procesie karnym*, Warsaw 2013, p. 91.

5 Model definition after J. Zagrodnik, *Model interakcji…*, p. 46.

6 Such elements are indicated in the Polish literature relating to the model of pre-trial proceedings, e.g. S. Waltoś, *Model postępowania przygotowawczego na tle prawnoporównawczym*, Warsaw 1968, p. 12; C. Kulesza, 'Ewolucja europejskich modeli postępowania przygotowawczego na przełomie wieków' in: P. Kruszyński, S. Pawelec, M. Warchoł (eds.), *Europejski kodeks postępowania karnego*, Warsaw 2010, p. 34; A. Lach, 'Spór o model postępowania przygotowawczego', *Kwartalnik KSSiP* 2012, Special issue no. 4, p. 52.

may be relevant from the point of view of the model of the judicial stage of the criminal proceedings.

Given the importance of the influence of the preparatory phase on the trial stage, this thesis first and foremost chooses to indicate the interaction concerning the normative shaping of the objectives of pre-trial proceedings and, consequently, the process of proof. The choice of an appropriate model at this level significantly affects the scope of activities undertaken at the trial stage, just as the extent to which procedural principles such as the principle of directness, material truth or the adversariality and right to defence apply. Thus, it is inextricably linked to shaping an appropriate model for the jurisdictional stage.

Although governed by similar values, European legislations, particularly those shaped by the Strasbourg Court case law, adopt different pre-trial proceedings models, which fundamentally affect the shape and importance of judicial proceedings. On the other hand, looking at the criminal process as a whole, the choice in this respect has an impact on the effectiveness of the entire criminal procedure, understood as the demand for a quick, efficient, but also fair (truthful and respectful of the guarantee rights of the parties and participants) examination of the criminal case.

This paper discusses the most important features of the pre-trial investigation models in force in France, Germany, Italy and Poland, indicating their objectives and the scope of the evidentiary activities carried out and, consequently, their impact on the stage of court proceedings. First, it is based on a dogmatic method, consisting of analysing the legal provisions in force. Finally, an attempt has been made to evaluate these solutions by pointing out the advantages and disadvantages of particular models.

2. Model Features of European Preparatory Proceedings

In continental criminal trials, the preparatory stage is now an intrinsic part of the criminal process and its design is code-based. German, Italian, French and Polish trials are based on the indictment model. The pre-trial phase is necessary for filing an indictment and initiating court proceedings, the essential function of which is to define the material and subjective limits of the court's examination of the case. During this phase of the process, it is therefore necessary to reveal the essential circumstances of the case so that the charge can be accurately constructed. In all the legislations indicated, the pre-trial procedure thus primarily fulfils a preparatory function, whereby evidence is disclosed to allow a decision on the future fate of the proceedings. However, depending on the model chosen, the evidence collected and recorded during the preparatory proceedings may have different relevance from the point of view of the main trial and the court's decision on the merits. The interaction between the first and second stages of the trial mainly relates to the impact of the pre-trial evidence on the content of the judicial decision concluding the proceedings[7].

Thinking of the pre-trial model in abstracto as a kind of hypothetical being, two extreme concepts can be distinguished. One of them, giving clear primacy to the judicial proceedings, reduces the preparatory stage to a subordinate stage. In its course, the collected evidence cannot be used during the main trial; it is only to serve the law enforcement authorities, who, on its basis, decide on the further fate of the proceedings and, if an indictment is filed to the court, on its basis carry out the functions of the prosecution within the framework of the adversarial evidentiary proceedings at the main trial. This concept is close to the model adopted by the Italian legislator. The second concept is somewhat the opposite of the first. Pre-trial proceedings are seen as a fully-fledged stage of the criminal procedure serving to collect, secure and record evidence not only for the needs of law enforcement authorities but first and foremost for the court, which may, on their basis – with the restriction of the principle of directness – issue the final decision. This conception is close to the models that can be observed in Germany and Poland, where in practise the preparatory proceedings are an extended and full-fledged stage of the criminal trial, and the evidence obtained as a result of them is subject to assessment by the court on the same principles as the evidence conducted at the trial.

The French model is characterised by the *instruction préparatoire*, which takes place after the *enquête de police* and is conducted by the *juge d'instruction* with the purpose to ascertain the truth (Art. 81 § 1 CCP-France). It follows that the pre-trial phase is of paramount importance: if the case is ordered to be transferred to the court for the judgment, the records collected by the *juge d'instruction* can be used to prove guilt[8]. However, except for the most serious offences (*crimes*), the public prosecutor is allowed to file an indictment to the competent court at the end of the *enquête de police*. As a consequence, the *instruction préparatoire* does not take place and the preparatory function of the pre-trial proceedings has a different

7 In the German literature, this influence is highlighted by, among others, H. Loritz, *Kritische Betrachtungen zum Wert des strafprozessualen Zwischenverfahrens*, Peter Lang 1996, p. 17. As for the Italian system see D. Negri, 'Modelli e concezioni' in: A. Camon et al., *Fondamenti di procedura penale*, 4th ed., Milan 2023, pp. 15 ff.

8 A different regulation is laid down for the judgement before the *cour d'assises*, which is competent for the most serious offences (*crimes*): the court decides the case without knowing the investigative dossier.

weight, which translates into a different scope of the activities undertaken, their degree of formalism and the scope of the procedural guarantees of the parties.

Historically, the European criminal process derives from the inquisitorial process, whose overriding feature was the strong position of investigation authorities. German literature from the turn of the 20th century pointed out that, for the sake of justice, the pre-trial procedure should be the central part of the criminal proceedings. The purpose of the pre-trial proceedings should be to clarify the circumstances of the case in such a way as to bring the criminal proceedings to an end[9]. In the German legal system, this thesis is still valid today despite the doctrinal assumption that pre-trial proceedings are preparatory and subordinate to court proceedings[10]. The German pre-trial procedure (*Ermittlungsverfahren*) being in practice the core of criminal proceedings[11] is characterised by the very strong position and role of the public prosecutor's office, which decides the fate of all criminal proceedings at this stage. In the opinion of F. Riklin, the German pre-trial procedure allows for the termination of criminal proceedings in their first stage, which results in the thesis that the conduct of court proceedings is only one of many possible ways of issuing the final substantive decision of a criminal case[12].

German doctrine strongly emphasises that the criminal process there is directed towards the investigation of material truth (*Wahrheitserforschung*)[13], whereby it is at the pre-trial stage that the findings of fact and the collection of evidence in the case are primarily made (Art. 160 §§ 2 and 3 CCP-Germany). The public prosecutor's office, as the body responsible for the pre-trial phase, is legally obliged to establish the truth and bring an accusation if there are grounds for prosecution[14]. The aim of the German preparatory proceedings is to comprehensively clarify the case's circumstances, including the act's consequences and record

---

9 Among others W. Kulemann, *Die Reform der Voruntersuchung. Vorschläge zu einer Änderung der Strafprozeßordnung nebst einen Gesetzentwurf mit Begründung*, Berlin 1904, pp. 9 ff.

10 Ł. Wiśniewski, 'Niemiecki proces karny' in: P. Kruszyński (ed.) *Proces karny. Rozwiązania modelowe w ujęciu prawnoporównawczym*, Warsaw 2014, p. 386.

11 C. Roxin, B. Schünemann, *Strafverfahrensrecht*, Munich 2009, p. 285.

12 F. Riklin, 'Die Strafprozessrechtsreform in der Schweiz', 7 *Goltdammer's Archiv für Strafrecht* 2006, p. 495.

13 For a broader discussion of the principle of material truth in the German criminal process, see, among others, W. Käßer, *Wahrheitserforschung im Strafprozess*, Berlin 2020, *passim*.

14 U. Moeller, 'Pre-trail procedure in Germany' in: E. Johnston, R. Erbaş, D. Jasinski (eds.), *A comparative analysis of pre-trial procedure in Europe: the search for an ideal model*, Istanbul 2020, p. 91.

evidence for future trial. Consequently, the public prosecutor's office (as well as the police) has a full range of investigative activities at its disposal (the so-called general investigation clause, *Ermittlungsgeneralklausel*)[15]. The jurisdictional phase of the German criminal procedure is, by design, described as the culminating stage of the proceedings. Characterised by orality and immediacy, it entails that all evidentiary steps are taken at the main trial. It would, therefore, seem that in such a model, the pre-trial procedure has only a servile role; however, in practice, there is a risk of the opposite interaction. Such a system may result in duplication of evidentiary actions and, in addition to an oral and immediance evidenciary proceedings, extensive use of the same evidence taken at an earlier stage of the proceedings. Which, due to the short time since the crime was committed, may be more significant in reaching the truth. In consequence, evidence taken during preparatory proceedings may be crucial for the final decision.

Similar model solutions can be observed against the background of the Polish legal system. The Polish Code of Criminal Procedure assumes that the main objective of pre-trial proceedings is to clarify the circumstances of the case and to collect, secure and, to the extent necessary, record evidence for the court (Art. 297 § 1(4) and (5) CCP-Poland). It must be emphasised here that these objectives are the same regardless of the form in which the pre-trial proceedings are conducted (*śledztwo* or *dochodzenie*). Moreover, in order to implement the provision of Art. 297 CCP-Poland, the investigating authorities, as in Germany, have at their disposal all evidentiary possibilities apart from those expressly prohibited by law. Thus, the evidentiary options remain identical to those at the court stage.

The history of the provision of Art. 297 CCP-Poland reveals clear doubts of the legislator as to the choice of the appropriate model of pre-trial proceedings. The differences in its wording were related to the scope of circumstances to be investigated in the course of investigative activities and the impact of evidence on the jurisdictional proceedings. Nowadays, the obligation to investigate the case comprehensively at the pre-trial stage has been abandoned, and only the duty to clarify the circumstances of the case has been left as an objective. At the same time, it has been decided that the evidence obtained at the preliminary stage of the trial is of equal value and may form the basis of the court's final substantive decision. However, it should be emphasised that the practice of law enforcement authorities indicates a tendency to investigate the case as extensively as possible, to collect strong and numerous evidence and to carry out actions with the greatest possible thoroughness, which can be regarded as a continuation of the influence

15 K. Volk, *Grundkurs stop*, Munich 2010, p. 53.

of the Soviet model, which was reflected in the previously applicable Criminal Procedure Code of 1968[16]. The possibility of conducting a limited investigation (the so-called *dochodzenie ograniczone*) provided for in Art. 325h CCP-Poland, which allows for a clear reduction of evidentiary actions, is not widely used in practice. Such a state of affairs leads to an evident elevation of the rank of preparatory proceedings at the expense of the stage of court proceedings, which takes on a secondary character and comes down primarily to the control of the evidentiary acts already performed and the duplication of evidence, often with a restriction of the principle of directness and adversarialism.

The models indicated above have undoubted advantages, mainly related to the efficiency of the evidentiary process. Firstly, as a rule, whereas trial takes place long after the alleged offence, pre-trial investigations are carried out within a short time after the crime has been committed, which allows for the detection and preservation of a greater amount and better quality of evidence (the risk of loss or distortion due to the passage of time, atmospheric, climatic, psycho-physical conditions, e.g., loss of memory, is reduced). Secondly, there is no doubt that law enforcement authorities in comparison to the trail judge have more experience and better personnel, as well as technical facilities, allowing for a high application of state-of-the-art forensic techniques[17]. These factors may render the search for truth more effective. However, one must recognise the disadvantages of such legislative solutions, which may consequently have the effect of limiting the principle of objectivity.

As already mentioned, the extensive use of pre-trial evidence leads to a *de facto* detraction of the role of court proceedings, which is reduced to verifying evidence carried out at an earlier stage and, at the same time, duplicating it at the trial (repeated questioning of the same witnesses, taking of the accused's explanations, examination of experts, etc.). Repeating the same evidence runs the risk of degrading its quality and, above all, of violating the guarantee rights of the parties. A witness who is questioned repeatedly already knows the subject matter of the proceedings, may verify their knowledge with other sources of evidence, and may, under the influence of time, fail to remember many relevant circumstances, which may lead to recourse to the imagination. In practice, in the

---

16 J. Głębocka, *Model francuskiego postępowania przygotowawczego w ujęciu prawnoporównawczym*, Warsaw 2023, p. 45.

17 J. Zagrodnik, 'An outline of the model of the interaction of preparatory proceedings and court proceedings in criminal procedure (considerations against the background of European systems of criminal procedure law)', 2(5) *Scholars International Journal of Law, Crime and Justice* 2019, p. 154.

indicated models, this leads to frequent recourse during the trial before the court to the preparatory material and basing the final decision primarily on it. The risk raised in the literature of a breach of objectivity through the suggestive influence of the pre-trial file on the members of the panel is also not insignificant[18]. Even before the trial is opened and the accused is heard, the court's perusal of the evidence – overwhelmingly in support of the prosecution – may raise concerns about impartiality and objectivity. It should also be stressed that the extensive use of evidence from pre-trial proceedings based on the inquisitorial principle significantly limits the possibility of exercising the parties' procedural rights and deprives them of participation in the adversarial evidence procedure. In turn, the lack of active participation of the parties in the evidentiary proceedings may negatively affect the reliability of the final decision. Concerns about the extent of the guaranteed rights of the parties, above all of the accused under such a model, are also highlighted by German doctrine, which advocates the need to increase the adversarial nature of pre-jurisdictional proceedings[19].

When comparing the German and Polish solutions, it should be noted that in the German pre-trial model, there is a judicial authority in the form of a pre-trial judge (*Ermittlungsrichter*), who upholds the legality of investigative activities and fundamental guaranteed rights. Their competence includes activities reserved for judicial authorities (e.g. the use of coercive measures) and the performance of certain evidentiary acts where there is a risk of loss. Notably, the evidence carried out by the *Ermittlungsrichter* may be directly usable in court proceedings. Although the principle of immediacy is clearly violated in such a case, evidence carried out by a judicial authority may be considered to better realise the guaranteed rights of the parties than evidence carried out by law enforcement authorities during the investigation.

The French model also provides for the presence of a judicial factor in the pre-trial phase, but its role and position is much stronger. Pre-trial proceedings conducted in the form of a judicial investigation (*instruction préparatoire*) are characterised by the fact that most of the evidentiary steps are carried out by or on the commission of an investigating judge (*juge d'instruction*)[20]. Some of them

---

18 Among others see M. Damaska, 'Of Hearsay and Its Analogues', 76 *Minnesota Law Review* 1992, p. 451; C. Guarnieri, 'Pubblico ministero e giudice: funzioni e carriere in discussione' in: *Pubblico ministero e riforma dell'ordinamento giudiziario*, Milan 2006, p. 45.

19 C. Roxin, B. Schünemann, *Strafverfahrensrecht…*, p. 285.

20 More extensively on the investigating judge see B. Bouloc, 'Le rôle du juge d'instruction dans la recherche de la vérité', *Petites affiches* 1986, p. 4.

have even been reserved to the exclusive competence of the judge, e.g. taking statements from a suspect or questioning a civil party. Furthermore, unlike the *enquête de police*, the *instruction préparatoire* contains some adversarial elements, e.g. the suspect's defense attorney has certain rights to participate in some evidentiary activities. In the course of the *instruction préparatoire*, the authorities have full evidentiary powers and may take all measures aimed at establishing the truth (Art. 81 § 1 CCP-France), even those which substantially interfere with the liberty rights of individuals (e.g. searches, seizures of property, control of correspondence, control of telephone calls). As a general rule, evidence from a judicial investigation may then form the basis of a judgment once the case is referred to the competent court. In French doctrine, it is considered that the presence of the *juge d'instruction* in pre-trial proceedings results in the implementation of the principle of the right to a court. The participation of the judicial factor that emerges legitimises pre-trial evidence, which can directly permeate the judicial proceedings. The investigating judge becomes, as it were, the guarantor of the legitimacy of the evidence gathered in the pre-trial proceedings, as well as the realisation of the guarantee function of this stage of the trial.

The impact of pre-trial proceedings on the judicial stage is quite different, at least from a theoretical point of view, in the case of the French *enquête de police*. Proceedings conducted in this form are, by definition, quick, informal proceedings in which the law enforcement authorities can only carry out certain evidentiary acts, in principle not interfering with the liberty rights of individuals. Characteristic of this form of procedure is that most of the actions interfering with the liberty rights (such as e.g. searches or seizures of property) generally require the consent of the person concerned or the approval of the public prosecutor or the liberty and detention judge (*juge des libertés et de la détention*)[21]. Some of the activities are not formally considered typical evidence. For example, in the course of this type of investigation, there is no formal hearing of a witness[22], only a kind of questioning. As a rule, no formal minutes are taken, only notes which constitute a report of the activity (*rapport*). The purpose of the *enquête de police* is, first and foremost, to gather basic data on the subject of the proceedings and the person of the potential perpetrator and to decide what will happen next. As a

21 S. Guinchard, J. Buisson, *Procédure pénale*, Paris 2010, pp. 664–665.

22 It is worth pointing out that the very term '*témoin*' does not occur in the *enquête de police* in which evidentiary acts are carried out with persons with possible knowledge of the subject matter of the proceedings, i.e. witnesses in the broad sense of the word. See J. Głębocka, 'Francuska procedura karna' in: P. Kruszyński (ed.), *Proces karny. Rozwiązania modelowe w ujęciu prawnoporównawczym*, Warsaw 2014, p. 282.

rule, therefore, it is conducted primarily for the benefit of the public prosecutor, who, as the investigator, decides whether to drop the case, to refer it to the *juge d'instruction* (*requisitoire introductif*) or to file an indictment to the competent court (*citation directe*).

In the last case primacy is given to the judicial stage of the proceedings, based on the principles of adversariality, directness and orality, reducing the pre-trial procedure to a subordinate role. However, it should be stressed that, in practice, the evidence gathered in the framework of the *enquête de police* permeates the judicial proceedings and, as written evidence from official notes and eventually protocols, as well as personal evidence from interviews with officers, forms the basis of judicial decisions. Moreover, the reforms of recent years indicate a trend towards the expansion of the powers of law enforcement authorities in the field of evidentiary proceedings, clearly extending their possibilities when it comes to interfering with citizens' guarantees[23].

It is also not without significance that the prosecutor has vast powers in terms of consensual forms of termination of proceedings, which, against the background of the opportunism prevailing in France, are a manifestation of the prosecutor's increasingly strong power and the transfer of part of the adjudicatory competence to him. Taken together, the reform trends of recent years are moving towards a real strengthening of the role of the pre-trial procedure.

Italian pre-trial proceedings have traditionally been modelled on the French *instruction préparatoire*, in which the investigating judge played a central role. Legislative work on the new Code of Criminal Procedure in the 1980s, however, resulted in a marked remodelling of the Italian criminal process towards a combination of features of the Anglo-American system and traditional continental solutions[24], which meant a turn away from the French model. Among other things, the institution of the investigating judge was permanently abandoned to be replaced by a pre-trial judge (*giudice per le indagini preliminari*). What is significant from the point of view of European models and characteristic of common law systems is that the Italian criminal process has been shaped in such a way as to explicitly give primacy to the judicial procedure, reducing the pre-trial procedure to a subservient role. Thus, the focal point of Italian criminal proceedings is now the main trial, where evidence is gathered and evaluated, respecting the principle

---

23 In this respect, attention should be drawn, first of all, to the last major reform introduced by Law no. 222/2019 on the programming and reform of the judiciary for years 2018–2022 (*Loi de programmation 2018–2022 et de réforme pour la justice*).

24 E. Amodio, 'Das Modell des Anklageprozess im neuen italienischen Strafverfahrensgesetzbuch', 102 *Zeitschrift für die gesamte Strafrechtswissenschaft* 1990, p. 195.

of equality of parties. In contrast, the pre-trial proceedings are primarily intended to acquire sources of evidence, which will only become evidence when they are collected at trial through cross-examination[25].

Italian preparatory proceedings are based on the premise that investigative acts do not constitute evidence in the strict sense and cannot, in principle, be used at the main trial and form the basis of the court's decision (Arts. 514 and 526 § 1 CCP-Italy). The argument in favour of such a solution is the inquisitorial nature of the pre-trial proceedings and the impossibility of guaranteeing the implementation of the adversariality, orality and publicity principles during such proceedings. These actions have the value of mere evidentiary sources (*fonti di prova*), and are therefore primarily relevant for the law enforcement authorities deciding how to conclude the pre-trial investigation and, if the case is referred to court, planning the relevant evidentiary proceedings in the jurisdictional phase[26]. As in the French *enquête de police*, persons questioned by law enforcement authorities do not have the status of witnesses; their statements are not referred to as testimonies[27]. From the point of view of the subsequent course of the proceedings, the role of the prosecution and law enforcement authorities is reduced to the obligation to secure evidentiary sources so they can be used at trial (Art. 326 CCP-Italy). At the same time, however, the Italian legislator notes certain risks and, recognising the needs of a pragmatic nature, allows for the use of evidence carried out in the pre-trial proceedings at a later stage, for example, if an examination is impossible for objective and unpredictable reasons (Art. 512 § 1 CCP-Italy) or the witness was threatened or corrupted (Art. 500 § 4 CCP-Italy). Moreover, the effects of the pre-jurisdictional proceedings provide a basis for several possible special procedures[28], interim proceedings[29] or intermediate stages between the pre-jurisdictional and the trial[30], which also allows the consensual function of the pre-trial proceedings to become a reality.

25 P. Ferrua, *Il 'giusto processo'*, 3rd ed., Bologna 2012, pp. 131 ff.

26 D. Negri, 'Modelli e concezioni'…, p. 64.

27 M. Warchoł, 'Włoski proces karny' in: P. Kruszyński (ed.), *Proces karny. Rozwiązania modelowe w ujęciu prawnoporównawczym*, Warsaw 2014, p. 573.

28 Among others, the 'abbreviated trial' (*giudizio abbreviato*), the 'deal at the request of the parties' (*applicazione della pena su richiesta delle parti*) and the 'proceeding by penal decree' (*decreto penale di condanna*).

29 Among others, proceedings on preventive measures or the judicial authorization to carry out wiretapping activities.

30 The so-called pre-trial hearing (*udienza preliminare*).

The realisation of the guarantee function in Italian pre-trial proceedings is based on the presence of a judge who is called *giudice per le indagini preliminari.* Their main role is to ensure the constitutional and judicial guarantees throughout the investigations (e.g. the preventive measures and the wiretapping activities shall be ordered by the judge upon request of the public prosecutor).

Moreover, upon request of the parties the *giudice per le indagini preliminari* is allowed to take the evidence in adversarial conditions (through cross-examination), but only in the cases provided for by the law (Art. 392 CCP-Italy): in particular where there is a risk of loss or where it is justified from the point of view of the principle of swiftness of the proceedings (e.g. in the case of an expert opinion, for which there is usually a long waiting time). If the required conditions are fulfilled, the parties may ask for evidence *sensu stricto* at the pre-trial stage so that it can then constitute full-fledged evidence (Art. 403 in conjunction with Art. 431 § 1(d) CCP-Italy). It is the so-called *incidente probatorio*[31].

In sum, the limited scope of the evidentiary steps taken during the pre-trial proceedings reduces the risk of infringement of the parties' procedural rights, above all falling within the broadly understood adversarial approach. Opponents of this concept point to the resulting risk of losing valuable evidence, thus limiting the possibility of ascertaining the facts. And this notwithstanding the possibility for the *incidente probatorio* to be celebrated, given its limited scope (Art. 392 CCP-Italy). In contrast, proponents of the Italian solution emphasise the advantages associated with the resulting pre-trial jurisdictional model based on a genuine adversarial approach.

3. Final Remarks

Analysing the issues raised above, it can be concluded that although all the legal systems indicated have the same origin and are an expression of the formation of a continental criminal procedural policy, one can notice apparent differences in the perception of the role and importance of the pre-court phase of criminal proceedings. The common goal remains, firstly, the realisation of justice in general and, secondly, the adaptation of normative provisions to the realities of current crime and the improvement of the administration of justice.

All the legislation described is based on the indictment model, which determines the indispensability of the pre-trial procedure. The primary function of this phase of the process is a preparatory one, which, in relation to complainability,

31 L. Giuliani, 'Indagini preliminari e udienza preliminare' in: M. Bargis (ed.), *Compendio di procedura penale*, 11th ed., Milan 2023, pp. 548 ff.

manifests itself in need to establish the circumstances concerning the subject matter of the criminal proceedings, at least to the extent that it is possible to construct a charge that is filed to the competent court for trial. Irrespective of the nature of the investigative steps, it is necessary to carry them out at least to a minimum extent that allows a decision to be made on the merits and grounds of the *notitia criminis*. Model solutions with regard to the taking of evidence and its impact on the judicial phase of the trial vary, and even in systems that are broadly similar in this respect, such as Germany and Poland, differences are apparent.

There are many dilemmas in choosing the appropriate pre-trial model. It seems evident that the main stage of a criminal proceedings should be the adversarial trial before an impartial court. At this stage, the evidence, based on which the court carries out the fact-finding and makes the final decision on the accused's criminal responsibility, should be directly conducted. It is only at the main hearing that procedural rights can be fully guaranteed, allowing the active participation of the parties in the trial, with the effect of creating greater opportunities to reach a trustworthy ascertainment of facts, as compared to inquisitorial solutions. Giving primacy to the main trial, however, should consequently lead to a reduced role for pre-trial proceedings, in which the evidence carried out should be of a preparatory and not of a final nature[32]. The Italian model seems to be closest to this concept.

Although all the indicated legislations, on a normative level, start from the assumption of the dominance of the main trial, the preparatory phase plays a central role. Even the French police investigation, intended to be a de-formalised procedure in which evidence should not infiltrate court proceedings, has become increasingly important in recent years.

Looking at the model's impact on the efficiency of the trial and the ascertainment of facts, purely pragmatic issues related to evidentiary possibilities could be pointed out. By carrying out actions within a short moment of disclosing a crime, law enforcement authorities have a greater chance to get to the truth. Moreover, they have specialised personnel and tools, allowing them to use forensic techniques to the fullest extent. Adequate technical and human resources and experience positively contribute to the fact-finding process. Furthermore, a broadly conducted evidentiary procedure in the preliminary phase of the trial may favour the implementation of the principle of concentration of evidence and, as a result, promote the speed and effectiveness of the adjudication of the case before the

32 In this context see S. Waltoś, *Model postępowania przygotowawczego na tle prawnoporównawczym*, Warsaw 1968, pp. 107–108.

court[33]. However, the inquisitorial nature of the preparatory proceedings remains a critical drawback, significantly limiting the guarantee rights of the parties to the proceedings, above all the suspect, who often has no real opportunity to participate in the evidence process. Although in all the systems indicated, the prosecutor's office not only plays an accusatory role but, being a state body, upholds the rule of law and justice without having a legal interest of its own, it primarily performs functions typical of law enforcement authorities, which may affect the directionality and scope of the investigative activities carried out, which, with the limited activity of the parties, may result in improper factual findings.

The strong emphasis on the discovery of truth is often linked to the principle of mandatory prosecution. In this respect, the exception is France, where the opportunity principle has traditionally been present, but even there, in recent years, there has been a clear limitation of discretion by imposing a clear framework on the prosecutor, narrowing the possibility of not prosecuting[34]. It follows that law enforcement authorities have the right and duty to take action to discover the truth, which justifies an extensive evidentiary investigation. A strong emphasis on the policy of mandatory prosecution can be seen in the Polish system, where, together with the principle of material truth, it results in a comprehensive and detailed explanation of the circumstances of the case already at the stage of preparatory proceedings. The German system is also based on the principle of legality and despite the introduction of solutions shaped on the opportunity principle[35], in most cases, the prosecution remains legally obliged to take all possible measures to bring the guilty party to justice, which, as a consequence, legitimises it to take extensive measures and to establish all the circumstances of the case in detail.

33 A strong emphasis on the principle of concentration of evidence and, simultaneously, speed of proceedings can be observed, inter alia, in French literature. In the context of ECtHR jurisprudence, see S. Guinchard, J. Buisson, *Procédure pénale*, Paris 2010, pp. 455–458.

34 Attention should be paid to the reforms introducing alternative methods of terminating pre-trial proceedings through the application of a specific criminal response, as well as the provisions obliging the prosecutor to justify the decision to discontinue, especially in the case of the detection of the perpetrator. See G. Stéfani, G. Levasseur, B. Bouloc, *Procédure pénale*, Paris 2006, p. 549; M. Rogacka-Rzewnicka, 'Środki racjonalizacji zasady legalizmu we współcze- snym procesie karnym' in: T. Grzegorczyk (ed.), *Funkcje procesu karnego. Księga jubileuszowa Profesora Janusza Tylmana*, Warsaw 2011, p. 106.

35 For more see S. Peters, 'Article 153' in: *Münchener Kommentar zur Strapfprozessordnung*, 1st ed., Munich 2016, references no. 1–2; U. Moeller, 'Pre-trail procedure in Germany' in: E. Johnston, R. Erbaş, D. Jasinski (eds.), *A comparative analysis of pre-trial procedure in Europe: the search for an ideal model*, Istanbul 2020, pp. 92–102.

In German doctrine, inquisitiveness is sometimes even explicitly equated with the principle of material truth[36].

At the same time, it is a regularity to be noted that the more strongly the preparatory function of the pre-trial proceedings is emphasised, the greater the influence of the evidence gathered in the preliminary phase of the trial, rather than at the main trial, on the final decision on criminal liability. The practice draws attention to the unfavourable effect of such solutions of reducing the court proceedings to a purely subordinate role, consisting only of controlling the activities of the pre-trial proceedings and duplicating them at the main trial, which negatively affects the length of the entire criminal trial and the time to wait for an appropriate criminal response. By promoting adversarialism, the Italian model clearly turns away from this concept and limits the tasks of the pre-trial procedure and, consequently, the possibility of evidence spilling over from this trial phase into the judicial phase.

At the same time, it should be noted that the last decades of the development of the continental criminal process clearly show a trend towards the introduction and expansion of consensualism, which entails making a final decision on criminal responsibility solely based on the evidence gathered during the pre-trial proceedings, without holding a trial. The growth of consensual but also opportunistic solutions is clearly moving European legislation towards extending judicial or *quasi*-judicial powers to prosecutors' offices. Consequently, this leads to a growing role for pre-trial proceedings, which increasingly constitute the only stage of criminal proceedings, with the final decision based on evidence carried out in an inquisitorial setting before the prosecuting authorities. Regarding the issue at hand, with a certain simplification, it should be pointed out that more and more often, it is the prosecuting authority at the preparatory stage that finally decides on the outcome of the entire case, not only by discontinuing the proceedings but also by submitting binding proposals to impose specific penalties in consensual modes or even applying a specific criminal response independently (as in France where the prosecutor may impose on the perpetrator certain orders or prohibitions under the *composition pénale* – Art. 41-1 CCP-France). It can be considered that this leads to a devaluation of jurisdictional proceedings and judicial settlement of criminal cases.

In this context, attention should be drawn even more emphatically to the guarantee function of pre-trial proceedings, for which the inclusion of a judicial factor

36 H. H. Kühne, *Strafprozessrecht: eine systematische Darstellung des deutschen und europäischen Strafverfahrensrechts*, Heidelberg 2010, p. 195.

in the preparatory phase is not without significance. However, it must be emphasised that from the point of view of the effectiveness of the trial (understood as compliance with the ascertainment of facts, efficiency and speed of the actions undertaken, but especially with the actual protection of guarantee rights), it is more advantageous to have a permanent judicial body involved in the proceedings than a judicial body appointed *ad hoc* from among the judges competent to hear the case at the judicial stage, as in the Polish model. In the Polish criminal process, the absence of a pre-trial judge, as in Germany and Italy, or an investigating judge, as in France, consequently entails the control of investigative actions by the court competent to hear the case. In practice, another judge may be personally appointed to each judicial action, for whom an in-depth knowledge of the case and a thorough analysis is often not even possible, with the consequence that a decision may be mechanically approved or the prosecution's request granted[37]. In this respect, having a judicial authority on the German model is preferable.

Continental systems of procedural criminal law clearly show a tendency to strengthen the role of pre-trial proceedings and increase their influence on judicial proceedings. This involves expanding the prosecutor's competence to decide the fate of the proceedings, increasing the mediation and consensual function and introducing alternative solutions in those models where the principle of legality is traditionally present[38]. The core of the proceedings seems to be tilting towards the preliminary phase of the trial. It can be observed from the examples of Germany and France that the legislator is moving towards an expansion of the procedural rights of the parties during the investigative stage rather than a strengthening of the trial phase. However, to strengthen the guarantee function in such a model, a judicial factor in the form of a permanent authority, such as a pre-trial judge, is a characteristic element. Such a body is conspicuously absent in Polish legislation, which concurrently uses pre-trial evidence extensively. Only the Italian model deviates significantly from the solution in which the primacy is actually given

37 For example, on the evident problem of being able to see the circumstances of the case and control the evidence when deciding on pre-trial detention, see S. Pawelec, 'Czas na podjęcie przez sąd decyzji w przedmiocie wniosku o zastosowanie tymczasowego aresztowania', 88 *Studia Iuridica* 2021, pp. 295–311.

38 B. Janusz-Pohl, 'Theoretical and methodological foundations for consensual models based on Polish example' in: S. Pawelec (ed.), *Consensual Mechanisms in Criminal Proceedings. Integrative and Comparative Perspective*, Peter Lang 2023, p. 19 points out that currently "real criminal justice system is not ideal and purely inquisitorial and adversarial oriented but contains a mixture of adversariality and inquisitoriality combined with opportunistically or legalistically oriented elements".

to the pre-trial phase. At the same time, it must be stressed that the widely used modes that allow the termination of proceedings before moving to the judicial phase, in fact, also allow a specific criminal response to be imposed solely based on the evidence carried out in the preparatory phase.

4. Bibliography

Literature

Amodio E., 'Das Modell des Anklageprozess im neuen italienischen Strafverfahrensgesetzbuch', 102 *Zeitschrift für die gesamte Strafrechtswissenschaft* 1990.

Bouloc B., 'Le rôle du juge d'instruction dans la recherche de la vérité', *Petites affiches* 1986.

Conchon H., L'évolution des nullités de l'instruction préparatoire, Paris 2002.

Damaska M., 'Of Hearsay and Its Analogues', 76 *Minnesota Law Review* 1992.

Ferrua P., *Il 'giusto processo'*, 3rd ed., Bologna 2012.

Giuliani L., 'Indagini preliminari e udienza preliminare' in: M. Bargis (ed.), Compendio di procedura penale, 11th ed., Milan 2023.

Głębocka J., 'Francuska procedura karna' in: P. Kruszyński (ed.), *Proces karny. Rozwiązania modelowe w ujęciu prawnoporównawczym*, Warsaw 2014.

Głębocka J., *Model francuskiego postępowania przygotowawczego w ujęciu prawnoporównawczym*, Warsaw 2023.

Gross H., 'Die Ausbildung des praktischen juristen', 14 *Zeitschrift für die Gesamte Strafrechtswissenschaft* 1894.

Guarnieri C., 'Pubblico ministero e Giudice: funzioni e carriere in discussione' in: *Pubblico ministero e riforma dell'ordinamento giudiziario*, Milan 2006.

Guinchard S., Buisson J., *Procédure pénale*, Paris 2010.

Janusz-Pohl B., 'Theoretical and methodological foundations for consensual models based on Polish example' in: S. Pawelec (ed.), *Consensual Mechanisms in Criminal Proceedings. Integrative and Comparative Perspective*, Peter Lang 2023.

Käßer W., *Wahrheitserforschung im Strafprozess*, Berlin 2020.

Kulemann W., *Die Reform der Voruntersuchung. Vorschläge zu einer Änderung der Strafprozeßordnung nebst einen Gesetzentwurf mit Begründung*, Berlin 1904.

Kulesza C., 'Ewolucja europejskich modeli postępowania przygotowawczego na przełomie wieków' in: P. Kruszyński, S. Pawelec, M. Warchoł (eds.), *Europejski kodeks postępowania karnego*, Warsaw 2010.

Kühne H. H., *Strafprozessrecht: eine systematische Darstellung des deutschen und europäischen Strafverfahrensrechts*, Heidelberg 2010.

Lach A., 'Spór o model postępowania przygotowawczego', *Kwartalnik KSSiP* 2012, Special Issue no. 4.

Loritz H., *Kritische Betrachtungen zum Wert des strafprozessualen Zwischenverfahrens*, Peter Lang 1996.

Moeller U., 'Pre-trail procedure in Germany' in: E. Johnston, R. Erbaş, D. Jasinski (eds.), *A comparative analysis of pre-trail procedure in Europe: the search for an ideal model*, Istanbul 2020.

Negri D., 'Modelli e concezioni' in: A. Camon, et al., *Fondamenti di procedura penale*, 4th ed., Milan 2023.

Peters S., 'Art. 153' in: *Münchener Kommentar zur Strapfprozessordnung*, 1st ed., Munich 2016.

Pawelec S., 'Czas na podjęcie przez sąd decyzji w przedmiocie wniosku o zastosowanie tymczasowego aresztowania', 88 *Studia Iuridica* 2021.

Riklin F., 'Die Strafprozessrechtsreform in der Schweiz', 7 *Goltdammer's Archiv für Strafrecht* 2006.

Rogacka-Rzewnicka M., 'Środki racjonalizacji zasady legalizmu we współczesnym procesie karnym' in: T. Grzegorczyk (ed.), *Funkcje procesu karnego. Księga jubileuszowa Profesora Janusza Tylmana*, Warsaw 2011.

Roxin C., Schünemann B., *Strafverfahrensrecht*, Munich 2009.

Spencer J. R., 'The English System' in: M. Delmas-Marty, J. R. Spencer (eds.), *European Criminal Procedures*, New York 2005.

Stéfani G., Levasseur G., Bouloc B., *Procédure pénale*, Paris 2006.

Volk K., *Grundkurs stop*, Munich 2010.

Waltoś S., *Model postępowania przygotowawczego na tle prawnoporównawczym*, Warsaw 1968.

Warchoł M., 'Włoski proces karny' in: P. Kruszyński (ed.), *Proces karny. Rozwiązania modelowe w ujęciu prawnoporównawczym*, Warsaw 2014.

Wawrzyńczak M., Janusz-Pohl B., 'Study on general characteristics of consensual procedures and reform trends' in: S. Pawelec (ed.), *Consensual Mechanisms in Criminal Proceedings. Integrative and Comparative Perspective*, Peter Lang 2023.

Wiśniewski Ł., 'Niemiecki proces karny' in: P. Kruszyński (ed.), *Proces karny. Rozwiązania modelowe w ujęciu prawnoporównawczym*, Warsaw 2014.

Zagrodnik J., *Model interakcji postępowania przygotowawczego oraz postępowania głównego w procesie karnym*, Warsaw 2013.

Zagrodnik J., 'An outline of the model of the interaction of preparatory proceedings and court proceedings in criminal procedure (considerations against the background of European systems of criminal procedure law)', 2(5) *Scholars International Journal of Law, Crime and Justice* 2019.

Konrad Burdziak*

VII. Applying the Achievements of 20th and 21st-Century Psychology to the Organisation of Justice: Remarks on the Improvement of Judicial Activity

Abstract: This work focuses on the analysis of the effectiveness of the justice system, but not from the perspective of the level of fairness of the decisions made by the courts, but from the perspective of the conditions created by the legislator for the courts (or rather judges) to make rational decisions, based on reason and logic, and not on accidental, unverifiable or fundamentally incorrect premises. Of course, one could say that it may happen that an irrational decision (based on irrational premises) turns out to be just and that a rational decision (based on rational premises) turns out to be not just, and argue that due to this, the issue of rationality of decisions and the creation of conditions for making them is of no importance. However, it can be assumed (although it is impossible to prove this empirically) that the authority that at least has conditions for making a rational decision will have a greater chance of making a just decision in a given case than the one that the matter of justice leaves entirely to chance. Moreover, it can be said that creating conditions for making a rational decision increases the chances of making such a (rational) decision, enabling the implementation of basic human rights. The general research method used in this work is the contextual method and the detailed research method used in the work is (primarily) the legal-dogmatic method. Thus, the study on the issue of the rationality of decisions made by courts was carried out through the analysis of normative material relating to all the issues raised. The work gives a negative answer to the question of whether the Polish legislator has created conditions for Polish courts to make rational decisions regarding the possibility and justification of applying the institution of pre-trial detention in a given case. At the same time, the work proposed – based on the findings of C. R. Sunstein, D. Kahneman and O. Sibony – several legal solutions (among others) that could lead to an increase in the chances of (Polish) courts making rational and fair decisions in matters of pre-trial detention. It was proposed, among others, solutions for building panels of judges, supporting the decision-making process of courts and appropriate justification of these decisions.

Keywords: Efficiency, rationality, legislation, criminal law, pre-trial detention

* Dr. hab., University of Szczecin, Poland.

1. Introduction

The effectiveness of the criminal justice system regarding criminal cases (the part of the system that is considered in this work) can be measured in a multitude of ways. It can be measured based on hard data, e.g. how quickly the proceedings are conducted (assuming that the sooner the final decision is made, the better it is) or the number of appeals against sentences in individual cases (again, assuming that the fewer appeals, the better), or based on soft data, e.g. to what degree the parties of the proceedings (prosecutors, aggrieved parties, and perpetrators) are pleased with final decisions, or to what degree the judges (as the primary ruling bodies in the criminal proceedings) believe their decisions were just.

At the same time, it is difficult not to value any of the above-mentioned or omitted but possible to imagine perspectives on the justice system. The subject of this work will be the perspective – in the opinion of the author of this work – of the utmost importance, and more specifically the perspective of verifying the conditions created for courts (or rather judges) to make rational decisions. Conditions – as should be added – created by the legislator, i.e. resulting directly from legal provisions (with particular emphasis on acts), and not from the way they are applied by individual entities, and ensuring – what should be emphasised once more – the possibility of making rational, and not just, decisions (although, ideally, the decisions made by the courts would be both rational and just). There is an enormous qualitative difference between justice understood, for example, as J. Hervada would have it, i.e. as providing everyone with what belongs to them[1], and rationality understood as showing clear thought or reason[2]. Not everything that is rational must be fair, just as not everything that is fair must be rational. Imposing a severe punishment on a man accused of rape may be completely rational because it results directly from the evidence collected in criminal proceedings; however, it does not have to be fair – after all, the collected evidence and the resulting facts do not have to correspond to reality (the accused does not have to be the actual perpetrator of the prohibited act). Similarly, imposing a life sentence on a 14-year-old perpetrator of murder with particular cruelty may, of course, be fair (all sentencing directives may support this)[3], but it does not

---

1 See J. Hervada, *Wprowadzenie do prawa naturalnego*, Kraków 2011, p. 14.

2 'Rational' in: *Cambridge Dictionary*, available at: https://dictionary.cambridge.org/dictionary/english/rational [accessed on: September 12th, 2023].

3 See A. Planas, 'Teen sentenced to life in prison for fatally stabbing Florida cheerleader 114 times', *NBC News*, available at: https://www.nbcnews.com/news/us-news/teen-sentenced-life-prison-fatally-stabbing-florida-cheerleader-114-rcna76550 [accessed on: September 12th, 2023].

have to be fully rational – the question arises whether if such a person leaves the prison, at least due to the application of the institution of conditional early release from serving the rest of the imprisonment, will they be able to function normally in society after spending most of their life in the closed environment of a total institution, which a prison undoubtedly is.

Thus, this work focuses – emphasising it once more – on the analysis of the effectiveness of the justice system not from the perspective of the level of fairness of the decisions made by the courts (this would be a nearly impossible task by definition), but from the perspective of the conditions created by the legislator for the courts (or rather judges) to make rational decisions, based on reason and logic, and not on accidental, unverifiable or fundamentally incorrect premises. Of course, one could say that it may happen that an irrational decision (based on irrational premises) turns out to be just and that a rational decision (based on rational premises) turns out to be not just, and argue that due to this, the issue of rationality of decisions and the creation of conditions for making them is of no importance. However, it can be assumed (although it is impossible to prove this empirically) that the authority that at least has conditions for making a rational decision will have a greater chance of making a just decision in a given case than the one that the matter of justice leaves entirely to chance. Moreover, it can be said that creating conditions for making a rational decision increases the chances of making such a (rational) decision, enabling the implementation of basic human rights, in particular, the right to defence (after all, a rational decision is a decision that can be discussed and try to effectively undermine it) and the right to equal treatment (again, it can be assumed that the rationality of the decision will influence the unification of decisions in cases of similar characteristics); ensuring the realisation of human rights and freedoms to the fullest possible extent is a need that cannot be overestimated.

It should be emphasised that creating the conditions for courts to make a rational decision by the legislator does not necessarily mean limiting in any way the freedom of judges in making decisions. Of course, this may happen, for example, when solutions introduced in a given legislation are analogous to those provided for in Art. 53 §§ 2a and 2b Polish Criminal Code (CC-Poland), according to which: "2a. Aggravating circumstances include in particular: 1) previous criminal record for a crime involving intent or a similar crime without intent; 2) taking advantage of vulnerability, disability, illness or old age of the aggrieved party; 3) manner of action leading to humiliation or torment of the aggrieved party; 4) committing a premeditated crime; 5) committing a crime with particularly reproachable malice; 6) committing a crime motivated by hatred due to the aggrieved party's national, ethnic, racial, political or religious affiliation or because of their lack of religious affiliation; 7) acting with particular cruelty; 8) committing a crime under the influence of alcohol or narcotic drugs, if this condition was a factor leading to the commission of the crime or a significant increase in its effects; 9) committing a crime in cooperation with a minor or using their participation. 2b. Mitigating circumstances include in particular: 1) committing a crime as a result of a motivation deserving consideration; 2) committing a crime under the influence of anger, fear or indignation, justified by the circumstances of the crime; 3) committing a crime in response to an emergency situation, the correct assessment of which was significantly difficult due to the personal circumstances, scope of knowledge or life experience of the perpetrator; 4) taking action to prevent damage or harm resulting from a crime or to limit its extent; 5) reconciliation with the aggrieved party; 6) compensation for damage caused by a crime or compensation for the harm resulting from a crime; 7) committing a crime with significant contribution from the aggrieved party; 8) voluntary disclosure of a crime committed by oneself to the authority responsible for prosecuting crimes".

The above-mentioned regulations of the CC-Poland require – as demonstrated – the need for courts adjudicating in criminal cases to consider certain circumstances in favour of and others to the detriment of the accused, limiting – as a result – the scope of judges' freedom, and are certainly intended – by the legislator – to increase the level of rationality of decisions made by criminal courts. However, they are not (or at least the initiator of the project has not demonstrated this[4]) based on any substantive premises, but rather on the initiator's intuition, and this does not guarantee that they will meet the expectations set for them (although this is of course not ruled out).

Nevertheless, such solutions, limiting the freedom of judges in the decisions they make, will not be considered in this work. It is impossible to formulate any factors in the context of criminal law solutions (or at least the author of this work does not feel able to indicate such factors), apart from those already formulated in the criminal law legislation of European countries (such as, for example, necessary self-defence, protective force, insanity), the consideration of which by the court in a given case would have to be absolute and obligatory. Naturally, elsewhere the author of the work formulated a proposal that in the decisions of individual authorities of a probabilistic nature (decisions regarding the possible manner of human behaviour in the future), such as, for example, the decision on the need to pre-trial detention the perpetrator of a prohibited act due to the fear reoffending,

4 See Explanatory Memorandum to the Government's Bill to amend the Criminal Code and certain other acts, available at: https://www.sejm.gov.pl/Sejm9.nsf/druk.xsp?nr=2024 [accessed on: September 12th, 2023].

the results of the application of the actuarial method and the SPJ (Structured Professional Judgment) method were considered, as methods ensuring objectivity of the assessment process due to their basis on risk factors and procedural methodologies developed in scientific research and extensive empirical practice[5]. It should be emphasised, however, that the proposed tools and the factors they consider – in the opinion of the author of the work – could not be the sole basis for decisions made by individual authorities and under no circumstances would they have to influence the way they assess a given circumstance or the number and type of circumstances constituting the basis for decisions made, and as a consequence, they would only provide additional information that could be considered in the decision-making process and could be rejected in the said process, without limiting in any way the judge's freedom.

Therefore, this work will focus on the analysis of the effectiveness of the justice system from the perspective of the conditions created by the legislator for courts (or rather judges) to make rational decisions, which do not or will not limit the courts in making procedural decisions.

It should also be declared from the beginning that this work is based solely on the example of Polish legislation, as it is best known to the author and, at the same time, requires legislative amendments. It should be noted, however, that the vast majority of considerations presented in this work can be applied (moreover, in a simple way) to the laws of other European countries, especially countries from Central and Eastern Europe. At the same time, this work will rely on only one selected aspect of the practice of Polish criminal courts, and more specifically on the issue of applying the above-mentioned preventive measure in the form of pre-trial detention. Narrowing the analysed issues to this one issue is justified by the following circumstances: firstly, analysing the entire criminal legislation of even one country in terms of creating conditions for making rational decisions vastly exceeds the scope of this work in the form of a chapter in a collective monograph. Secondly, the issue of applying the institution of pre-trial detention encompasses all the most difficult issues that may be faced by criminal justice authorities, i.e. the need to quickly make a decision, based on unspecified grounds, as to what the future of a potential perpetrator may look like (risk assessment), and how to react in such a situation (risk management); decisions – land it need to be emphasised – that may result in the deprivation of a person's liberty, and therefore the most far-reaching interference in their rights and freedoms, which also indicates the

5 See K. Burdziak, 'Przeciwdziałanie przemocy domowej w perspektywie karnoprawnej praktyki prokuratorskiej', submitted to a scientific publisher.

justification for undertaking analysis in the context of the above-mentioned issues. Thirdly, and finally, the analysis of the institution of pre-trial detention from the perspective of the judicial practice of Polish courts allows to conclude that in its context it deals with basic problems in the form of bias and noise (which will be discussed later), which are worth solving as an appropriate legislative measures based on the achievements of modern psychology.

This work will therefore be accompanied by the following research question: 'Has the Polish legislator created conditions for Polish courts to make rational decisions regarding the possibility and justification of applying the institution of pre-trial detention in a given case?' and the following research hypotheses: '1. The Polish legislator has not created conditions for Polish courts to make rational decisions regarding the possibility and justification of applying the institution of pre-trial detention in a given case. 2. It is necessary to make changes in the procedure for making decisions by Polish courts regarding the possibility and justification of applying the institution of pre-trial detention in a given case based on the solutions of modern psychology'. It should be emphasised once again that the solutions proposed in this work can be easily extrapolated to legal systems other than the Polish one, and also to issues other than the issue of pre-trial detention that courts have and will encounter in the administration of justice in criminal cases.

2. Research Method

The general research method used in this work is the contextual method due to two circumstances. Namely: 1) it allows for a multi-sided approach to the studied phenomena; 2) it aims to determine all relevant contexts: genetic, historical, functional, logical, axiological and others[6].

The detailed research method used in the work is (primarily) the legal-dogmatic method. Thus, the study on the issue of the rationality of decisions made by courts in the context of pre-trial detention was carried out through the analysis of normative material relating to all the issues raised, in particular through the analysis of the Polish Code of Criminal Procedure. This analysis was carried out – as should be added – using the derivational concept of legal interpretation by M. Zieliński[7].

---

6 See R. Tokarczyk, *Komparatystyka prawnicza*, Warszawa 2008, p. 74.

7 See M. Zieliński, *Wykładnia prawa. Zasady, reguły, wskazówki*, Warszawa 2012, p. 360; M. Zieliński, 'Derywacyjna koncepcja wykładni jako koncepcja zintegrowana', 68(3) *Ruch Prawniczy, Ekonomiczny i Socjologiczny* 2006, pp. 93 ff.

It is also worth emphasising that in terms of methods developed by psychology to increase the rationality of decisions made, reference was made primarily to the findings of C. R. Sunstein, D. Kahneman and O. Sibony[8].

3. Pre-trial Detention in Poland

Pre-trial detention is one of the most well-known preventive measures, i.e. measures intended to secure the proper conduct of the proceedings, and exceptionally, to prevent a new serious offence from being committed by the accused. Significantly, its application is possible (in Poland) only if the evidence collected indicates a high probability that they have committed an offence (Art. 249 § 1 CCP-Poland), and only on the basis of a court decision (Art. 250 § 1 CCP-Poland).

The exact reasons for applying the indicated measure include: 1) justified fear that the accused may take flight or go into hiding, particularly if their identity cannot be established or if they have no permanent residence in this country; 2) justified fear that the accused would induce other persons to give false testimony or attempt to obstruct the criminal proceedings in some other unlawful manner; 3) the accused being charged with a crime or with a misdemeanour carrying the statutory maximum penalty of imprisonment for a minimum of 8 years, or if the court of the first instance sentenced them to imprisonment for no less than 3 years; and also 4) justified fear that the accused charged with a crime or an intentional misdemeanour would commit an offence against life, health or public safety, particularly if they threatened to commit such an offence (Art. 258 CCP-Poland).

Pre-trial detention is, therefore, a measure whose application requires the court to make at least several decisions based on previously made assessments regarding, on the one hand, the past (the matter of assessing whether the accused is highly likely to have committed the crime they were charged with), and, on the other hand, the future, and more specifically, what the accused may do in connection with the criminal proceedings pending in their case (will they obstruct criminal proceedings, and if so, in what form: will they go into hiding, will they encourage persons to give false testimony?) or what danger it may create for legally protected interests important for society (will they commit a prohibited act, and if so, in what form and against what interests will this act be directed: will it be a misdemeanour or a crime? Will it be a crime against personal interests, or perhaps against public safety?).

---

8 C. R. Sunstein, D. Kahneman, O. Sibony, *Szum, czyli skąd się biorą błędy w naszych decyzjach*, Poznań 2022, *passim*. The English translation of the title is *Noise. A Flaw in Human Judgment*.

The decisions that need to be made by the court and the assessments that precede them are not only important from the perspective of the accused (after all, they result in far-reaching interference with their rights and freedoms), but above all, extremely complicated. This is particularly obvious in the context of the need to assess the defendant's future. How should this be done? What factors should be considered? Should these be only objective factors or also subjective ones? Should those be only static factors or also dynamic ones? Should those be factors related only to the prohibited act that the accused allegedly committed, or also factors unrelated to the accusation? If factors directly relating to the accused are to be considered, should only their characteristics be considered or should their personal situation also be considered? Are there any factors at all that could indicate, for example, the risk of taking flight or going into hiding? Should the above-mentioned data be considered individually in favour of applying pre-trial detention, or is their quantum enough? What should be done if some data is not available or impossible to obtain? Should the data obtained before making a decision be assessed only from the perspective of a given, specific case analysed at a given moment, or should they be compared with statistical data on similar people and similar cases? These and other questions must be asked by the court before making the assessments and decisions that are considered in this work.

However, regardless of what data the court considers, what rank it assigns to the data and how it evaluates them, it is also important what scenarios it constructs based on this data and which of the scenarios it considers the most likely (the question is on what basis each scenario will be assessed in this respect). Among the potential scenarios, it will be necessary to consider at least the following: 1) a scenario in which a person has committed the crime of which they have been accused, in connection with: a) a scenario in which the course of proceedings is obstructed (the question is of what nature: whether the perpetrator will go into hiding or will they encourage persons to give false testimony?), or b) a scenario in which the accused reoffends (the question is of what nature: will it be a crime against human life or health, or will it be a crime against public safety?); 2) a scenario in which a person committed the crime of which they were accused, related to a scenario in which there is: a) no obstruction of the proceedings, or b) no new crime committed; 3) a scenario in which the person did not commit the crime they were charged with; as well as 4) scenarios related to the situation in which a measure in the form of pre-trial detention is applied (the question is for what period: for 3 months, or maybe shorter or longer?), and 5) scenarios related to the situation in which the measure in the form of pre-trial detention does not occur (the question is whether another measure is applied, for example in the form of police supervision, or not).

However, one question immediately arises: based on what criteria should these scenarios be constructed and one of them selected as the most likely? Is appropriate knowledge, life experience and principles of logic enough? Is using algorithms or the SPJ methods necessary? Are there any circumstances or tools that could indicate that a given solution is more or less likely? After all, decisions made in the matters that this work focuses on cannot be verified even post factum, let alone ipso factum. How can be verified whether the court's decision on the need to apply pre-trial detention due to the fear of the perpetrator reoffending while free was correct, if in fact they (the perpetrator) were deprived of the potential possibility of committing a prohibited act by placing them in a detention facility? This type of verification would only be possible if pre-trial detention had not been imposed. However, another question automatically arises: which court will risk waiving pre-trial detention in a situation where it sees even the slightest risk of the perpetrator reoffending? The pressure that weighs on a decision-maker in this type of situation seems to be at least very difficult to overcome, especially since it is not only internal pressure caused by one's own fears, feelings, and beliefs, but also external pressure – coming from the police, prosecutor's office, but also victims, the general public, and often from the media.

Nevertheless, verification of the decision made will also be exceptionally difficult if the decision is made to not apply pre-trial detention due to the existing fear of the possibility of, for example, inciting by the perpetrator to give false testimony; however, the suspicion of fraud by the perpetrator may be exceptionally difficult to verify and prove.

The characteristics presented above may suggest that making a decision to apply or not to apply pre-trial detention is extremely difficult. However, making a decision in this regard may become even more difficult for the decision-maker when they consider the far-reaching consequences of applying this preventive measure and realise the related need to exercise great caution in its application. After all, pre-trial detention amounts to imprisonment for a long time[9]. Pursuant

9 As Court Watch Polska points out: "The average length of pre-trial detention that lasts until the end of court proceedings with a final verdict, which results from the analysis of the files made available to us, is 439 days in cases where the material jurisdiction was a regional court and 223 days for cases that were pending before district courts. The longest waiting time in custody for a final judgment that we examined was 43 months (more than 3 years). However, we did not have access to cases that were still pending in mid-2019. It can therefore be presumed that, in reality, the average length of pre-trial detention may be longer in Poland and has certainly been increasing in recent years" (Z. Branicka et al., *Aktualna praktyka stosowania tymczasowego aresztowania w Polsce. Raport z badań empirycznych*, Toruń 2019, p. 18).

to Art. 263 CCP-Poland, when applying pre-trial detention, the court must specify its period, which generally cannot be longer than three months. Yet, it may happen that the application of this measure will be extended: if, due to the special circumstances, it is not possible to complete the preparatory proceedings within the previously set period of time, at the request of the prosecutor, the court of first instance competent to hear the case will, if necessary, be able to extend pre-trial detention for a period which may not exceed twelve months in total. At the same time, in accordance with the will of the legislator, the total period of pre-trial detention until the first judgment is issued by the court of first instance cannot exceed two years. However, the deadlines indicated above do not have to be final. Pre-trial detention may be extended for a specified period exceeding these periods; this will be able to be done by the court of appeal in whose district the proceedings will be conducted at the request of the court before which the case will be heard, and in preparatory proceedings at the request of the competent prosecutor directly superior to the prosecutor conducting or supervising the investigation, if such a need arises in connection with the suspension of criminal proceedings, activities aimed at establishing or confirming the identity of the accused, carrying out evidentiary activities in a case of particular complexity or outside the country, as well as an intentional delay of the proceedings by the accused. It is also worth adding that if there is a need to apply pre-trial detention after the first judgment is issued by the court of first instance, each extension will be possible for a period not longer than six months (Art. 263 CCP-Poland).

In view of the above, it should be repeated that pre-trial detention is therefore a measure that greatly interferes with the rights and freedoms of a person (potential perpetrator), and therefore carries far-reaching consequences for them. Court Watch Polska even points out that it is not only for them; as Z. Branicka et al. point out: "The application of pre-trial detention affects not only the person subjected to this measure, but also his/her immediate surroundings. Social consequences of detainment is borne, first of all, by the family of the accused, especially their children. There are also economic consequences because a detained person cannot perform his/her duties as an employee, debtor or entrepreneur. The consequence of prolonged detention may be the fading of social, economic and even personal ties. The accused is not the only one who suffers, but also all persons isolated from him, with whom he or she has any ties. Even short-term deprivation of liberty by the judiciary, e.g. pre-trial detention lifted after a few weeks as a result of a complaint, can undoubtedly leave a mark on the psyche of the person subjected to this preventive measure, and also damage his/her good name"[10].

10 Z. Branicka et al., *Aktualna praktyka…*, p. 3.

Pre-trial detention should therefore be a measure applied with great caution. In such a way as to ensure, on the one hand, the possibility of achieving the objectives of criminal proceedings and its proper course and (possibly) to protect society against the perpetrator reoffending, and, on the other hand, to ensure an appropriate guarantee of protection of the rights and freedoms of the accused by not interfering in them when it is not actually needed. This is confirmed by the legislator, who in Art. 257 CCP-Poland clearly indicates that pre-trial detention shall not be applied if another preventive measure is sufficient, and at the same time that in applying pre-trial detention, the court may reserve that the measure will be amended when an agreed bail is posted with the court within the prescribed time-limit. However, as it turns out, the discussed preventive measure is treated (in Poland) as a rule, not an exception to it. According to Court Watch Polska: "Analysis of the collected data leads to the conclusion that in Poland pre-trial detention plays in practice a role of a default and not final preventive measure. Most judges, instead of reaching for them after considering alternatives such as bail, police custody or passport impounding, seem to start their analysis with the belief that the prosecutor's request for pre-trial detention alone generates a presumption of the need for this preventive measure"[11]. This is a global problem, typical for many countries, not only in Central and Eastern Europe[12].

In the case of the practice of applying the institution of pre-trial detention, there is a matter of errors in the form of bias and noise, as mentioned by Kahneman et al. As the mentioned researchers claim: "Some judgments are biased; they are systematically off target. Other judgments are noisy, as people who are expected to agree end up at very different points around the target"[13]. In the case of the practice of applying pre-trial detention, however, it is – in the opinion of those who research this issue empirically – a matter of widespread abuse of the preventive measure in question, that is, its use when it is not actually necessary, and this is an example of a clear divergence of opinions regarding individual analysed cases by people specialising in legal issues, i.e. by the courts on the one hand and by researchers on

---

11 Z. Branicka et al., *Aktualna praktyka*…, pp. 5–6.

12 See K. Kamber, 'The overuse of pre-trial detention as a public policy and human rights problem', available at: https://www.cep-probation.org/the-overuse-of-pre-trial-detention-as-a-public-policy-and-human-rights-problem/ [accessed on: September 12th, 2023]; A. Martufi, C. Peristeridou, 'The Purposes of Pre-Trial Detention and the Quest for Alternatives', 28(2) *European Journal of Crime, Criminal Law and Criminal Justice* 2020, pp. 153–174.

13 D. Kahneman, O. Sibony, C. R. Sunstein, *Szum, czyli skąd się biorą błędy w naszych decyzjach* (trans. P. Szymczak), Poznań 2022, p. 14.

the other (noise), and an example of the courts systematically missing the target (bias). Court Watch Polska even clearly states that: "Data obtained on a random sample of 310 cases of this preventive measure show that some of the irregularities identified by the Court are widely duplicated by Polish courts, and thus constitute evidence that we are dealing with a systemic problem in our country. Pre-trial detention is sometimes applied even in cases where the evidence contained in the case files does not indicate the need to imprison a person to whom the principle of the presumption of innocence applies"[14].

The above-mentioned errors should, of course, be strictly counteracted, as they clearly suggest that decisions made in matters of pre-trial detention may not be rational; in the next subsection, the author will therefore attempt to indicate potential legislative changes (but not only those) that could serve to solve the problems diagnosed in this way. It should be emphasised, however, that noise and bias are, to some extent, natural phenomena when making such complex and, at the same time, unverifiable decisions and assessments as those made in the case of the institution of pre-trial detention, and impossible to completely eliminate, at least to the extent that concerns noise. Differences of opinion on particular issues will exist always and everywhere, and it is impossible to fight them. Just as people differ from each other, so do the situations in which decisions will be made, the situations to which decisions will concern, and our assessments of these situations. The author of this work only wants to create conditions in which decisions and assessments will be made in conditions in which detecting potential errors will be possible even at the stage before the decision is made, and easier than it is currently, giving a chance to immediately implement any corrections and preventing the accused or society from suffering disproportionate harm that could be associated with clearly erroneous decisions entering circulation. Paraphrasing Kahneman et al., one could say that the author of this work wants to create a process of formulating judgments regarding the justification, or lack thereof, of using the institution of pre-trial detention that will ensure the best possible judgments for the entire set of possible cases; judgments – it should be added – not necessarily proper from the perspective of the result of their application, but consistent with the facts of a given case[15].

---

14 Z. Branicka et al., *Aktualna praktyka…*, p. 5.

15 See D. Kahneman, O. Sibony, C. R. Sunstein, *Szum, czyli skąd…*, pp. 65–66.

4. Possible Approaches to Remove Bias and Noise in the Use of Pre-Trial Detention

Imagine subject X, call him James, that was accused of raping a 10-year-old girl. The case is shocking, attracts attention, and even leads to lynching. Much evidence collected during the preparatory proceedings (pre-jurisdictional phase of criminal proceedings) indicates that the prohibited act actually occurred and was committed by James; the prosecutor is even convinced of this, as are the accused's closest circle and the media (and also through them many other third parties, not directly related to the case). However, there is also evidence pointing to the view that the rape did not actually take place or that the rape was committed by someone else, and at the same time, as to many circumstances important from the perspective of the decision, there are no premises, much less evidence regarding them. The prosecutor who accused the alleged perpetrator requests the court to apply pre-trial detention because, according to the prosecutor, the fact that James committed an act with such a high degree of social consequences suggests that there is a high risk that, if left free, he will again offend public order, or at least impede criminal proceedings by, for example, taking flight. The court that is to hear the prosecutor's application, or rather one judge, because this is the type of panel that hears such cases, must make a number of assessments in the shortest possible time (after all, the fate of a potentially endangered society is at stake), including, in particular, the extent to which the probability that James actually committed the crime he was accused of, and to assess whether there is an actual risk on James's part to important social goods or to the proper course of the proceedings. There are no guidelines or assistance from experts. At the same time, he is bombarded with messages about social dissatisfaction with the alleged perpetrator being free, which is a significant psychological pressure for him. Enormous pressure and relying solely on evidence indicating that a prohibited act has been committed lead to the decision to apply pre-trial detention and, in fact, to imprisonment. The criminal proceedings continue and more evidence is being collected. Time passes and there is still no decision, and the pre-trial detention is constantly extended. After twelve months spent in isolation, James receives the final decision – he is innocent. He leaves the detention facility and returns home. Mentally and physically suppressed, with a tarnished reputation, unemployed.

The above-mentioned situation is, of course, fiction, but there is nothing to prevent it – in the light of the previous considerations – from actually happening. Polish courts (but probably not only Polish) use pre-trial detention – as already mentioned – not as a last resort, but as a first-choice measure, in the opinion of researchers – as should be recalled – even in "cases where the evidence contained in the case files does not indicate the necessity of imprisonment of a person to whom the principle of presumption of innocence applies". Considering this, the question arises what to do to prevent this. This section will try to answer this question, looking at this issue – as indicated in the introduction – from the perspective of the legislator and what they can do to create the best conditions for courts to make rational decisions and, consequently (one can hope) also fair, or at least creating the impression that they were undertaken in a procedure guaranteeing the best possible protection of human rights and freedoms.

4.1. The right people in the right place

It is clear that people differ from each other in many respects. These differences concern both the physical and mental spheres; just as people differ in terms of height, weight, eye colour or hair, people also differ in terms of personality, memory, ability to concentrate or speed of information processing. Individual characteristics that differentiate people (especially in the psychological sphere) may be of great importance when choosing a person who would hold, for example, the position of a judge. In the context of the issue considered in this work, differences in training, intelligence and cognitive style emerge. After all, as Kahneman et al. suggest: "Judgments are both less noisy and less biased when those who make them are well trained, are more intelligent, and have the right cognitive style. In other words: good judgements depend on what you know, how well you think, and how you think"[16].

For obvious reasons, from the perspective of the accuracy of assessments and decisions made, the most eligible people should be well-trained, experts with appropriate knowledge and experience in a given field, and, above all, those who achieve the best results in that field. After all, you can have a lot of knowledge and experience and still be wrong at every step; the fact of having knowledge and experience does not mean the ability to use them correctly in practice. Unfortunately, in the case of judges it is difficult to rely on this last criterion[17]. How to measure the accuracy of assessments and decisions constituting the basis of individual judgments? How to verify whether the pre-trial detention applied by a given judge in individual cases was actually accurate, in a situation where it is impossible to check what would have happened if the pre-trial detention had not been applied? How to verify whether the sentence was accurate in a situation where in most cases it is not possible to find evidence that clearly reveals all aspects of a given incident?

16 D. Kahneman, O. Sibony, C. R. Sunstein, *Szum, czyli skąd...*, p. 265.
17 See D. Kahneman, O. Sibony, C. R. Sunstein, *Szum, czyli skąd...*, p. 266.

In the case of judges, they are people making judgments in which the real value (one can even risk calling it 'truth' per se) is neither easy to discover nor easy to define. Therefore, they cannot be evaluated as experts based on their results (it is not possible to make an assessment even based on the number of repealed judgments, because this type of factor basically proves nothing, apart from the fact that the appellate bodies found or did not find errors in the reasoning of the body of first instance), but – at most – based on the trust and respect they enjoy among other professionals (other judges, prosecutors, lawyers, etc.); trust and respect – it needs to be added – which should be (and hopefully are) based on: 1) appropriate knowledge acquired during studies of an appropriate high level, as well as during professional apprenticeship; 2) many years of life and professional experience; and 3) the ability to appropriately formulate and explain one's judgments[18].

In order to ensure a sufficiently high accuracy of assessments and decisions made in matters of pre-trial detention, the selection should (having no other choice) be guided primarily by the esteem of individual lawyers, and therefore by the degree of their respect in the community. Therefore, the judges should be people (assuming, of course, that a reduction in noise and bias is expected, and, consequently, also something like assessments made in a rational manner) who carry with them a certain amount of baggage: intellectual and emotional. These cannot be young people who suddenly (although probably with appropriate training and after acquiring as comprehensive theoretical knowledge as possible) move on to making decisions that may result in dramatic consequences for other people (and such consequences occur in the case of the use of measures involving imprisonment). The highest grades and recognition in the eyes of lecturers or patrons are not enough to conclude that in the case of a given person one will have a greater chance of accurate judgments. It should also be necessary to demonstrate appropriate knowledge and effectiveness in matters that are the subject of analysis in individual criminal cases, to learn different perspectives on these matters (preferably both the perspective of the prosecutor and the defence lawyer), to actually understand the consequences of applying individual institutions provided for by law, developing cooperation with specialists from various fields (in particular in the field of psychology, psychiatry and criminology) and gaining knowledge from them about the nature of man and the world, etc.

In Poland, however, people at the age of twentynine can become judges, and the path to a career as a judge requires completing 'only' the following procedure: 1) graduating from law school (three-five years); 2) completing judicial

---

18 See D. Kahneman, O. Sibony, C. R. Sunstein, *Szum, czyli skąd…*, pp. 266–269.

apprenticeship (three years); and 3) passing the judicial examination. The question arises whether this type of solution is beneficial. Considering the previous considerations, it should be concluded that this is not the case and that it could be worth returning to the concept of the position of a judge as the culmination of a legal career, at least as far as the examination of criminal cases is concerned. As far as the competence to apply measures that interfere the most with human rights and freedoms (and such measures are available in criminal law) is concerned, expertise measured by knowledge, experience and the resulting respect in the community must appear to be necessary.

Another issue that requires consideration in the context of striving to ensure appropriate judgments in pre-trial detention cases is the selection of people to take up the position of judge from among individuals characterised by the highest level of intelligence and the appropriate cognitive style. It is suggested to verify the mental abilities of people applying for the position of judge and those already holding such a position through standardised tests containing verbal, quantitative and spatial tasks[19]. Of course, it could be said that people aspiring to be judges after graduating from law school and requiring professional training have already proven their intellectual predispositions through their achievements, and this is probably the case. However, Kahneman rightly points out that: "Even among the top 1% of people as measured by cognitive ability (…) exceptional outcomes are strongly correlated with GMA. Compared with those who are in the bottom quartile of this top 1%, those who are in the top quartile are two to three times more likely to earn a doctoral-level degree, publish a book, or be granted a patent. In other words, not only does the difference in GMA matter between the 99th percentile and the 80th or 50th, but it still matters – a lot! – between the 99.88th percentile and the 99.13th"[20]. Therefore it should be expected to select people with the highest performance to serve as a judge adjudicating in criminal cases.

It could also be said, of course, that standardised tests of intelligence are inherently discriminatory and that they should therefore not be used. However, in the author's opinion, such doubts will be non-existent in a situation where these tests cannot constitute the only basis for the selection of criminal judges; they will only constitute an additional indicator that will be considered in this respect, but will not be a decisive indicator.

---

19 See D. Kahneman, O. Sibony, C. R. Sunstein, *Szum, czyli skąd…*, p. 270.

20 D. Kahneman, O. Sibony, C. R. Sunstein, *Szum, czyli skąd…*, pp. 271–272.

Finally, it is suggested to verify the cognitive style of people who will hold the position of judge. It concerns choosing people who, when faced with a problem, will not trust their first intuition, but will take action to verify or even refute it, or teach future judges this type of behaviour (if possible, of course). A judge making decisions in criminal cases should not be a person who decides quickly, but a person who decides deliberately, striving to obtain as much information as possible and able to verify this information in a way that will not lead to its adjustment to a predetermined solution. This should be a person who is open to the opinions of other people, ready to accept the fallacy of their position, and therefore, in a sense, a humble person and not a person convinced of their own infallibility or so self-confident that they reject other people's views in advance. This should be a person who, based on the presented arguments, will make a preliminary assessment and make a preliminary decision, but will also ask themselves the following, among others, questions: 1) are the arguments I based on my decision fully convincing? 2) have I omitted any circumstances that are important from the perspective of a given case? 3) are there any alternative solutions? 4) are the alternative solutions less convincing than the solution I assumed? 5) have I made any errors in reasoning along the way? etc. Therefore, it should be a person who is – to use the phrase proposed by J. Baron[21] – actively open-minded[22].

To sum up, the judges deciding on pre-trial detention cases should be people: 1) with extensive knowledge, experience and respect in the community; 2) achieving the highest scores on intelligence tests; and 3) characterised by the need to verify the assessments they make and the positions they take.

4.2. Single-person or group adjudication?

In the Polish legal system, the rule is that the court adjudicates in single-person judicial panels; one judge and two lay judges or three judges adjudicate in a given case only as an exception (Art. 28 CCP-Poland). The situation is similar in the context of pre-trial detention – the decision in this respect is made by a single judge, who is not even obliged to seek the opinion of another expert (another judge) in a given case. Considering this, the question arises whether it would not be better if decisions on matters as important as imprisonment were made by at least two people. In other words – the question arises whether group decisions lead to better results than decisions made by a single person.

---

21 See J. Baron, *Thinking and Deciding*, Cambridge 2008, p. 584.

22 See D. Kahneman, O. Sibony, C. R. Sunstein, *Szum, czyli skąd…*, p. 276.

On the one hand, single-person decision-making ensures the speed and efficiency of the proceedings (and also reduces their cost), which is particularly important in the context of measures such as pre-trial detention, i.e. measures aimed at securing the course of the proceedings and preventing the commission of a new crime. On the other hand, however, single-person decision-making leads to it being based solely on the knowledge and experience of that one person (therefore, the number of perspectives on the matter, the number of arguments considered, the number of alternative solutions perceived, etc. are also limited). As mentioned above, when making judgments, one should care about maximising both the knowledge and experience of decision-making entities; the knowledge and experience of a group (or, in fact, the combined scope of knowledge and experience of several people forming this group) may be better, and therefore also more adequate than the knowledge and experience of a single person. What's more, it may be that participation in other people's decision-making will allow for spotting cognitive errors, made by a given person that they would not have caught on their own, and for a better understanding of the analysed issue/discussed problem as a result of discussion that includes more than one interpretation. The decisions made by a group may also be bolder (after all, the responsibility is shared among several people), and therefore, in the case of pre-trial detention, the group will decide to refrain from applying it more often than a single person does (too often).

The issue of group decisions has become the subject of social psychology research. As indicated, group can make good decisions, but there are also disadvantages to this type of decision-making; these disadvantages include: 1) social pressure toward conformity (if the need for cohesion and consensus among individual group members becomes stronger than the need to make the best possible decisions and if individuals are afraid that other group members will consider them uncooperative, it may result in subordination to the direction chosen by the group, even if this direction is wrong in the opinion of these individuals); 2) individual domination (it may happen that an individual with a strong position, rank or personality will dominate other people and what appears to be a group decision will actually be an individual's decision); 3) conflicting secondary goals (it may happen that internal frictions in the group or internal competition between its individual members lead to a wrong decision, but beneficial for part of the group); 4) undesirable compromises (in the case of controversial issues and opposing views of group members, discussion within the group may lead to the conclusion that a decision favouring either party is unacceptable and the selection of a compromise solution that may be wrong); 5) ambiguous responsibility (in the case of group decisions, responsibility is dispersed and it is not known who should be expected to take responsibility for the mistake made); and 6) time (making and agreeing on a decision by many people takes more time than making a decision by one person)[23].

The above-mentioned potential disadvantages of group decisions largely determine the lack of justification for introducing collegial panels of judges in deciding whether to apply or not to apply pre-trial detention. However, decisions in this regard should be made as quickly and adequately as possible (compromises cannot be considered). That said, it was mentioned earlier that due to the dispersion of responsibility in the case of group decisions, it could be expected that decisions not to apply pre-trial detention, which are exceptionally risky decisions due to the potential possibility of, for example, the perpetrator taking flight or reoffending, will be undertaken more often than before (to the benefit of protecting the freedom and rights of the accused). Additionally, in the case of a group decision, external pressure (e.g. by media) will lose its impact and may not have such an impact on the final shape of the decisions made. Unfortunately (or fortunately), group decisions are not always riskier than decisions made by an individual. As Lunenburg points out: "Subsequent research refutes the conclusion that groups consistently take greater risk than individuals (Bordley, 1983). For some groups and some decisions, cautious shifts were observed; that is, groups arrived at decisions that were less risky than those of individuals. Thus, both risky and cautious decisions are possible in groups. A key factor in determining which kind of shift occurs – more risky or more cautious – is the position assumed by the members before group interaction occurs. If the members lean initially toward risk, group discussion results in a shift toward greater risk; and if members lean initially toward caution, discussion leads to a cautious shift"[24].

Does the above mean that decision-making in matters of pre-trial detention should belong to the individual and not to the group? In a sense, yes, provided that the group and group decisions are considered as decisions made in cooperation between individual people, and not as decisions made by several individuals, but independently of each other. It turns out that "averaging the independent judgments of different people generally improves accuracy"[25]. That said, a similar

23 See F. C. Lunenburg, 'Group Decision Making', 20(3) *National Forum of Teacher Education Journal* 2010, pp. 3–5, available at: http://www.nationalforum.com/Electronic%20Journal%20Volumes/Lunenburg,%20Fred%20C.%20Group%20Decision%20Making%20NFTEJ%20V20%20N3%202010.pdf [accessed on: September 12th, 2023].

24 F. C. Lunenburg, *Group Decision…*, p. 5.

25 D. Kahneman, O. Sibony, C. R. Sunstein, *Szum, czyli skąd…*, p. 102.

thing happens when one person's estimates are averaged (the result is then better than in the case of only one estimate)[26]; however, as Kahneman et al. point out, "Averaging two guesses by the same person does not improve judgments as much as does seeking out an independent second opinion"[27]. Decisions to apply or not to apply pre-trial detention should therefore be (or at least could be) made by at least two people (two judges), each of whom would make an estimate independently of each other (preferably in the form of a percentage) and who would then average the received results by themselves. This type of solution does not seem to be very expensive, either in terms of time or personnel (it simply requires the involvement of a second judge in the custody case), and could give much better results than a decision made by only one person.

An alternative to the solution proposed above (especially for people who believe that there is no reason to additionally engage already overloaded judges in custody cases) is to use a method called 'dialectical bootstrapping'. More specifically, forcing individual judges considering the issue of pre-trial detention to prepare, in addition to the first judgment (considered appropriate by a given judge), another judgment, equally reliable as the first one, but completely different from it; in the case of pre-trial detention, it would obviously be about preparing a second judgment which would indicate – contrary to the original judgment – that the application of pre-trial detention is not justified. This type of additional task would force the judge to adopt a new perspective, verify the circumstances taken into account, consider the use of additional arguments, etc. It would make it possible to overcome at least some cognitive errors by thinking about the case once again, but with a completely different attitude[28]. However, this type of solution seems to be more risky than the solution of seeking someone else's independent opinion, due to the fact that controlling and enforcing the actual conduct of a given judge may turn out to be impossible, or at least very difficult. This solution is also strictly dependent on the cognitive skills of a given person, and these may, unfortunately, be limited.

Additionally, regardless of the above findings, introducing in pre-trial detention cases the institution of an observer judge should be considered an institution unknown to Polish (but not only Polish) law whose task would be to detect cognitive errors underlying decisions, but not after they have been made, but during them. Such a judge would be obliged to check in real-time whether any or several

26 See D. Kahneman, O. Sibony, C. R. Sunstein, *Szum, czyli skąd…*, p. 103.
27 D. Kahneman, O. Sibony, C. R. Sunstein, *Szum, czyli skąd…*, p. 103.
28 See D. Kahneman, O. Sibony, C. R. Sunstein, *Szum, czyli skąd…*, p. 104.

cognitive errors occurred in the process of making the decision to apply or not to apply pre-trial detention. This type of control could be a sort of discussion with the judge appointed to make a decision about the premises of their reasoning, the focuses of this reasoning and its expected effects, and indicating, based on the information obtained, suggestions about potential observed or imminent errors. Of course, the task of such a person would not be easy, and consequently, it would have to be a person who was properly trained and had the appropriate tools[29]; in this last respect, however, there are instructions; as Kahneman et al. claim: "One such tool is a checklist of the biases they are attempting to detect. The case for relying on a checklist is clear: checklists have a long history of improving decisions in high-stakes contexts and are particularly well suited to preventing the repetition of past errors"[30].

The functioning of the above-mentioned judge observer would not have to be a formalised institution resulting from applicable legal provisions. It would be enough for judges to support each other in this respect on the basis of camaraderie and with a sense of responsibility for the administration of justice, acting as reliable supervisors for each other.

4.3. Appropriate preparation of applications for pre-trial detention

Pursuant to the Polish Code of Criminal Procedure, pre-trial detention may only occur by a court decision and is applied (or rather – may be applied) at the request of the prosecutor at the stage of preparatory proceedings (Art. 250 CCP-Poland). Importantly, according to the ordinance of the Polish legislator, in the application for pre-trial detention, the prosecutor is obliged to mention evidence indicating a high probability that the accused has committed a crime, circumstances indicating the existence of threats to the proper course of proceedings or the possibility of the accused committing a new, serious crime and the basis for applying this preventive measure and the necessity of its application (Art. 250 § 2 CCP-Poland). In other words, the prosecutor's duty is to indicate in their application only the circumstances to the detriment of the accused, and therefore they do not have to (and they would probably never do it if they were fully convinced of the justification for using pre-trial detention) indicate the circumstances in favour of the accused and, consequently, also in favour of not applying pre-trial detention.

A certain counterweight to the prosecutor's arguments is (or, at least, can be) the arguments of the accused themselves or their defence attorney, after all, in

29 See D. Kahneman, O. Sibony, C. R. Sunstein, *Szum, czyli skąd…*, pp. 283–286.

30 D. Kahneman, O. Sibony, C. R. Sunstein, *Szum, czyli skąd…*, p. 285.

accordance with Art. 249 § 3 CCP-Poland: "Before applying a preventive measure, the court or the prosecutor applying the measure interrogates the accused, unless this is impossible due to their hiding or absence from the country. The appointed defence attorney should be allowed to participate in the hearing if they appear". However, the accused may not be able to defend themselves against the application of pre-trial detention, and the participation of a defence lawyer is rare. According to the file study: "Defence attorneys were least likely to be present at these key hearings – they appeared at 26.6% of the hearings when a case was heard by a district court, and 15.8% when it was heard by a regional court"[31].

The above means that the main arguments faced by the judge deciding on pre-trial detention are the prosecutor's arguments; the prosecutor – what should be recalled – who is certainly convinced of the justification for applying pre-trial detention (otherwise they would not have submitted an appropriate application to the court), has no interest in having their application rejected and, therefore, has no interest in presenting arguments that may raise doubts in the court as to the validity of its application (of pre-trial detention). This type of situation may, however, lead to numerous cognitive errors in the court. It may, for example, cause confirmation bias, which is the tendency to ignore contradictory data once a judgment has been made in advance[32] (and such a judgment will certainly be made by the court after the first, even preliminary, reading of the indictment). Of course, the court has the opportunity (and even the obligation, see Art. 249a § 2 CCP-Poland) to also consider *ex officio* circumstances that the prosecutor did not disclose after their disclosure at the hearing if they are favourable to the accused. It should be emphasised, however, that not every judge must be characterised by a sufficiently high level of being 'actively open-minded', and this justifies the fear that favourable information may not be found or may be incorrectly interpreted and adjusted to the previously considered view on the justification for applying pre-trial detention in a given case.

Therefore, it is worth expecting the prosecutor to indicate in the application for pre-trial detention not only the arguments in favour of its application (of pre-trial detention), but also the arguments against the application of this preventive measure, along with considerations on why the arguments against its application should not be accepted and conceivable alternative solutions (assuming,

---

31 B. Pilitowski, B. Kociołowicz-Wiśniewska, Z. Branicka, 'Obecność oskarżonych, obrońców i prokuratorów na posiedzeniach w przedmiocie zastosowania tymczasowego aresztowania' in: P. Karlik, B. Pilitowski (eds.), *Stosowanie tymczasowego aresztowania. Analiza praktyczna*, Warszawa 2022.

32 See D. Kahneman, O. Sibony, C. R. Sunstein, *Szum, czyli skąd...*, p. 204.

for example, that the accused would not reoffend if pre-trial detention was not applied) should be rejected. Only this type of justification for application for pre-trial detention will, in the opinion of the author of this work, create conditions appropriate for the court to make a rational decision. At the same time, conditions would then be created for the prosecutor to make a rational decision. It should be noted that the current solutions lead the prosecutor to confirm their previously made decision by having to indicate in the justification only those arguments that are consistent with their narrative (consistent with the decision to submit an application for pre-trial detention to the court). Creating the need for a broader justification of the application may force the prosecutor to reconsider the decision and may even reduce the number of applications for the preventive measure that is in the interest of this work to a minimum. In connection with the above, it is suggested to introduce in the Polish Code of Criminal Procedure the following regulation: "The application for applying pre-trial detention shall list all the evidence collected, in particular evidence indicating a high probability that the accused has committed a crime, together with the justification for the decision made in this respect, all circumstances of the case, including in particular circumstances supporting the existence of threats to the proper course of proceedings or the possibility of the accused committing a new, serious crime, together with the justification for the assessment made in this respect. The application shall also indicate the specific basis for applying this preventive measure, and justify the necessity of its use and not being able to use alternative measures" (instead of the current Art. 250 § 2a CCP-Poland).

4.4. Justifications prepared before or after the decision was made?

In Poland, one of the requirements related to the use of pre-trial detention is, in addition to issuing an appropriate decision, its proper justification. The justification should include evidence that the accused has committed a crime, circumstances indicating the existence of threats to the proper course of proceedings or the possibility of the accused committing a new, serious crime in case this preventive measure is not applied, as well as the specific basis for its application and the need to apply a given measure. It should also be explained why another preventive measure was not considered sufficient (Art. 251 CCP-Poland). The court is therefore obliged to indicate evidence in favour of the application of pre-trial detention and may omit evidence against its application, or at least it is not obliged to indicate it. Therefore, the purpose of the justification is – as it seems – for the court to create a coherent and convincing narrative for the application of the discussed solution in a given case.

The question that should be asked in the context of the above is as follows: should the main purpose of justifying the decision to apply a preventive measure be to create a coherent narrative aimed at convincing potentially interested entities (including, in particular, the accused) of the justification for applying this measure? In the opinion of the author of this work, the answer to this question should be negative. The justification for the decision to apply pre-trial detention (or, in fact, every justification) should reflect the judge's thinking – first of all. Secondly, it should give them a chance to verify the decision they made through a subsequent autopsy, i.e. breaking it down into prime factors and assessing its individual fragments, and not only the overall picture, whether it creates a good impression or not[33]. As such, the justification should include: 1) information about all the circumstances that the court considered when making its decision, and about all the circumstances that it did not consider (but was aware of); 2) information about all analysed scenarios – both those related to, for example, the possibility of the perpetrator reoffending, and those in which the perpetrator does not commit another crime; 3) a justification for why certain circumstances were found convincing and others were rejected; 4) justification for why a given scenario was selected and the others were rejected; 5) information on considered preventive measures; 6) information on all scenarios analysed by them related to the application of given preventive measures; 7) justification for why applying pre-trial detention was the only solution in the analysed situation.

It seems that the best solution would be to introduce a requirement for courts to prepare justifications with a standardised structure, which could include points corresponding to those mentioned in the previous paragraph. It would also be possible to prepare a kind of checklist for judges, based on which they would verify whether the justification prepared by them includes all the information necessary to be considered. This type of justification would not only actually reflect the judge's actual thinking, but also – as already mentioned – it would give them a chance to verify their decision. By writing down individual arguments and the course of the decision-making process, and reading them several times, the judge would be able to detect any errors in reasoning and make – if necessary – a decision different from the one that was already made. This type of justification should therefore be prepared before issuing the decision for the pre-trial detention, and not only after it is issued; otherwise it would no longer be possible to modify a previously made decision.

33 See E. Samborski, 'Forma postanowienia' in: E. Samborski, *Zarys metodyki pracy sędziego w sprawach karnych*, Warszawa 2011.

The introduction of the above-mentioned solutions seems justified also because the justifications prepared by the courts do not seem appropriate. As Court Watch Polska points out: "Most of the decisions on pre-trial detention are justified only seemingly. It meets formal requirements, but does not include an analysis of the actual grounds for the application of pre-trial detention, nor the circumstances determining whether the deprivation of the accused's freedom at this stage of criminal proceedings is necessary"[34].

4.5. Status quo bias – is cognitive error salvation for human rights and freedoms?

One way to overcome the tendency of courts to order pre-trial detention even where it is not needed is to use cognitive bias (sic!). The bias in question is status quo bias, i.e. a person's tendency to maintain the status quo. An excellent example of the use of status quo bias is the strategy commonly used by cable networks where specific channels are offered for free, e.g. for a period of twelve months, and after that period these channels can be cancelled by performing a specific action (e.g. calling the cable network operator) or they can be kept and after a period of twelve months, it will be necessary to pay an appropriate fee. The author of this work has often forgotten to turn off the indicated option or delayed cancelling the service for some time, unable to bring himself to turn it off. As it turns out, this is nothing unusual[35]. Regardless of the reasons for the indicated phenomenon[36], the fact is that it exists, i.e. individuals tend to choose the default option; as Thaler and Sunstein point out: "The combination of loss aversion with mindless choosing implies that if an option is designated as the 'default', it will attract a large market share. Default options thus act as powerful nudges. In many contexts, defaults have some extra nudging power because consumers may feel, rightly or wrongly,

---

34 Z. Branicka et al., *Aktualna praktyka…*, p. 6.

35 See R. H. Thaler, C. R. Sunstein, *Impuls. Jak podejmować właściwe decyzje dotyczące zdrowia, dobrobytu i szczęścia* (trans. J. Grzegorczyk), Poznań 2017, pp. 51–52.

36 See W. Samuelson, R. Zeckhauser, 'Status Quo Bias in Decision Making', 1(1) *Journal of Risk and Uncertainty* 1988, p. 39; A. Bernecker, 'Is Status Quo Bias Explained by Anchoring? Evidence from Survey Experiments', available at: https://www.vwl.uni-mannheim.de/media/Lehrstuehle/vwl/Gruener/StatusQuoBiasAnchoring.pdf [accessed on: September 12th, 2023]; J. Blasch, C. Daminato, 'Behavioral Anomalies and Energy-related Individual Choices: The Role of Status-quo Bias', 41(6) *Energy Journal* 2020, pp. 181–214; R. Cialdini, *Wywieranie wpływu na ludzi. Teoria i praktyka* (trans. B. Wojciszke), Sopot 2020, pp. 75–132.

that default options come with an implicit endorsement from the default setter, be it the employer, government, or TV scheduler"[37].

But how can status quo bias be used in such a way as to limit the number of pre-trial detentions applied? Well, it is very simple. The first step is to introduce a regulation listing in points the individual preventive measures that can be applied by the court. A regulation introducing such a list could, for example, have the following form: "Preventive measures are: 1) measure X; 2) measure Y; 3) pre-trial detention; 4) measure Z". The pre-trial detention is clearly placed in the middle; this is due to the fact that the first and last options usually have the strongest impact on a person (this is confirmed by research by social psychologists)[38]; moreover, such an order of measures could suggest to the court that, in the legislator's opinion, a measure in the form of pre-trial detention should be applied only when two previous measures (including e.g. police supervision) prove to be insufficient or ineffective. All this together could increase the chance of using pre-trial detention only as a last resort.

The second step, making full use of the status quo bias, would be changing the content of the regulation, which currently allows for the use of pre-trial detention in cases where there is a fear of obstruction of the proceedings by the accused or a fear of reoffending. It should be recalled that currently this regulation in Poland reads as follows: "1. Pre-trial detention and other preventive measures may be applied if 1) there is a justified fear that the accused may take flight or go into hiding, especially when their identity cannot be established or they do not have permanent residence in the country; 2) there is a justified fear that the accused may induce other persons to give false testimony or may otherwise unlawfully obstruct criminal proceedings. 2. If the accused is charged with a crime or a misdemeanour punishable by imprisonment for at least eight years, or if the court of first instance sentenced them to imprisonment for not less than three years, the need to apply pre-trial detention in order to secure the proper course of the proceedings may be justified by the severe penalty threatening the accused. 3. The preventive measure may also be applied in exceptional cases when there is a justified fear that the accused who has been charged with a crime or an intentional misdemeanour may commit an offence against life, health or public safety, especially when they have threatened to commit such an

37 R. H. Thaler, C. R. Sunstein, *Impuls. Jak podejmować…*, p. 52.

38 See J. Murphy, Ch. Hofacker, R. Mizerski, 'Primacy and Recency Effects on Clicking Behavior', 11(2) *Journal of Computer-Mediated Communication* 2006, pp. 522–535; C. Li, 'Primacy effect or recency effect? A long-term memory test of Super Bowl commercials', 9(1) *Journal of Consumer Behaviour* 2010, pp. 32–44.

offence. 4. When deciding on the application of a specific preventive measure, the type and nature of the concerns indicated in §§ 1–3, accepted as the basis for applying a given measure, and the severity of their threat to the proper course of the proceedings at a specific stage of the proceedings shall be considered" (Art. 258 CCP-Poland).

As demonstrated, the regulation mentions pre-trial detention first, making it (intentionally or not) a kind of default option for the court compared to other preventive measures that are listed later. In order to use the status quo bias to reduce the number of pre-trial detention orders, the default option should be another measure that is less interfering with human rights and freedoms, in the form of e.g. police supervision, reserving – of course – the possibility of adjudicating another measure (including pre-trial detention), if police supervision turned out to be insufficient or too far-reaching. This type of solution may, on the one hand, make police supervision the default option, and on the other hand, it may make it difficult for the court to order pre-trial detention, requiring it to properly justify why the default measure is insufficient and an alternative measure is necessary. However, it should be noted that this type of solution may prove to be appropriate only temporarily. After all, after some time it may lead to the abuse of police supervision and its use in situations where a better solution would be to order pre-trial detention. The situation would therefore require ongoing monitoring and file and statistical research to verify the current state of affairs.

A potential new regulation could take the following form: "1. Police supervision applies if: 1) there is a justified fear that the accused may take flight or go into hiding, especially when their identity cannot be established or they do not have permanent residence in the country; 2) there is a justified fear that the accused may induce other persons to give false testimony or may otherwise unlawfully obstruct criminal proceedings. 2. If the accused is charged with a crime or a misdemeanour punishable by imprisonment for at least eight years, or if the court of first instance sentenced them to imprisonment for not less than three years, the need to apply police supervision or another preventive measure in order to secure the proper course of proceedings may be justified by the severe penalty threatening the accused. 3. Police supervision or another preventive measure may also be applied in exceptional cases when there is a justified fear that the accused who has been charged with a crime or an intentional misdemeanour may commit an offence against life, health or public safety, especially when they have threatened to commit such an offence. 4. In the situation specified in § 1, instead of police supervision, the court may order another preventive measure. When deciding on the application of a specific preventive measure, the type and nature of the concerns indicated in §§ 1–3, accepted as the basis for applying a given measure, and the severity of their threat to the proper course of the proceedings at a specific stage of the proceedings shall be considered"[39].

To conclude this issue, it should be added that status quo bias may also be important from the perspective of extending pre-trial detention, revoking it or changing it. If the decision on the indicated issues is made by the same panel of judges, it will most likely strive to maintain the consistency of the decision. As indicated in the literature, the choices made in the past are rationalised by the individual, while rejecting or suppressing information that indicates that the decision made in the past was wrong. The rationalisation process extends to current and future choices, ultimately leading to maintaining the current choice. Moreover, according to the self-perception theory of attitudes, individuals establish their basic attitudes and preferences by observing their own behaviour, just as they do in the context of third parties. So they refer to their past decisions when making current and future choices, thinking 'If it was good enough for me then, it is (must be) good enough for me now'. This type of reasoning may lead to maintaining the previously made choice and, consequently, to maintaining the current state of affairs; in the context of pre-trial detention, it may lead to its further application, non-repealing and non-amending)[40]. The existence of this type of situation seems to be confirmed by file research, which shows that: "pre-trial detention in most cases is applied not only throughout the preparatory proceedings, but also during the court proceedings. It very rarely happened that pre-trial detention was revoked or replaced by other preventive measures before a final judgment was issued"[41] and further that: "The average duration of pre-trial detention lasting until the end of court proceedings with a final judgment, which results from the analysis of the files made available to us, is 439 days for cases being heard in regional courts and 223 days for cases being heard in district courts. The longest waiting time in custody for a final judgment that we examined was fortythree months (over three years). However, we did not have access to cases that were still pending in mid-2019. It can therefore be assumed that in reality the average length of pre-trial detention in Poland may be longer and has certainly been increasing in recent years. There are approximately 5,000 people who have been

39 A similar solution, but related to the implicit adjudication of property surety, is suggested by Court Watch Polska (see Z. Branicka et al., *Aktualna praktyka…*, p. 8).

40 See K. Burdziak, 'Dawstwo organów w kontekście skłonności człowieka do bycia konsekwentnym. Rozważania z pogranicza prawa i psychologii', 3 *Probacja* 2021, pp. 118–119.

41 B. Pilitowski, B. Kociołowicz-Wiśniewska, Z. Branicka, 'Kiedy kończy się stosowanie tymczasowego aresztowania' in: P. Karlik, B. Pilitowski (eds.), *Stosowanie tymczasowego aresztowania. Analiza praktyczna*, Warszawa 2022.

in detention facilities in Poland for over a year at the moment (487 people at the end of 2018), although only two years earlier there were only 151 of them"[42]. It cannot be denied that if such a long period of pre-trial detention were to result from a cognitive error, it would be an absolutely unacceptable situation.

It is also worth mentioning another effect, similar to status quo bias; as Kahneman et al. point out: "Professionals who make a series of decisions in sequence, including judges, loan officers, and baseball umpires, lean toward restoring a form of balance: after a streak, or a series of decisions that go in the same direction, they are more likely to decide in the opposite direction than would be strictly justified. As a result, errors (and unfairness) are inevitable"[43]. This is the so-called gambler's fallacy, i.e. not admitting the possibility that the streak may be the result of pure chance[44]. Dockets in custody cases, or rather the method of determining them, may also be of significant importance from the perspective of the situation of the accused.

To avoid the above-mentioned errors, it is suggested to clearly separate the decisions issued in individual custody cases in time and to appoint completely new panels of judges to rule on the issue of extending, revoking and changing pre-trial detention.

4.6. Use of appropriate scales

One way to reduce noise in court decisions on pre-trial detention may also be formulating appropriate standards for the courts regarding the conduct in this type of case, not necessarily resulting from statutory legal acts; standards – what should be emphasised – and not rules, that would strictly bind individual panels of judges, or similarly operating guidelines. These are some general suggestions on how decisions should be made, but without limiting judicial freedom. Such standards could include, among others, the previously mentioned issues of factors that are worth considering when making a decision (it would be worth, for example, suggesting the use of tools based on algorithms, i.e. ensuring the so-called

42 B. Pilitowski, B. Kociołowicz-Wiśniewska, Z. Branicka, 'Czas trwania tymczasowego aresztowania' in: P. Karlik, B. Pilitowski (eds.), *Stosowanie tymczasowego aresztowania. Analiza praktyczna*, Warszawa 2022.

43 See D. Kahneman, O. Sibony, C. R. Sunstein, *Szum, czyli skąd…*, p. 110.

44 See D. Kahneman, O. Sibony, C. R. Sunstein, *Szum, czyli skąd…*, p. 110.

external view[45]), cognitive errors, to which judges are exposed, and how to avoid these mistakes, issues of using the help of a reliable supervisor, etc.

However, regardless of the best-formulated standards, it is necessary to provide appropriate grounds for adjudicating the measure of interest of this work (pre-trial detention) in the form of appropriately formulated conditions for its adjudication. Even the best standards will not be able to overcome, for example, incorrectly constructed scales used by the legislator. It should be recalled that in Poland the conditions for applying pre-trial detention are: 1) establishing that the collected evidence indicates a high probability that the accused has committed a crime (Art. 249 § 1 CCP-Poland); 2) determining that there is, for example, a justified fear that the accused may take flight or go into hiding, especially when their identity cannot be established or they have no permanent place of residence in the country, or a justified fear that the accused may induce other persons to give false testimony or may otherwise unlawfully obstruct criminal proceedings. In the context of the above, a question arises – and not a new one – what the phrases "high probability" and "reasonable fear" mean. Are there any objective scales in this regard? Is there any chance that the indicated wordings will be understood by everyone in the same way, both theoretically and practically?[46]

It is obvious that the legislator had to formulate some condition that would limit the scope of application of the preventive measure of the interest of this work in to a minimum. However, the use of such ambiguous wordings as it is currently encountered in the Polish Code of Criminal Procedure may intensify the noise, which – as previously indicated – should be counteracted. Kahneman et al. rightly point out that: "Judgments that are expressed in such phrases ['beyond a reasonable doubt', 'clear and convincing evidence' or 'unlikely'] are inevitably noisy because they are interpreted differently by both speakers and listeners"[47].

---

45 As D. Kahneman, O. Sibony, C. R. Sunstein, *Szum, czyli skąd…*, p. 438 point out: "When one bases one's view of an issue on one's own individual experience, the result is regularity noise. A statistical outsider's perspective solves this problem: when experts use the same reference class, the noise in their judgements decreases - not to mention the fact that a statistical perspective often yields valuable insights about a particular case". Algorithm-based tools, meanwhile, are based on scientifically developed risk factors and on accumulated, usually very extensive statistical data on cases that have already happened. Such knowledge and tools do not, of course, make it possible to determine without error what will happen in a specific, unique case. They do, however, broaden the perspective of the evaluator or decision-maker and thus increase the objectivity of the process carried out.

46 See M. Żbikowska, 'Prawdopodobieństwo w procesie karnym', 3 *Państwo i Prawo* 2018, pp. 69–81.

47 See D. Kahneman, O. Sibony, C. R. Sunstein, *Szum, czyli skąd…*, p. 224.

Therefore, it is suggested to consider changing the conditions for applying pre-trial detention in such a way that the ambiguity of the wording used is kept to a minimum. How to do this? According to the author, this can be done as follows:

A) In accordance with the current wording of Art. 249 § 1 CCP-Poland: "Preventive measures may be applied to secure the proper course of proceedings, and, in exceptional cases, also to prevent the accused from committing a new, serious crime; they can only be applied when the evidence shows a high probability that the accused has committed a crime". It is suggested to give the indicated regulation the following wording: "Preventive measures may be applied to secure the proper course of proceedings, and, in exceptional cases, also to prevent the accused from committing a new, serious crime; they can only be applied when the evidence collected shows that the accused has committed a crime". In other words, it is suggested to give up on the imprecise scale of probability, discussions about what it is, whether it is greater or lesser, and pointless disputes about whether the level of probability has been properly determined or not (one cannot count on agreement in this regard); it is suggested to move on to the level of substantive discussion, and more specifically, the discussion on whether the collected evidence indicates that the accused has committed a crime or not.
B) In accordance with the current wording of Art. 258 § 1 CCP-Poland: "Pre-trial detention and other preventive measures may be applied if: 1) there is a justified fear that the accused may take flight or go into hiding, especially when their identity cannot be established or they have no permanent place of residence in the country; 2) there is a justified fear that the accused may induce other persons to give false testimony or may otherwise unlawfully obstruct criminal proceedings". It is suggested to give the indicated regulation the following wording: "Pre-trial detention and other preventive measures may be applied if the collected evidence indicates the possibility of: 1) the accused taking flight or going into hiding, especially when their identity cannot be established or they do not have a permanent place in the country stay; 2) the accused inducing other persons to give false testimony or otherwise unlawfully obstructing the criminal proceedings" (subsequent paragraphs of Art. 258 CCP-Poland should be amended similarly). In other words, it is again suggested to move away from discussions about what are supposedly subjective fears and the level of their justification, in favour of – it should be emphasised once more – a substantive discussion about what the collected evidence indicates.In the opinion of the author of this work, the suggested amendments may lead to greater objectivity of decisions on pre-trial detention and thus – reduce noise in this area.

5. Summary

Briefly summarising the above considerations, it should be stated that the work gives a negative answer to the question of whether the Polish legislator has created conditions for Polish courts to make rational decisions regarding the possibility and justification of applying the institution of pre-trial detention in a given case. In other words, the following research hypotheses were confirmed in the work: 1. The Polish legislator has not created conditions for Polish courts to make rational decisions regarding the possibility and validity of applying the institution of pre-trial detention in a given case. 2. It is necessary to make changes in the procedure for making decisions by Polish courts regarding the possibility and validity of applying the institution of pre-trial detention in a given case based on the solutions of modern psychology.

At the same time, the work proposed – based on the findings of C. R. Sunstein, D. Kahneman and O. Sibony – several legal solutions (among others) that could lead to an increase in the chances of (Polish) courts making rational and fair decisions in matters of pre-trial detention. It was proposed, among others, solutions for building panels of judges, supporting the decision-making process of courts and appropriate justification of these decisions[48].

6. Bibliography

Literature

Baron J., *Thinking and Deciding*, Cambridge 2008.

Bernecker A., 'Is Status Quo Bias Explained by Anchoring? Evidence from Survey Experiments', available at: https://www.vwl.uni-mannheim.de/media/Lehrstuehle/vwl/Gruener/StatusQuoBiasAnchoring.pdf [accessed on: September 12th, 2023].

Blasch J., Daminato C., 'Behavioral Anomalies and Energy-related Individual Choices: The Role of Status-quo Bias', 41(6) *Energy Journal* 2020.

Branicka Z. et al., *Aktualna praktyka stosowania tymczasowego aresztowania w Polsce. Raport z badań empirycznych*, Toruń 2019.

48 Irrespective of the decision to make appropriate changes, it is still necessary to verify the level of implementation in practice. As it turns out, legal solutions do not always have a significant impact on practice. See T. Smith, 'The Practice of Pre-trial Detention in England & Wales – Changing Law and Changing Culture', 28 *European Journal on Criminal Policy and Research* 2022, pp. 435–449.

Burdziak K., 'Dawstwo organów w kontekście skłonności człowieka do bycia konsekwentnym. Rozważania z pogranicza prawa i psychologii', 3 *Probacja* 2021.

Burdziak K., 'Przeciwdziałanie przemocy domowej w perspektywie karnoprawnej praktyki prokuratorskiej', submitted to a scientific publisher.

Cialdini R., *Wywieranie wpływu na ludzi. Teoria i praktyka* (trans. B. Wojciszke), Sopot 2020.

Hervada J., *Wprowadzenie do prawa naturalnego*, Kraków 2011.

Kahneman D., Sibony O., Sunstein C. R., *Szum, czyli skąd się biorą błędy w naszych decyzjach* (trans. P. Szymczak), Poznań 2022.

Kamber K., 'The overuse of pre-trial detention as a public policy and human rights problem', available at: https://www.cep-probation.org/the-overuse-of-pre-trial-detention-as-a-public-policy-and-human-rights-problem/ [accessed on: September 12th, 2023].

Li C., 'Primacy effect or recency effect? A long-term memory test of Super Bowl commercials', 9(1) *Journal of Consumer Behaviour* 2010.

Lunenburg F. C., 'Group Decision Making', 20(3) *National Forum of Teacher Education Journal* 2010, available at: http://www.nationalforum.com/Electronic%20Journal%20Volumes/Lunenburg,%20Fred%20C.%20Group%20Decision%20Making%20NFTEJ%20V20%20N3%202010.pdf [accessed on: September 12th, 2023].

Martufi A., Peristeridou C., 'The Purposes of Pre-Trial Detention and the Quest for Alternatives', 28(2) *European Journal of Crime, Criminal Law and Criminal Justice* 2020.

Murphy J., Hofacke Ch., Mizerski R., 'Primacy and Recency Effects on Clicking Behavior', 11(2) *Journal of Computer-Mediated Communication* 2006.

Pilitowski B., Kociołowicz-Wiśniewska B., Branicka Z., 'Obecność oskarżonych, obrońców i prokuratorów na posiedzeniach w przedmiocie zastosowania tymczasowego aresztowania' in: P. Karlik, B. Pilitowski (eds.), *Stosowanie tymczasowego aresztowania. Analiza praktyczna*, Warszawa 2022.

Pilitowski B., Kociołowicz-Wiśniewska B., Branicka Z., 'Kiedy kończy się stosowanie tymczasowego aresztowania' in: P. Karlik, B. Pilitowski (eds.), *Stosowanie tymczasowego aresztowania. Analiza praktyczna*, Warszawa 2022.

Pilitowski B, Kociołowicz-Wiśniewska B., Branicka Z., 'Czas trwania tymczasowego aresztowania' in: P. Karlik, B. Pilitowski (eds.), *Stosowanie tymczasowego aresztowania. Analiza praktyczna*, Warszawa 2022.

Planas A., 'Teen sentenced to life in prison for fatally stabbing Florida cheerleader 114 times', *NBC News*, available at: https://www.nbcnews.com/news/us-news/teen-sentenced-life-prison-fatally-stabbing-florida-cheerleader-114-rcna76550 [accessed on: September 12th, 2023].

Samborski E., 'Forma postanowienia' in: E. Samborski, *Zarys metodyki pracy sędziego w sprawach karnych*, Warszawa 2011.

Samuelson W., Zeckhauser R., 'Status Quo Bias in Decision Making', 1(1) *Journal of Risk and Uncertainty* 1988.

Smith T., 'The Practice of Pre-trial Detention in England & Wales – Changing Law and Changing Culture', 28 *European Journal on Criminal Policy and Research* 2022.

Thaler R. H., Sunstein C. R., *Impuls. Jak podejmować właściwe decyzje dotyczące zdrowia, dobrobytu i szczęścia* (trans. J. Grzegorczyk), Poznań 2017.

Tokarczyk R., *Komparatystyka prawnicza*, Warszawa 2008.

Żbikowska M., 'Prawdopodobieństwo w procesie karnym', 3 *Państwo i Prawo* 2018.

Zieliński M., 'Derywacyjna koncepcja wykładni jako koncepcja zintegrowana', 68(3) *Ruch Prawniczy, Ekonomiczny i Socjologiczny* 2006.

Zieliński M., *Wykładnia prawa. Zasady, reguły, wskazówki*, Warszawa 2012.

Marcin Rau*

VIII. Challenging Legal Education in Pursuit of Judicial Efficiency: A Comparative Analysis of Poland and Italy

Abstract: This article presents a critical comparative analysis of legal education systems in Poland and Italy, juxtaposed against the innovative model at Berkeley Law School in the United States. It underscores the urgent need for challenging traditional legal education to enhance judicial efficiency. The research reveals a significant disconnect between the conventional academic approach and the evolving demands of the legal profession, particularly in the digital age. The study highlights the dissatisfaction among law students in Poland and Italy with predominantly theoretical courses, underscoring their preference for more practical, experiential learning methods. It also examines the influence of Millennials and Generation Z on legal practice, noting their digital fluency and expectations for education that integrates theory with practical application. The article delves into Berkeley's successful integration of Socratic teaching, clinical experiences, and technology-enhanced learning, demonstrating its effectiveness in preparing students for the modern legal landscape. Proposed reforms include a shift from passive to active learning methodologies, the introduction of new, practical courses, and the gradual elimination of outdated subjects. These reforms aim to align legal education with the expectations of new generations, incorporating interactive and technologically advanced teaching methods. In conclusion, the article emphasizes that redefining legal education is crucial for improving the efficiency of the justice system. By enhancing the quality of legal representation, adapting to the dynamic legal environment, and fostering improved communication and negotiation skills, these changes can significantly impact the efficiency of legal proceedings. The article calls for further research in common law countries to explore the implementation and effects of these reforms on legal education and practice.

Keywords: Legal education, judicial efficiency, comparative analysis, Berkeley Law School, Generation Z, pedagogical strategies, educational reforms

1. Introduction

Faced with escalating societal expectations and the dynamic changes within the legal environment, the system of legal education is confronted with challenges that demand immediate attention and reform. In Poland and Italy, this model is

* Assistant Professor, Cardinal Stefan Wyszyński University, Warsaw, Poland.

deeply rooted in a nineteenth-century positivist legal doctrine that reduces law to written texts, thereby marginalizing its practical application. The dominance of a theoretical approach to legal studies, often based on rote memorization, leads to a situation where law graduates enter the professional realm not only unprepared for the effective application of legal knowledge but also devoid of essential soft skills and digital competencies. Such educational deficiencies inevitably reflect on the efficiency of the judiciary system, both in Poland and Italy. This study aims to diagnose the primary causes of this discourse and to suggest possible solutions that may be inspired by the achievements of psychological and cognitive sciences. It will outline the contrasts in legal teaching methods between the countries under analysis and those of common law systems, which will serve as a foundation for formulating recommendations aimed at modernizing the educational process at law universities. Methodologically, this research falls into a niche that has not yet been fully explored in Poland and Italy. Due to the limited availability of extensive empirical research, this analysis is based on available statistical data from selected universities, comparative literature review, and legal doctrine. This methodology, combining comparative and doctrinal analysis, allows for outlining the current state of knowledge and identifying potential paths for educational reform. In the pursuit of understanding and transforming legal education, it will be crucial to apply an interdisciplinary approach that will capture the complexity of the problem and develop practical and theoretically substantiated recommendations.

2. Historical and Contextual Background

The pedagogical philosophy underpinning legal education in Poland, Italy, and indeed across the continental legal tradition, draws heavily from the experiences of nineteenth-century legal positivism. This school of thought predicates the application of law as a purely technical activity, one that involves the objective methodology of applying legal principles to relevant facts[1]. As a consequence of this enduring legacy, today's law graduates often find themselves in a state of professional isolation, ensconced within the autonomous realms of various dogmatic legal sciences and disconnected from the advancements of related disciplines[2].

The academic world has traditionally been oriented towards the projection of the lawyer-scholar archetype. The foundation of knowledge within this particular

1 A. Czarnota, M. Paździora, M. Stambulski, 'Ukryty program w edukacji prawniczej', 2 *Krytyka Prawa* 2018, p. 98.

2 P. Jabłoński, 'Na czym polega poznawanie prawa? O konsekwencjach myśli Gadamerowskiej dla edukacji prawniczej', 3 *Krytyka Prawa* 2016, p. 50.

paradigm lies in the dogmatics of law, wherein the lawyer is anticipated to possess a comprehensive understanding of the established legal framework and the art of scholarly discourse. The evaluation of said knowledge is based on the capacity to articulate and advocate for one's comprehension and analysis of legal principles.

The twentieth-century evolution of universities from institutions serving the elite to those accommodating the masses has precipitated a tripartite estrangement within the academic sphere. As highlighted by P. Jabłoński, the first dimension of this alienation is evident in the diluted interactions between educators and learners[3]. The prevailing model casts the academic teacher in the role of the sole knowledge provider, with students relegated to the passive role of information receivers. This one-directional flow of knowledge from lecturer to student undermines the potential for a more engaging and interactive educational experience.

Simultaneously, the second aspect of this estrangement manifests in the compartmentalization of academic disciplines[4]. The resultant fragmentation has transformed the university landscape into a collection of vocational silos, each insulated from the other. This insularity is not only counterproductive for interdisciplinary learning but also for students within cognate disciplines such as the social sciences and humanities, who find themselves isolated from one another and from the advancements in their respective fields. This isolation is compounded by a pedagogical approach that remains anchored to antiquated nineteenth-century didactic methods, which are increasingly recognized as ineffective for long-term retention and critical engagement with complex material.

The third facet of this academic alienation concerns the diminished role of students in the research process[5]. The current educational climate places undue emphasis on quantitative assessment metrics, often at the expense of qualitative learning processes. This overemphasis on testing and examination can inadvertently prioritize the acquisition of grades over the cultivation of inquiry and research skills, which are vital for the intellectual and professional development of students. This shift towards an assessment-centric model not only narrows the scope of learning but also potentially stifles the development of the analytical and critical thinking skills that are indispensable in the practice of law and the advancement of a robust civic society.

Nevertheless, this methodology has not been devoid of its drawbacks, a reality that has been emphasized in the age of the Internet and further solidified with

3 P. Jabłoński, 'Na czym polega…', p. 50.
4 P. Jabłoński, 'Na czym polega…', p. 51.
5 P. Jabłoński, 'Na czym polega…', p. 51.

the emergence of artificial intelligence. The dissemination of knowledge in the field of legal studies has exhibited inefficiencies and a lack of alignment with student expectations. Despite the incorporation of insights from disciplines like sociology, psychology, and cognitive science, the teaching methods employed in this domain still largely adhere to passive instructional approaches reminiscent of the nineteenth century. These methodologies demonstrate a lack of efficacy in effectively engaging the Millennial and Generation Z cohorts. Moreover, law graduates are often equipped with knowledge that is ill-suited to the rapidly evolving societal context. Today's law graduates are unprepared for independent thought or for contributing to the foundations of a civic society. A state devoid of true elites, competent officials, or lawyers—those who are cognizant of the complex social reality that surrounds them—is fundamentally unable to function properly. As emphasized by A. Skibińska, the situation bears resemblance to an organism suffering from a grave ailment. If this condition remains unaddressed, it will ultimately result in its demise. This can be observed through the emergence of internal chaos, the breakdown of communal bonds, deterioration in international relations, and in extreme cases, the potential for economic and political collapse[6]. To avert such a fate, a thoughtful reconsideration of legal education is imperative, one that aligns it with the current realities. It is essential to harness the potential of other sciences and interdisciplinary insights to reform legal studies, thereby rejuvenating the system to meet the exigencies of contemporary society.

3. Analysis of the Contemporary Legal Education Paradigm

In the realm of legal education, the aspirational model posits that a lawyer should not only utilize the skills acquired at university in their professional practice but also approach their application with a critical eye. Such a professional should be well-equipped to tackle the multifaceted problems of legal practice and capable of effective action. The hallmark of a law graduate should be a nimble intellect, capable of rapid adaptation to the fluctuating conditions of our modern era and the progressively legalistic nature of societal interactions.

Yet, the current state of legal education in Poland and Italy reveals a bifurcation between academic instruction and the vocational training offered by legal corporations. This dichotomy has given rise to two distinct educational objectives and, consequently, two disparate lawyer archetypes[7]. The academic sector remains

---

6 A. Skibińska, 'Prawniczy dataizm ex cathedra', 2 *Krytyka Prawa* 2020, p. 160.

7 G. Resta, 'Quale formazione, per quale giurista' in: B. Pasciuta, L. Loschiavo (eds.), *La formazione del giurista. Contributi a una riflessione*, Romatre-Press 2018, p. 127.

entrenched in the production of the compliant and uncritical lawyer-scholar, with a curriculum steeped in legal dogmatism and a pedagogical approach that often limits students to passive absorption of information. The process of knowledge verification in this setting is reminiscent of a theatrical school, where students are expected to memorize and regurgitate scripted dialogues, albeit without the emotional and reflective nuances that one would associate with the dramatic arts.

Conversely, legal corporations are invested in cultivating the lawyer-practitioner, valuing the practical application of law, innovative thinking, and the craft of argumentation. Here, the emphasis is on the ability to navigate legal challenges, to think creatively, and to clothe legal arguments in the persuasive garb of rhetoric and influence. The measure of success in this context is predicated on efficacy, defined by the judicious application of legal tools to achieve desired outcomes[8].

The present preliminary analysis highlights a significant division within the legal education system, wherein the realms of academia and practice shape distinct lawyer identities. If the primary objective of legal education is to prepare individuals for an unpredictable future and for difficulties that beyond our current understanding, then it is imperative that it cultivates skills that enable students to navigate this uncertain world and make informed decisions. Legal education, therefore, must evolve beyond the mere transmission of knowledge to actively nurturing the critical faculties, problem-solving abilities, and adaptability that are indispensable in the legal profession amidst the complex and dynamic tapestry of contemporary society.

4. Shortcomings in the Current Legal Education System

The present condition of legal education, as indicated by research done at the University of Wrocław in 2017 and the University of Catania in 2022, presents a troubling depiction of a system that emphasizes discipline over education. The present system exhibits a deficiency in effectively connecting the transfer of knowledge with its practical implementation in both professional contexts and within a democratic society[9]. The absence of perceived relevance results in students perceiving their education as an external imposition, only a barrier to professional qualification rather than a purposeful preparation for their future jobs. The lack of connection between the learning process and the students leads to an educational experience that is both unengaging and easily forgotten. This issue is worsened by concerns of

8 A. Czarnota, M. Paździora, M. Stambulski, 'Ukryty program…', p. 101.

9 A. Czarnota, M. Paździora, M. Stambulski, *Nużąca konieczność. Powody podjęcia i ocena studiów prawniczych na WPAE UWr*, Wrocław 2017, p. 14.

an overwhelming amount of coursework and bad relationships between students and teachers. The law faculty in Catania exhibits the lowest degree of satisfaction with the quality of the educational experience compared to other faculties surveyed[10]. The deficiencies inherent in the present-day legal education system can be identified as three fundamental elements, which are applicable to both Poland and Italy: the inadequate method of imparting knowledge, the neglect in instructing new and essential subjects, and the mismanagement of time allocated to subjects that lack relevance in the context of the contemporary legal landscape. In order to enhance comprehensibility and mitigate potential misinterpretations, a thorough examination will be conducted on each of these constituent elements.

4.1. The inadequate method of imparting knowledge

Within the realm of educational techniques, there has been a growing critique of passive learning paradigms. These paradigms primarily rely on instructors as the central source of knowledge transmission. However, they have been found to be inadequate in promoting critical thinking skills and deep understanding. These paradigms place a greater emphasis on the memorizing of information and the reproduction of facts, rather than fostering a comprehensive understanding and practical utilization of the acquired knowledge. Passive learning, although it may sometimes function as an initial stage leading to more interactive educational experiences, has been largely overshadowed by the dominant pedagogical trend favoring active learning methodologies[11]. Active learning, in clear opposition to passive learning, requires students to actively and critically engage with the content being studied. The act of engaging students is frequently achieved by using novel pedagogical frameworks, like project-based learning, the flipped classroom model, and interactive conversations. Research has demonstrated that these approaches effectively improve the retention and practical application of knowledge. The active approaches mentioned are based on constructivist learning theories, which propose that learners engage in the active construction of new

10 F. Verzì, S. G. Cosentino, *Relazione annuale del Nucleo di Valutazione - anno 2022*, UO Ufficio del Nucleo di Valutazione, available at: https://www.unict.it/sites/default/files/files/Relazione_Finale_NdV_2022_completa.pdf [accessed on: October 10th, 2023].

11 L. Deslauriers et al., 'Measuring actual learning versus feeling of learning in response to being actively engaged in the classroom', 116 *Proceedings of the National Academy of Sciences* 2019, pp. 19251–19257.

knowledge by connecting it to their previous cognitive frameworks[12]. The active learning process entails more than the passive acquisition of factual information; it is distinguished by the learner's deliberate production of knowledge. This educational exercise serves as a means of furthering the students' existing knowledge and recognizing their active participation in the learning process. Active learning requires students to engage in critical thinking and reflection, thereby transitioning them from passive recipients of information to active contributors in the generation of knowledge. The transition from a focus on consuming knowledge to actively producing knowledge not only improves learning results but also fosters a deeper and more critical involvement with the subject matter[13]. The assessment of pedagogical efficacy necessitates a critical analysis of certain prevailing educational techniques that need inspection due to their low effectiveness, as extensively documented in psychological and pedagogical literature:

1. Verbal-Only Lectures: The traditional lecture format, predicated on passive listening and note-taking, has been subject to considerable critique for its failure to sufficiently engage students. Empirical studies reveal a stark retention deficit, with students preserving only a fraction of the imparted information[14]. This stands in stark contrast to the demonstrably superior outcomes of active learning—where experience, action, and the practical application of knowledge in tangible contexts reign supreme.
2. Direct Information Transmission: There is a growing recognition that pedagogies which simply transmit knowledge without promoting critical engagement or inquiry are considered inadequate. According to Biggs and Tang, the exclusive focus of educators on delivering content without adequately considering student comprehension might undermine the effectiveness of the learning process[15].

12 Y. Solomon, *Comparison between problem-based learning and lecture-based learning: Effect on nursing students immediate knowledge retention. Advances in medical education and practice*, Taylor & Francis 2020, pp. 947–952.

13 D. Roberts, 'Higher education lectures: From passive to active learning via imagery?', 20 *Active Learning in Higher Education*, 2019, pp. 63–77.

14 See J. D. Bransford, A. L. Brown, R. R. Cocking, *How people learn*, Washington DC 2000.

15 See J. Biggs, C. Tang, *Teaching for Quality Learning at University 5e*, McGraw-Hill Education 2022, *passim*.

3. Memorization-Centric Assessment: Assessment paradigms that place excessive emphasis on rote memorization, as demonstrated by traditional multiple-choice testing, have been criticized for their detrimental effects on fostering profound learning and genuine comprehension. Gardner provides a critical analysis of these approaches, arguing that they restrict creative thinking and do not effectively measure a student's authentic understanding of the subject matter. There is a recommended movement in pedagogy towards a process-oriented approach to learning, which prioritizes the process of acquiring knowledge and developing skills over the final outcome of grades[16].
4. One-Size-Fits-All Materials: There is a growing recognition that educational resources lacking accommodation for the various learning styles and demands of students are deemed useless. The idea of multiple intelligences sheds light on the diverse cognitive profiles of learners, promoting the adoption of a more individualized approach to the design of instructional materials[17].
5. Feedback Deficiency: The lack of regular and constructive feedback poses a substantial obstacle to the enhancement of students' performance and the development of instructors' skills. In the absence of this crucial element, pupils may remain unaware of their academic deficiencies, while educators continue to employ antiquated teaching methods. Hattie and Timperley advocate for the significant impact of feedback on student motivation and learning results, emphasizing its transformative potential[18].
6. Cognitive Overload: Passive learning environments, which involve the unidirectional transfer of large amounts of information, frequently result in cognitive overload, hindering immediate understanding and long-term memory retention. This phenomena highlights the importance of implementing interactive and structured learning experiences that take into consideration the cognitive capacity of students[19].

---

16 See J. Gardner, *Assessment for learning: A compelling conceptualization*, Routledge 2006, pp. 197–204.

17 See H. Gardner, T. Hatch, 'Educational implications of the theory of multiple intelligences', 18 *Educational researcher* 1989, pp. 4–10.

18 J. Hattie, H. Timperley, 'The power of feedback', 77 *Review of educational research* 2007, pp. 81–112.

19 D. Roberts, 'Higher education lectures: From passive to active learning via imagery?', 20 *Active Learning in Higher Education* 2019, pp. 63–77.

7. Andragogical Neglect: The exclusion of andragogy, which pertains to the art and science of adult education and its cognitive research roots, is a notable oversight in current pedagogical practices. According to the concepts of andragogy, effective learning requires active engagement in problem-solving, the involvement of both hemispheres of the brain, and the incorporation of learners' prior experiences. However, the existing absence of mutual communication between educators and learners leads to instructional approaches that do not effectively utilize the diverse range of students' experiences and knowledge[20].

4.2. The omission of essential learning

The examination of present-day legal education necessitates a thorough consideration of the significant inadequacies pertaining to the instruction of fundamental skills: critical thinking, selective information processing and soft skills[21]. Critical thinking is an essential aspect that legal education should cultivate. It entails adopting a thoughtful and introspective approach, allowing legal professionals to scrutinize and assess their own acts, as well as the actions of others, in light of moral principles. The capacity for reflection, referred to as "judgment competence" by L. Kohlberg, pertains to an individual's ability to connect their behavior with their deeply ingrained moral principles[22]. A lack of proficiency in this particular skill frequently results in the emergence of a binary perspective, which in turn predisposes individuals to either resort to violent behavior or surrender to authoritative figures when confronted with circumstances that question their personal actions or views. This can be attributed to their incapacity to provide nuanced justifications for their positions.

Selective information processing has become more important in the legal profession due to the overwhelming amount of data available to practitioners. The ability to distinguish between relevant and extraneous information has become a crucial talent in this era. Hence, it is imperative for the legal educational program to give precedence to the development of discerning information processing

20 D. J. Merritt, 'Legal Education in the Age of Cognitive Science and Advanced Classroom Technology', 63 *Center for Interdisciplinary Law and Policy Studies Working Paper Series* 2007, p. 6.

21 E. Conte, 'Educare il giurista. Le sfide del terzo millennio e le tentazioni della conservazione accademica' in: B. Pasciuta, L. Loschiavo (eds.), *La formazione del giurista. Contributi a una riflessione*, Romatre-Press 2018, p. 115–120.

22 A. Czarnota, M. Paździora, M. Stambulski, 'Ukryty program...', p. 105.

abilities. This will enable aspiring attorneys to effectively navigate the overwhelming volume of information and choose and analyze data that is relevant, reliable, and suitable for their legal pursuits[23].

The growing acknowledgement within the legal industry about the significance of soft skills requires that individuals pursuing a career in law possess a comprehensive understanding of personal branding, self-presentation, as well as the fundamental principles of reasoning and rhetoric. Moreover, it is essential that modern legal practitioners have an extensive knowledge of business principles, as they are required to adeptly traverse the complexities of both legal intricacy and the commercial dynamics inherent in their clients' matters[24]. These talents are not simply supplementary to legal expertise, but rather essential in shaping a legal professional who possesses adaptability, persuasive abilities, and the capacity to excel in the intricate and always changing legal environment.

4.3. Elimination of certain mandatory academic subjects

The findings derived from an extensive study carried out from 2020 to 2023 on a group of 333 students at Cardinal Stefan Wyszyński University in Warsaw reveal a noticeable lack of enthusiasm towards subjects pertaining to the history of law, including Roman Law, Political-Legal Doctrines, and the History of Legal Systems. The quantitative representation of the study's findings is as follows: a total of 27 participants stated a high level of interest, 76 persons indicated a moderate level of interest, and a substantial majority of 220 individuals reported no interest[25]. The evidence presented indicates a distinct inclination among students to view these disciplines as optional rather than obligatory elements of the legal curriculum, appealing mostly to individuals with a particular fascination for the historical aspects of law.

Nevertheless, it is important to highlight the lack of comparable data from Italy, which could potentially reflect the opinions of Polish students. It is possible to hypothesize that the outcomes would exhibit similarity, considering the prevailing patterns in legal education worldwide. However, such conjectures require

---

23 R. Garlati, 'Formazione e professionalizzazione per il giurista del terzo millennio (c'è qualcosa di nuovo…forse di antico…)' in: B. Pasciuta, L. Loschiavo (eds.), *La formazione del giurista. Contributi a una riflessione*, Romatre-Press 2018, p. 162.

24 M. R. Marella, 'Per un'introduzione allo studio del diritto: costruire le competenze di base' in: B. Pasciuta, L. Loschiavo (eds.), *La formazione del giurista. Contributi a una riflessione*, Romatre-Press 2018, p. 69–71.

25 The author conducted a study on a cohort of 333 fourth-year law students, encompassing both full-time and part-time participants, during the period of 2020–2023.

empirical validation through extensive investigation conducted in analogous academic contexts inside Italy. The validation of the findings from Poland, in addition to contributing to a more nuanced comprehension of the educational preferences of law students across many cultural and legal traditions, would be achieved through this approach.

The implications of these investigations can be classified into two separate dimensions. The author's main goal is to emphasise the significance of incorporating curricular adjustments that align more effectively with the interests and professional aspirations of contemporary law students. Furthermore, the author highlights the potential benefits of integrating history-focused legal courses as elective offerings, so enabling students to tailor their academic trajectory in accordance with their individual interests and career aspirations. Additionally, this method facilitates a more focused core curriculum that prioritizes courses that are directly applicable to current legal practice.

5. Comparison with the Common Law System. Case Study Berkeley Law School

The issues discussed in the previous sections pertaining to legal education in Poland and Italy are not only the author's subjective opinion, but rather align with the critical viewpoints of experts from common law nations. According to the observations made by Alberto Alemanno and Lamin Khadar, there appears to be a notable disparity between legal education and real-world practice, notably in Europe. Lawyers and their academic institutions in this region have shown a historical tendency to avoid introspection and critical examination of their own practices[26]. The European legal academic community continues to exhibit a greater inclination towards engaging in discussions over the content of legal education, rather than focusing on pedagogical methodologies[27]. Consistent with this perspective, Oppenheimer claims that a law school is classified as a professional institution, so imposing upon each professor the professional responsibility of imparting knowledge to aspiring legal practitioners[28]. While it is true that a portion of

26 A. Alemanno, L. Khadar, *Reinventing Legal Education: How Clinical Education is Reforming the Teaching and Practice of Law in Europe*, Cambridge University Press 2018, p. 15.

27 A. Alemanno, L. Khadar, *Reinventing…*, p. 15.

28 D. B. Oppenheimer, 'Un modello di formazione giuridica esperienziale', 3 *Questione Giustizia* 2019, p. 106.

students may pursue scholarly paths and engage in academic pursuits, the majority are more likely to enter the legal field and establish themselves as practitioners. Consequently, the conventional approach has been to impart legal analytical skills to students, enabling them to adopt a lawyer's mindset and leverage insights from the legal field in preparation for their future legal profession.

In the realm of Polish and Italian literature, it is widely recognized that legal education in common law jurisdictions does not neglect the study of legal writings[29]. However, the pedagogical method employed in these countries entails a critical examination of both the texts themselves and the underlying doctrines they embody. The Socratic pedagogical approach, which involves the examination of texts within small group settings, is based on the underlying principle that truth is derived through democratic discourse rather than being presented as authoritative doctrine by the instructor[30]. Law schools have also transformed into institutions that foster democratic principles, since students are actively engaged in discussions and are encouraged to articulate their viewpoints and present arguments. The grading system that disallows evaluation just based on a single paper or exam, but rather emphasizes class involvement and essay composition, facilitates the development of participatory and persuasive skills.

Oppenheimer argues that a notable distinction between the United States and Europe lies in the functioning of legal clinics. During the early 20th century, a number of influential figures within the American legal education community advocated for the integration of clinical teaching into law schools as a means to enhance student education[31]. These proponents frequently drew comparisons between the traditional teaching methods employed in law schools and the clinical approaches commonly found in American medical schools, often expressing a preference for the latter[32]. In response to the support of corporate entities, law schools have initiated the provision of legal assistance courses to students, albeit frequently scheduled outside of regular class hours and overseen by professional attorneys. Despite some initial limitations, a movement emerged that regarded the inclusion of clinical training as an essential component of legal education[33].

---

29 V. Zeno-Zencovich, 'Una diversa idea del corso di laurea in giurisprudenza' in: B. Pasciuta, L. Loschiavo (eds.), *La formazione del giurista. Contributi a una riflessione*, Romatre-Press 2018, p. 181–191.

30 D. B. Oppenheimer, 'Un modello...', p. 107.

31 R. Sandefur, J. Selbin, 'The Clinic Effect', 16 *Clinical Law Review* 2009, p. 57

32 P. A. Joy, 'The Uneasy History of Experiential Education in U.S. Law Schools', 122 *Dickinson Law Review* 2018, p. 551.

33 P. A. Joy, 'The Uneasy History...', p. 552.

The advancement of this movement was strengthened by study that concentrated on learning approaches, uncovering that experiential learning, sometimes referred to as "learning by doing" is frequently more efficacious than lectures or Socratic dialogue, even when the objective is to impart analytical abilities[34]. Additional investigation into the fundamental elements that contribute to the professional achievement of a proficient lawyer has broadened our comprehension of the competencies that aspiring students must possess. The traditional view of lawyering emphasized the importance of analytical prowess and writing proficiency. However, contemporary understanding acknowledges that aspiring lawyers must also cultivate additional competencies, such as active listening, task delegation, effective management, negotiation skills, and the cultivation of empathy and compassion.

The Berkeley Law School serves as a notable example of a revolutionary model in legal education, which could potentially serve as a valuable point of reference for Poland and Italy to consider adopting. The incorporation of practical learning into the curriculum of this school has shown to be effective, as it has facilitated the development of a collaborative atmosphere between the judiciary and legal professionals. From the commencement of their legal education, students are fully engaged in experiential learning opportunities. During the initial week, students are encouraged to engage in one of the 33 'Student-Initiated Legal Services Projects' (SLPS)[35]. The aforementioned projects, which are completely driven by students and originated, offer highly valuable practical experience with the supervision of more than 50 active legal professionals[36]. This proactive approach goes beyond undertakings that are undertaken voluntarily. First-year students are required to enroll in a winter semester course that centers on the development of legal research and writing abilities[37]. This is subsequently followed by a summer semester course that aims to refine their skills in both written and oral defense, encompassing simulated trials involving the participation of volunteer lawyers and judges. During the intermission between the initial and subsequent years of academic pursuit, students are presented with an additional prospect to get practical exposure, commonly by engaging in employment at legal offices or law firms. Compared to previous groups, Berkeley students commence their

34 D. B. Oppenheimer, 'Using a Simulated Case File to Teach Civil Procedure', 4 *Journal of Legal Education* 2016, pp. 819–821.
35 D. B. Oppenheimer, 'Un modello…', p. 108.
36 D. B. Oppenheimer, 'Un modello…', p. 109.
37 D. B. Oppenheimer, 'Un modello…', p. 109.

jobs equipped with a solid grounding in reflective practice, owing to their active engagement in SLPS or BLAST initiatives[38].

The curriculum of Berkeley Law School exemplifies the efficacy of experiential learning. The school's prioritization of meaningful involvement in legal cases, especially in the absence of prior legal preparation, stands in stark contrast to the conventional methodologies employed in Poland and Italy. Furthermore, the educational institution cultivates a climate that encourages pro bono endeavors and engagement in community service, wherein students are inspired by their fellow peers to actively partake in such activities. The presence of agency and responsibility is not only a highly influential factor but also an essential component for the advancement of one's professional growth within the legal domain.

The Berkeley model serves as a prime example of how a dynamic and immersive learning environment can successfully align with high educational requirements. This exemplifies the efficacy of integrating conventional legal education with the cultivation of practical skills and a robust professional ethos. The aforementioned method has promise as a constructive foundation for the reformation of legal education in Poland and Italy, offering a more comprehensive, relevant, and practical training for aspiring legal professionals.

6. The Evolution of Legal Education in Response to Generation Z Preferences

The imperative to adapt legal education arises from the necessity to address the evolving requirements and characteristics of Millennials and Generation Z. These generational groups have been significantly influenced by their upbringing in a society that is totally digitalized. The current transition between generations has resulted in a distinct set of anticipations for the field of legal education, placing significant emphasis on the necessity of adopting a pragmatic and career-focused approach. Students born after 1996, belonging to Generation Z, are not only technologically adept but also entrepreneurial, favoring rapid information retrieval from digital sources over traditional methods. Despite their inclination towards digital mediums, they value meaningful personal interactions, indicating a need for a balanced integration of digital and interpersonal skills in their education.

Generation Z students anticipate that legal courses will extend beyond theoretical knowledge to actively develop practical skills such as legal problem-solving

38 D. B. Oppenheimer, 'Un modello...', p. 109.

and negotiation. They seek an educational experience that is tailored to their individual needs, offering personalized options and clear career pathways. Furthermore, they expect their education to leverage their digital capabilities, utilizing technologies like online legal databases, virtual collaboration tools, and courtroom simulation software. Within the field of legal education, students belonging to Generation Z possess the ability to proficiently employ digital tools in order to engage in legal research, access educational resources, and simulate the processes involved in making legal decisions. The integration of technology has the potential to greatly increase active learning approaches, such as Problem-Based Learning (PBL) and courtroom simulations. For example, the utilization of online trial simulation platforms and tools designed for legal data analysis can enhance the educational experience by offering a more engaging and interactive learning environment. These generations may favor more interactive and engaging legal classes that leverage their digital skills. Virtual legal clinics, for example, could allow students to work on real cases through the Internet. They are likely to engage more with interactive e-learning platforms that offer diverse multimedia resources, including video content, online quizzes, and other digital learning tools. Educational institutions face the challenge of providing current and innovative teaching methods that align with the rapid changes in the legal field and technology. The evolution of legal education to meet the needs of Generation Z is not just desirable but essential. This evolution necessitates the adoption of teaching methodologies that are interactive, technologically sophisticated, and focused on preparing students for the practical realities of a legal career in a digital age. By integrating modern technologies and interactive learning strategies, legal education can be restructured to equip the new generation of lawyers for the dynamic and evolving demands of the legal profession.

7. Rethinking Law School: Cutting-Edge Proposals for Reform

The imperative for reform in legal education, a task both challenging and necessary, arises from an inherent human resistance to change. This resistance, deeply rooted in our psychology, stems from a preference for the familiar and a fear of the unknown. It manifests as a reluctance to break away from established thought patterns and an aversion to learning new methodologies. However, the transformation of legal education, particularly in the Polish and Italian contexts, is essential. A paradigm shift towards a model resembling that of Berkeley Law School is likely achievable only when the decision-making is in the hands of the millennial generation. This generation, having grown up in both analog and digital realms, possesses a nuanced understanding of our rapidly evolving reality, making them well-suited to spearhead such changes. The process of managing this transformation is multifaceted and requires a phased approach. It necessitates actions that are gradual and based on a pre-determined current state. The recommended sequence, as outlined in § 4 of the article, involves initially transitioning from passive to active teaching methodologies. This shift would be followed by the introduction of new subjects relevant to contemporary legal practice, and finally, the gradual phasing out of certain traditional subjects that may no longer align with the current needs of the legal profession. In terms of teaching methodology, it is worth considering the adoption of some practices from Berkeley Law School. This includes the introduction of clinical classes that emphasize the practical application of law, thereby bridging the gap between theoretical knowledge and real-world legal practice. Additionally, the development of workshop-style classes focusing on soft skills, such as the psychology of witness testimony, interrogation techniques, and legal argumentation, would significantly enhance the practical skillset of law students. The suggested revisions have the objective of fostering a learning environment that is characterized by dynamism, interactivity, and direct alignment with the practical requirements of the legal field. By incorporating experiential learning and problem-solving activities, legal education can enhance its ability to adequately equip students for the complex and diverse issues encountered in the legal profession. This method is in accordance with the preferences and values of Millennials and Generation Z, guaranteeing that upcoming legal practitioners possess not only a comprehensive understanding of legal principles but also proficiency in analytical reasoning, persuasive communication, and ethical judgment. The main goal is to develop a top-tier team of legal experts that have the know-how to successfully negotiate the complex and dynamic legal landscape, which is constantly influenced by social and technological developments.

8. Final Observations and Future Research Directions

The primary objective of this article has been to illuminate the integral role of legal education in shaping the efficacy of the justice system. This exploration leads to the conclusion that transformative changes in legal education should commence with a reevaluation of the perception of human skills, knowledge, and experience as pivotal elements in this intricate matrix. Education in law begins from the inaugural day at the law faculty, and it is evident that in countries like Poland and Italy, the pedagogical methodologies significantly trail behind those employed in the United States, where active and engaging teaching techniques are the norm. Should the implementation of even a fraction of the proposed reforms prove successful, the justice system could witness substantial enhancements in several key areas:

- Elevated Quality of Legal Representation: The introduction of courses aimed at cultivating soft skills such as communication and empathy could lead to a new generation of lawyers who are more adept at understanding and advocating for their clients. This enhancement in representation skills could translate into more effective courtroom argumentation and a heightened propensity for finding mutually beneficial resolutions.
- Adaptability to the Dynamic Legal Landscape: A curriculum that places significant emphasis on technical literacy has the potential to enhance the abilities of lawyers in properly managing huge data sets and digital tools. This transition has the potential to enhance accuracy and efficiency in the processing of legal cases, potentially transforming certain areas of the legal process by means of automation and advanced data analysis.
- Refined Communication in Legal Processes: Enhanced training in communication skills could enable lawyers to elucidate complex legal matters to their clients more clearly, thereby reducing misunderstandings and elevating client satisfaction. This improvement in client-lawyer communication is crucial for the smooth functioning of the legal process.
- Acceleration of Legal Proceedings: Incorporating project management skills into the legal curriculum could lead to more efficient time and resource management by lawyers. This efficiency could result in expedited legal procedures and progress in cases, thereby reducing the duration of legal proceedings and the associated waiting times for judgments.
- Increased Effectiveness in Negotiations: A focus on negotiation skills within the legal education framework could improve lawyers' proficiency in reaching out-of-court settlements. This skill is invaluable in alleviating the burden on the judicial system and contributes to a more efficient allocation of court resources, offering quicker and potentially less costly dispute resolution alternatives.

This article serves as a preliminary step in a broader research agenda, highlighting the need for further studies that delve into the impact of these educational reforms in common law countries. Such research should aim to track the changes implemented in these jurisdictions, particularly focusing on how they enhance legal awareness and empower law students. The main takeaway is straightforward: in order to educate prospective lawyers for both the opportunities and challenges of the contemporary legal environment, legal education must adapt to the shifting needs of society and the legal profession by incorporating technical know-how and practical skills into its foundation.

9. Bibliography

Literature

Alemanno A., Khadar L., *Reinventing Legal Education: How Clinical Education is Reforming the Teaching and Practice of Law in Europe*, Cambridge University Press 2018.

Biggs J., Tang C., *Teaching for Quality Learning at University 5e*, McGraw-Hill Education 2022.

Bransford J. D., Brown A. L., Cocking R. R., *How people learn*, Washington DC 2000.

Conte E., 'Educare il giurista. Le sfide del terzo millennio e le tentazioni della conservazione accademica' in: Pasciuta B., Loschiavo L. (eds.), *La formazione del giurista. Contributi a una riflessione*, Romatre-Press 2018.

Czarnota A., Paździora M., Stambulski M., 'Ukryty program w edukacji prawniczej', 2 *Krytyka Prawa* 2018.

Czarnota A., Paździora M., Stambulski M., *Nużąca konieczność. Powody podjęcia i ocena studiów prawniczych na WPAE UWr*, Wrocław 2017.

Deslauriers L. et al., 'Measuring actual learning versus feeling of learning in response to being actively engaged in the classroom', 116 *Proceedings of the National Academy of Sciences* 2019.

Gardner H., Hatch T., 'Educational implications of the theory of multiple intelligences', 18 *Educational researcher* 1989.

Gardner J., *Assessment for learning: A compelling conceptualization*, Routledge 2006.

Garlati R., 'Formazione e professionalizzazione per il giurista del terzo millennio (c'è qualcosa di nuovo…forse di antico…)' in: Pasciuta B., Loschiavo L. (eds.), *La formazione del giurista. Contributi a una riflessione*, Romatre-Press 2018.

Hattie J., Timperley H., 'The power of feedback', 77 *Review of educational research* 2007.

Jabłoński P., 'Na czym polega poznawanie prawa? O konsekwencjach myśli Gadamerowskiej dla edukacji prawniczej', 3 *Krytyka Prawa* 2016.

Joy P. A., 'The Uneasy History of Experiential Education in U.S. Law Schools', 122 *Dickinson Law Review* 2018.

Marella M. R., 'Per un'introduzione allo studio del diritto: costruire le competenze di base' in: Pasciuta B., Loschiavo L. (eds.), *La formazione del giurista. Contributi a una riflessione*, Romatre-Press 2018.

Merritt D. J., 'Legal Education in the Age of Cognitive Science and Advanced Classroom Technology', 63 *Center for Interdisciplinary Law and Policy Studies Working Paper Series* 2007.

Oppenheimer D. B., 'Un modello di formazione giuridica esperienziale', 3 *Questione Giustizia* 2019.

Oppenheimer D. B., 'Using a Simulated Case File to Teach Civil Procedure', 4 *Journal of Legal Education* 2016.

Resta G., 'Quale formazione, per quale giurista' in: Pasciuta B., Loschiavo L. (eds.), *La formazione del giurista. Contributi a una riflessione*, Romatre-Press 2018.

Roberts D., 'Higher education lectures: From passive to active learning via imagery?' 20 *Active Learning in Higher Education*, 2019.

Sandefur R., Selbin J., 'The Clinic Effect', 16 *Clinical Law Review* 2009.

Skibińska A., 'Prawniczy dataizm ex cathedra', 2 *Krytyka Prawa* 2020.

Solomon Y., *Comparison between problem-based learning and lecture-based learning: Effect on nursing students' immediate knowledge retention. Advances in medical education and practice*, Taylor & Francis 2020.

Verzì F., Cosentino S. G., Relazione annuale del Nucleo di Valutazione - anno 2022, UO Ufficio del Nucleo di Valutazione, available at: https://www.unict.it/sites/default/files/files/Relazione_Finale_NdV_2022_completa.pdf

Zeno-Zencovich V., 'Una diversa idea del corso di laurea in giurisprudenza' in: Pasciuta B., Loschiavo L. (eds.), *La formazione del giurista. Contributi a una riflessione*, Romatre-Press 2018.

Part II
Digital Justice

Alejandro Hernández López*

I. The European Union's Strategy on Digitalisation of Judicial Cooperation in Criminal Matters: Towards a More Effective Justice in Cross-Border Scenarios?

Abstract: The Commission presented in December 2021 a package of measures to move forward on the objective of digitalisation of judicial cooperation in civil and criminal matters in the European Union. These included the Proposal for a Regulation COM (2021) 759 and the Proposal for a Directive COM (2021) 760 on the digitalisation of judicial cooperation and access to justice in cross-border civil, commercial and criminal matters, whose main objective was to establish the default use of secure digital channels in cross-border judicial cooperation instruments, increasing the effectiveness and swiftness of all proceedings. This paper (drafted in mid-2023) aims to analyse the main aspects of those proposals, which subsequently led to the adoption of Regulation 2023/2844/EU.

Keywords: European Union, digitalisation, judicial cooperation in criminal matters, Proposal for a Regulation COM (2021) 759 final, Proposal for a Directive COM (2021) 760 final

1. Introduction and Background

The digitalization of justice and, specifically, of judicial cooperation in criminal matters, is one of the great unresolved issues in the process of consolidating the Area of Freedom and Justice[1]. The latest Commission data on the digitalization of justice in the European Union show the enormous differences that still exist today between the Member States in terms of the level of digitalization of their justice administration systems[2]. There is an uneven use of digital solutions and

* Associate Professor of Procedural Law, University of Valladolid, Spain. This work is part of the national research project 'Criminal Procedure and the European Union. Analysis and Proposals' (Ref. PID2020-116848GB-I00).

1 European Comission, *Study on the Digitalisation of Cross-Border Judicial Cooperation in the EU – Final Report*, 2021, pp. 28–31 (DOI 10.2838/174474).

2 *The 2023 EU Justice Scoreboard*, pp. 32–38 (DOI 10.2838/619558).

disruptive technologies in justice at national level, which means that most formal exchanges of information between judicial authorities and natural and legal persons still take place in paper format.

From the outset, the digitalization of the Area of Freedom, Security and Justice has always been one of the European Union's objectives. Thus, the JHA Council decided in June 2007 that the use of ICT should be promoted in the field of Justice[3], leading to the creation of the European e-Justice portal[4]. This strategy was gradually developed through the multiannual European e-Justice Action Plan 2009–2013, its successive reissues[5], as well as through the actions and recommendations issued by the European institutions[6]. The use of digital solutions in the field of judicial cooperation in criminal matters started even early on: the use of videoconferencing was already provided for in the 2000 Convention on Mutual Assistance in Criminal Matters between Member States of the European Union (Art. 10). In the same vein, the now repealed Framework Decision 2001/220/JHA allowed for the hearing of victims residing abroad by videoconference (Art. 11).

The COVID-19 pandemic situation has been a real turning point, making the need to push forward the process of digitalization of justice more evident. When face-to-face proceedings were not possible or were severely limited, Member States had to resort to transitional solutions, often supported by digital means, in order to continue with the proceedings. This exceptional situation logically spilled over into the field of cross-border judicial cooperation, slowing down or even paralysing the implementation of most cooperation instruments, including those giving effect to the principle of mutual recognition[7]. The temporary

---

3 F. Bueno de Mata, 'Justicia online y ciudadanía: el portal europeo E-Justicia como medio de información y apoyo a los ciudadanos para solventar sus litigios transfronterizos', 18 *Revista Europea de Derechos Fundamentales* 2011, pp. 194–195.

4 F. Gascón Inchausti, 'La e-Justicia en la Unión Europea: balance de situación y planes para el futuro (en diciembre de 2009)' in: C. Senés Motilla (ed.), *Presente y futuro de la E-Justicia en España*, Cizur Menor: Aranzadi 2010, pp. 83–125.

5 Multi-annual Action Plan 2014–2018 on European e-Justice; Multi-annual Action Plan 2019–2023.

6 See Council Recommendations 'Promoting the use of cross-border video conferencing in the field of justice in the Member States and at EU level and sharing best practices', July 31st, 2015.

7 See *The impact of COVID-19 on Judicial Cooperation in Criminal Matters. Analysis of Eurojust Casework*, May 2021 (DOI: 10.2812/083631).

adoption of solutions based on digital means, solutions that have so far only been applied on an exceptional basis, prevented the total paralysis of these procedures. However, the use of these digital solutions often lacked sufficient legal coverage or even precise technical support and specifications to back them up.

The lessons learned during this fateful period have led Member States and the European Union to consider the need to standardise the use of ICT, making the digitalization of all areas of our society, including judicial cooperation and access to justice, a priority strategy. In this context, in June 2020 the Council adopted its Conclusions on 'Shaping Europe's Digital Future', which included as a priority objective the digitalization of Member States' judicial systems to improve access to justice. As part of this broad objective, the Council asked the Commission to propose measures to facilitate cross-border digital exchanges between Member States in both civil and criminal matters, ensuring the sustainability and continuous development of the technical solutions used for such exchanges. The same month saw the completion of the final report commissioned by the Cross-border Digital Criminal Justice Commission[8], a document that analyses in depth the digital problems and dysfunctions detected over the years by the judicial authorities, bodies and agencies of the Union with an active role in judicial cooperation, including some *lege ferenda* proposals for different future scenarios.

In October 2020, the Council again called on the Commission to present concrete measures to undertake the digitalization of justice. Specifically, in the criminal area, it asked to assess the extension of the Electronic Evidence Exchange Digital System (eEDES), which was already being used in the framework of the European Investigation Order (EIO), to other instruments of judicial cooperation in criminal matters[9]. In December 2020, the Commission published a new Communication on the digitalization of Justice in the European Union[10], including a series of measures aimed at boosting this digitalization at both national and European level. Specifically, it considered the need to increase the resilience of European judicial systems to contingency situations such as the one experienced during the pandemic and foresaw as one of the main lines of action the modernisation of all legislative procedures for judicial cooperation towards the application of the 'digital by default' principle, i.e. the preferential

8 *Cross-border Digital Criminal Justice. Final Report*, June 2020. DOI: 10.2838/118529.

9 See Council Conclusions 'Access to justice: seizing the opportunities of digitalization', in particular Conclusion 27.

10 Document COM(2020) 710 final of December 2nd, 2020.

application of digital channels of communication as a means to improve the efficiency and flexibility of communication, as well as to reduce costs and the administrative burden.

Thus, the Commission incorporated in its work programme for 2021[11] the provision to adopt new specific measures within the so-called 'digital judicial cooperation package'. Among these measures, the creation of a mechanism for the digital exchange of information in cross-border terrorism cases; the creation of a collaborative platform for Joint Investigation Teams; and the proposal of common standards on the digitalization of cross-border judicial cooperation were expressly envisaged. All these initiatives were scheduled to be launched in the fourth quarter of 2021.

As foreseen, the Commission published on December 1st, 2021 a set of proposals aimed at realising some of the objectives formulated on the digitalization of judicial cooperation[12]. In the criminal area, these initiatives are: the Proposal for a Regulation establishing a collaborative platform to support the functioning of the Joint Investigation Teams[13]; the Proposal for a Regulation on the exchange of digital information in terrorism cases[14]; the Proposals for a Regulation and a Directive on the digitalization of judicial cooperation in civil, commercial and criminal matters[15]. As of the date of presentation of this chapter, only the proposal on the collaboration platform for Joint Investigation Teams has been finally adopted[16]. To this legislative package, we must add the recent adoption of Regulation 2022/850/EU on the e-CODEX system, the content of which undoubtedly affects the processing of the rest of the proposals.

Due to its wider material scope, in the following lines we will focus our analysis on the Proposal for a Regulation (and Directive) on digitalization of judicial cooperation and access to justice in cross-border civil, commercial and criminal

11 Document COM(2020) 690 final of October 19th, 2020, *Commission Work Programme 2021: a Union of vitality in a world of fragility*, Annex I, p. 5.

12 D. Reynders, 'Digitalising Justice Systems to Bring Out the Best in Justice', 4 *Eucrim* 2021, pp. 236–237.

13 Document COM(2021) 756 final of December 1st, 2021.

14 Document COM(2021) 757 final of December 1st, 2021.

15 Documents COM(2021) 759 final and COM(2021) 760 final of December 1st, 2021.

16 Regulation 2023/969/EU establishing a collaboration platform to support the functioning of joint investigation teams.

matters (hereinafter, Proposal for a Regulation and Directive DIG), for which legislative negotiations are still ongoing[17].

2. The Proposal for a Regulation on Digitalization of Judicial Cooperation COM(2021) 759 Final

2.1. Objective and scope

The main objective of this initiative is to establish the default use of secure digital channels in the application of all cross-border judicial cooperation mechanisms adopted to date, with the aim of improving efficiency, speed and contributing to savings in material and time costs.

In this respect, the proposed DIG Regulation seeks to introduce a new legal framework for electronic communication between competent authorities, and between natural and legal persons and competent authorities in the field of judicial cooperation in civil, commercial and criminal matters. Specifically, the Commission's initiative seeks to establish common minimum rules on the following issues[18]:

- Electronic communication between competent authorities and between natural or legal persons and competent authorities.
- The use of videoconferencing or similar means of distance communication for purposes other than the taking of evidence in civil and commercial matters[19].
- The implementation of electronic trust services.
- Regulation of the legal effects of electronic documents.
- Electronic payment of fees.

As can be seen, the material scope of the proposed DIG Regulation includes aspects related to cross-border judicial cooperation in civil, commercial and criminal matters. As regards specifically judicial cooperation in criminal matters,

17 Digitalisation of cross-border judicial cooperation, 2021/0394(COD), available at: https://oeil.secure.europarl.europa.eu/oeil/popups/ficheprocedure.do?reference=2021/0394(COD)&l=en, [accessed on: June 15th, 2023]; Digitalisation of cross-border judicial cooperation (amendment of certain directives and framework decisions), 2021/0395(COD), available at: https://oeil.secure.europarl.europa.eu/oeil/popups/ficheprocedure.do?reference=2021/0395(COD)&l=en, [accessed on: June 15th, 2023].

18 X. Kramer, 'Digitising access to justice: the next steps in the digitalisation of judicial cooperation in Europe', 56 *Revista General de Derecho Europeo* 2022, p. 5.

19 The latter is already covered by Regulation 2020/1783/EU.

the material scope proposed by this initiative would concern exclusively the following areas:

- Electronic communication between competent authorities in the context of the acts of Union law specifically identified in Annex II of the proposed DIG Regulation. These acts include all instruments giving effect to the principle of mutual recognition adopted to date[20].
- Use of videoconferencing and other similar means of remote communication in the conduct of criminal proceedings and, in particular, for the hearing of defendants, accused persons and convicted persons.
- Use of trust services and regulation of the legal effectiveness of electronic documents.
- Protection of information transmitted through these media.

As regards its spatial scope, the proposed DIG Regulation would apply to all Member States except Ireland and Denmark in accordance with the *opt in* and *opt out* clauses of their respective protocols[21]. However, Ireland may notify its intention to participate in the instrument at any time.

---

20 Annex II Document COM(2021) 759 final: Framework Decision 2002/465/JHA on joint investigation teams; Framework Decision 2002/584/JHA on the European arrest warrant and the surrender procedures between Member States; Framework Decision 2003/577/JHA on the execution in the European Union of orders freezing property or evidence; Framework Decision 2005/214/JHA on the application of the principle of mutual recognition to financial penalties; Framework Decision 2006/783/JHA of October 6th, 2006 on the application of the principle of mutual recognition to confiscation orders; Framework Decision 2008/909/JHA on the application of the principle of mutual recognition to judgments in criminal matters imposing custodial sentences or measures involving deprivation of liberty for the purpose of their enforcement in the European Union; Framework Decision 2008/947/JHA on the application of the principle of mutual recognition to judgments and probation decisions for the supervision of probation measures and alternative sanctions; Framework Decision 2009/829/JHA on the application, between Member States of the European Union, of the principle of mutual recognition to decisions on supervision measures as an alternative to provisional detention; Framework Decision 2009/948/JHA on prevention and settlement of conflicts of exercise of jurisdiction in criminal proceedings; Directive 2014/41/EU on the European Investigation Order in criminal matters (EIO Directive); Regulation 2018/1805/EU on the mutual recognition of freezing and confiscation orders.

21 See Arts. 1, 2 and 4 *bis* § 1 Protocol no. 21 to the Treaty on the Functioning of the European Union on the position of the United Kingdom and Ireland in respect of the area of freedom, security and justice; Arts. 1 and 2 Protocol no. 22 to the Treaty on the Functioning of the European Union on the position of Denmark.

2.2. Digital communication by default between competent authorities

Chapter II of the proposed DIG Regulation regulates communication by digital means between the competent authorities of the Member States. For the purposes of this initiative, competent authority should be understood to mean the judicial authorities *lato sensu* of the Member States – judges and prosecutors –, bodies and agencies of the Union (e.g. European Public Prosecutor's Office, Eurojust) and other authorities involved in judicial cooperation procedures in accordance with the provisions of legal acts of Union law falling within its scope[22].

The text uses for this purpose a general wording which will make communication by electronic means the default option for the exchange of information between competent authorities. Thus, all references to communications that must or may be established between competent authorities in each of the legal acts covered by the list of cooperation instruments in Annex II of the initiative, including the exchange of forms, will be carried out by digital means using a decentralised, secure and reliable IT system[23]. Therefore, not only will digital communication be the default means to be used by the authorities, but also this communication will have to be carried out through an *ad hoc* IT system with the specific characteristics mentioned above – decentralised, secure, and reliable. The decentralised nature of such an IT system should allow for secure data exchanges exclusively between one Member State and another, without any third party intervention in the content. Although not specified in the Articles of the proposed DIG Regulation, the access points of the system should be based on the e-CODEX platform technology[24].

Despite the mandatory introduction of the 'digital by default' principle for communications between authorities through a decentralised system, the proposed DIG Regulation itself provides for exceptions to the mandatory use of this system. Firstly, it expressly provides for the possibility that the electronic communication cannot be transmitted through the *ad hoc* decentralised IT system because it is not operational due to a temporary outage, or because the nature of the material to be transmitted or exceptional circumstances make its use inadvisable. In such cases, the current wording of the proposed DIG Regulation would allow communication

---

22 E.g. national competent authorities as set out in Art. 2 (c) (ii) EIO Directive, in accordance with Art. 2 (1) of the Proposal for a Regulation COM(2021) 759 final.

23 Art. 3 § 1 Proposal for a Regulation COM(2021) 759 final.

24 See Recital 11 Proposal for a Regulation COM(2021) 759 final in relation to Regulation 2022/850/EU on a computerised system for the electronic cross-border exchange of data in the field of judicial cooperation in civil and criminal matters (e-CODEX system).

to take place by the fastest and most appropriate alternative means, while taking into account the need to ensure that the exchange of information takes place in a secure and reliable manner[25]. This will in practice translate into the possibility of using an alternative transmission system for the exchange of information, provided that this system offers adequate standards of security and reliability. In the absence of further specification in the current text of the initiative, it seems that it will be up to the Member States to determine what kind of alternative systems (e.g. secure e-mail, registered mail) can validly replace the decentralised system in case of temporary disruption of the system or the occurrence of any of the other listed - and currently ambiguously worded - exceptions.

Secondly, where the use of the decentralised computer system is not deemed appropriate in view of the specific circumstances of the communication to be transmitted, any other means of communication may be used[26]. This clause would allow for the subsidiary and exceptional use of more informal means of communication between national authorities, such as conventional e-mail. Again, the current wording of the proposed DIG Regulation is silent as to what specific circumstances might motivate this subsidiary use of non-secure and unreliable communication, so it must be understood that its use will be subject to the prudent discretion of the authorities carrying out the communication themselves. However, the text does expressly prohibit the use of this exception for the exchange of forms provided for in the instruments listed in Annex II (e.g. the exchange of EAW or EIO forms), which should therefore be transmitted using secure and reliable means and preferably electronically[27].

2.3. Use of videoconferencing or other similar means of distance communication in cross-border criminal proceedings

2.3.1. Basic common requirements: the prevalence of consent

Chapter IV, Art. 8 of the proposed DIG Regulation regulates the use of videoconferencing or other remote communication technologies in the course of criminal proceedings with cross-border elements in the Member States of the European Union.

Where the competent national authority of a Member State requests the hearing of an investigated, accused or sentenced person in proceedings under any of

25 Art. 3 § 2 Proposal for a Regulation COM(2021) 759 final.

26 Art. 3 § 3 Proposal for a Regulation COM(2021) 759 final.

27 Art. 3 § 4 Proposal for a Regulation COM(2021) 759 final.

the legal acts listed in Annex II, the competent authority receiving the request should allow participation in the hearing by videoconference or other means of remote communication, provided that the technology is available[28]; the particular circumstances of the case justify the use of such technology[29] and the investigated or sentenced person expresses his or her consent[30]. In relation to the latter requirement, the investigated, accused or convicted person must have the possibility to be advised by a lawyer in accordance with Union law[31] before validly giving his or her consent. Therefore, the proposed DIG Regulation, unlike other EU instruments, makes the express consent of the investigated, accused or convicted person a mandatory precondition for the valid delivery of his statement by videoconference.

The above provision should be considered a general and particularly protective rule, but it must nevertheless coexist with other specific provisions regulating the use of videoconferencing and other similar means in other instruments of judicial cooperation in criminal matters. In this sense, the Proposal for a DIG Regulation itself limits its material scope of application by establishing that its provisions are without prejudice to the provisions of the legal acts set out in Annex II[32]. One of these legal acts is precisely the EIO Directive, which in Art. 24 already regulates in detail the hearing by videoconference of witnesses and experts as well as of the investigated or accused person himself. In relation to the latter case, the EIO Directive, unlike the current Proposal for a DIG Regulation, contemplates the lack of consent of the investigated or accused person as an optional and specific ground for refusal, so that its necessity will depend, to a large extent, on the manner in which each Member State has transposed this provision and on the judicial praxis at the national level[33]. Equally, the EIO Directive is silent on the time and manner

28 Art. 8 § 1 (a) Proposal for a Regulation COM(2021) 759 final.

29 Art. 8 § 1 (b) Proposal for a Regulation COM(2021) 759 final.

30 Art. 8 § 1 (c) Proposal for a Regulation COM(2021) 759 final.

31 In line with the provisions of Directive 2013/48/EU on the right to legal counsel in criminal proceedings and in European Arrest Warrant proceedings and on the right to have a third party informed at the time of deprivation of liberty and to communicate with third parties and consular authorities during deprivation of liberty. For an in-depth analysis of the instrument, C. Arangüena Fanego, 'El derecho a la asistencia legal en la directiva 2013/48/UE', 51 *Revista General de Derecho Europeo* 2014, pp. 1 ff.

32 Art. 8 § 2 Proposal for a Regulation COM(2021) 759 final.

33 From the Spanish perspective, see M. De Hoyos Sancho, 'La Orden Europea de Investigación: reflexiones sobre su potencial efectividad a la vista de los motivos de denegación del reconocimiento y ejecución en España', 49 *Revista General de Derecho Procesal* 2019.

in which this consent must be given and, especially, whether or not it must be informed with the concurrence of legal assistance.

Thus, the general regulation currently pictured in the proposed DIG Regulation differs in key aspects (such as the consent regime) with the specific pre-existing regulation in other instruments already adopted, such as the EIO Directive. The current wording of the proposed DIG Regulation emphasises its subsidiary nature, so it must be understood that more restrictive regulations from the point of view of procedural safeguards will prevail. In our opinion, this approach is erroneous, since the generic and more protective wording proposed in the Proposal for a DIG Regulation, which is also in line with the most current guidelines of the CEPEJ[34] and the case law of the ECtHR on this matter[35], should prevail over any other specific regulations that are less protective. Furthermore, the direct effectiveness and non-transposition requirement of the regulation would allow, once adopted, for a uniform minimum standard throughout the Union, thus putting an end to the current regulatory fragmentation resulting from the disparity of national provisions and the uneven transposition of the EIO Directive in the legal systems of the different Member States. Consequently, during the negotiations, it would be advisable to discuss the possibility of making the regulation on the use of video-conferencing and similar means contained in the Proposal for a DIG Regulation prevail, so that all the specific provisions on the same subject contained in the other legal acts listed in Annex II would only be considered compatible insofar as they do not conflict with the provisions of the new DIG Regulation. This would mean reversing the Commission's current approach and turning what is today a proposal for supplementary regulation into a proposal for preferential application.

2.3.2. Applicable law: the problematic referral back to national law

With regard to the rules applicable to the procedure for holding videoconferences or other means of distance communication, the Proposal for a DIG Regulation merely states that it must be governed by the law of the Member State where the videoconference or other means of distance communication is held, this being

34 *Guidelines on videoconferencing in judicial proceedings*, document adopted by the CEPEJ at its thirty-sixth plenary meeting (June 2021), pp. 14 ff.

35 See ECtHR, *Marcello Viola v. Italia*, October 5th, 2006; ECtHR, *Asciutto v. Italy*, November 27th, 2007; ECtHR, *Shulepov v. Russia*, June 26th, 2008. On the use of videoconferencing and its impact on fundamental rights during the pandemic, P. Gori, A. Pahladsingh, 'Fundamental rights under COVID-19: an European perspective on videoconferencing in court', 21(4) *ERA Forum* 2021, pp. 561–577.

understood as the Member State that organises the videoconference[36]. Naturally, it is on this point that we can find the greatest problems and heterogeneous applications in practice, depending on the provisions of each national legal system.

This issue is particularly relevant from a Spanish perspective[37]. In Spain, there is a Draft Law on Procedural Efficiency Measures (PLEP)[38] that contemplates the limitation of the use of videoconferencing in criminal proceedings. According to its most current wording, the physical presence of the defendant and his or her lawyer will be required, regardless of whether or not the defendant consents to give evidence by videoconference, in all trials for crimes with a custodial sentence of more than five years[39]. This restriction is no more than the maintenance of the restriction that was temporarily introduced due to the pandemic situation[40] by virtue of Law no. 3/2020[41]. Therefore, if the current wording of the PLEP finally succeeds, Spanish law will continue to maintain a strong restriction on the use of videoconferencing for the statements of accused persons that is not contemplated in the Proposal for a DIG Regulation.

It will be also particularly interesting to determine whether the restrictions currently applied at the national level should also be applied, where appropriate, in the execution of videoconferences requested by virtue of cooperation instruments based on the principle of mutual recognition such as the EIO, given the existence of specific regulations in the EIO Directive – the aforementioned Art. 24 – and the current supplementary application of the Proposal for a DIG Regulation in these cases. On this issue, from the Spanish perspective, it is true that neither the

---

36 Art. 8 § 3 in conjunction with recital 19 Proposal for a Regulation COM(2021) 759 final.

37 For an in-depth analysis from the Spanish perspective, see A. Hernández López, 'La digitalización de la cooperación judicial en materia penal en la Unión Europea: propuestas y perspectivas legislativas' in: C. Arangüena Fanego, M. De Hoyos Sancho, E. Pillado González, (eds.), *El proceso penal ante una nueva realidad tecnológica*, Cizur Menor: Aranzadi 2023, pp. 281–306.

38 Available at: https://www.congreso.es/public_oficiales/L14/CONG/BOCG/A/BOCG-14-A-97-1.PDF [accessed on: June 15th, 2023].

39 See Eighth additional provision to the LECrim included in the Draft Law on Procedural Efficiency Measures for the Public Justice Service (PLEP).

40 Regarding the temporal application of this restriction, Supreme Court, Judgment no. 652/2021 is particularly clarifying.

41 See Art. 14 § 2 in relation to the Second Transitional Provision Law no. 3/2020 on procedural and organisational measures to deal with COVID-19 in the field of the Administration of Justice.

EIO Directive nor our transposing law[42] limit the penal scope of application of videoconferencing, nor do they contemplate a specific ground for refusal based on this circumstance[43], so that the restrictions currently contained in Spanish law for domestic proceedings and which will virtually be maintained in the future should not be applied to the cross-border context of execution of an EIO, under penalty of incurring a breach of EU law. It is true that the EIO Directive does provide as a specific optional ground for non-execution that its use in the specific case is contrary to the fundamental principles of the law of the executing State[44], a ground that our transposing law has also made mandatory[45]. But this European public policy clause[46], which is nothing more than a specification of the due protection of fundamental rights[47], should not be applicable in the present case. Given the express consent of the investigated or accused person, the true pillar on which, unless there is a conflict with a relevant public interest examined in the light of the principles of proportionality and necessity, the use of videoconferencing in criminal proceedings should be established, it does not seem reasonable to consider that the application of national restrictions could serve as an additional guarantee of protection of their fundamental rights or act as a fundamental legal principle, especially when the hearing by videoconference may be much more convenient

42 Law 23/2014, on the mutual recognition of criminal decisions in the European Union (BOE no. 282 of November 21st, 2014).

43 It is established case law of the Court of Luxembourg that the application of any ground for refusal in the framework of mutual recognition instruments must be considered as the exception. Cf., inter alia, ECJ, *Aranyosi and Căldăraru*, Joined Cases C-404/15 and C-659/15, April 5th, 2016; ECJ, *Bob-Dogi*, C-241/15, June 1st, 2016; ECJ, *Tupikas*, C-270/17, August 10th, 2017; ECJ, *Piotrowski*, C-367/16, January 23rd, 2018; ECJ, *ML*, C-220/18, July 25th, 2018; ECJ, *Minister for Justice and Equality*, C-216/18, July 25th, 2018; ECJ, *Dorobantu*, C-128/18, October 15th, 2019.

44 Art. 24 § 2(b) Directive 2014/41/EU.

45 Art. 216 § 1 LRM: 'The competent Spanish authority shall refuse the recognition and execution of the European Investigation Order for an appearance by videoconference or other means of audiovisual transmission (…) in cases where the execution of such an investigative measure in a specific case would be contrary to the fundamental legal principles of Spanish law'.

46 L. Bachmaier Winter, 'Prueba transnacional penal en Europa: la Directiva 2014/41 relativa a la Orden Europea de Investigación', 36 *Revista General de Derecho Europeo*, 2015.

47 In the same vein, C. Rodríguez-Medel Nieto, *Obtención y admisibilidad en España de la prueba penal transfronteriza. De las comisiones rogatorias a la orden europea de investigación*, Cizur Menor: Thomson Reuters-Aranzadi 2016, *passim*.

for all parties involved, including the accused, when the specific circumstances make it advisable to do so.

2.3.3. *Conducting the videoconference, confidentiality and documentation of the event*

As for the way in which the procedural act of videoconferencing is carried out and conducted, the Proposal for a DIG Regulation just states that this aspect will also be governed by the provisions of the legal system of each Member State.

The Proposal also establishes that the confidentiality of communications between persons under investigation, accused or convicted and their respective lawyers must be guaranteed both before and during the hearing by videoconference or other means of remote communication[48]. Actually, it means generalising the application of the same rules that already apply in the Member States of the European Union for physical hearings following the national transposition of the directive on the right to legal assistance for investigated and accused persons[49]. Therefore, the challenge really lies in ensuring that the digital IT environment used technically and effectively allows for this confidential communication between the person appearing and his or her lawyer, a condition that it will normally be up to the authority conducting the act to provide[50]. This challenge is even greater when the videoconference takes place in the framework of an EAW and the requested person exercises his or her right to dual legal assistance[51], as confidentiality will not only extend also to the communication with the lawyer appointed in the issuing State, but also to the communications that both lawyers may have in order to coordinate their defence strategy[52].

48 Art. 8 § 4 Proposal for a Regulation COM(2021) 759 final.

49 Art. 3 in conjunction with recital 23 of Directive 2013/48/EU.

50 According to the established case law of the ECtHR, the declarant must be guaranteed a secure and confidential line of communication with his lawyer, or his physical presence under the same conditions. Cf. ECtHR, *Shulepov v. Russia*, June 26th, 2008; ECtHR, *Gorbunov and Gorbachev v. Russia*, March 1st, 2016; ECtHR, *Sakhnovskiy v. Russia*, March 1st, 2018; ECtHR, *Sakhnovskiy v. Russia*, November 27th, 2018.

51 Art. 10 Directive 2013/48/EU; Art. 50 LRM.

52 On this issue, see Opinion 1/21 of the State Prosecutor's Office, pp. 30–31.

Similarly, where the recording of physical hearings is provided for in the national law of the Member State for purely domestic cases, the same rules shall apply to hearings conducted by videoconference or other means of distance communication in cross-border cases[53]. In any event, Member States should take all necessary measures to ensure that these recordings are stored securely and that they are not disclosed publicly.

2.3.4. Protection of minors and the right to effective judicial protection

The initiative provides for the application of special rules in cases where the person under investigation, accused or convicted is a minor[54]. In such cases, in accordance with the provisions of the Directive on procedural safeguards for minors under investigation or accused persons in criminal proceedings[55], the holders of parental authority or another appropriate adult designated by the minor and accepted as such by the competent authority must be notified without delay and before the hearing takes place. The competent authority should take into account the best interests of the child when deciding to agree to the child's appearance by video conference or other means of remote communication.

On the other hand, the Proposal for a DIG Regulation provides that the investigated, accused or convicted person is in any case entitled to effective judicial protection under the national law of each Member State when he/she considers that any of the general provisions of this Article has been infringed[56]. It seems clear that the Commission's intention is to recognise the possibility for the person investigated, accused or convicted to denounce the infringement of any of the general provisions it lays down by means of a judicial remedy in accordance with the applicable rules of national law. However, taking again into account the limited scope and the subsidiary nature of the current text of the proposed DIG Regulation with respect to its own provisions, it is not clear what exactly will be the scope of application of this right of appeal, which could also collide with the

---

53 Art. 8 § 6 Proposal for a Regulation COM(2021) 759 final.

54 Art. 8 § 5 Proposal for a Regulation COM(2021) 759 final.

55 Arts. 3 § 2 and 5 § 2 Directive 2016/800/EU. On the application of this rule from a practical perspective, see F. Garrido Carrillo, J. Jiménez Martín, 'Guide to Good Practices in Procedural Treatment of Minor Offenders. The Procedural Guarantees of Suspected or Accused Minors in Criminal Proceedings' in: C. Arangüena Fanego, M. De Hoyos Sancho, A. Hernández López, (eds.), *Procedural Safeguards for Suspects and Accused Persons in Criminal Proceedings. Good Practices Throughout the European Union*, Cham: Springer 2021, pp. 73–80.

56 Art. 8 § 7 Proposal for a Regulation COM(2021) 759 final.

current regulation of the Member States in the application of certain cross-border cooperation instruments[57].

2.4. Electronic identification and legal effects of electronic documents

Chapter V of the proposed DIG Regulation seeks to standardise the use and recognition of digital document and signatures in the field of judicial cooperation. On this point, the proposed DIG Regulation again uses a referral clause[58] to Regulation 910/2014/EU on electronic identification and trust services for transactions in the internal market. Thus, the provisions on trust services set out in Regulation 910/2014/EU should apply to all communications by electronic means that will be introduced by default in the proposed DIG Regulation[59]. Similarly, for electronic communications between competent authorities where a document transmitted as part of the communication requires or contains a handwritten seal or signature, qualified electronic seals and signatures may be used interchangeably in accordance with the provisions of the above-mentioned Regulation[60].

With regard to the legal effectiveness of electronic documents, the proposed DIG Regulation expressly prohibits that their effectiveness can be denied in the context of cross-border judicial proceedings solely on the grounds that they are submitted in electronic form[61]. This clause will prevent the acceptance of such documents from being made conditional on their format, thus equating the validity and effectiveness of physical and electronic documents submitted in the proceedings. Obviously, the judicial authorities will have to apply the same admission

57 This could be the case in Spain in those cases in which the recognition and enforcement of an EIO is carried out by the Public Prosecutor's Office, since according to Art. 24 § 4 LRM, the decree adopted cannot be appealed against, without prejudice to possible challenges on the merits before the issuing authority and its subsequent assessment in the criminal proceedings in the issuing State. On the latter issue, *cf.* ECJ, *Gavanozov II*, C-852/19, November 11th, 2021. From the perspective of the Spanish issuing authorities of OEI, see F. J. Garrido Carrillo, 'Debilidades de la Orden Europea de Investigación (OEI) en la lucha contra la delincuencia organizada' in: F. J. Garrido Carrillo, V. Faggiani (eds.), *Lucha contra la criminalidad organizada y cooperación judicial en la UE: instrumentos, límites y perspectivas en la era digital*, Cizur Menor: Thomson Reuters-Aranzadi 2022, pp. 53–54.

58 Art. 9 § 1 Proposal for a Regulation COM(2021) 759 final.

59 Art. 9 § 2 Proposal for a Regulation COM(2021) 759 final.

60 Art. 9 § 3 Proposal for a Regulation COM(2021) 759 final.

61 Art. 10 Proposal for a Regulation COM(2021) 759 final.

regime as for documents in physical format, so that they will still be able to justifiably refuse their effectiveness, even when the cause is specific to electronic documents. However, they will in no case be able to require their mandatory production in physical format as a condition for their full validity.

2.5. Establishment of the decentralised IT system and costs

The proposed DIG Regulation provides for an obligation on the Commission to adopt implementing acts to establish the decentralised IT system. This includes the following[62]:

- The technical specifications defining the methods of communication by electronic means for the purpose of the decentralised IT system.
- The technical specifications of the communication protocols.
- Information security objectives and relevant technical measures to ensure a minimum standard of information security and a high level of cybersecurity in the processing and communication of information through the decentralised IT system.
- The minimum availability objectives and possible technical requirements related to the services provided by the decentralised IT system.

The timeframe for the adoption of these implementing acts differs widely depending on the instrument to which they are to apply. The initiative proposes a staggered implementation, ranging from a minimum of two years from entry into force (e.g. EAW Framework Decision) to a maximum period of six years (e.g. JIT Framework Decision).

As regards the implementation costs of the system, the Commission will be responsible for the creation, maintenance and development of the reference implementation software that Member States may choose to apply as their *back-end* system instead of their own national IT system[63]. This system will be funded from the EU budget and the Commission will be required to provide, maintain and support this software free of charge[64].

As regards the costs of the decentralised IT system and the national IT portals, these will be shared between the different actors involved in cross-border judicial cooperation – Member States, bodies, offices and agencies of the Union. The costs of installing, operating and maintaining the access points of the decentralised

62 Art. 12 Proposal for a Regulation COM(2021) 759 final.
63 Art. 13 § 1 Proposal for a Regulation COM(2021) 759 final.
64 Art. 13 § 2 Proposal for a Regulation COM(2021) 759 final.

system will be borne by the Member State in which they are located[65]. They will also have to bear the costs of setting up and aligning their national IT systems with the access points to make them interoperable - one of the pillars of the digitalization strategy - as well as the costs of administering, operating and maintaining these systems[66]. To meet these costs, Member States may apply for support under EU funding programmes[67], following the model of the e-CODEX project.

The Union agencies and bodies shall also bear their own costs of installation, operation and maintenance of the components comprising the decentralised IT system for which they are responsible[68]. They shall also bear the costs of adjusting their case management systems to make them interoperable with the national access points, as well as their administration, operation and maintenance costs[69]. For its part, the Commission shall bear all costs related to the European electronic access point[70].

2.6. Protection of transmitted information

One of the major concerns for Member States and for the Union institutions, bodies, offices and agencies is to ensure the security and confidentiality of information and data transmitted by digital means[71]. On this point, in the criminal field, the Proposal for a DIG Regulation does not add anything new, as it merely establishes that the competent authority under the applicable legal act in each case must be considered the controller for the purposes of the provisions of Directive 2016/680/EU[72] with respect to the processing of data sent or received through the decentralised computer system[73]. Similarly, the Commission itself should be

65 Art. 14 § 1 Proposal for a Regulation COM(2021) 759 final.
66 Art. 14 § 2 Proposal for a Regulation COM(2021) 759 final.
67 Art. 14 § 3 Proposal for a Regulation COM(2021) 759 final.
68 Art. 14 § 4 Proposal for a Regulation COM(2021) 759 final.
69 Art. 14 § 5 Proposal for a Regulation COM(2021) 759 final.
70 Art. 14 § 6 Proposal for a Regulation COM(2021) 759 final.
71 In this regard, see the conclusions of the Opinion of the European Economic and Social Committee on the Proposal for a Regulation COM(2021) 759 final and the Proposal for a Directive COM(2021) 760 final (Document SOC/711-EESC-2022, May 18th, 2022), in which the security and confidentiality of communications are considered essential features for the viability of the system.
72 Art. 3 § 8 Directive 2016/680/EU.
73 Art. 15 (1) Proposal for a Regulation COM(2021) 759 final.

considered as the controller for the purposes of Regulation 2018/1725/EU with regard to personal data processed by the European electronic access point[74].

In any case, the competent authorities should ensure that information considered confidential and transmitted to another competent authority in the context of judicial proceedings of a cross-border nature is kept confidential in accordance with the national law of the Member State receiving such information[75].

2.7. Amendment of legislative acts

In the area of judicial cooperation in criminal matters, the text of the proposed DIG Regulation incorporates provisions for the reform of the only legislative instrument of all those listed in Annex II that was adopted by means of a regulation: Regulation 2018/1805/EU on the mutual recognition of freezing and confiscation orders.

The amendments proposed for this legislative act are essentially limited to introducing in its Articles the obligation of communication by electronic means by default between competent authorities derived from Art. 3 Proposal for a DIG Regulation[76] in the terms that have already been analysed previously.

3. The Proposal for a Directive COM(2021) 760 Final

3.1. Rationale and objective scope

In parallel to the Proposal for a DIG Regulation, the Commission has launched a proposal for a Directive on the digitalization of judicial cooperation (Proposal for a DIG Directive). In fact, this directive does not introduce anything new with respect to what is already provided for in the Proposal for a DIG Regulation but is a complementary and purely instrumental legislative act that serves as a suitable channel for reforming certain legislative instruments - mostly in the criminal field - listed in the annexes of the Proposal for a DIG Regulation. Thus, the use of an additional legal act for this work is exclusively due to the constraints imposed by primary law, which means that certain acts – framework decisions and directives – need to be amended using a directive[77].

---

74 Art. 15 § 2 Proposal for a Regulation COM(2021) 759 final.

75 Art. 15 § 3 Proposal for a Regulation COM(2021) 759 final.

76 Art. 23 Proposal for a Regulation COM(2021) 759 final.

77 In this regard, see the Explanatory Memorandum to the Proposal for a Directive COM(2021) 760 final.

Consequently, the main and only objective of the proposed DIG Directive is to transpose the new provisions of the proposed DIG Regulation, especially those deriving from its Art. 3 – transmission of information between competent authorities by electronic means – and Art. 8 – use of videoconferencing – to all those acts that cannot be reformed by a regulation[78]. In criminal matters, these acts are all those listed in Annex II, with the exception of Regulation 2018/1805/EU.

3.2. Spatial scope and deadlines for transposition

As with the proposed DIG Regulation, in principle all Member States except Ireland and Denmark will participate and will be obliged to transpose the provisions of the proposed DIG Directive in the event that it is finally adopted.

As regards transposition deadlines, a general common deadline of two years is set, but this must be linked to the deadlines for implementation of the implementing acts set out in the Proposal for a DIG Regulation for each of the legislative acts in Annex II[79]. As a result, the following transposition table is proposed:

- Framework Decision 2002/584/JHA (EAW), Council Framework Decision 2008/909/JHA and Directive 2014/41/EU (EIO): two years from the adoption of the implementing act referred to in Art. 12 (3) of the proposed DIG Regulation. In other words, a maximum of four years (2+2) from its adoption.
- Framework Decision 2003/577/JHA, Framework Decision 2005/214/JHA, Framework Decision 2006/783/JHA and Framework Decision 2009/948/JHA: two years from the adoption of the implementing act referred to in Art. 12 (5) of the proposed DIG Regulation. In other words, a maximum of seven years (5+2) from its adoption.
- Framework Decision 2002/465/JHA, Framework Decision 2008/947/JHA and Framework Decision 2009/829/JHA: two years from the adoption of the implementing act referred to in Art. 12 (6) of the proposed DIG Regulation. That is, a maximum of eight years (6+2) from its adoption.

4. Conclusions

Following the analysis above, it can be concluded that the proposed DIG Regulation - and the accompanying DIG Directive - introduces a general legal framework and provides legal certainty on key aspects of cross-border judicial

78 See Arts. 1–11 Proposal for a Directive COM(2021) 760 final.

79 See Arts. 12–15 Proposal for a Directive COM(2021) 760 final.

cooperation, such as the exchange of information by digital means, the use of videoconferencing, or the legal effect of electronic signatures and documents. This should lead to faster and more efficient cooperation, in line with the EU strategy, with a positive impact in terms of material, time and environmental costs[80].

Notwithstanding, the initiative sometimes suffers from a lack of ambition and a lack of concreteness. Communication by default between national authorities through a decentralised, secure and reliable digital system, one of the main objectives of this initiative, is in fact tempered by the inclusion of up to two different exceptions that allow its use to be circumvented. Likewise, the general framework it establishes for the hearing of persons under investigation, accused or convicted by videoconference, which is broadly protective and built around consent, is overshadowed by its subsidiary nature and the constant reference to the national law of the Member States. This greatly reduces its actual scope of application and its harmonising capacity.

In addition to the current proposal's lack of ambition and specificity on certain issues, there are other general problems that affect the text as a whole. There is a lack of attention to the impact that this digitalization process may have on individuals - the so-called digital divide - and, in particular, on the guarantees of those under investigation, accused and convicted. On the other hand, the impact of this digital divide on legal operators themselves, as well as the volume of costs derived from the implementation of digital media and systems and, above all, from training in the use of these systems, are not reflected with sufficient clarity in their impact assessment. The long implementation and transposition periods in the current texts, which in certain cases can be up to eight years after the adoption of the DIG Regulation, do not help either, which can lead to a kind of premature obsolescence of its provisions.

The legislative iteration of the package of proposals presented by the Commission is proceeding smoothly. The Economic and Social Committee has recommended the improvement of key aspects of security, the application

80 According to data from the impact assessment of the Proposal for a Regulation COM(2021) 759 final, the overall average annual savings at EU level are estimated at € 23,372,900 in postage costs and € 2,216,160 in paper costs, for a total of € 25,589,060. Individuals and legal entities will save € 4,098,600 in postage and € 388,800 in paper costs. Furthermore, 874 person/years will be saved in the processing effort at the level of courts and competent authorities. The use of the digital channel is also expected to have a positive environmental impact, due to the use of less paper and postage.

of the open justice principle and the avoidance of the digital divide[81]. For its part, the European Parliament has already proposed a set of amendments to the proposal aimed at improving the guarantees and rights of the parties in the proceedings, extending and improving the wording of key aspects of the proposal[82]. It is expected that in the coming months an agreement will be reached on the Proposals for a Regulation and the DIG Directive that have been analysed here. The adoption of the e-CODEX Regulation has undoubtedly given a major boost to this process by providing internal consistency and legal certainty to the provisions of the proposals relating to the use of a decentralised, secure and trusted information exchange system.

Despite the problems highlighted throughout this brief study, this is a legislative package that has real potential to bring judicial cooperation in the European Union into the digital age. However, we should not lose sight of the fact that all these proposals are still in the legislative debate period, so it is very possible that their content will change substantially before their final adoption. In any case, the process of digital transition of judicial cooperation in criminal matters is already underway, and its inevitable culmination will represent a qualitative leap for the Area of Freedom, Security and Justice in terms of greater efficiency and resilience.

5. Bibliography

Literature

Arangüena Fanego C., 'El derecho a la asistencia letrada en la directiva 2013/48/UE', *Revista General de Derecho Europeo* 2014, 51.

Bachmaier Winter L., 'Prueba transnacional penal en Europa: la Directiva 2014/41 relativa a la Orden Europea de Investigación', 36 *Revista General de Derecho Europeo* 2015.

Bueno de Mata F., 'Justicia online y ciudadanía: el portal europeo E-Justicia como medio de información y apoyo a los ciudadanos para solventar sus litigios transfronterizos', 18 *Revista Europea de Derechos Fundamentales* 2011.

De Hoyos Sancho M., 'La Orden Europea de Investigación: reflexiones sobre su potencial efectividad a la vista de los motivos de denegación del reconocimiento y ejecución en España', 49 *Revista General de Derecho Procesal* 2019.

81 EESC, *Digitalisation. Challenges for Europe*, available at: https://www.eesc.europa.eu/sites/default/files/files/qe-01-19-295-en-n.pdf [accessed on: June 15th, 2023].

82 Report A9-0062/2023, March 9th, 2023, available at: https://www.europarl.europa.eu/doceo/document/A-9-2023-0062_EN.pdf [accessed on: June 15th, 2023].

Garrido Carrillo F., Jiménez Martín J., 'Guide to Good Practices in Procedural Treatment of Minor Offenders. The Procedural Guarantees of Suspected or Accused Minors in Criminal Proceedings' in: Arangüena Fanego C., De Hoyos Sancho M., Hernández López, A. (eds.), *Procedural Safeguards for Suspects and Accused Persons in Criminal Proceedings. Good Practices Throughout the European Union*, Cham: Springer 2021.

Garrido Carrillo F. J., 'Debilidades de la Orden Europea de Investigación (OEI) en la lucha contra la delincuencia organizada' in: Garrido Carrillo, F. J., Faggiani V. (eds.), *Lucha contra la criminalidad organizada y cooperación judicial en la UE: instrumentos, límites y perspectivas en la era digital*, Cizur Menor: Thomson Reuters-Aranzadi 2022.

Gascón Inchausti I F., 'La e-Justicia en la Unión Europea: balance de situación y planes para el futuro (en diciembre de 2009)' in: Senés Motilla, C. (ed.), *Presente y futuro de la E-Justicia en España*, Cizur Menor: Aranzadi 2010.

Gori P., Pahladsingh, A., 'Fundamental rights under COVID-19: an European perspective on videoconferencing in court', 21(4) *ERA Forum* 2021.

Hernández López A., 'La digitalización de la cooperación judicial en materia penal en la Unión Europea: propuestas y perspectivas legislativas' in: Arangüena Fanego C., De Hoyos Sancho M., Pillado González E. (eds.), *El proceso penal ante una nueva realidad tecnológica*, Cizur Menor: Aranzadi 2023.

Kramer X., 'Digitising access to justice: the next steps in the digitalisation of judicial cooperation in Europe', 56 *Revista General de Derecho Europeo* 2022.

Reynders, D., 'Digitalising Justice Systems to Bring Out the Best in Justice', 4 *Eucrim* 2021.

Rodríguez-Medel Nieto C., *Obtención y admisibilidad en España de la prueba penal transfronteriza. De las comisiones rogatorias a la orden europea de investigación*, Cizur Menor: Thomson Reuters-Aranzadi 2016.

Marianna Biral*

II. The Italian Route towards Digitalisation of Criminal Proceedings – The Latest Developments in the Field of Remote Justice

Abstract: On the path towards the digitalisation of the criminal proceedings pursued by the Legislative Decree n. 150/2022 the enhancement of remote justice paradigm plays a key role. By exploiting the experience gained during the COVID-19 pandemic, when audiovisual links have shown their potential in terms of time saving and efficiency for the judicial system, the legislator decided to make participation by videoconference a stable and general alternative to in-presence participation for a wide range of acts and hearings (evidence-taking procedure included) provided that concerned persons give their consent. After an overview of the milestones in the evolution of meaning and scope of remote justice within the realm of the Italian criminal procedure the paper tries to answer two questions: how does the new piece of legislation fit within the academic and jurisprudential debate developed on the matter over the years? Is the current framework capable of combining in a satisfactory manner efficiency and guarantees?

Keywords: Remote justice, participation by videoconference, virtual hearing, defense rights, right to confrontation

1. Introduction

In 2022 the Italian legislator promulgated an ambitious reform (the so-called 'Cartabia reform') aimed at meeting three demanding imperatives: to reduce by 25% the so-called 'disposition-time', i.e. the average time needed to adjudicate the case; to reduce the backlog in the courts; to simplify and rationalise the criminal justice system[1].

One of the pillars of the reform is digitalisation, with a wide range of measures aimed at making criminal proceedings faster, more technology-oriented and possibly 'paperless'. In addition to the implementation of the digital dossier and notification mechanisms, which largely take advantage of the digital domicile, the consistent expansion of remote justice stands in this perspective. As has been noted in literature, this is one of the most sensitive aspects of the reform

---

* Junior Assistant Professor of Criminal Procedure, University of Trento, Italy. The paper has already been published in 10(2) *Revista brasileira de direito processual penal* 2024.

1 Legislative Decree no. 150/2022.

as it calls into question the rights of the defence and the adversarial nature of criminal proceedings. At the same time, it is clear that the push towards remote participation in acts and hearings may well satisfy the demands for efficiency on which the new legislation is based.

Against this background, the aim of this essay is to analyse the new broad regulation on remote justice. In this perspective, after reviewing the milestones in the implementation of the remote justice paradigm in the field of criminal procedure and the related academic and jurisprudential debate from early 1990s to the present day, particular attention is paid to the key role played by the consent clause, which appears in each of the new cases of remote participation in acts and hearings. The thesis presented here is that, despite its theoretical suitability for facilitating the technological 'switch' without significant cost to fundamental rights, it may not function properly in practice. In this respect, some proposals are made to smooth out the identified criticalities and to improve the perspective of a knowing and intelligent waiver to the right to physical presence in criminal proceedings.

2. First Steps, Stabilization and Growth

At the dawn remote justice was enclosed within narrow bounds. It was in 1992 that the Italian legislator first opened the doors to audiovisual links as a means of participating in criminal hearings (Art. 7 Law Decree no. 306/1992, converted into Law n. 356/1992). That was a dramatic year for Italy: two of the most famous anti-Mafia magistrates (Giovanni Falcone and Paolo Borsellino) were assassinated by the criminal organization they were investigating. In response to these tragic events, the legislator introduced numerous measures, both substantive and procedural, to strengthen the fight against organised crime. One of these measures was the introduction of the first case of 'remote examination' (*esame a distanza*) of witnesses[2]. In particular, under (the early version of) Art. 147 *bis* CCP-Italy Implementing Provisions (from here on CCP-Italy Imp. Prov.) it was provided that testimony of collaborators of justice[3] could be taken remotely, provided that the technological facilities were available. The purpose of this provision was to protect these

---

2 The term is used here in a broad sense, including also co-accused persons.

3 As is well known, the term refers to persons accused or convicted of participating in a criminal organisation, who agree to cooperate with the judicial authorities, in particular by testifying about the criminal organisation and the crimes committed by its members, in exchange for protection) from the State. At the European level on this matter see Recommendation n. 5/2009 and, more recently, Recommendation n. 9/2022, available at: https://search.coe.int/cm/pages/result_details.aspx?objectid=0900001680a5fe33 [accessed on: May 27th, 2024].

people – who were often the target of deadly attacks, especially in those years – by avoiding their presence in the courtroom and by keeping the remote location secret[4].

A further step forward was taken in 1998 (Law no. 11/1998), when Art. 147 *bis* CCP-Italy Imp. Prov. was broadened in scope[5] and another application of video-conferencing was regulated: 'remote participation' (*partecipazione a distanza*) in organised crime trials[6] for defendants serving a custodial sentence or in pre-trial detention, in the event of serious threats to security or the complexity of the trial (with the exception of dangerous inmates, who must in any case participate remotely). The rationale in this case was to avoid the transfer of these persons from one prison to another (in order to allow them to attend the numerous trials in which they were involved as defendants), mainly in order to prevent the possibility of contacts between the members of the criminal association (Art. 146 *bis* CCP-Italy Imp. Prov.)[7].

These early implementations of remote justice were conceived as special measures to be adopted for security reasons, typically in criminal proceedings against organised crime. They were also designed to be in force for a limited period of time and not as a permanent feature of procedural law. For these reasons, the response of the majority of scholars has not been one of total rejection. Although the detrimental effects on the rights of the defence and on the adversarial model – particularly in terms of the reduced fluidity and effectiveness of cross-examination, and the greater difficulty for the remotely connected defendant to follow what happens in the courtroom and to consult his or her lawyer in confidence – were not ignored, and indeed were clearly highlighted, the rules on video-links were essentially accepted as the outcome of a fair balancing between the protection of fundamental rights and the public interest[8].

---

4 See D. Curtotti, 'Esame a distanza', *Enciclopedia del diritto* 2008, Annali II, 1, p. 201.

5 This is mainly due to the fact that the remote examination of witnesses (unless in case the presence of the witness in the courtroom was necessary) become mandatory for collaborators of justice but also for co-accused persons when they were called to testify in organised crime proceedings.

6 And also in hearings in chambers (Art. 45 *bis* CCP-Italy Imp. Prov.) such as preliminary hearing and the hearing of abbreviated proceedings.

7 See D. Curtotti, 'Dibattimento a distanza', *Enciclopedia del diritto* 2008, Annali II, 1, p. 164.

8 At least with respect to the cases strictly tight to the said rationale and not inspired by the need to speed up the proceedings. See G. P. Voena, 'Il telesame' in: E. Zappalà (ed.), *L'esame e la partecipazione a distanza nei processi di criminalità organizzata*, Milano 1999, pp. 104 ff.; M. Bargis, 'Videoconferenza' in: E. Zappalà (ed.), *L'esame e la partecipazione a distanza nei processi di criminalità organizzata*, Milano 1999, pp. 48 ff.; D. Curtotti, *I collegamenti audiovisivi nel processo penale*, Milano 2006, pp. 285 ff.

The Constitutional Court has also given the green light. In 1999 it ruled that the use of video-links as an alternative means of participating in court hearings is in line with the rights of the defence (Art. 24 of Italian Constitution, hereinafter IC), in so far as the technology guarantees effective and concrete participation on the part of the accused and confidential communication with defence counsel[9]. In this perspective, technical aspects have played a significant role in the recognition of the constitutional legitimacy of 146 *bis* CCP-Italy Imp. Prov. In particular, the fact that the provision required a two-way (bidirectional) link capable of guaranteeing mutual visibility between the persons present in the courtroom and those – the defendants – at the remote location has been positively highlighted.

The effect of the decision of the Constitutional Court, together with the substantial approval by the European Convention of Human Rights[10] and the reduction in the costs of IT equipment led to the conversion of the cases of remote justice from temporary to permanent solutions (Law no. 279/2022). Moreover, in the following years the scope of Arts. 146 *bis* and 147 *bis* CCP-Italy Imp. Prov. experienced a steady growth.

---

9 Constitutional Court, Judgment no. 342/1999. For a critical comment on the judgement, see C. Conti, 'Partecipazione e presenza dell'imputato nel processo penale: questione terminologica o interessi contrapposti da bilanciare?', 6(1) *Diritto penale e processo* 2000, pp. 79 ff.

10 In the case *Marcello Viola v. Italy* the Strasbourg Court found that the virtual participation in the appeal hearings (under Art. 146 *bis* CCP-Italy Imp. Prov.) by the defendant: *a)* "pursued legitim aim" under the Convention "namely prevention of disorder, prevention of crime, protection of witnesses and victims [...] and compliance with the 'reasonable time' requirement in judicial proceedings" as the applicant was accused of serious crimes related to Mafia's activities; *b)* did not put the defense at a substantial disadvantage as compared with the other parties to the proceedings as the accused by taking advantage of the audiovisual link had an opportunity to exercise the rights and entitlements inherent in the concept of a fair trial (ECtHR, *Marcello Viola v. Italy*, October 27th, 2006, §§ 71–76). Manifestly ill-funded was evaluated also the application in the case *Asciutto v. Italy* (ECtHR, November 27th, 2007). On the contrary, in the case *Zagaria v. Italy* (ECtHR, November 27th, 2007) the Court found a violation of Art. 6 ECHR, but not due to the fact that participation by videoconferencing is as such contrary to the Convention neither is Art. 146 *bis* CCP-Italy Imp. Prov. The problem was with how the provision, in particular the part concerning the confidentiality of the communications between lawyer and defendant, had been actually applied.

In 2010 a new case of 'remote examination' was introduced for undercover agents (Art. 147 *bis* § 3 (*c bis*) CCP-Italy Imp. Prov.): unless their presence in the courtroom is considered absolutely necessary by the judge, they are examined remotely and their face is shaded[11].

Then in 2017 an important change to remote participation's scheme[12]. By virtue of Law no. 103/2017 the use of video-links, in case of security needs and great complexity of the trial, has become possible also in criminal proceedings other than those against organised crime and regardless of the fact that the defendant is *in vinculis* or not (Art. 146 *bis* § 1 *quater* CCP-Italy Imp. Prov.). Furthermore, it has been provided that persons detained for offences related to organised crime and defendants benefiting from protection programs (*id est* collaborators of justice) shall always participate in their proceedings remotely, the only exception being if their physical presence at the hearing is deemed necessary by the judge (Art. 146 *bis* §§ 1, 1 *bis* and 1 *ter* CCP-Italy Imp. Prov.)[13].

The remarkable extension of participation through videoconferencing has been accompanied by a new approach to it. The fact that the use of audiovisual links has become the rule (rather than the exception) for some categories of persons[14], and is now possible in all criminal proceedings provided, *inter alia*, that the trial is complex, has altered the original rationale for the provision: not only the needs of public safety but also efficiency justify the sacrifice of the physical presence of the accused. This in turn reflects the idea that virtual presence, if supported by appropriate technology, can be a perfect substitute for physical presence.

The new regulation and its conceptual premises have caused a stir among scholars. A wave of polemical voices has filled the pages of law journals. The majority view has always been (ant still is) that virtual presence, even when supported by

---

11 Art. 8 Law no. 136/2010.

12 For a detailed perspective on the piece of legislation, see N. Triggiani, 'La partecipazione a distanza' in: E. Mezzetti, L. Luparia (eds.), *La legislazione antimafia*, Bologna 2020, pp. 538 ff.

13 Stands still the special rule concerning maximum-security prisoners who remotely participate to the proceedings in each and every case, with no exception.

14 See S. Signorato, 'L'ampliamento dei casi di partecipazione a distanza dell'imputato tra logiche efficientistiche e menomazioni difensive', *La legislazione penale* 2017, p. 5, available at: https://www.lalegislazionepenale.eu/wp-content/uploads/2017/11/S.-Signorato-Lampliamento-dei-casi-di-partecipazione-a-distanza.pdf [accessed on: May 27th, 2024].

the best technology, cannot be equated with physical presence[15]. This is because, when the accused is behind the screen, the exercise of the rights and entitlements is far from ideal. This is not only because of the less fluid and rapid communication with the lawyer standing elsewhere, but also because of the (far from insignificant) risk that less care and attention will be paid by the judge to what the defendant says, does and asks, with the effect of weakening the impact of self-defence. On a different level, participation by videoconference has a negative impact on the adversarial model of criminal proceedings, in that the physical distance makes cross-examination less sharp and 'biting'[16] - it ends up resembling an interview rather than a proper examination with adverse effects on the ability of such a method to expose and discourage lies and fabrications[17]. Immediacy and orality also seem to be curtailed, even where the most sophisticated software and instruments are used. As it has been noted, since it is extremely difficult, if not even impossible, in videoconferencing looking at both the camera lens and the image

15 Among those who support such opinion with a variety of arguments and perspectives, see M. Daniele, *La formazione digitale delle prove dichiarative. L'esame a distanza tra regole interne e diritto sovranazionale*, Torino 2012. p. 19; A. De Caro, 'La partecipazione al dibattimento a distanza', 23(10) *Diritto penale e processo* 2017, pp. 1136–1137; S. Lorusso, 'La mutata fisionomia della partecipazione a distanza al dibattimento e il *vulnus* alle garanzie difensive' in: S. Lorusso (ed.), *Il fragile mosaico delle garanzie difensive. Dalla legge Orlando alle scelte della XVIII legislatura*, Torino 2020, pp. 220 ff.; D. Negri, 'Atti e udienze "a distanza"': risvolti inquisitori di una transizione maldestra alla giustizia penale' in: D. Castronuovo, M. Donini, E. M. Mancuso, G. Varraso (eds.), *Riforma Cartabia: la nuova procedura penale*, Milano 2023, pp. 454 ff.; S. Signorato, 'L'ampliamento dei casi di partecipazione a distanza…', pp. 12 ff.; G. P. Voena, 'Il teleseme…', p. 83.

16 For example, without a full perception of the source of evidence and his or her reactions, the parties lack the information needed to decide whether to 'squeeze' the witness or avoid insisting on a particular issue.

17 The argument is refuted by R. Susskind, *Online courts and the future of justice*, Oxford University Press 2019, pp. 231 ff. The Author claims that: "there is nothing inherent in the concept of online courts that requires the abandonment of the adversarial system […]. At the heart of the adversarial system is not the oral hearing but that the arguments are presented from both sides and that a judge sits impartially in deciding between competing accounts of facts and law. An online court can happily accommodate this mode of disputation and decision-making – parties set out their arguments through online argument and submission of evidence, while judges can sit as impartially at their dining room tables as they do in the courtroom".

of other participants at the same time, this would compromise the impression of eye contact[18].

If all this is true – this is the conclusion of the reasoning – it is highly questionable whether the remarkable expansion of participation by videoconference and, in particular, its transformation from a solution to be enforced when it is necessary to protect sources of testimony or to prevent the planning and commission of crimes by members of dangerous criminal associations to an option in the service of the efficiency of the criminal justice system is in conformity with the Italian Constitution, in particular with Art. 24 § 2 IC, which declares the inviolability of the right of defense, and Art. 111 § 4 IC, according to which the evidence in criminal proceedings must be gathered through the cross-examination in accordance with the adversarial model[19]. The guarantee of a reasonable duration of the trial is not a legitimate objective for the use of audiovisual technologies, since efficiency cannot be pursued at the expense of fundamental rights - quite the opposite, an efficient criminal proceedings assumes as its premises the acknowledgement of guarantees[20].

The suspicions of constitutional illegitimacy raised by scholars have so far been neither confirmed nor rejected by the Constitutional Court so far. Meanwhile exceptional circumstances have fostered a huge resorting to remote justice, like never before.

---

18 A. Falcone, 'Online Hearings and the Right to Effective Defence in Digitalized Trials' in: L. Bachmaier Winter, S. Ruggeri (eds.), *Investigating and Preventing Crime in the Digital Era*, Springer 2022, p. 204.

19 See M. Daniele, 'La partecipazione a distanza allargata', *Diritto penale contemporaneo* 2017, pp. 6 ff., available at: https://archiviodpc.dirittopenaleuomo.org/upload/9865-daniele2017a.pdf [accessed on: May 27th, 2024]; D. Negri, 'La gigantesca espansione della videoconferenza come alternativa alla presenza fisica dell'imputato in giudizio', LXX(1) *Archivio penale* 2018, Special issue, pp. 582 ff.

20 See Corte Cost., Judgment no. 317/2009 where the Court clarified that the right of defence and the principle of reasonable duration of the trial cannot be compared, for balancing purposes, independently of the completeness of the system of guarantees. What matters is exclusively the duration of the 'fair' trial. A different solution would introduce a logical and legal contradiction within Art. 111 IC itself, which on the one hand would impose full protection of the confrontation principle and on the other would authorise all the exceptions deemed useful for the purpose of shortening the duration of proceedings. A trial that is not 'fair', because it lacks guarantees, does not conform to the constitutional model, whatever its duration.

3. Anti-COVID 19 Legislation

The tendency to employ audiovisual links as a substitute for physical presence of the persons involved in the criminal proceedings – not only witnesses and defendants but also other parties and the judicial authority – hit a peak after the outbreak of the COVID-19 pandemic[21].

In order to avoid the paralysis of judicial activities during the toughest phases of contagion, the legislator has relied heavily on remote justice[22]. The regulatory interventions that took place between 2020 and 2022 were many and fast-paced. They followed a fluctuating trend, alternating pushes and backs up in line with the various phases of worsening and easing of the contagion in Italy[23].

The most innovative development was the decision to implement something close to the 'virtual hearing' model, i.e. a hearing where all participants are outside the courtroom. The discrepancy with the model depended on the exception concerning the judge assistant who had to be present in the courtroom in every case in order to fulfil his reporting duties.

It represented a significant step forward: under the anti-COVID 19 regulation video-links moved from being an option designed for selected people or specific evidentiary acts to a generalised and overarching solution covering the entire trial and affecting all those involved in it with the effect of making the proceedings a sum of virtual connections. This has been described as a form of 'dematerialization' of the criminal proceedings[24].

This remarkable progression was made under the pressure and urgency imposed by the spreading of the pandemic and with a short time horizon, in the sense that the solutions adopted were clearly seen as temporary.

---

21 For an overview on the approach undertaken beyond the Italian borders during the pandemic period, see A. Falcone, 'Online Hearings and the Right to Effective Defence…', pp. 194 ff.

22 Similarly to what has happened in other States. An overview of how European courts have dealt with videoconferencing during the COVID-19 pandemic is available at: https://www.osce.org/files/f/documents/5/5/469170.pdf [accessed on: May 27th, 2024].

23 For a close perspective on this, see B. Galgani, *Forme e garanzie nel prisma dell'innovazione tecnologica*, Milano 2022. pp. 235 ff.; S. Napolitano, 'Dall'udienza penale a distanza all'aula virtuale', *Sistema penale* 2020, available at: https://www.sistemapenale.it/pdf_contenuti/1594123110_napolitano-2020a-udienza-penale-a-distanza-aula-virtuale-teams-dalla-legge-27-2020-alla-legge-70-2020.pdf [accessed on: May 27th, 2024].

24 E. M. Mancuso, 'La dematerializzazione del processo al tempo del COVID-19', *Giurisprudenza penale* 2020, available at: https://www.giurisprudenzapenale.com/wp-content/uploads/2020/05/EMMancuso_gp_2020_5.pdf [accessed on: May 27th, 2024].

This has had an impact on the way the legislator has worked. Scarce attention was paid to the rule of law (Art. 111 § 1 IC). In this sense, it has been highlighted the absence of a legislative regulation on the technical aspects of the virtual hearing (operating system, connection mode, etc.) and the decision to give the Director of the information technology services in the field of criminal justice the authority and capacity to determine these essential aspects[25]. On a different note, it was also noted that the chosen IT platforms (*Microsoft Teams* and *Skype for business*) were structured in such a way that did not guarantee the openness of the trial since they were accessible by a limited number of people and only by invitation[26], which had a negative impact on the principle of publicity, which is an expression of the principle of popular sovereignty (Art. 1 IC) and one of the ways in which the participation of the people in the administration of justice is fulfilled (Art. 102 § 3 IC).

However, it was another aspect that attracted the strongest criticism. Initially the 'quasi-virtual hearing' model was also to be applied to the sensitive phases of the trial namely the gathering of evidence and the closing statements of the parties. But due to the strong disapproval of scholars and lawyers' associations the rule was soon abolished.

The criticism surrounding the perspective of an entire evidence-taking procedure carried out remotely called (and calls) into question Art. 111 § 4 IC, the constitutional provision according to which evidence in criminal proceedings must be gathered through the cross-examination in accordance with the adversarial model. As already mentioned[27], the main opinion in the Italian literature is that confrontation, when carried out remotely, loses its strength and becomes something different from what is prescribed at the constitutional level. This means that audiovisual links are lawfully adopted only if one of the exceptions allowing a departure from the confrontation principle established by Art. 111 § 5 IC is met (consent, misconduct, impossibility of carrying out face-to-face confrontation)[28]. At the time, the legislator did not follow this path (at least not immediately and not in a consistent and systematic way) and the proposal of an online evidence-taking procedure was strongly opposed. With the Cartabia reform things turned out differently, as we will see in a moment.

---

25 See O. Mazza, 'Distopia del processo a distanza', LXXII(1) *Archivio penale* 2020, p. 4.

26 See G. Borgia, 'Dibattimento a distanza e garanzie costituzionali: spunti di riflessione a partire dall'emergenza sanitaria', *Osservatorio AIC* 2023, p. 196, available at: https://www.osservatorioaic.it/images/rivista/pdf/2020_6_23_Borgia.pdf [accessed on: May 27th, 2024].

27 See *supra*, § 2.

28 G. Borgia, 'Dibattimento a distanza e garanzie costituzionali...', pp. 191–192.

4. Current Setting: Cases

We are now back to the starting point namely the Legislative Decree no. 150/2022 which is the latest piece in the legislative puzzle concerning remote justice. As already mentioned, the assumption underlying this piece of legislation is one of deep trust in technology and its ability to achieve the goals of the reform – making the proceedings faster and more efficient – without prejudice for defence rights and the general principles of criminal proceedings. In this perspective, the proposition was to provide a solid and comprehensive basis for the use of audiovisual links in order to make it a stable and secure (in terms of guarantees) mode of participation in the proceedings, also in light of the experience gained during the pandemic.

The legislator decided to work 'by addition'. Basically the old cases provided for by Arts. 146 *bis* and 147 *bis* CCP-Italy Imp. Prov. have been retained and many new ones have been added. In this respect, the articulated framework resulting from the juxtaposition between pre-existent and new provisions can be examined from two different perspectives: one focused on the acts and hearings included within the scope of videoconferencing (objective perspective) and another one that looks at the subjects whose participation in the proceedings can be supported by technological facilities (subjective perspective).

From the first point of view, it can be said that the use of audiovisual links has no limits today, as it is an option not only at the trial phase, but also – at the request of the person concerned – at the preliminary stage and within the framework of precautionary measures' procedures (re-examination procedure for orders directing a coercive measure according to Art. 309 CCP-Italy, confirmation hearings in case of arrest or temporary detention pursuant to Art. 391 CCP-Italy). It also covers both hearings (in whole or in part) and individual acts (questioning of the suspected person, non-repeatable technical ascertainments etc.).

The choice to apply the remote justice paradigm also to the preliminary phase is, on the whole, commendable in the sense that it allows a concrete saving of time and resources without having a significant negative impact on guarantees. However, there are two options that seem to be controversial. The first concerns non-repeatable technical ascertainments. If remote participation appears to be perfectly suitable for preliminary activities, such as the appointment of experts, the same cannot be said for the technical assessment itself, which normally consists of complex activities and procedures[29]. The case of confirmation hearings

29 See E. A. A. Dei-Cas, 'La partecipazione "parzialmente smaterializzata": il grimaldello del consenso a favore dell'economia processuale', *La legislazione penale* 2023, p. 18, available at: https://www.lalegislazionepenale.eu/wp-content/uploads/2023/04/DEI-CAS-Definitivo.pdf [accessed on: May 27th, 2024].

following arrest or temporary detention can also be criticised. In this respect, it should be stressed that, even if the judicial control of the measure does not explicitly include an assessment of the detained person's state of health, these are aspects that should nevertheless be taken into account, given the particular vulnerability of the person concerned[30]. After all, the evocative phrase used to refer to the need for judicial control of deprivation of liberty measures – *habeas corpus* – suggests a physical dimension of such an assessment – a physical dimension that is inevitably cut off by video-links[31].

As for the trial phase, the rule contained in the new § 2 *bis* of Art. 496 CCP-Italy represents a step forward as compared to the previous regime (including pandemic legislation[32]). It provides that, upon consent of the parties, the entire evidence-taking procedure may be carried out remotely.

Turning to the second perspective, there is also a broad and permissive approach at the subjective level. Under the new legislation, all private parties, legal representatives and sources of testimonial evidence (lay persons, experts, co-accused persons etc.) can participate in acts and hearings via audiovisual links. Only the judge and the public prosecutor are required to be physically present in court[33]. It can be said that the legislator decided to maintain something in between a virtual and a traditional – physical – hearing: a *phygital* hearing[34].

Overall, the new scenarios are remarkable. The combination of innovations occurred at the objective and subjective levels gives us the image of an institution that is deeply and stably rooted in the system.

---

30 There is support for such a view in the document elaborated in October 2020 by OCSE on 'The functioning of courts in the Covid-19 pandemic. Primer', available at: https://www.osce.org/files/f/documents/5/5/469170.pdf [accessed on: May 27th, 2024]. In the section dedicated to "fair trial concerns" relating to the use of audiovisual links it is recalled that the UN Human Rights Committee has clarified that detainees have the right to appear in person – physically – before the court when the legality of the restriction of personal liberty must be assessed by the competent legal authority.

31 On structure and essential contents of the guarantee, see M. Daniele, *Habeas corpus. Manipolazioni di una garanzia*, Torino 2017, *passim*.

32 See § 3.

33 It can be inferred by the joint consideration of Arts. 496 § 2-*bis* CCP-Italy and 146 *bis* § 4-*bis* CCP-Italy Imp. Prov. For the shared view that such provision is in breach of the equality of arms principle (Art. 111 § 3 Cost.) see D. Negri, 'Atti e udienze "a distanza"...', p. 454.

34 An evocative neologism referring to the coexistence and reciprocal interaction between digital and physical dimensions. It is available at: https://www.treccani.it/vocabolario/figitale_(Neologismi)/?search=figitale [accessed on: May 27th, 2024].

5. … and Mode of Videocoferencing

The wide recognition of videoconferencing and the aim of giving it a stable and rational allocation within the system can also be inferred from the introduction of a general and comprehensive regulation on the technical aspects of the use of video links and the range of guarantees to be recognised (Art. 133 *ter* CCP-Italy).

Firstly, it is stated that, under the penalty of nullity, videoconferencing facilities must ensure "contextual, effective and reciprocal" visibility and audibility between those present in the courtroom and those connected from remote locations, in order to guarantee the right to confrontation and an effective participation in the act or hearing (§ 3).

As far remote locations are concerned, there is a fundamental distinction to be made: people facing custodial sentence or pre-trial detention participate from the place of detention, whereas people not subject to restrictions on their personal liberty participate from a judicial office (or police office) designated by the court, subject to verification of the availability of the necessary technical equipment (§§ 4 and 5). In the latter case, the court may also authorise the connection from another place, provided that the parties have been heard (§ 6). Special rules apply to lawyers who may connect from their offices or any other adequate place, unless they prefer to be with the person they are assisting. In any event, the right to confidential communication between lawyers and clients is guaranteed (§ 7).

An assistant to the judge or the public prosecutor or a police officer must be present at the place where the persons participating to the act or hearing by remote access are located in order to certify and report on the regularity of the procedure and the absence of obstacles to the excercise of rights (§ 8). It is also prescribed that the Ministry of Justice shall ensure the security and integrity of the transmission of data between the courtroom and the remote locations (Art. 147 *quater* CCP-Italy Imp. Prov.).

In case of public hearing, the court ensures that what happens in the remote location can be seen and heard not only by the parties and the judicial authority but also by the public.

The influence of the constitutional jurisprudence (Judgement no. 342/1999) and also of the Guidelines on videoconferencing in judicial proceedings delivered in 2021 by the European Commission for the Efficiency of Justice (CEPEJ) can be seen behind this articulated set of rules. Both convey the idea that the quality, integrity and security of technological facilities play an essential role in guaranteeing the enjoyment of rights. With regard to these aspects, the introduction of a nullity (of the decree authorizing the use of video links) in the event that the technological equipment does not guarantee effective participation in the act or hearing, and the attention paid to the need for security and integrity of the data transmitted over the links deserve particular recognition. On the other hand, more could have been done with regard to the description of the type, number and direction of the cameras, which are aspects of paramount importance in order to guarantee the realism of remote participation and the effective excercise of rights[35].

6. Due Process by Remote: Where Are We?

Despite the faith in technology on which the broadening of remote justice is based, the new legislation does not support the idea that videoconferencing is perfectly comparable to the experience of being present. This is clear from the fact that, in all the cases recently introduced, in order for remote participation to be authorised, it is necessary for the persons concerned to express their will and for all the parties involved to agree when the use of audiovisual links relates to the taking of evidence (at the preliminary hearing or at trial).

Such a requirement reflects the view, shared by the majority of scholars[36], that virtual participation is not the same as in-person participation, that cross-examination is somewhat different when parties and witnesses are not face-to-face and, more generally, that justice is better served when litigants gather in the same place – a public physical space where everyone accommodated can look each other in the eyes.

Against this background, consent plays a key role in the new legal framework for remote justice, as already mentioned. With the exception of cases where participation by videoconference is based on Arts. 146 *bis* and 147 *bis* CCP-Italy Imp. Prov., the authorisation of audiovisual links depends on the expression of the persons concerned. Such an expression of will is essential in order to respect the constitutional guarantees. By requesting or accepting to participate in the act or hearing by videoconference the parties, and in particular the defendant, freely waive that part of the right of defence which is impeded by the virtual connection without prejudice to Art. 24 IC. Moreover, the consent of the defendant is one of the conditions under which the constitutional rule that the the evidence-taking procedure must be adversarial may be derogated from (Art. 111 § 5 IC).

---

35 See B. Galgani, 'La c.d. remote justice nella riforma Cartabia', 175(5) *Giurisprudenza italiana* 2023, p. 1183.

36 See *supra*, § 2.

Is the overall picture satisfactory? Does it dispel any doubts of constitutional illegitimacy? Leaving aside the opinion that the extent of the dematerialization of judicial activities achieved by the 'Cartabia reform' is such that the new virtual proceedings is so different from the traditional and constitutionally-driven criminal process that it cannot be considered constitutional despite the introduction of the consent clause[37], there is room for doubt that the legislator has achieved a satisfactory balance between efficiency and guarantees. If we look at the way in which consent is obtained, we can see that little or no attention is paid to essential aspects: is the consent to be expressed explicitly or implicitly? Is it a personal or a technical choice, in the sense that it can be validly expressed by the lawyer without special authorisation (*procura speciale*) from the client? Is the declaration of will revocable?

The vagueness of the law makes it difficult to find sure answers to these questions even though they are important and sensitive matters. Given the structural asymmetry of powers between the State and the individual in the realm of criminal proceedings, provisions on the waiver of guarantees may in practice encourage haggling and bargaining to the detriment of the 'weak part' in the proceedings – the accused – who may be tempted to give up his rights in order to obtain a 'reward'[38]. We see this, for example, in the area of agreements on the use of evidence gathered during preliminary investigation for the establishment of facts. The judge is more inclined to be lenient and to recognise mitigating circumstances if the defendant agrees to the use of such acts. However, it is clear that behind this approach there is a recognition on the part of the system that consent is not a 'neutral' choice as it should be[39].

Against this background, it is important to minimise the risk of expressions of will which are not personal, knowing and intelligent. Although the structural and unavoidable asymmetry of powers between the State and the individual will always make the criminal proceedings a slippery slope for negotiation – in the

37 The opinion is upheld by D. Negri, 'Atti e udienze "a distanza"...', p. 457.

38 For a broad perspective on the relationship between procedural agreements and criminal justice, see A. Camon, 'Accordi processuali e giustizia penale: la prova patteggiata', 63(1) *Rivista di diritto processuale* 2008, pp. 55 ff.

39 See F. Nicolicchia, 'Consenso del difensore all'acquisizione dibattimentale degli atti d'indagine e riconoscimento delle attenuanti generiche. Riflessioni all'incrocio tra diritto e processo penale', *La legislazione penale* 2020, available at https://www.lalegislazionepenale.eu/wp-content/uploads/2020/06/Nicolicchia-opinioni.pdf [accessed on: May 27th, 2024].

field of remote justice as well as in any other field where it is allowed – strict rules on the waiver of rights could certainly help to prevent injustice and abuse.

7. Conclusive Remarks: the Importance to Take the Consent Seriously

The scenario described above invites the elaboration of a solid and clear scheme for the interpretation of the 'consent clause' provided for in each of the new rules on participation in acts and hearings by videoconference. Given the importance of the consent clause for the respect of constitutional guarantees (Arts. 24 and 111 IC), a strong commitment to take it seriously would be a (small but) decisive step to open up the perspective of remote justice as a technological switch capable to pursue efficiency without (undue) prejudice to fundamental rights.

This means, on the one hand, that an explicit expression of will should always be required, even in cases where the implementation of audiovisual links is not subjected to a specific request on the part of the persons concerned but the wording of the law refers generally to the 'consent' of these persons[40].

Secondly, the choice should not be considered as a 'technical' one, in order to avoid the risk that the decision to accept the participation by videoconference could be driven by the personal interest of the lawyer (who may be tempted to give the consent in order to win the good will of the judge also with regard to other proceedings) or by his/her negligence[41].

Thirdly, revocation of consent should be allowed. This is particularly important where the waiver does not relate to a single act or examination, but potentially to the entire evidence-taking procedure (Art. 496 § 2 *bis* CCP-Italy). The parties should be given the opportunity to reconsider their decision at any time during the trial, if circumstances so warrant.

---

40 In order to increase the awareness in relation to the potential disadvantages of virtual participation, there has been discussion about the possibility of introducing information requirements in favour of the accused. Moreover, it has been argued that consent should refer not only to the acceptance of the virtual connection but also to the lawyer's decision to be connected from a location other than that of the defendant. See A. Falcone, 'La videoconferenza nel procedimento penale italiano: riflessioni a margine della recente riforma Cartabia in materia di partecipazione a distanza', *La legislazione penale* 2023, pp. 33 and 37, available at: https://www.lalegislazionepenale.eu/wp-content/uploads/2023/09/A.Falcone_La-videoconferenza.pdf [accessed on: May 27th, 2024].

41 See E. A. A Dei-Cas, 'La partecipazione "parzialmente smaterializzata"...', p. 34.

8. Bibliography

Literature

Bargis M., 'Videoconferenza' in: E. Zappalà (ed.), *L'esame e la partecipazione a distanza nei processi di criminalità organizzata*, Milano 1999.

Borgia G., 'Dibattimento a distanza e garanzie costituzionali: spunti di riflessione a partire dall'emergenza sanitaria', *Osservatorio AIC* 2020, available at: https://www.osservatorioaic.it/images/rivista/pdf/2020_6_23_Borgia.pdf [accessed on: May 27th, 2024].

Camon A., 'Accordi processuali e giustizia penale: la prova patteggiata', 63(1) *Rivista di diritto processuale* 2008.

Conti C., 'Partecipazione e presenza dell'imputato nel processo penale: questione terminologica o interessi contrapposti da bilanciare?', 6(1) *Diritto penale e processo* 2000.

Curtotti D., *I collegamenti audiovisivi nel processo penale*, Milano 2006.

Curtotti D., 'Esame a distanza' in: *Enciclopedia del diritto*, Annali II, 1, 2008.

Curtotti D., 'Dibattimento a distanza' in: *Enciclopedia del diritto*, Annali II, 1, 2008.

Daniele M., 'La partecipazione a distanza allargata', *Diritto penale contemporaneo* 2017, available at: https://archiviodpc.dirittopenaleuomo.org/upload/9865-daniele2017a.pdf. [accessed on: May 27th, 2024].

Daniele M., *Habeas corpus. Manipolazioni di una garanzia*, Torino 2017.

Daniele M., *La formazione digitale delle prove dichiarative. L'esame a distanza tra regole interne e diritto sovranazionale*, Torino 2012.

De Caro A., 'La partecipazione al dibattimento a distanza', 23(10) *Diritto penale e processo* 2017.

Dei-Cas E. A. A., 'La partecipazione "parzialmente smaterializzata": il grimaldello del consenso a favore dell'economia processuale', *La legislazione penale* 2023, available at: https://www.lalegislazionepenale.eu/wp-content/uploads/2023/04/DEI-CAS-Definitivo.pdf. [accessed on: May 27th, 2024].

Falcone A., 'Online Hearings and the Right to Effective Defence in Digitalized Trials' in: L. Bachmaier Winter, S. Ruggeri (eds.), *Investigating and Preventing Crime in the Digital Era*, Cham: Springer 2022.

Falcone A., 'La videoconferenza nel procedimento penale italiano: riflessioni a margine della recente riforma Cartabia in materia di partecipazione a distanza', *La legislazione penale* 2023, available at: https://www.lalegislazionepenale.eu/wp-content/uploads/2023/09/A.Falcone_La-videoconferenza.pdf [accessed on: May 27th, 2024].

Galgani B., 'La c.d. remote justice nella riforma Cartabia', 175(5) *Giurisprudenza italiana* 2023.

Galgani B., *Forme e garanzie nel prisma dell'innovazione tecnologica*, Milano 2022.

Lorusso S., 'La mutata fisionomia della partecipazione a distanza al dibattimento e il *vulnus* alle garanzie difensive' in: S. Lorusso (ed.), *Il fragile mosaico delle garanzie difensive. Dalla legge Orlando alle scelte della XVIII legislatura*, Torino 2020.

Mancuso E. M., 'La dematerializzazione del processo al tempo del COVID-19', *Giurisprudenza penale* 2020, available at: https://www.giurisprudenzapenale.com/wp-content/uploads/2020/05/EMMancuso_gp_2020_5.pdf. [accessed on: May 27th, 2024].

Mazza O., 'Distopia del processo a distanza', LXXII(1) *Archivio penale* 2020.

Napolitano S., 'Dall'udienza penale a distanza all'aula virtuale', *Sistema penale* 2020, available at: https://www.sistemapenale.it/pdf_contenuti/1594123110_napolitano-2020a-udienza-penale-a-distanza-aula-virtuale-teams-dalla-legge-27-2020-alla-legge-70-2020.pdf. [accessed on: May 27th, 2024].

Negri D., 'Atti e udienze "a distanza": risvolti inquisitori di una transizione maldestra alla giustizia penale' in: D. Castronuovo, M. Donini, E. M. Mancuso, G. Varraso (eds.), *Riforma Cartabia: la nuova procedura penale*, Milano 2023.

Negri D., 'La gigantesca espansione della videoconferenza come alternativa alla presenza fisica dell'imputato in giudizio', LXX(1), *Archivio penale* 2018, Special issue.

Nicolicchia F., 'Consenso del difensore all'acquisizione dibattimentale degli atti d'indagine e riconoscimento delle attenuanti generiche. Riflessioni all'incrocio tra diritto e processo penale', *La legislazione penale* 2020, available at: https://www.lalegislazionepenale.eu/wp-content/uploads/2020/06/Nicolicchia-opinioni.pdf [accessed on: May 27th, 2024].

Signorato S., 'L'ampliamento dei casi di partecipazione a distanza dell'imputato tra logiche efficientistiche e menomazioni difensive', *La legislazione penale* 2017, available at: https://www.lalegislazionepenale.eu/wp-content/uploads/2017/11/S.-Signorato-Lampliamento-dei-casi-di-partecipazione-a-distanza.pdf [accessed on: May 27th, 2024].

Susskind R., *Online courts and the future of justice*, Oxford University Press 2019.

Triggiani N., 'La partecipazione a distanza' in: E. Mezzetti, E. Luparia (eds.), *La legislazione antimafia*, Bologna 2020.

Voena G. P., 'Il telesame' in: E. Zappalà (ed.), *L'esame e la partecipazione a distanza nei processi di criminalità organizzata*, Milano 1999.

Ewa Aleksandra Płocha*

III. The Impact of AI-based Recidivism Risk Assessment Instruments on Human Decision-Making in Criminal Justice: COMPAS Case Study in the Context of Polish and European Union Law

Abstract: The possibility to use Artificial Intelligence systems as a substitute of judges or as an assistive tool on human decision-making in criminal cases has been criticized for a long time for many reasons. However, the discussion regarding these issues has got more vivid and intensive when AI applications were in particular implemented for needs of Chinese and United States' criminal justice systems. This paper is focused on AI-based (also referred to as algorithmic) recidivism risk assessment instruments, which are one of the assistive tools having an impact on human decision-making in criminal justice. The analysis of this matter is based on U.S. experiences with controversial AI software called COMPAS (Correctional Offender Management Profiling for Alternative Sanctions). The author will shortly present the generations of recidivism risk assessments and then describe the COMPAS, in particular how it works, where it was implemented and how it is currently evaluated in American jurisprudence and by researchers. Subsequently, she will analyze the possibility of using such an algorithm under Polish and European Union legal conditions. Finally, the author will attempt to describe the impact of AI-based recidivism risk assessment on human decision-making in criminal justice.

Keywords: Artificial Intelligence, risk assessment instruments, recidivism, COMPAS

1. Introduction

The developments in Artificial Intelligence (hereinafter referred to as 'AI') technology, which have taken place in recent years, have significantly contributed to accelerating the digital transformation of criminal justice around the world. Some of the AI systems have been applied to such areas as, for example, e-filing, document anonymization, triaging, allocation, workflow automation, automated online dispute resolution, prediction of litigation outcomes, decision-support and

* PhD Candidate, Cardinal Stefan Wyszyński University, Warsaw, Poland.

decision-making[1,2]. Among them, the recidivism risk assessment instruments are particularly noteworthy. They are standardized tools for estimating the risk of recidivism[3] and the criminogenic needs of the offender, which are used in criminal proceedings (e.g., in the application of some precautionary measures, sentencing) and criminal enforcement proceedings (e.g., in the execution of a prison sentence, parole, the application of a protective measure in the form of placement in a psychiatric institution[4]). To be more precise, they are used to prepare criminological prognoses[5].

The AI-based recidivism risk assessment instruments have already been implemented in many countries, e.g., the OASys (Offender Assessment System) application in Estonia and the United Kingdom[6], Cassandra in Ukraine[7] or the Sexual

1 Reliable information on artificial intelligence systems and other key cyberjustice tools used in the digital transformation of the judiciary in different countries around the world is available on the official website of the Resource Centre on Cyberjustice and AI, available at: https://www.coe.int/en/web/cepej/resource-centre-on-cyberjustice-and-ai#{%22202452374%22:[0]} [accessed on: June 1st, 2023].

2 Among the AI systems used in the judiciary, a distinction can be made between applications of a general-procedural nature (they can be used in any type of court proceedings; they are universal and concern, in particular, the court infrastructure and the work of the secretariats) and those dedicated to a specific type of proceedings, e.g. criminal, civil or administrative (it is about issuing judgements, which requires knowledge of the provisions of a specific branch of law and court case law). See more E. A. Płocha, 'O pojęciu sztucznej inteligencji i możliwościach jej zastosowania w postępowaniu cywilnym', 44 *Prawo w Działaniu. Sprawy cywilne* 2020, pp. 284–287, available at: https://pwd.iws.gov.pl/tom-44-prawo-cywilne/ [accessed on: June 1st, 2023].

3 Due to the various understandings of the notion of recidivism in different nations' legal orders, for the purposes of this paper, it is understood in a general way, i.e., as a return to crime, regardless of whether it is a similar crime or not.

4 See more E. A. Płocha, 'Sztuczna inteligencja w postępowaniu w sprawach dotyczących wykonania środka zabezpieczającego w postaci pobytu w zakładzie psychiatrycznym' in: J. Piskorski, M. Błaszczak (eds.), *Nowe technologie. Wyzwania i perspektywy dla prawa karnego*, ArchaeGraph 2023, pp. 206–226, available at: https://www.archaegraph.pl/lib/l231bv/978-83-67527-87-3-e-book-lmyp4svo.pdf [accessed on: September 23rd, 2023].

5 K. Mamak, 'Prognoza kryminologiczna' in: K. Mamak, *Rewolucja cyfrowa a prawo karne*, Krakowski Instytut Prawa Karnego Fundacja 2019, pp. 101 ff.

6 K. Burdziak, E. Rüütel, *Prognoza kryminologiczna. Porównanie rozwiązań estońskich i polskich*, Wydawnictwo Naukowe Tygiel 2022, *passim*.

7 Fair Trials, *Automating Injustice: The Use of Artificial Intelligence & Automated Decision-Making Systems in Criminal Justice in Europe*, p. 25, available at: https://www.fairtrials.org/app/uploads/2021/11/Automating_Injustice.pdf [accessed on: December 6th, 2023].

Violence Risk-20 and Risk for Sexual Violence Protocol in Australia[8]. However, the United States of America appears to have the greatest and most diverse experience in the implementation and use of such tools. They were implemented there at both the state and federal levels[9]. Apart from this, it was there that the first attempts were made in the 1920s to develop predictive tools for estimating the risk of recidivism[10]. It should be noted that COMPAS (Correctional Offender Management Profiling for Alternative Sanctions) is one of the longest and most widely used AI-based recidivism risk assessment instruments in the U.S. criminal justice system. There have been dozens of academic studies, including legal analyses, and court decisions concerning this predictive algorithm. Although COMPAS has been implemented in the common law system, good practices, as well as remarks, objections and concerns, should be taken into account when evaluating the utility and trustworthiness of all AI-based recidivism risk assessment instruments. Importantly, the possibility of using such applications in the Polish criminal justice system has also been under consideration for some time[11]. Hence, it is imperative to inquire: Can and should Polish criminal justice authorities adopt the use of such tools?

In order to answer this question, the generations of recidivism risk assessment will be briefly described, and the COMPAS algorithm will be characterized. Following that, a selection of judicial rulings from the United States and

8 A. Alan et al., 'Assessing the Risk of Australian Indigenous Sexual Offenders Reoffending: A Review of the Research Literature and Court Decisions', 26(2) *Psychiatry, Psychology and Law* 2019, pp. 274–294.

9 For a more detailed analysis of the matter, see T. H. Cohen et al., 'The Federal Post-Conviction Risk Assessment Instrument: A Tool for Predicting Recidivism for Offenders on Federal Supervision' in: J. P. Singh et al. (eds.), *Handbook of recidivism risk/needs assessment tools*, New York: John Wiley & Sons 2018, pp. 79 ff.; A. B. Cyphert, 'Reprogramming Recidivism: The First Step Act and Algorithmic Prediction of Risk', 51 *Seton Hall Law Review* 2020, pp. 331–381.

10 See more B. Stańdo-Kawecka, 'Ruch What works i „technologie szacowania ryzyka"' in: B. Stańdo-Kawecka, *Polityka karna i penitencjarna między punitywizmem i menedżeryzmem*, Wolters Kluwer Polska 2020, pp. 227–235; K. Burdziak, E. Rüütel, *Prognoza kryminologiczna…*, p. 50.

11 For more, see D. Wójcik, 'Stosowanie w postępowaniu karnym narzędzi diagnostyczno-prognostycznych służących oszacowaniu ryzyka powrotności do przestępstwa', 16 *Prawo w Działaniu. Sprawy karne* 2013, pp. 59–102; M. Kowalewska-Łukuć, K. Burdziak, 'The use of AI in formulating a criminological prognosis of an offender', 25 *Technium Social Sciences Journal* 2021, pp. 115–125; K. Burdziak, E. Rüütel, *Prognoza kryminologiczna…*, pp. 67–88.

scholarly viewpoints about this algorithm will be presented. Moreover, due to editorial requirements, the applicability of recidivism risk assessment tools in Poland will only be discussed in relation to selected national and EU legislation. Finally, comments will be made in this context on the impact of such tools on human decision-making in criminal justice. The main methodologies used in this paper are comparative and dogmatic methods.

2. From Unstructured Professional Judgment to AI-based Recidivism Risk Assessment Instruments

In the United States of America in the early years of the 20th century, judges, prison officers, probation officers, psychologists, psychiatrists and social workers assessed criminogenic risk based on their own experience and intuition (the so-called first generation risk assessment)[12]. There, in 1928, E. W. Burgess developed the first criminogenic risk assessment tool for the Illinois parole system, which was based on the actuarial (statistical) method of risk assessment, i.e. a numerical prediction made on the basis of an analysis of static risk factors[13]. This instrument analyzed only static risk factors (second generation risk assessment), such as marital status, criminal and employment history and institutional misconduct. During the 1930s, '40s, and '50s Illinois was the only state using an actuarial risk assessment instrument, Ohio was experimenting with such tools in the 1960s, California and the federal government implemented them in 1970s and some other states in the late 1970s and early 1980s[14]. The third generation of risk assessment instruments also characterized assessments of some dynamic risk factors. They can be used not only to assess the likelihood of reoffending but also to identify criminogenic needs. One of the most well-known tools of this type are the Assessment and Case Evaluation System (ACE) and Level of Service Inventory-Revised (LSI-R)[15]. To maximize treatment and supervision benefits, the fourth generation instruments

12 U.S. Department of Justice, Bureau of Justice Assistance, *History of Risk Assessment. Public Safety Risk Assessment Clearinghouse*, available at: https://bja.ojp.gov/program/psrac/basics/history-risk-assessment#gcov4e [accessed on: September 23rd, 2023].

13 K. Burdziak, E. Rüütel, *Prognoza kryminologiczna…*, p. 50.

14 B. E. Harcourt, *Against Prediction. Profiling, Policing, and Punishing in an Actuarial Age*, University of Chicago Press 2006, pp. 47 ff.

15 D. Wójcik, Stosowanie w postępowaniu karnym…, pp. 70–71; E. Chelioudakis, 'Risk Assessment Tools in Criminal Justice: Is There a Need for such Tools in Europe and would Their Use Comply with European Data Protection Law?', 1(2) *Australian National University Journal of Law and Technology* 2020, p. 78.

emphasize the integration of "systematic intervention and monitoring with the assessment of a broader range of offender risk factors heretofore not measured and other personal factors important to treatment"[16]. Examples of these tools are the Level of Service/Case Management Inventory (LS/CMI) and COMPAS (Correctional Offender Management Profiling for Alternative Sanctions), the latter of which is based on Artificial Intelligence technologies (Machine Learning)[17]. The AI-based risk assessment tools are also called "algorithmic risk assessment instruments" (ARAI)[18].

3. General Characteristics of the COMPAS Application and Its Legal Assessment in the Jurisprudence of U.S. Courts

COMPAS was developed in 1998[19], but the primary version of this software has been modified and improved many times over the years[20]. The application is periodically updated and adapted to developments in science and new technologies, at the forefront of AI. COMPAS is one of the most widely used predictive algorithms by criminal justice system authorities in the United States of America

16 J. Bonta, D. A. Andrews, *Risk-Need-Responsivity Model for Offender Assessment and Rehabilitation*, Canada 2007, p. 4, available at: https://www.publicsafety.gc.ca/cnt/rsrcs/pblctns/rsk-nd-rspnsvty/index-en.aspx [accessed on: September 23rd, 2023].

17 The Machine Learning methods used in COMPAS are random forests and support vector machines. For a more detailed analysis of the matter, see M. Ghasemi et al., 'The Application of Machine Learning to a General Risk–Need Assessment Instrument in the Prediction of Criminal Recidivism', 48 *Criminal Justice and Behavior* 2021, pp. 518–538; Australian Lawyers Alliance, *Predicting recidivism – the questionable role of algorithms in the criminal justice system*, available at: https://www.lawyersalliance.com.au/opinion/predicting-recidivism-the-questionable-role-of-algorithms-in-the-criminal-justice-system [accessed on: September 23rd, 2023]; Equivant, *Practitioner's Guide to COMPAS Core – April 4th, 2019*, p. 1, available at: https://www.equivant.com/practitioners-guide-to-compas-core/ [accessed on: September 23rd, 2023].

18 T. Greene et al., 'Forks Over Knives: Predictive Inconsistency in Criminal Justice Algorithmic Risk Assessment Tools', 185 *Journal of the Royal Statistical Society Series A: Statistics in Society* 2022, Issue Supplement_2, pp. 692–723.

19 The recidivism risk scale, which is a component of COMPAS responsible for recidivism prediction, has been in use since 2000 (J. Dressel, H. Farid, 'The accuracy, fairness, and limits of predicting recidivism', 4 *Sciences Advances* 2018, pp. 1–5).

20 Equivant, *Practitioner's Guide*..., p. 1.

(in particular in New York State, Wisconsin, California and Florida)[21]. It is used for estimating the risk of recidivism and the criminogenic needs of the offender, which are taken into consideration in the human decision-making process in criminal justice (preparatory proceedings, court proceedings and criminal executive proceedings). This concerns in particular the application, modification or revocation of precautionary measures, sentencing (imposing, inter alia, penalty of deprivation of liberty, probative measures or protective measures) and the execution of penalties and other criminal sanctions. Depending on the type of crime, the characteristics of the offender and the needs of the criminal procedural authorities (stage of criminal proceedings and type of decision), apart from the main component (COMPAS Core), different versions of the COMPAS are used, such as, for example, Youth COMPAS, Reentry COMPAS, Women's COMPAS (also known as COMPAS-WRNA) and Recidivism Risk Screen, Pretrial Release Risk Scale II. The specific modules of the software are tailored to the individual needs of the contracting authority; they not only take into account the purpose of its use (the stage of the procedure), but also require in particular relevant input data (e.g., on populations or subpopulations in the territory).

COMPAS has two scales: the risk scale estimates the general recidivism risk and the violent recidivism risk, while the needs scale refers to the extent and type of therapeutic interventions. Data concerning the offender is obtained from the criminal case file and during an interview with him (based on a questionnaire consisting of 137 questions that deal with facts and evaluations[22])[23]. Based on this information, the predictive algorithm prepares a report consisting of two parts: General Risk Potential (in which it distinguishes between Violence, Recidivism and Failure to Appear) and Criminogenic Profile and Needs (in which it separately assesses: Criminal Involvement, History of Non-Compliance, History of Violence, Criminal Attitude, Resentful/Mistrust, Responsivity Problems, Few Pro-Social Peers, Criminal Associates/Peers, Impulsivity, Anger, Few Family

---

21 E. A. Płocha, 'Narzędzia oceny ryzyka powrotności do przestępstwa oparte na sztucznej inteligencji: uwagi na przykładzie aplikacji COMPAS', 2 *Problemy Prawa Karnego* 2023, pp. 1–22.

22 The answers can be intentionally manipulated by offenders themselves or by persons interviewing them. To avoid such situations, COMPAS has a mechanism for a 'data validity check' in self-reported questionnaires. For more, see T. Brennan, W. Dieterich, 'Correctional offender management profiles for alternative sanctions (COMPAS)' in: J. P. Singh et al. (eds.), *Handbook of recidivism risk/needs assessment tools*, New York: John Wiley & Sons 2018, pp. 49 ff.

23 For more, see Equivant, *Practitioner's Guide…*, *passim*.

Supports, Family Criminality, Substance Abuse, Life Goals/Idleness, Financial Problems, Vocational/Educational Problems, Social Environment, Social Isolation, Depression)[24]. Only the first part of the report is predictive, while the second part only contains data useful for describing the offender. The results in both parts of the report are presented graphically, using bar charts (a scale from 1 to 10, where score from 1 to 4 may be regarded as low risk, above 4 to 7 – medium, above 7 to 10 – high). The prediction made by COMPAS represents the risk of the individual reoffending within two years. Importantly, it is generated by comparing the information obtained about the offender with a similar group of data. In other words, the algorithm assigns him or her to one of eight categories of offenders[25] and then analyzes statistics regarding persons with the same set of characteristics ('similar' persons) to assess recidivism probability.

It should be noted that, in the United States of America, the use of Recidivism Risk Assessment Instruments by criminal justice system authorities has been regulated under state law, either as an obligation (Kentucky, Ohio, Pennsylvania, Oklahoma) or an option (e.g. Idaho, some courts in Louisiana)[26]. On the other hand, in terms of federal law, it is significant that on December 21st, 2018, former President Donald J. Trump signed the First Step Act of 2018 (FSA), on the basis of which an attempt was made to create an effective new risk and needs assessment system and, in particular, a new recidivism risk assessment instrument (PATTERN – the Prisoner Assessment Tool Targeting Estimated Risk and Needs) was developed[27].

In the beginning, it happened that the authorities of the criminal justice system did not use risk assessment tools. However, with regard to the activities of the parole board, judicial case law has clarified that it must carry out a factual assessment of each petitioner, whereby it should also consider the results generated by

24 A sample case report is available at: https://assets.documentcloud.org/documents/2839240/Sample-Risk-Assessment-COMPAS-Results.pdf [accessed on: September 23rd, 2023].

25 There are separate classifications for men and women. For a more detailed analysis of the matter, see Equivant, *Practitioner's Guide...*, pp. 54–61.

26 *State of Wisconsin v. Loomis*, 881 N.W.2d 749 (Wis. 2016), § 42. For more, see Ch. Bavitz et al., 'Assessing the Assessments: Lessons From Early State Experiences in the Procurement and Implementation of Risk Assessment Tools', Berkman Klein Center for Internet & Society 2018, available at: https://dash.harvard.edu/handle/1/37883502 [accessed on: September 23rd, 2023].

27 See e.g. U.S. Department of Justice, Office of the Attorney General, *The First Step Act of 2018: Risk and Needs Assessment System*, available at: https://www.ojp.gov/First-Step-Act-of-2018-Risk-and-Needs-Assessment-System [accessed on: September 23rd, 2023].

an instrument that measures rehabilitation and the likelihood of parole success[28]. Moreover, even if such an assessment report is generated and attached to the case file, the failure to evaluate it (as part of a free assessment of the evidence) is a violation of the law[29]. It should be made clear at this point that the results contained in the report are only of a subsidiary nature and do not bind the authorities[30].

Special attention should also be paid to the judicial case-law on the use of such tools at the sentencing stage. It was explained that "COMPAS is only one of the tools available to the court at the time of adjudication"[31]. It is important to signal that some restrictions regarding using this type of evidence have been placed on. Firstly, the assessments generated by these instruments cannot be an aggravating or mitigating circumstances. Secondly, they cannot be used to determine the total duration of the sentence, but they can be used to determine how the sentence is to be served[32].

One of the most frequently cited and discussed rulings on the use of the COMPAS tool is that in Loomis v. State. The Wisconsin Supreme Court examined whether the mere use of a COMPAS-generated risk assessment at the sentencing stage violated Eric Loomis' due process rights[33]. The offender explained in detail what this breach consisted of. In his opinion, by using a methodology in COMPAS that is covered by commercial confidentiality and was not disclosed during the proceedings, his right to a conviction on the basis of accurate information was violated (it is not known how the factors are weighted, the scores assigned, the results determined, and whether this is in accordance with the applicable scientific standards). In addition, his right to an individualized conviction has been violated,

---

28 *Diaz v. New York State Board of Parole*, available at: https://law.justia.com/cases/new-york/other-courts/2013/2013-ny-slip-op-23422.html [accessed on: September 23rd, 2023].

29 *Morris v. New York State Department of Corrections and Community Supervision et al.*, available at: https://law.justia.com/cases/new-york/other-courts/2013/2013-ny-slip-op-50604-u.html [accessed on: September 23rd, 2023].

30 Compare the judgments in the following cases: *Partee v. Evans*, 40 Misc. 3d 896 (N.Y. Sup. Ct. 2013); *Williams v. New York*, 49 Misc. 3d 732 (N.Y. Sup. Ct. 2015).

31 *State of Wisconsin v. Samsa*, 2015 WI App 6 (Wis. Ct. App. 2014), § 13.

32 See e.g. *Malenchik v. State of Indiana*, 928 N.E.2d 564, 574 (Ind. 2010). Although the judgment concerns the LSI-R tool, the court's opinion remains valid for other applications of this kind as well.

33 "At Loomis's sentencing hearing, the trial court referred to the COMPAS assessment in its sentencing determination and, based in part on this assessment, sentenced Loomis to six years of imprisonment and five years of extended supervision" (*State v. Loomis*, 881 N.W.2d 749 (Wis. 2016), 130(5) *Harvard Law Review* 2017, pp. 1530–1537).

as COMPAS is compiling the report with reference to group data. Furthermore, in his opinion, the contested ruling discriminated against him based on his gender (the recidivism risk assessment generates separate results for men and women).

In the opinion of the Wisconsin Supreme Court, the described violations of the law did not occur. The circumstance that determined this was the trial court's conclusion that the same judgment would have been reached even without the COMPAS risk assessment. However, the literature points out that the mere allegation of a violation of the due process right had already given the Wisconsin Supreme Court the opportunity to analyze in detail the legal issues surrounding the use of risk assessment tools at the sentencing stage in criminal cases. The Wisconsin Supreme Court's grounds were found to be unsatisfactory. This is because some did not agree with the statement that, in order to challenge the COMPAS report, it is sufficient to read it without knowing how the algorithm estimates risk. Meanwhile, the report only contains bar charts without any further explanation or justification of the scores. It is therefore unclear how the value of each indicator was estimated and why. In the opinion of the Wisconsin Supreme Court, the explanations in 'Practitioner's Guide to COMPAS Core' are enough in this regard. While others find the document too superficial[34].

Importantly, this judgment in Loomis v. State indicates that the Pre-Sentence Investigation (PSI) report containing the risk assessment generated by COMPAS must include a caution to the sentencing courts regarding the accuracy of the assessment. This caution should include the following information: "(1) the proprietary nature of COMPAS has been invoked to prevent disclosure of information relating to how factors are weighed or how risk scores are to be determined; (2) risk assessment compares defendants to a national sample, but no cross-validation study for a Wisconsin population has yet been completed; (3) some studies of COMPAS risk assessment scores have raised questions about whether they disproportionately classify minority offenders as having a higher risk of recidivism; and (4) risk assessment tools must be constantly monitored and re-normed for accuracy due to changing populations and subpopulations. Providing information to sentencing courts on the limitations and cautions attendant with the use of COMPAS risk assessments will enable courts to better assess the accuracy of the assessment and the appropriate weight to be given to the risk score"[35].

34 *State v. Loomis*, 881 N.W.2d 749 (Wis. 2016). See, e.g. E. Israni, 'Algorithmic Due Process: Mistaken Accountability and Attribution in State v. Loomis', *JOLT Digest*, available at: https://jolt.law.harvard.edu/digest/algorithmic-due-process-mistaken-accountability-and-attribution-in-state-v-loomis-1 [accessed on: September 23rd, 2023].

35 *State v. Loomis*, 881 N.W.2d 749 (Wis. 2016), § 66.

The Wisconsin Supreme Court also explained that "if a COMPAS risk assessment were the determinative factor considered at sentencing this would raise due process challenges regarding whether a defendant received an individualized sentence. As the defense expert testified at the post-conviction motion hearing, COMPAS is designed to assess group data. He explained that COMPAS can be analogized to insurance actuarial risk assessments, which identify risk among groups of drivers and allocate resources accordingly"[36]. Furthermore, the Court pointed out that gender is not used as a criminogenic factor but only serves for statistical normalization, as confirmed by scientific studies[37]. The appellant did not provide evidence to prove that the prohibition of discrimination had been violated.

Detailed information on the working of the COMPAS tool was also attempted through access to public information. For instance, on November 15th, 2022, Martha Rayner, Professor of Law, initiated proceedings in the Albany County Supreme Court against the New York State Department of Corrections and Community Supervision (DOCCS)[38]. The case was conducted under a different procedure, i.e., inter alia, based on the Freedom of Information Law (FOIL), and concerned the Department's denial of a request for information on the operation and robustness of COMPAS Re-entry, which is mandatorily used by the New York State Parole Board in every parole proceeding. Under FOIL, agency records presumptively are available for public inspection unless they fall within a specific exemption set forth in Public Officers Law. In opinion of the petitioner, the records she requested are not exempt from disclosure by state or federal statute.

The Albany County Supreme Court explained that agency records are exempt from disclosure if they "contain bona fide trade secrets". However, "even records that do not qualify for trade secret protection are exempt if 'submitted to the agency by a commercial enterprise' and disclosure 'would cause substantial injury to the competitive position of the subject enterprise'"[39]. After hearing

36 *State v. Loomis*, 881 N.W.2d 749 (Wis. 2016), § 68.

37 *State v. Loomis*, 881 N.W.2d 749 (Wis. 2016), § 72.

38 The text of the submitted petition is available at: https://law.yale.edu/sites/default/files/documents/pdf/mfia_rayner_nys.pdf [accessed on: August 1st, 2023]. See M. Rayner, 'Commentary: This algorithm is used to deny inmates parole. We're not allowed to know anything about it', *Times Union*, available at: https://www.timesunion.com/opinion/article/commentary-proprietary-algorithm-deny-inmate-18001304.php [accessed on: August 1st, 2023].

39 *Rayner v. New York State Department of Corrections and Community Supervision*, available at: https://law.justia.com/cases/new-york/other-courts/2023/2023-ny-slip-op-23293.html [accessed on: December 11th, 2023].

from a representative of the company's research team, the court found that the requested information was covered by trade secrets. The Court determined "that the formulae, algorithms, risk and needs scales, and norming data underlying COMPAS-NY – including the manner in which risk and needs scores are derived from the Board's questionnaire, the decile cut-off points used by COMPAS-NY, and the manner in which deciles are assigned to qualitative categories [...] – were developed, identified, gathered and/or analyzed by Equivant, 'a private, for-profit corporation' [...], through substantial investments of time, money and effort. To recoup these investments and continue its research and development into risk and needs assessment instruments, Equivant licenses software incorporating its proprietary technology to DOCCS [...]. But if petitioner's FOIL application were granted and equivant's technology opened to the public, it would be a simple matter for one of the State's information technology vendors to supply DOCCS with the functionality of COMPAS-NY at a much lower cost. [...] Thus, continued secrecy of COMPAS-NY has real value to Equivant and gives it a clear 'advantage over competitors' that do not have access to the scales, norming data, and cut-off points incorporated into the program [...]. The Court therefore concludes that the value of the risk and needs assessment technology embodied in COMPAS-NY, both to Equivant and to potential competitors, 'is self-evident and its disclosure would almost assuredly complicate, if not compromise, [Equivant's] competitive position' in New York (and perhaps in other states) [...]"[40]. Thus, in the Court's opinion, the technology underlying COMPAS-NY is a bona fide trade secret belonging to Equivant, and agency records containing such material are exempt from disclosure. Importantly, any change in this scope based on the "exceptionally important public interest" of parole supervision requires action by the State Legislature.

4. Predictive Inconsistency and Algorithmic Unfairness

There is an ongoing debate in the literature about the usage of COMPAS applications and other comparable prediction algorithms in criminal justice. Experts from a diverse array of scientific fields are participating in it, including economics, Machine Learning, statistics, sociology, criminology, law, and philosophy. This is due not only to the mere nature of the recidivism risk assessment tools and AI technologies being applied but also to the area in which they are implemented

40 *Rayner v. New York State Department of Corrections and Community Supervision*, available at: https://law.justia.com/cases/new-york/other-courts/2023/2023-ny-slip-op-23293.html [accessed on: December 11th, 2023].

and their impact on the rights and fundamental freedoms of individuals. The AI-based Recidivism Risk Assessment Tools have both their supporters and opponents. But particular consideration needs to be given to any critiques, objections, or uncertainties regarding the use of these algorithms. They concern the use of such tools in general or only specific software.

Experts observe that different, equally legitimate choices during the development, testing and implementation of these tools (technical aspects) can lead to divergent predicted risk outcomes for the same individual[41]. They refer to this phenomenon as "predictive inconsistency"[42]. It is important to note that although certain disparities might seem acceptable when analyzed through a technical or statistical lens, they give rise to valid concerns regarding their legality, in particular whether they guarantee the right to a fair trial.

As for the COMPAS tool, the first criticisms and concerns about its functioning were raised after its implementation in the U.S. justice system. They were the impetus for changes and improvements to this software. It should be clarified that the producer of this algorithm is cooperating with authorities in this regard (public and private partnership)[43]. Despite the fact that the results of research and evaluation are widely available (e.g. post-conference publications, technical reports), the use of COMPAS in criminal justice still raises a number of concerns.

A report published by ProPublica in 2016, alleging that the algorithm discriminates against black people, was widely echoed. According to it, black offenders' recidivism risk assessment scores were more often inflated than those of white defendants. On the other hand, the scores of white perpetrators were underrated more often[44]. A team of researchers from Equivant carefully reviewed the findings of the ProPublica report and announced that they had found statistical and

---

41 As an illustration, in the case *State of Iowa v. Gordon*, the three-category SOTIPS instrument categorized Gordon's pre-sentencing report for sexual recidivism as high-risk, whereas the five-category STATIC-99R categorized him as average risk. For more, see *State of Iowa v. Gordon*, available at: https://www.iowacourts.gov/courtcases/754/briefs/1162/embedBrief [accessed on: December 1st, 2023].

42 T. Greene et al., *Forks Over Knives…, passim.*

43 Equivant, *Practitioner's Guide…*, p. 12.

44 For extended analysis, see J. Angwin et al., 'Machine bias. There's software used across the country to predict future criminals. And it's biased against blacks', *ProPublica*, available at: https://www.propublica.org/article/machine-bias-risk-assessments-in-criminal-sentencing [accessed on: December 1st, 2023]; J. Larson et al., 'How We Analyzed the COMPAS Recidivism Algorithm', available at: https://www.propublica.org/article/how-we-analyzed-the-compas-recidivism-algorithm [accessed on: December 1st, 2023].

technical errors in the report, which resulted in the incorrect finding that the algorithm allowed for racial discrimination[45]. However, some researchers note that the two studies used different research methods, which led to different results[46]. Significantly, this controversy has not yet been clearly resolved. In this context it should be noted, nevertheless, that algorithmic discrimination is challenging to detect. When carried out by human beings, it predominantly manifests itself through the conduct of both the victims and the perpetrators. However, the identification of algorithmic unfairness of this nature necessitates the participation of experts.

Another study published in 2018 also caused a credibility crisis. The study involved 400 non-expert volunteers who were able to estimate the risk of re-offending at a level (63%) similar to the COMPAS score (65%) based on just seven pieces of information about the offender, rather than 137[47]. The outcomes of this experiment reinforced some people's beliefs that the U.S. justice system collects too much information about offenders and that algorithmic predictions are no better than human ones. Interestingly, the producers of the COMPAS software did not take these claims as criticism, but on the contrary, as confirmation that it achieves good predictability[48].

The experience of the U.S. criminal justice system described above highlights that recidivism risk assessment tools must be reliable, i.e., lawful, ethical and robust (in technical and social terms)[49]. Meeting these conditions, however, is not easy. Indeed, there is no consensus even on what data should be analyzed for the prediction. The consideration of dynamic factors is questioned. For example, some scholars take the view that information on place of residence, salary level

---

45 See T. Brennan, W. Dieterich, Ch. Mendoza, 'COMPAS Risk Scales: Demonstrating Accuracy Equity and Predictive Parity. Performance of the COMPAS Risk Scales in Broward County, July 8th, 2016', available at: https://go.volarisgroup.com/rs/430-MBX-989/images/ProPublica_Commentary_Final_070616.pdf [accessed on: December 1st, 2023].

46 L. Eckhouse et al., 'Layers of Bias: A Unified Approach for Understanding Problems With Risk Assessment', 46 *Criminal Justice and Behavior* 2019, pp. 185–209.

47 See J. Dressel, H. Farid, 'The accuracy, fairness, and limits of predicting recidivism', 4 *Science Advances* 2018, pp. 1–5.

48 E. Yong, 'A Popular Algorithm Is No Better at Predicting Crimes Than Random People', *The Atlantic*, available at: https://www.theatlantic.com/technology/archive/2018/01/equivant-compas-algorithm/550646/ [accessed on: December 1st, 2023].

49 On the topic of trustworthy AI see E. A. Płocha, 'O pojęciu sztucznej inteligencji i możliwościach jej zastosowania w postępowaniu cywilnym', 44 *Prawo w Działaniu. Sprawy cywilne* 2020, pp. 280–284.

or education may indirectly lead to discrimination based on gender, race, ethnic minority, social class[50].

Moreover, the presented court rulings show that, in fact, it is not clear how COMPAS works. Neither the perpetrator, his defence counsel, nor the court know this. There is a lack of information on how: 1) the algorithm compares the offender's data with a specific population, 2) the training data are prepared (the problem of so-called biases in the data), 3) groups are created, 4) weights are assigned to individual characteristics (criteria). The report generated by the tool does not contain a justification. Due to the refusal to disclose trade secrets in this regard, there is even talk of the phenomenon of the "privatization of sentencing"[51].

It is crucial to remember that the credibility of AI is a prerequisite for its diffusion. Studies conducted so far have indicated that individuals possess trust in AI, exhibit a highly favorable attitude towards it, and hold the belief that it is greater intelligence than themselves. Consequently, they acquiesce to all its suggestions, regardless of their correctness (displaying blind obedience). It is contended that this mechanism exerts influence on the majority of individuals and that this influence will probably increase in the future[52].

5. European Union and Polish Legal Perspective

There is no doubt that the legal situation of AI systems is governed by acts that concern them as products in general or that regulate the particular area in which the algorithms would be applied (sector-specific regulations). However, legislative work is still ongoing at the international, EU and national levels on regulation directly or solely dedicated to artificial intelligence. One of the most anticipated regulations was Regulation 2024/1689/EU laying down harmonised rules on artificial intelligence (Artificial Intelligence Act, hereinafter referred to as 'AI Act'), part of whose provisions entered into force on August 1st, 2024. It should be made clear that, prior to the entry into force of the AI Act within the structures of the European Union, a number of documents have been also produced that

---

50 L. Eckhouse et al., *Layers of Bias…*, pp. 185–209.

51 See A. Nishi, 'Privatizing Sentencing: A Delegation Framework for Recidivism Risk Assessment', 119 *Columbia Law Review* 2019, *passim*.

52 See e.g. M. Klichowski, 'People Copy the Actions of Artificial Intelligence', 11 *Frontiers in Psychology* 2020, available at: https://www.frontiersin.org/articles/10.3389/fpsyg.2020.01130/full [accessed on: December 23rd, 2023].

deal directly with Artificial Intelligence[53]. Despite their usefulness, however, they are not sources of law and are not binding.

According to Art. 3(1) AI Act, "'AI system' means a machine-based system that is designed to operate with varying levels of autonomy and that may exhibit adaptiveness after deployment, and that, for explicit or implicit objectives, infers, from the input it receives, how to generate outputs such as predictions, content, recommendations, or decisions that can influence physical or virtual environments"[54].

In Recital 42 AI Act, it is clarified that "In line with the presumption of innocence, natural persons in the Union should always be judged on their actual behaviour. Natural persons should never be judged on AI-predicted behaviour based solely on their profiling, personality traits or characteristics, such as nationality, place of birth, place of residence, number of children, level of debt or type of car, without a reasonable suspicion of that person being involved in a criminal activity based on objective verifiable facts and without human assessment thereof. Therefore, risk assessments carried out with regard to natural persons in order to assess the likelihood of their offending or to predict the occurrence of an actual or potential criminal offence based solely on profiling them or on assessing their personality traits and characteristics should be prohibited. In any case, that prohibition does not refer to or touch upon risk analytics that are not based on the profiling of individuals or on the personality traits and characteristics of individuals, such as AI systems using risk analytics to assess the likelihood of financial fraud by undertakings on the basis of suspicious transactions or risk analytic tools to predict the likelihood of the localisation of narcotics or illicit goods by customs authorities, for example on the basis of known trafficking routes".

With regard to AI-based Recidivism Risk Assessment Instruments, the most meaningful provision is Art. 5 § 1(d) AI Act, which stipulates that: "The following

53 In particular: European Commission, *Communication from the Commission to the European Parliament, the Council, the European Economic and Social Committee and the Committee of Regions, Building Trust in Human-Centric Artificial Intelligence*, COM/2019/168 final; European Commission, Directorate-General for Communications Networks, Content and Technology, *Ethics guidelines for trustworthy AI*, Publications Office, 2019, available at: https://data.europa.eu/doi/10.2759/346720 [accessed on: December 23rd, 2023]; European Commission, *White Paper on Artificial Intelligence – A European approach to excellence and trust*, COM/2020/65 final.

54 See, e.g. G. van Dijck, 'Predicting Recidivism Risk Meets AI Act', 28 *European Journal on Criminal Policy and Research* 2022, p. 411.

AI practices shall be prohibited: the placing on the market, the putting into service for this specific purpose, or the use of an AI system for making risk assessments of natural persons in order to assess or predict the risk of a natural person committing a criminal offence, based solely on the profiling of a natural person or on assessing their personality traits and characteristics; this prohibition shall not apply to AI systems used to support the human assessment of the involvement of a person in a criminal activity, which is already based on objective and verifiable facts directly linked to a criminal activity".

Exceptions to this prohibition are "AI systems intended to be used by law enforcement authorities or on their behalf or by Union institutions, bodies, offices or agencies in support of law enforcement authorities for assessing the risk of a natural person offending or re-offending not solely on the basis of the profiling of natural persons as referred to in Art. 3(4) Directive 2016/680/EU, or to assess personality traits and characteristics or past criminal behaviour of natural persons or groups", which are classified as a high-risk AI systems (Annex III, § 6(d)). Classifying an algorithm into the 'high-risk AI systems' group entails meeting the most stringent requirements set out in this regulation (regarding registration of system, having a risk management system, training of models, rigoristic quality criteria for data sets).

High-risk AI systems should only be placed on the Union market, put into service or used if they comply with certain mandatory requirements (e.g. an adequate risk management system, quality of training, validation and testing data sets, technical documentation, automatic recording of events, called 'logs'). It should be underlined that making them available or putting into service can take place only when they comply with all applicable Union harmonisation legislation. Currently, it is uncertain whether COMPAS and other similar tools will face a ban in Poland and other Member States unless they adapt to the requirements set out for high-risk AI systems.

Due to the sensitive area of application, which is the criminal justice system, this paper focuses only on selected legal regulations that guarantee and implement fundamental human rights and, for editorial limitations, provides just an overview of the most important issues. Then the review of legal regulations should therefore be done through the prism of the right to a court, the presumption of innocence, the principle of individualized justice, the principle of equality of arms, or the principle of equality before the law. These rights are stipulated in the European Convention on Human Rights (ECHR).

Although this study focuses on selected EU and Polish legislation, the stance and activity of the Council of Europe, which is Europe's most important human rights organization, cannot be ignored in this respect. Among numerous documents, the following deserve special mention European ethical Charter on the use of Artificial Intelligence in judicial systems and their environment[55], which, through the prism of the U.S. experience with the COMPAS tool, formulates demands for the implementation of such instruments. The Charter requires to "fully guarantee to respect for the principle of equality of arms and presumption of innocence established by Art. 6 ECHR. The party concerned should have access to and be able to challenge the scientific validity of an algorithm, the weighting given to its various elements and any erroneous conclusions it comes to whenever a judge suggests that he/she might use it before making his/her decision. Moreover, this right of access is also covered by the fundamental principle of personal data protection. All people have the right not to be subject to decisions affecting them significantly made solely on the basis of automated data processing, without their point of view having been taken into account beforehand. […] In this respect, there is a difference between Europe and the United States with regard to the right of access to algorithms: while in the United States the judicial authorities are still reluctant to recognize this right fully and weigh private interests (particularly the protection of intellectual property) against the rights of defence, in Europe the framework is more protective because of the GDPR, which establishes a right to information on the underlying logic of decisions made using algorithms".

Apart from that, the Council of Europe was developing a legally binding instrument, which is the Council of Europe Framework Convention on Artificial Intelligence and Human Rights, Democracy and the Rule of Law, signed in Vilnius on September 5th, 2024[56]. It is fully compatible with EU law in general, in particular the AI Act, which is the first comprehensive AI regulation globally.

From a Polish legal perspective, the most meaningful regulations in this regard are the Constitution of the Republic of Poland and the Polish Code of Criminal Procedure, which establish the right to a court, the presumption of innocence, the principle of individualized justice, the principle of equality of arms, or the principle of equality before the law. Despite the fact that a rich and varied jurisprudence of the courts has developed on the grounds of these legal acts, they still

---

55 Council of Europe, European Commission for the Efficiency of Justice (CEPEJ), *European ethical Charter on the use of Artificial Intelligence in judicial systems and their environment (2018)*, pp. 51–61, available at: https://rm.coe.int/ethical-charter-en-for-publication-4-december-2018/16808f699c [accessed on: December 23rd, 2023].

56 For more, see https://www.coe.int/en/web/artificial-intelligence/the-framework-convention-on-artificial-intelligence [accessed on: September 10th, 2024].

require constant interpretation and it is difficult to predict how they will rule on AI-based Recidivism Risk Assessment Tools. This will depend not only on the features of the algorithm itself, but also on how it is implemented in the national legal order (i.e., the stage of the proceedings, the requirements for application and questioning, procedural guarantees).

The criticisms and concerns described, based on the experience of the U.S. criminal justice system, indicate that the implementation of algorithmic recidivism risk assessment tools may violate the principle of individualization of criminal responsibility. However, if it were to be assumed that there was no such breach, the deployment of these instruments would require changes to criminal procedural law in particular. Firstly, the place of the report generated by the algorithm in the evidence catalogue needs to be determined. Indeed, it has to be decided whether these algorithms are to function as research tools to be used by court experts (to develop opinions/expertises) or probation officers (for the purpose of preparing a background interview), or whether they should constitute a separate (stand-alone) type of evidence (to be prepared by a specialist or expert who would operate the program and provide additional explanations, or whether the reports should be generated by the court itself and attached to the case file). Depending on which of the above approaches is implemented, the algorithms will be able to influence the outcome of the case either directly or indirectly. It is important to bear in mind that the reports will be subject to a free evaluation of the evidence, which means that the courts may find them either wholly or partly credible or unreliable.

Most importantly, however, mechanisms must be put in place to eliminate or reduce the risk of the court submitting to the results of the report, ruling automatically in accordance with them. Indeed, a judge cannot become 'managerial' and rely on the power of information systems to quickly resolve disputes.

Firstly, it must be made clear that the predictions contained in the reports are only supportive and cannot be aggravating or mitigating circumstances. Secondly, there must be an obligation to inform participants in the proceedings of the intention to use AI-based Recidivism Risk Assessment Instrument. Thirdly, as in the United States of America, judges should be instructed about the objections to the predictions developed by such an algorithm. Fourthly, the report generated by the algorithm should include a justification of the results. The lack of an explanation makes the document non-transparent (a black box phenomenon). Such a justification is particularly desirable when there is more than one report in the casefile generated by different algorithms (or just different models) and their results are not consistent. In its absence, the court is unable to trace the thought process and determine why the prediction is the way it is. The court should then consider both reports to be untrustworthy and make his own assessment of the risk of re-offending, guided by personal experience, knowledge standards and principles of sound reasoning. Fifthly, the reasons for court decisions should include an explanation of why the court found the report credible or unreliable. Finally, there is a concern that challenging the results of such a report by a party will be made much more difficult. Not only because of the lack of special knowledge but also because of the court's belief in the robustness and infallibility of the tool. This issue requires separate analysis and research from a psychological perspective. However, consideration should be given to the creation of a 'fast-track' verification of allegations that the algorithm is working correctly. It would be recommended to establish a team of experts within an existing institute or other entity, such as AI system certifier.

Notwithstanding the above, attention should be paid to the need for training for judges, prosecutors, probation officers, representatives, defense attorneys, and other participants in the proceedings.

6. Final Remarks

In conclusion, it is important to point out that the experience of U.S. criminal justice authorities with the use of predictive algorithms provides an understanding of how complex a process it is to implement such recidivism risk assessment tools. The algorithm should be objective and neutral. More precisely, such an algorithm is supposed to meet the requirements characteristic of trustworthy Artificial Intelligence, as well as comply with constitutional and EU standards regarding human rights (e.g. the right to a court, the presumption of innocence, the principle of individualized justice or the principle of equality before the law) and criminal law. The analysis shows that this has not yet been achieved in the United States. It is therefore not surprising that the EU legislator, in order to ensure respect for the fundamental rights of the individual, has chosen such a restrictive approach to algorithmic tools for assessing the risk of recidivism. The enactment of the AI Act is undoubtedly decisive in terms of permitting the implementation of such instruments. This is because a determination will need to be made as to whether the tool in question is prohibited or admissible as a high-risk AI system.

Despite this, it is important to keep in mind that these tools are still being improved and perhaps in the future they will become trustworthy (legal, ethical and robust) and EU will change her attitude to them. However, the implementation of such tools in Poland is not recommended at the moment. The risk of violation of fundamental human rights and freedoms is too great.

7. Bibliography

Literature

Alan A. et al., 'Assessing the Risk of Australian Indigenous Sexual Offenders Reoffending: A Review of the Research Literature and Court Decisions', 26(2) *Psychiatry, Psychology and Law* 2019.

Angwin J. et al., 'Machine bias. There's software used across the country to predict future criminals. And it's biased against blacks', *ProPublica*, available at: https://www.propublica.org/article/machine-bias-risk-assessments-in-criminal-sentencing [accessed on: December 1st, 2023].

Bavitz Ch. et al., 'Assessing the Assessments: Lessons From Early State Experiences in the Procurement and Implementation of Risk Assessment Tools', Berkman Klein Center for Internet & Society 2018, available at: https://dash.harvard.edu/handle/1/37883502 [accessed on: September 23rd, 2023].

Bonta J., Andrews D. A., *Risk-Need-Responsivity Model for Offender Assessment and Rehabilitation*, Canada 2007, available at: https://www.publicsafety.gc.ca/cnt/rsrcs/pblctns/rsk-nd-rspnsvty/index-en.aspx [accessed on: September 23rd, 2023].

Brennan T., Dieterich W., 'Correctional offender management profiles for alternative sanctions (COMPAS)' in: J. P. Singh et al. (eds.), *Handbook of recidivism risk/needs assessment tools*, New York: John Wiley & Sons 2018.

Brennan T., Dieterich W., Mendoza Ch., 'COMPAS Risk Scales: Demonstrating Accuracy Equity and Predictive Parity. Performance of the COMPAS Risk Scales in Broward County, July 8th, 2016', available at: https://go.volarisgroup.com/rs/430-MBX-989/images/ProPublica_Commentary_Final_070616.pdf [accessed on: December 1st, 2023].

Burdziak K., Rüütel E., *Prognoza kryminologiczna. Porównanie rozwiązań estońskich i polskich*, Wydawnictwo Naukowe Tygiel 2022.

Chelioudakis E., 'Risk Assessment Tools in Criminal Justice: Is There a Need for such Tools in Europe and would Their Use Comply with European Data Protection Law?', 1(2) *Australian National University Journal of Law and Technology* 2020.

Cohen T. H. et al., 'The Federal Post-Conviction Risk Assessment Instrument: A Tool for Predicting Recidivism for Offenders on Federal Supervision' in: J. P. Singh et al. (eds.), *Handbook of recidivism risk/needs assessment tools*, New York: John Wiley & Sons 2018.

Criminal Law – Sentencing Guidelines – Wisconsin Supreme Court Requires Warning Before Use of Algorithmic Risk Assessments in Sentencing – State v. Loomis, 881 N.W.2d 749 (Wis. 2016), 130(5) *Harvard Law Review* 2017.

Cyphert A. B., 'Reprogramming Recidivism: The First Step Act and Algorithmic Prediction of Risk', 51 *Seton Hall Law Review* 2020.

van Dijck G., 'Predicting Recidivism Risk Meets AI Act', 28 *European Journal on Criminal Policy and Research* 2022.

Dressel J., Farid H., 'The accuracy, fairness, and limits of predicting recidivism', 4 *Sciences Advances* 2018.

Eckhouse L. et al., 'Layers of Bias: A Unified Approach for Understanding Problems With Risk Assessment', 46 *Criminal Justice and Behavior* 2019.

Ghasemi M. et al., 'The Application of Machine Learning to a General Risk–Need Assessment Instrument in the Prediction of Criminal Recidivism', 48 *Criminal Justice and Behavior* 2021.

Greene T. et al., 'Forks Over Knives: Predictive Inconsistency in Criminal Justice Algorithmic Risk Assessment Tools', 185 *Journal of the Royal Statistical Society Series A: Statistics in Society* 2022, Issue Supplement_2.

Harcourt B. E., *Against Prediction. Profiling, Policing, and Punishing in an Actuarial Age*, University of Chicago Press 2006.

Israni E., 'Algorithmic Due Process: Mistaken Accountability and Attribution in State v. Loomis', *JOLT Digest*, available at: https://jolt.law.harvard.edu/digest/algorithmic-due-process-mistaken-accountability-and-attribution-in-state-v-loomis-1 [accessed on: September 23rd, 2023].

Klichowski M., 'People Copy the Actions of Artificial Intelligence', 11 *Frontiers in Psychology* 2020, available at: https://www.frontiersin.org/articles/10.3389/fpsyg.2020.01130/full [accessed on: December 23rd, 2023].

Kowalewska-Łukuć M., Burdziak K., 'The use of AI in formulating a criminological prognosis of an offender', 25 *Technium Social Sciences Journal* 2021.

Larson J. et al., 'How We Analyzed the COMPAS Recidivism Algorithm', available at: https://www.propublica.org/article/how-we-analyzed-the-compas-recidivism-algorithm [accessed on: December 1st, 2023].

Mamak K., 'Prognoza kryminologiczna' in: K. Mamak (ed.), *Rewolucja cyfrowa a prawo karne*, Krakowski Instytut Prawa Karnego Fundacja 2019.

Nishi A., 'Privatizing Sentencing: A Delegation Framework for Recidivism Risk Assessment', 119 *Columbia Law Review* 2019.

Płocha E. A., 'O pojęciu sztucznej inteligencji i możliwościach jej zastosowania w postępowaniu cywilnym', 44 *Prawo w Działaniu. Sprawy cywilne* 2020, available at: https://pwd.iws.gov.pl/tom-44-prawo-cywilne/ [accessed on: June 1st, 2023].

Płocha E. A., 'Narzędzia oceny ryzyka powrotności do przestępstwa oparte na sztucznej inteligencji: uwagi na przykładzie aplikacji COMPAS', 2 *Problemy Prawa karnego*, 2023.

Płocha E. A., 'Sztuczna inteligencja w postępowaniu w sprawach dotyczących wykonania środka zabezpieczającego w postaci pobytu w zakładzie psychiatrycznym' in: J. Piskorski, M. Błaszczak (eds.), *Nowe technologie. Wyzwania i perspektywy dla prawa karnego*, ArchaeGraph 2023, available at: https://www.archaegraph.pl/lib/l231bv/978-83-67527-87-3-e-book-lmyp4svo.pdf [accessed on: September 23rd, 2023].

Rayner M., 'Commentary: This algorithm is used to deny inmates parole. We're not allowed to know anything about it', *Times Union*, available at: https://www.timesunion.com/opinion/article/commentary-proprietary-algorithm-deny-inmate-18001304.php [accessed on: August 1st, 2023].

Stańdo-Kawecka B., 'Ruch What works i „technologie szacowania ryzyka"' in: B. Stańdo-Kawecka, *Polityka karna i penitencjarna między punitywizmem i menedżeryzmem*, Wolters Kluwer Polska 2020.

Wójcik D., 'Stosowanie w postępowaniu karnym narzędzi diagnostyczno-prognostycznych służących oszacowaniu ryzyka powrotności do przestępstwa', 16 *Prawo w Działaniu. Sprawy karne* 2013.

Yong E., 'A Popular Algorithm Is No Better at Predicting Crimes Than Random People', *The Atlantic*, available at: https://www.theatlantic.com/technology/archive/2018/01/equivant-compas-algorithm/550646/ [accessed on: December 1st, 2023].

Other sources

Australian Lawyers Alliance, *Predicting recidivism – the questionable role of algorithms in the criminal justice system*, available at: https://www.lawyersalliance.com.au/opinion/predicting-recidivism-the-questionable-role-of-algorithms-in-the-criminal-justice-system [accessed on: September 23rd, 2023].

Council of Europe, European Commission for the Efficiency of Justice, *European ethical Charter on the use of Artificial Intelligence in judicial systems and their environment (2018)*, available at: https://rm.coe.int/ethical-charter-en-for-publication-4-december-2018/16808f699c [accessed on: December 23rd, 2023].

Equivant, *Practitioner's Guide to COMPAS Core. April 4th, 2019*, available at: https://www.equivant.com/practitioners-guide-to-compas-core/ [accessed on: September 23rd, 2023].

European Commission, Directorate-General for Communications Networks, Content and Technology, *Ethics guidelines for trustworthy AI*, Publications Office, 2019, available at: https://data.europa.eu/doi/10.2759/346720 [accessed on: December 23rd, 2023].

European Commission, *White Paper on Artificial Intelligence – A European approach to excellence and trust*, COM/2020/65 final.

Fair Trials, *Automating Injustice: The Use of Artificial Intelligence & Automated Decision-Making Systems in Criminal Justice in Europe*, available at:

https://www.fairtrials.org/app/uploads/2021/11/Automating_Injustice.pdf [accessed on: December 6th, 2023].

U.S. Department of Justice, Bureau of Justice Assistance, *History of Risk Assessment. Public Safety Risk Assessment Clearinghouse*, available at: https://bja.ojp.gov/program/psrac/basics/history-risk-assessment#gcov4e [accessed on: September 23rd, 2023].

U.S. Department of Justice, Office of the Attorney General, *The First Step Act of 2018: Risk and Needs Assessment System*, available at: https://www.ojp.gov/First-Step-Act-of-2018-Risk-and-Needs-Assessment-System [accessed on: September 23rd, 2023].

Kristjan Kask*, Annegrete Palu**,
Mari-Liis Tohvelmann***, Pekka Santtila****

IV. Systematic Literature Review of Associations Between Question Type and Adult Witnesses' Accuracy: A Step in Creating a Digital Solution to Train Law Enforcement Personnel's Investigative Interviewing Skills

Abstract: It is known that investigative interviewing of child and adult victims and witnesses is a challenge for law enforcement personnel. Research suggests that the interviewers should ask open questions which facilitate the interviewee recalling what happened in their own words. Instead, research demonstrates that interviewers tend to use a lot of not recommended questions such as closed, option-posing, suggestive and misleading questions. There are several solutions that aim to train law enforcement personnel how to interview child witnesses but there is a lack of solutions to train their adult witness interviewing skills. One main factor in creating this type of solution is to know how accurately adult witnesses respond to different question types. We conducted a literature review to clarify this shortcoming. The initial database search yielded 63,083 hits out of which 53 studies met our inclusion criteria. Free recall questions produced most accurate responses where the accuracy rate in different studies ranged from 76 to 98%. For other question types, the accuracy rates were lower ranging from 44 to 87%.

Keywords: Investigative interviewing, question types, interviewer training, avatars, victims, witnesses

* Associate Professor of Legal Psychology, School of Natural Sciences and Health, Tallinn University, Tallinn, Estonia.

** Junior Lecturer in Experimental Psychology, Institute of Psychology, University of Tartu, Tartu, Estonia.

*** Junior Researcher, School of Natural Sciences and Health, Tallinn University, Tallinn, Estonia.

**** Professor of Psychology, Faculty of Arts and Sciences, NYU Shanghai, Shanghai, China.

1. Introduction

Investigative interviewing of adult witnesses can be challenging to law enforcement personnel. Literature suggests that for interviewing adult witnesses structured interviewing techniques such as the cognitive interview should be used to elicit detailed and accurate accounts[1]. Cognitive interview is a sequence of activities the interviewer should follow when planning, conducting and evaluating interviews with adult victims or witnesses[2]. One crucial aspect in conducting the interview is, first, to let the witnesses recall what happened in their own words and, second, support them elaborating their account with open questions[3]. Meta-analyses[4] conducted in the field demonstrate that by using cognitive interview the proportion of correct details in interviewees' answers increases compared to control interviews.

Experimental studies with adult witnesses have demonstrated that their answers are influenced by question types[5] with most accurate accounts being obtained in answer to questions supporting free recall[6]. Open questions also help adults report more accurate answers[7]. However, research has also demonstrated that interviewers tend to use a lot of not recommended question types such as

1 A. Memon, C. A. Meissner, J. Fraser, 'The Cognitive Interview: A meta-analytic review and study space analysis of the past 25 years', 16(4) *Psychology, Public Policy, and Law* 2010, pp. 340–372.

2 R. P. Fisher, R. E. Geiselman, *Memory-enhancing Techniques in Investigative Interviewing: The Cognitive Interview*, Springfield 1992, *passim*.

3 R. M. Paulo, P. B. Albuquerque, R. Bull, 'The Enhanced Cognitive Interview: Towards a better use and understanding of this procedure', 15(3) *International Journal of Police Science & Management* 2013, pp. 190–199.

4 A. Memon, C. A. Meissner, J. Fraser, *The Cognitive Interview…*, pp. 340–372.

5 J. P. Lipton, 'On the psychology of eyewitness testimony', 62 *Journal of Applied Psychology* 1977, pp. 90–95; R. Sutherland, H. Hayne, 'The effect of postevent information on adults' eyewitness reports', 15 *Applied Cognitive Psychology* 2001, pp. 249–263.

6 J. P. Lipton, *On the psychology…*, pp. 90–95; C. M. Allwood et al., 'Children's and adults' realism in their event-recall confidence in responses to free recall and focused questions', 14(6) *Psychology, Crime & Law 2008*, pp. 529–547; W. S. Cassel, C. E. M. Roebers, D. F. Bjorklund, 'Developmental patterns of eyewitness responses to repeated and increasingly suggestive questions', 61(2) *Journal of Experimental Child Psychology* 1996, pp. 116–133.

7 J. P. Lipton, *On the psychology…*, pp. 90–95; I. Ibabe, S. L. Sporer, 'How you ask is what you get: On the influence of question form on accuracy and confidence' 18(6) *Applied Cognitive Psychology* 2004, pp. 711–726.

closed, option-positing, suggestive or misleading questions[8]. Research indicates that option-posing[9], repeated[10], negative and double negative[11], and complex question forms[12] decrease accuracy of adult witnesses' answers. Also, it has been demonstrated that adult witnesses are also susceptible to misleading information in questions[13]. Launey and Py[14] found that there is not much scientific literature focusing on the methods and goals for investigative interviewing of adult witnesses. Their overview demonstrated that free recall was rarely used[15] in those interviews and that focused questions were often used.

Thus, in this chapter we first give an overview about solutions that have been created to train law enforcement personnel's interviewing skills of child witnesses. Then we move on to a literature review of adult witnesses response accuracy to

---

8 M. R. Kebbell, S. D. Johnson, 'Lawyers' questioning: The effect of confusing questions on witness confidence and accuracy', 24(6) *Law and Human Behavior* 2000, pp. 629–641.

9 I. Ibabe, S. L. Sporer, *How you ask…*, pp. 711–726.

10 M. J. Sharps et al. 'Repetition and reconfiguration: Demand-based confabulation in initial eyewitness memory', 9 *Journal of Investigative Psychology and Offender Profiling* 2012, pp. 149–160.

11 K. A. Wade, E. R. Spearing, 'The effect of cross-examination style questions on adult eyewitness accuracy depends on question type and eyewitness confidence', 31(2) *Memory* 2022, pp. 1–16.

12 Q. M. Chrobak, E. J. Rindal, M. S. Zaragoza, 'The impact of multifaceted questions on eyewitness accuracy following forced fabrication interviews', 142(3) *The Journal of General Psychology* 2015, pp. 150–166; F. Jack, R. Zajac, 'The effect of age and reminders on witnesses' responses to cross-examination-style questioning', 3 *Journal of Applied Research in Memory and Cognition* 2015, pp. 1–6; T. Valentine, K. Maras, 'The effect of cross-examination on the accuracy of adult eyewitness testimony', 25 *Applied Cognitive Psychology* 2011, pp. 554–561.

13 C. V. Molyneaux, J. D. Larsen, 'Acceptance of misleading information by children and adults', 71 *Psychological Reports* 1992, pp. 267–274; C. M. Roebers, W. Schneider, 'The impact of misleading questions on eyewitness memory in children and adults', 14 *Applied Cognitive Psychology* 2000, pp. 509–526; L. R. Shapiro, C. Blackford, C. F. Chen, 'Eyewitness memory for a simulated misdemeanor crime: The role of age and temperament in suggestibility', 19 *Applied Cognitive Psychology* 2005, pp. 267–289.

14 C. Launay, J. Py, 'Methods and aims of investigative interviewing of adult witnesses: An analysis of professional practices', 21(1) *Pratiques Psychologiques* 2015, pp. 55–70.

15 See M. Ginet, J. Py, 'A technique for enhancing memory in eye witness testimonies for use by police officers and judicial officials: the cognitive interview', 64 *Le travail humain* 2001, pp. 173–191; A. M. Wright, L. Alison, 'Questioning sequences in Canadian police interviews: Constructing and confirming the course of events?', 10 *Psychology, Crime & Law* 2004, pp. 137–154.

different question types which can give an input in creating a similar solution to train law enforcement personnel's interviewing skills of adult witnesses.

2. Digital Solutions Aimed at Child Witnesses

Trainings aimed to improve interviewing skills often focus on increasing the participants' knowledge of the topic with possibly some practical exercises. Unfortunately, it seems that translating this theoretical knowledge into actual interviewing situations is difficult. Further, if skills are not practiced repeatedly the effects of any training will disappear rapidly[16].

These trainings can be roughly grouped[17] into (i) short and intensive theory-based trainings, (ii) trainings that focus on practice and ongoing feedback, and (iii) training using computerised methods and 'serious gaming'[18].

Short and intensive theory-based trainings is the most common training format[19]. However, such traditional classroom-based trainings are not very successful in facilitating applying the theoretical skills into practice[20] - while theoretically oriented trainings enhance knowledge of interview skills, transferring this knowledge into practical skills may not automatically ensue[21].

One prevalent component of practical training are lectures about the use of a structured interview protocol followed by practising using the protocol in interviews with mock victims or witnesses[22]. Continuous practice is important

---

16 F. Pompedda, *Training in Investigative Interviews of Children: Serious Gaming Paired with Feedback Improves Interview Quality*, Doctoral thesis, Åbo Akademi University 2018.

17 F. Pompedda, *Training in Investigative…, passim.*

18 See also M. L. Tohvelmann, K. Kask, 'From Child to Adult Victims and Witnesses: Ways of Improving the Quality of Investigative Interviews', 31 *Juridica International* 2022, pp. 136–146.

19 F. Pompedda, *Training in Investigative…, passim.*

20 M. Lamb, 'Difficulties Translating Research on Forensic Interview Practices to Practitioners: Finding Water, Leading Horses, but Can We Get Them To Drink?', 71(8) *American Psychologist* 2016, pp. 710–718.

21 J. Hattie, H. Timperley, 'The power of feedback', 77(1) *Review of Educational Research* 2007, pp. 81–112; M. Johnson et al. 'Best practice recommendations still fail to result in action: A national 10-year follow-up study of investigative interviews in CSA cases', 29(5) *Applied Cognitive Psychology* 2015, pp. 661–668.

22 M. L. Tohvelmann, K. Kask, *From Child to Adult…*, pp. 136–146.

in mastering complex skills such as investigative interviewing[23]. It is known that interviewer performance is improved when practice is combined with expert feedback[24]. Explicit feedback assists in narrowing the gap between interviewers' subjective perceptions of their abilities and actual performance[25]. The type and number of feedback opportunities needed to produce optimal benefits in investigative interview training has not yet been specified. However, it has been established that feedback is more effective if learners play an active role in appraising their performance and in generating strategies to overcome limitations[26]. Immediate feedback is important[27], and interactive feedback given during a mock interview can be effective because the interviewers can be helped to identify and correct behavior in real time[28]. A recent overview analyzing mock interviews as a training tool for interviewers of children[29] pointed out that although mock interviews where children are portrayed by adult actors enable the interviewers to obtain immediate feedback to their performance, this method is expensive and time-consuming. Also, it is not clear to what extent the adult actors can mimic the behavior of real children.

It is known that interviewing child witnesses in sexual abuse cases is very challenging to investigators as there is a threat to contaminate child witness statement which could lead to the statement not being usable as an evidence later in court.

---

23 J. J. Donovan, D. J. Radosevich, 'A meta-analytic review of the distribution of practice effect', 84(5) *Journal of Applied Psychology* 1999, pp. 795–805; K. A. Ericsson, R. T. Krampe, C. Tesch-Römer, 'The role of deliberate practice in the acquisition of expert performance', 100(3) *Psychological Review* 1993, pp. 363–406.

24 M. B. Powell, R. P. Fisher, C. H. Hughes-Scholes, 'The effect of intra-versus post-interview feedback during simulated practice interviews about child abuse', 32(2) *Child Abuse & Neglect* 2008, pp. 213–227; M. B. Powell, R. P. Fisher, C. H. Hughes-Scholes, 'The effect of using trained versus untrained adult respondents in simulated practice interviews about child abuse', 32(11) *Child Abuse & Neglect* 2008, pp. 1007–1016.

25 M. B. Powell, S. P. Brubacher, G. A. Baugerud, 'An overview of mock interviews as a training tool for interviewers of children', 129 *Child Abuse & Neglect* 2022, pp. 1–11.

26 D. Boud, E. Molloy, 'Rethinking models of feedback for learning: The challenge of design', 38(6) *Assessment & Evaluation in Higher Education* 2013, pp. 698–712.

27 J. Gigante, M. Dell, A. Sharkey, 'Getting beyond good job: How to give effective feedback', 127(2) *Pediatrics* 2011, pp. 205–207; G. P. Wiggins, *Assessing student performance: Exploring the purpose and limits of testing*, Jossey-Bass/Wiley 1993, *passim*.

28 M. B. Powell, R. P. Fisher, C. H. Hughes-Scholes, *The effect of intra-versus…*, pp. 213–227.

29 For an overview see M. B. Powell, S. P. Brubacher, G. A. Baugerud, *An overview of mock…*, pp. 1–11.

Therefore, in recent decade, there have been several attempts to create digital solutions to create simulated interview experiences with avatars portraying child witnesses in sexual abuse cases[30].

Avatar Based Interview Training (AvBIT) consists of a web-based solution simulating a face-to-face conversation with a virtual representation of a child, that is, avatar[31]. This solution can be used to train specialists who have to conduct forensic investigative interviews with child victims or witnesses. AvBIT can overcome several limitations of traditional training methods that use role-play in training the investigators' interviewing skills[32]. Namely, this solution makes it possible for the interviewer to interact with an adult behind the avatar of a child on a computer screen in real time[33]. More specifically, an interviewer using one computer can be in one location and the adult interviewee (whose face and voice are converted into a child avatar outlook and high-pitched voice) in another location. The interviewee has a script to follow and tries to answer interviewers' questions as a typical child in this case would answer. AvBIT allows therefore to practice the whole structure of an interview protocol (such as NICHD protocol[34]) from the start to the end. To our knowledge there are no studies conducted that have investigated the effectiveness of this method for increasing the use of recommended questions in interviewers' questions. Also, the problem of understanding to what extent the adult is able to mimic child-like response patterns remains unsolved.

One solution created to train investigators to use a larger proportion of recommended questions when interviewing child victims and witnesses is Empowering Interviewer Training (EIT)[35]. In this web-based software, four or six-years-old child avatars who have either been or not been sexually abuse can be interviewed by the trainees. This corresponds to real life in that not all allegations that are reported

30 A. Dalli, *Technological Acceptance of an Avatar Based Interview Training Application*, Master's thesis, Linnaeus University 2021; F. Pompedda et al., 'Simulations of child sexual abuse interviews using avatars paired with feedback improves interview quality', 21(1) *Psychology, Crime & Law* 2015, pp. 28–52; G. A. Baugerud et al., 'Multimodal Virtual Avatars for Investigative Interviews with Children' in: *Proceedings of the 2021 Workshop on Intelligent Cross-Data Analysis and Retrieval (ICDAR '21)*, Association for Computing Machinery New York 2021, pp. 2–8.

31 A. Dalli, *Technological Acceptance of an Avatar…, passim.*

32 A. Dalli. *Technological Acceptance of an Avatar…, passim.*

33 See also M. L. Tohvelmann, K. Kask, *From Child to Adult…*, pp. 136–146.

34 For an overview see M. E. Lamb et al., *Tell me what happened: Questioning children about abuse*, 2nd ed., Chichester: John Wiley & Sons Ltd 2018.

35 F. Pompedda et al., *Simulations of child…*, pp. 28–52.

have actually happened. These child avatars can also be emotional (e.g., crying)[36]. The training works as follows: First the interviewer reads a scenario describing an allegation and provides a preliminary opinion as to what has happened. After that the interviewer has ten minutes to interview the child avatar to understand what happened, and then make a summary of what they think took place. During the interview, an operator (who can be present or participate from distance) listens and categorizes the questions asked after which the software launches the child's response by displaying the appropriate video clip which may contain accurate or inaccurate information. Every avatar has pre-specified memory content about what happened. The answers given by the avatar are dependent on algorithms that have been created based on a literature review of how accurately children of certain age have answered certain type of questions in experimental studies where question types have been varied[37]. The benefit of using algorithms is that, in this way, avatars behave as real children would in this situation. As the ground truth is known in these cases, feedback can be given not only regarding the question types used in the interviews but also regarding the final conclusion the interviewer makes[38]. EIT has been tested repeatedly and proved to be effective in increasing the proportion of interviewers' recommended questions not only within avatar interviews but also in transferring the skills learned during the simulations into interviews with both mock and actual child victims and witnesses[39].

Another research team is constructing an avatar solution to train investigators' child witness interviewing skills as well[40]. They propose a training program that utilizes different system components and multimodal data from the field of artificial intelligence such as chatbots, generation of visual content, text-to-speech, and speech-to-text. This program will be able to generate an almost unlimited amount of interview and also training data. The goal of combining all these different technologies and datatypes is to create an immersive and interactive child

---

36 F. Pompedda et al., 'Transfer of simulated interview training effects into interviews with children exposed to a mock event', 73 *Nordic Psychology* 2020, pp. 43–67.

37 F. Pompedda. *Training in Investigative…, passim.*

38 N. Krause et al., 'The effects of feedback and reflection on the questioning style of untrained interviewers in simulated child sexual abuse interviews', 31(2) *Applied Cognitive Psychology* 2017; F. Pompedda et al., *Simulations of child…*, pp. 28–52; F. Pompedda, *Training in Investigative…, passim.*

39 K. Kask et al., 'Transfer of avatar training effects to investigative field interviews of children conducted by police officers', 13 *Frontiers in Psychology* 2022; F. Pompedda et al., *Transfer of simulated…*, pp. 43–67.

40 G. A. Baugerud et al., *Multimodal Virtual Avatars…*, pp. 2–8.

avatar that responds in a realistic way, to help to support the training of police interviewers, but can also produce synthetic data of interview situations that can be used to solve different problems in the same domain.

3. Literature Review of Adult Witnesses' Accuracy in Response to Different Question Types

To our knowledge, there has been no attempts to create a similar software to simulate adult witness interviews with avatars[41]. An important factor in creating such software (similarly to EIT), is to know based on experimental studies how adult witnesses are responding to different question types. The associations between question types and the accuracy of child interviewees' answers has been extensively examined[42]. However, surprisingly, much less is known about how accurately adults respond to different types of questions. Thus, the aim of this review was to conduct a literature review of research concerning different question types and accuracy of details in response to the question types among adult witnesses. We wanted to find out what is the accuracy of details reported by adult witnesses in response to different question types. The result of such a review can provide the necessary input to create algorithms that will allow the creation of adult victim and witness avatars whose responses will realistically mimic those of actual adult victims and witnesses.

3.1. Search strategy

In November 2021, three electronic databases (PsycArticles and PsycInfo via EBSCOhost, Web of Science) as well as Google Scholar were searched to identify studies that have measured or reported how adults respond to different question types in investigative interviews. There were no restrictions in terms of the year of the study; however, we limited our search to peer-reviewed articles in English.

Our search criteria were broad and intended to elicit a large sample of possible studies (in order to, for example, include studies that have not specifically researched adults but have used adults as a control group) for inclusion in the analyses. The Boolean search strings we used are reported in Table 1 (slightly modified for each database where necessary). First, we did a separate

41 A recently published overview gives the state of the art concerning these issues. See M. L. Tohvelmann, K. Kask, *From Child to Adult…*, pp. 136–146.

42 For an overview see M. E. Lamb et al., *Tell me what happened…, passim.*

search for two separate search terms: 'post-event information' and 'Gudjonsson Suggestibility Scale'. For other strings, we categorised them to five main and nine additional categories. We first did a search with all combinations of the five main categories. Then we proceeded with combining each main category with each additional category.

Table 1: Systematic review search terms

Category	Search string
Separate	post-event information
Separate	gudjonsson suggestibility scale
Main	('Investigative interview*' OR 'police interview*' OR 'cognitive interview*')
Main	forensic
Main	suggesti*
Main	(witness* OR victim OR eyewitness*)
Main	question*
Extra	(questioning OR 'question type*' OR 'question format*' OR 'question style*' OR 'question wording' OR 'question order')
Extra	('Recall accuracy' OR 'accuracy of answers' OR 'erroneous information' OR 'eyewitness accuracy')
Extra	('Amount of information' OR 'free*recall details' OR 'number of details' OR 'free*recall report*')
Extra	bias
Extra	('interview* style' OR 'interview* strateg*' OR 'interview* practice*' OR 'interview* technique')
Extra	Rapport
Extra	'false memor*'
Extra	('person description' OR 'person recollection' OR description of faces)
Extra	('repeat* question*' OR 'question repetition*' OR 'free*recall prompt*' OR 'free*recall invitation*' OR 'general invitation*' OR 'cued invitation*' OR invitation* OR 'time segmentation invitation*' OR facilitator* OR 'forced*choice question*' OR 'multiple*choice question*' OR 'open*ended question*' OR 'open*ended invitation*' OR 'directive question*' OR 'closed question*' OR 'yes*no question*' OR 'closed*ended question*' OR 'option*posing question*' OR 'closed*ended directive*' OR 'suggestive question*' OR suggestion OR 'misleading question*')

3.2. Criteria for inclusion and exclusion of studies

During the search, we only included studies that were written in English and published in a peer-reviewed journal. Empirical studies were included if they: (a) investigated how adults respond in mock investigative interviews (i.e., participants first witness a mock event and then are interviewed about the event which gives the researchers opportunity to assess the accuracy of their responses to different question types); (b) included adult participants (even if adults were in a control group); (c) assessed at least one question type (free recall, cued recall, open questions, closed or yes/no questions, suggestive/leading questions, misleading questions, forced-choice questions); (d) a dependent measure of accuracy was reported. We did not include qualitative studies or meta-analyses.

3.3. Screening and study selection

Studies were screened and selected based upon pre-specified inclusion/exclusion criteria. We used a three-stage process: title review, abstract review, full-text screening. In the first round of screening, titles that had no relevance to disclosure of information in investigative interviews were eliminated. The abstracts of the articles that were not excluded were checked for whether the study involved adults as participants and question types. Those studies that did not meet these inclusion criteria were eliminated at this stage. Articles that passed the abstract screening were progressed to full-text screening. Articles were deemed ineligible at this stage if they did not have an adult group for which at least one question type was reported or where the question types were reported but not in terms of the proportion of accurateness but only in terms of means. The articles that passed the full-text screening stage and were then coded for sample characteristics (number of participants, age or participants), question types (free recall, cued recall, open questions, closed or yes/no questions, suggestive/leading questions, misleading questions, forced-choice questions), proportion of accurate responses, event realism (mock crime in video, non-crime in video, live event of non-crime); medium of registering the victim/witness statements in the study (oral or written), retention interval (immediate or number of days between seeing the stimuli and providing statements).

3.4. Results

The initial database search yielded 63 083 hits (see Table 2). After removing duplicates (n = 26,651), 36.432 articles remained for title screening. During the title screening, 33,818 articles were excluded, and thus, 2,614 articles remained for abstract screening. After excluding 2,312 articles based on the abstracts, we assessed 302 full-text articles to identify whether they met the inclusion criteria. Altogether, 249 articles were excluded (either not having an adult group for which at least one question type was reported or where the question types were reported but not in terms of the proportion of accurateness but only in terms of means). Finally, 53 studies[43] met the inclusion criteria (15 of them involved two or more experiments).

43 C. M Allwood, J. Knutsson, P. A. Granhag, 'Eyewitnesses under influence: How feedback affects the realism in confidence judgements', 12(1) *Psychology, Crime & Law* 2006, pp. 25–38; C. M. Allwood et al., Children's and adults' realism in their event-recall confidence in responses to free recall and focused questions', 14(6) *Psychology, Crime & Law* 2008, pp. 529–547; D. F. Bjorklund et al., 'Social demand characteristics in children's and adults' eyewitness memory and suggestibility: the effect of different interviewers on free recall and recognition', 14(5) *Applied Cognitive Psychology* 2000, pp. 421–433; N. Brackmann et al., 'Testing a new approach to improve recall in different ages: Providing witnesses with a model statement', 3(2) *Translational Issues in Psychological Science* 2017, pp. 131–142; S. P. Brubacher et al., 'The effect of question type on resistance to misinformation about present and absent details', 34(6) *Applied Cognitive Psychology* 2020, pp. 1323–1334; A. J. Bonham, C. González-Vallejo, 'Assessment of calibration for reconstructed eye-witness memories', 131(1) *Acta Psychologica* 2009, pp. 34–52; J. Boon, E. Noon, 'Changing perspectives in cognitive interviewing, Psychology', 1 *Crime & Law* 1994, pp. 59–69; R. Boon et al., 'Demonstrating detail in investigative interviews – An examination of the DeMo technique', 34(5) *Applied Cognitive Psychology* 2020, *passim*; S. Buratti, C. M. Allwood, M. Johansson, 'Stability in the metamemory realism of eyewitness confidence judgments', 15(1) *Cognitive Processing* 2015, pp. 39–53; G. A. Bärthel et al., 'Collaboration enhances later individual memory for emotional material', 25(5) *Memory* 2017, pp. 636–646; R. N. Carol et al., 'Being a good witness: The roles of benevolence and working memory capacity in rapport's effect on eyewitness memory', 51(7) *Journal of Applied Social Psychology* 2021, pp. 730–745; W. S. Cassel, D. F. Bjorklund, 'Developmental patterns of eyewitness memory and suggestibility: An ecologically based short-term longitudinal study', 19(5) *Law and Human Behavior* 1995, pp. 507–532; W. S. Cassel, C. E. M. Roebers, D. F. Bjorklund, 'Developmental patterns of eyewitness…', pp. 116–133; R. Collins, R. Lincoln, M. G. Frank, 'The effect of rapport in forensic interviewing', 9(1) *Psychiatry, Psychology and Law* 2002, pp. 69–78; M. Dahl et al., 'Old and very old adults as witnesses: Event memory and metamemory', 21(8) *Psychology, Crime & Law* 2015, pp. 764–775; C. J. Dando et al., 'Modifying the cognitive interview: Countenancing forensic application by enhancing practicability', 17(6)*Psychology, Crime & Law* 2011, pp. 491–511; M. L. Eisen, D. Y. Morgan, L. Mickes,

'Individual differences in eyewitness memory and suggestibility: examining relations between acquiescence, dissociation and resistance to misleading information', 33(4) *Personality and Individual Differences* 2002, pp. 553–571; J. Eastwood, B. Snook, K. Luther, 'Establishing the most effective way to deliver the sketch procedure to enhance interviewee free recall', 25(5) *Psychology, Crime & Law* 2019, pp. 482–493; J. R. Evans, R. P. Fisher, 'Eyewitness memory: Balancing the accuracy, precision and quantity of information through metacognitive monitoring and control' 25(3) *Applied Cognitive Psychology* 2011, pp. 501–508; A. Hagsand et al., 'Bottled memories: on how alcohol affects eyewitness recall', 54(3) *Scandinavian Journal of Psychology* 2013, pp. 188–195; M. H. Karlén et al., 'To wait or not to wait? Improving results when interviewing intoxicated witnesses to violence', 58(1) *Scandinavian Journal of Psychology* 2017, pp. 15–22; L. Hope et al., 'Protecting and enhancing eyewitness memory: The impact of an initial recall attempt on performance in an investigative interview', 28(3) *Applied Cognitive Psychology* 2014, pp. 304–313; J. Gawrylowicz et al., 'Intoxicated eyewitnesses: The effect of a fully balanced placebo design on event memory and metacognitive control', 33(3) *Applied Cognitive Psychology* 2019, pp. 344–357; J. Gawrylowicz, A. Memon, A. Scoboria, 'Equipping witnesses with transferable skills: The Self-Administered Interview', 20(4) *Psychology, Crime & Law* 2020, pp. 315–325; M. Ginet, J. Py, C. Colomb, 'The differential effectiveness of the cognitive interview instructions for enhancing witnesses' memory of a familiar event', 73(1) *Swiss Journal of Psychology* 2014, pp. 25–34; I. Ibabe, S. L. Sporer, *How you ask…*, pp. 711–726; F. Jack, J. Leov, R. Zajac, 'Age-related differences in the free recall accounts of child, adolescent, and adult witnesses', 28(1) *Applied Cognitive Psychology* 2014, pp. 30–38; M. R. Kebbell, S. D. Johnson, 'Lawyers' questioning: The effect of confusing questions on witness confidence and accuracy', 24(6) *Law and Human Behavior* 2000, pp. 629–641; J. Knutsson, C. M. Allwood, M. Johansson, 'Child and adult witnesses: the effect of repetition and invitation-probes on free recall and metamemory realism', 6 *Metacognition Learning* 2011, pp. 213–228; A. C. Krix et al., 'Providing eyewitnesses with initial retrieval support: What works at immediate and subsequent recall?', 20(10) *Psychology, Crime & Law* 2014, pp. 1 005–1 027; A. C. Krix et al., 'Eyewitness evidence obtained with the Self-Administered Interview is unaffected by stress', 30(1) *Applied Cognitive Psychology* 2016, pp. 103–112; J. Ma, H. M. Paterson, M. Temler, 'The effects of immediate recall and subsequent retrieval strategy on eyewitness memory', 29(5) *Psychiatry, Psychology & Law* 2021, pp. 788–805; K. Matsuo, H. Miura, 'Effectiveness of the Self-Administered Interview and drawing pictures for eliciting eyewitness memories', 24(5) *Psychiatry, Psychology & Law* 2016, pp. 643–654; V. Murnikov, K. Kask, 'Recall accuracy in children: Age vs. conceptual thinking', 12 *Frontiers in Psychology* 2021, *passim*; Z. Nahouli et al., 'Rapport building and witness memory: Actions may 'speak' louder than words', 16(8) *PloS One* 2021; J. Rechdan et al., 'Computer mediated social comparative feedback does not affect metacognitive regulation of memory reports', 8 *Frontiers in Psychology* 2017; C. M. Roebers, 'Confidence judgments in children's and adult's event recall and suggestibility', 38(6) *Developmental Psychology* 2002, pp. 1052–1067; C. M. Roebers, N. von der Linden, P. Howie, 'Favourable and unfavourable conditions for children's confidence judgments', 25(1) *British Journal of Developmental Psychology* 2007, pp. 109–134; C. M. Roebers, W. Schneider, 'The strategic regulation of children's memory performance and suggestibility', 91(1) *Journal of Experimental Child Psycholology* 2005, pp. 24–44; C. M. Roebers, K. M. McConkey, 'Mental reinstatement of the misinformation context and the misinformation effect in children and adults', 17(4) *Applied Cognitive Psychology* 2003, pp. 477–493; C. M. Roebers, N. Moga, W. Schneider, 'The role of accuracy motivation on children's and adults' event recall', 78(4) *Journal of Experimental Child Psychology* 2001, pp. 313–329; C. M. Roebers, W. Schneider, 'Memory for an observed event in the presence of prior misinformation: Developmental patterns of free recall and identification accuracy', 19(4) *British Journal of Developmental Psychology* 2001, pp. 507–524; C. M. Roebers, O. Fernandez, 'The effects of accuracy motivation and children's and adults' event recall, suggestibility, and their answers to unanswerable questions', 3(4) *Journal of Cognition and Development* 2002, pp. 415–443; C. M. Roebers, P. Howie, 'Confidence judgments in event recall: developmental progression in the impact of question format', 85(4) *Journal of Experimental Child Psychology* 2003, pp. 352–371; C. M. Roebers, W. Schneider, 'The impact of misleading questions on eyewitness memory in children and adults', 14 *Applied Cognitive Psychology* 2000, pp. 509–526; F. Sarwar, C. M. Allwood, Å. Innes-Ker, 'Effects of communication with non-witnesses on eyewitnesses' recall correctness and meta-cognitive realism', 25 *Applied Cognitive Psychology* 2011, pp. 782–791; R. B. Saraiva et al., 'Using metamemory measures and memory tests to estimate eyewitness free recall performance', 28(4) *Memory* 2020, pp. 94–106; N. Schreiber Compo et al., 'Witness memory and alcohol: The effects of state-dependent recall', 41(2) *Law & Human Behavior* 2017, pp. 202–215; A. Scoboria, G. Mazzoni, I. Kirsch, '"Don't know" responding to answerable and unanswerable questions during misleading and hypnotic interviews', 14(3) *Journal of Experimental Psychology: Applied* 2008, pp. 255–265; A. Scoboria et al., 'Improving responding to questioning using a brief retrieval training', 2(4) *Journal of Applied Research in Memory and Cognition* 2013, pp. 210–215; A. de la Fuente Vilar et al., 'Effects of cooperation on information disclosure in mock-witness interviews', 25(5) *Legal and Criminological Psychology* 2020, pp. 133–149; L. Wysman et al., 'The cognitive interview buffers the effects of subsequent repeated questioning in the absence of negative feedback', 32(2) *Behavioral Sciences and the Law* 2014, pp. 207–219; E. Wang, H. Paterson, R. Kemp, 'The effects of immediate recall on eyewitness accuracy and susceptibility to misinformation', 20(7) *Psychology, Crime & Law* 2014, pp. 619–634.

Table 2: Search Strategy for the Review

Identification	Database searches: PsycArticles and PsycInfo via EBSCOhost and Web of Science, Google Scholar (N = 63 083)	
Screening	Records screened after duplicates removed (n = 26 651)	
	Titles screened (n = 26 651)	Records excluded (n = 24 037)
	Abstracts screened (n = 2 614)	Records excluded (n = 2 312)
Eligibility	Full text (n = 302)	Excluded (n = 249) – no adults – no question type – no proportion of accuracy
Included	Studies included (n = 53)	

The mean age of witnesses in the experiments was 24.5 years (range from 18 to 66 years). For 33 experiments the recall followed immediately to witnessing the event in question. For three experiments the time delay was 1–2 days, for 22 experiments 7–8 days (a week), for three experiments 14 days (two weeks), for seven experiments 21 days (three weeks) and for one experiment 42 days (six weeks). Concerning stimulus event, for 58 experiments it was a video of a crime episode, for one experiment a live event of a non-crime and for ten experiments a video of a non-crime event. Information from the witnesses was gathered orally in 41 experiments and in written form 28 experiments. A 'don't know' option was present in nine experiments.

The question types in the experiments could be classified into seven broad categories: free and cued recall, and open, closed, suggestive/leading, misleading and forced-choice questions. Free recall indicated that the witnesses were asked very broadly to recall what happened (e.g., 'Tell me what you remember about the witnessed event?'). In cued recall, the witnesses were directed to remember details about specific topics (e.g., 'Tell me what you remember about that person?'). Open questions specified what the witness had mentioned already with wh-questions (e.g., what, where, who). Closed questions were formed from questions indicating a yes or no response (e.g., 'Did he go away?'). In suggestive/leading questions the interviewees were targeted to answer in a specific way indicating a correct response (e.g., 'They were pushing the man, didn't they?'). In misleading questions, a false details was introduced to interviewees (e.g., the colour of the car was not mentioned by a witness but they were asked 'Was the car green?'). Finally, the witnesses were given choice how to respond (e.g., 'Did it happen once or twice or many times?').

Most popular category examined in the studies was free recall (see Table 3). Other question types were asked less frequently. Free recall questions produced most accurate responses where the accuracy rate in different studies ranged from 76 to 98%. For other question types, the accuracy rates were lower.

Table 3: Accuracy range by question types

Question type	Number of experiments	Accuracy range
free recall	37	76–98
cued recall	12	52–87
open questions	14	45–82
closed or yes/no questions	11	54–89
suggestive/leading questions	3	63–79
misleading questions	14	44–87
forced-choice questions	1	67

We also grouped the question types also as recommended questions (recommended to be used by structured interview methods such as free and cued recall, and open questions, see Kask et al., 2022) and non-recommended questions (closed, suggestive/leading, misleading and forced-choice questions). For recommended questions, the accuracy rates ranged from 45 to 87% and for non-recommended questions, the range was 44 to 87%.

4. Conclusion

Based on the results of the literature analysis, we found how accurately adult witnesses respond to different types of questions. We found that free recall produces more accurate accounts compared to other question types confirming some of the previous findings[44]. Thus, the result of this literature review provides us valuable input of creating algorithms how adult avatars would answer in such a software when an interviewer asks them a certain sort of question.

44 J. P. Lipton, *On the psychology…*, pp. 90–95; C. M. Allwood et al., *Children's and adults' realism…*, pp. 529–547; W. S. Cassel, C. E. M. Roebers, D. F. Bjorklund, 'Developmental patterns of eyewitness…', pp. 116–133.

However, the literature review also identified gaps in our knowledge of these issues which are now discussed more in detail. First, there is overall surprisingly little research conducted solely focusing on the accuracy of adult witnesses in response to different question types. Often adult sample accompanies research conducted with child witnesses ability to recall events using different types of questions[45] or are used as a control group in examining the effect of alcohol on the event recall[46]. Even more, research comparing structured interviewing methods to unstructured interviewing methods usually compare the number of details in free recall between the different methods such as the cognitive interview[47] or self-administered interview[48] to a control group at the level of the interview not analysing the associations between question types and responses at the level of question-answer pairs. It is known that in structured interviewing methods a free recall is usually first elicited from witnesses followed by a clarification phase. However, our knowledge of the question types and the accuracy of answers to those question types is still sparse.

Second, there were only limited number of experiments where a 'don't know' option was included as a possible choice for the witness[49]. In future studies, we encourage to involve 'don't know' or 'don't remember' options as in structured interviewing methods of adult witnesses such as the cognitive interview, this type of instruction is a common standard to educate the witness what is expected to answer as it lowers the possibility to guess in cases where the witness memory of what happened is vague[50].

---

45 For example, see C. M. Roebers, N. Moga, W. Schneider, *The role of accuracy…*, pp. 313–329.

46 A. Hagsand et al., A. Söderpalm-Gordh, *Bottled memories…*, pp. 188–195.

47 M. Ginet, J. Py, C. Colomb, *The differential effectiveness…*, pp. 25–34.

48 J. Gawrylowicz, A. Memon, A. Scoboria, *Equipping witnesses…*, pp. 315–325.

49 W. S. Cassel, D. F. Bjorklund, *Developmental patterns of eyewitness memory…*, pp. 507–532; J. R. Evans, R. P. Fisher, *Eyewitness memory: Balancing…*, pp. 501–508; N. Schreiber Compo et al., *Witness memory and alcohol…*, pp. 202–215; W. S. Cassel, C. E. M. Roebers, D. F. Bjorklund, 'Developmental patterns of eyewitness…,' pp. 116–133; C. M. Roebers, *Confidence judgments…*, pp. 1052–1067; C. M. Roebers, W. Schneider, *The strategic regulation…*, pp. 24–44; A. Scoboria et al., *Improving responding to questioning…*, pp. 205–210; C. M. Roebers, O. Fernandez, 'The effects of accuracy…,' pp. 414–443; C. M. Roebers, P. Howie, *Confidence judgments in event…*, pp. 352–371.

50 R. P. Fisher, R. E. Geiselman. *Memory-enhancing Techniques…, passim.*

To conclude, there are several software solutions that have been develop to train investigators' interviewing skills of child witnesses[51]. However, there is lack of similar softwares targeted for practicing investigative interviews with adult witnesses. For creating such a software, an essential component to know would be how accurately adult witnesses respond to different types of questions. The literature review conducted indicated that most accurate accounts are provided by free recall followed by other question types.

5. Bibliography

Literature

Allwood C. M, Knutsson J., Granhag P. A., 'Eyewitnesses under influence: How feedback affects the realism in confidence judgements', 12(1) *Psychology, Crime & Law* 2006.

Allwood C. M., et al., 'Children's and adults' realism in their event-recall confidence in responses to free recall and focused questions', 14(6) *Psychology, Crime & Law* 2008.

Bärthel G. A. et al., 'Collaboration enhances later individual memory for emotional material', 25(5) *Memory* 2017.

Baugerud G. A. et al., 'Multimodal Virtual Avatars for Investigative Interviews with Children' in: *Proceedings of the 2021 Workshop on Intelligent Cross-Data Analysis and Retrieval (ICDAR '21)*, Association for Computing Machinery New York 2021.

Bjorklund D. F. et al., 'Social demand characteristics in children's and adults' eyewitness memory and suggestibility: the effect of different interviewers on free recall and recognition', 14(5) *Applied Cognitive Psychology* 2000.

Bonham A. J., González-Vallejo C., 'Assessment of calibration for reconstructed eye-witness memories', 131(1) *Acta Psychologica* 2009.

Boon J., Noon E., 'Changing perspectives in cognitive interviewing, Psychology', 1 *Crime & Law* 1994.

Boon R. et al., 'Demonstrating detail in investigative interviews – An examination of the DeMo technique', 34(5) *Applied Cognitive Psychology* 2020.

Boud D., Molloy E., 'Rethinking models of feedback for learning: The challenge of design', 38(6) *Assessment & Evaluation in Higher Education* 2013.

---

51 A. Dalli, *Technological Acceptance of an Avatar…*, *passim*; F. Pompedda et al., *Simulations of child…*, pp. 28–52; G. A. Baugerud et al., *Multimodal Virtual Avatars…*, pp. 2–8.

Brackmann N. et al., 'Testing a new approach to improve recall in different ages: Providing witnesses with a model statement', 3(2) *Translational Issues in Psychological Science* 2017.

Brubacher S. P. et al., 'The effect of question type on resistance to misinformation about present and absent details', 34(6) *Applied Cognitive Psychology* 2020.

Buratti S., Allwood C. M., Johansson M., 'Stability in the metamemory realism of eyewitness confidence judgments', 15(1) *Cognitive Processing* 2015.

Carol R. N. et al., 'Being a good witness: The roles of benevolence and working memory capacity in rapport's effect on eyewitness memory', 51(7) *Journal of Applied Social Psychology* 2021.

Cassel W. S., Bjorklund D. F., 'Developmental patterns of eyewitness memory and suggestibility: An ecologically based short-term longitudinal study', 19(5) *Law and Human Behavior* 1995.

Cassel W. S., Roebers C. E. M., Bjorklund D. F., 'Developmental patterns of eyewitness responses to repeated and increasingly suggestive questions', 61(2) *Journal of Experimental Child Psychology* 1996.

Chrobak Q. M., Rindal E. J., Zaragoza M. S., 'The impact of multifaceted questions on eyewitness accuracy following forced fabrication interviews', 142(3) *The Journal of General Psychology* 2015.

Collins R., Lincoln R., Frank M. G., 'The effect of rapport in forensic interviewing', 9(1) *Psychiatry, Psychology and Law* 2002.

Dahl M. et al., 'Old and very old adults as witnesses: Event memory and metamemory', 21(8) *Psychology, Crime & Law* 2015.

Dalli A., *Technological Acceptance of an Avatar Based Interview Training Application*, Master's thesis, Linnaeus University 2021.

Dando C. J. et al., 'Modifying the cognitive interview: Countenancing forensic application by enhancing practicability', 17(6) *Psychology, Crime & Law* 2011.

de la Fuente Vilar A. et al., 'Effects of cooperation on information disclosure in mock-witness interviews', 25(5) *Legal and Criminological Psychology* 2020.

Donovan J. J., Radosevich D. J., 'A meta-analytic review of the distribution of practice effect', 84(5) *Journal of Applied Psychology* 1999.

Eastwood J., Snook B, Luther K., 'Establishing the most effective way to deliver the sketch procedure to enhance interviewee free recall', 25(5) *Psychology, Crime & Law* 2019.

Eisen M. L., Morgan D. Y., Mickes L., 'Individual differences in eyewitness memory and suggestibility: examining relations between acquiescence, dissociation and resistance to misleading information', 33(4) *Personality and Individual Differences* 2002.

Ericsson K. A., Krampe R. T., Tesch-Römer C., 'The role of deliberate practice in the acquisition of expert performance', 100(3) *Psychological Review* 1993.

Evans J. R., Fisher R. P., 'Eyewitness memory: Balancing the accuracy, precision and quantity of information through metacognitive monitoring and control', 25(3) *Applied Cognitive Psychology* 2011.

Fisher R. P., Geiselman R. E., *Memory-enhancing Techniques in Investigative Interviewing: The Cognitive Interview*, Springfield 1992.

Gawrylowicz J. et al., 'Intoxicated eyewitnesses: The effect of a fully balanced placebo design on event memory and metacognitive control', 33(3) *Applied Cognitive Psychology* 2019.

Gawrylowicz J., Memon A., Scoboria A., 'Equipping witnesses with transferable skills: The Self-Administered Interview', 20(4) *Psychology, Crime & Law* 2020.

Gigante J., Dell M., Sharkey A., 'Getting beyond good job: How to give effective feedback', 127(2) *Pediatrics* 2011.

Ginet M., Py J., 'A technique for enhancing memory in eye witness testimonies for use by police officers and judicial officials: the cognitive interview', 64 *Le travail humain* 2001.

Ginet M., Py J., Colomb C., 'The differential effectiveness of the cognitive interview instructions for enhancing witnesses' memory of a familiar event', 73(1) *Swiss Journal of Psychology* 2014.

Johnson M. et al., 'Best practice recommendations still fail to result in action: A national 10-year follow-up study of investigative interviews in CSA cases', 29(5) *Applied Cognitive Psychology* 2015.

Hagsand A. et al., 'Bottled memories: on how alcohol affects eyewitness recall', 54(3) *Scandinavian Journal of Psychology* 2013.

Hattie J., Timperley H., 'The power of feedback', 77(1) *Review of Educational Research* 2007.

Hope L. et al., 'Protecting and enhancing eyewitness memory: The impact of an initial recall attempt on performance in an investigative interview', 28(3) *Applied Cognitive Psychology* 2014.

Ibabe I., Sporer S. L., 'How you ask is what you get: On the influence of question form on accuracy and confidence' 18(6) *Applied Cognitive Psychology* 2004.

Jack F., Leov J., Zajac R., 'Age-related differences in the free-recall accounts of child, adolescent, and adult witnesses', 28(1) *Applied Cognitive Psychology* 2014.

Jack F., Zajac R., 'The effect of age and reminders on witnesses' responses to cross-examination-style questioning', 3 *Journal of Applied Research in Memory and Cognition* 2015.

Matsuo K., Miura H., 'Effectiveness of the Self-Administered Interview and drawing pictures for eliciting eyewitness memories', 24(5) *Psychiatry, Psychology & Law* 2016.

Karlén M. H. et al., 'To wait or not to wait? Improving results when interviewing intoxicated witnesses to violence', 58(1) *Scandinavian Journal of Psychology* 2017.

Kask K. et al., 'Transfer of avatar training effects to investigative field interviews of children conducted by police officers', 13 *Frontiers in Psychology* 2022.

Kebbell M. R., Johnson S. D., 'Lawyers' questioning: The effect of confusing questions on witness confidence and accuracy', 24(6) *Law and Human Behavior* 2000.

Knutsson J., Allwood C. M., Johansson M., 'Child and adult witnesses: the effect of repetition and invitation-probes on free recall and metamemory realism', 6 *Metacognition Learning* 2011.

Krause N. et al., 'The effects of feedback and reflection on the questioning style of untrained interviewers in simulated child sexual abuse interviews', 31(2) *Applied Cognitive Psychology* 2017.

Krix A. C. et al., 'Eyewitness evidence obtained with the Self-Administered Interview is unaffected by stress', 30(1) *Applied Cognitive Psychology* 2016.

Krix A. C. et al., 'Providing eyewitnesses with initial retrieval support: What works at immediate and subsequent recall?', 20(10) *Psychology, Crime & Law* 2014.

Lamb M., 'Difficulties Translating Research on Forensic Interview Practices to Practitioners: Finding Water, Leading Horses, but Can We Get Them To Drink?', 71(8) *American Psychologist* 2016.

Lamb M. E. et al., *Tell me what happened: Questioning children about abuse*, 2nd ed., Chichester: John Wiley & Sons Ltd 2018.

Launay C., Py J., 'Methods and aims of investigative interviewing of adult witnesses: An analysis of professional practices', 21(1) *Pratiques Psychologiques* 2015.

Lipton J. P., 'On the psychology of eyewitness testimony', 62 *Journal of Applied Psychology* 1977.

Ma J., Paterson H. M., Temler M., 'The effects of immediate recall and subsequent retrieval strategy on eyewitness memory', 29(5) *Psychiatry, Psychology & Law* 2021.

Memon A., Meissner C. A., Fraser J., 'The Cognitive Interview: A meta-analytic review and study space analysis of the past 25 years', 16(4) *Psychology, Public Policy, and Law* 2010.

Molyneaux C. V., Larsen J. D., 'Acceptance of misleading information by children and adults', 71 *Psychological Reports* 1992.

Murnikov V., Kask K., 'Recall accuracy in children: Age vs. conceptual thinking', 12 *Frontiers in Psychology* 2021.

Nahouli Z. et al., 'Rapport building and witness memory: Actions may 'speak' louder than words', 16(8) *PloS One* 2021.

Paulo R. M., Albuquerque P. B., Bull R., 'The Enhanced Cognitive Interview: Towards a better use and understanding of this procedure', 15(3) *International Journal of Police Science & Management* 2013.

Pompedda F. et al., 'Simulations of child sexual abuse interviews using avatars paired with feedback improves interview quality', 21(1) *Psychology, Crime & Law* 2015.

Pompedda F. et al., 'Transfer of simulated interview training effects into interviews with children exposed to a mock event', 73 *Nordic Psychology* 2020.

Pompedda F., *Training in Investigative Interviews of Children: Serious Gaming Paired with Feedback Improves Interview Quality*, Doctoral thesis, Åbo Akademi University 2018.

Powell M. B., Brubacher S. P., Baugerud G. A., 'An overview of mock interviews as a training tool for interviewers of children', 129 *Child Abuse & Neglect* 2022.

Powell M. B., Fisher R. P., Hughes-Scholes C. H., 'The effect of intra- versus post-interview feedback during simulated practice interviews about child abuse', 32(2) *Child Abuse & Neglect* 2008.

Powell M. B., Fisher R. P., Hughes-Scholes C. H., 'The effect of using trained versus untrained adult respondents in simulated practice interviews about child abuse', 32(11) *Child Abuse & Neglect* 2008.

Rechdan J. et al., 'Computer mediated social comparative feedback does not affect metacognitive regulation of memory reports', 8 *Frontiers in Psychology* 2017.

Roebers C. M., 'Confidence judgments in children's and adult's event recall and suggestibility', 38(6) *Developmental Psychology* 2002.

Roebers C. M., Fernandez O., 'The effects of accuracy motivation and children's and adults' event recall, suggestibility, and their answers to unanswerable questions', 3(4) *Journal of Cognition and Development* 2002.

Roebers C. M., Howie P., 'Confidence judgments in event recall: developmental progression in the impact of question format', 85(4) *Journal of Experimental Child Psychology* 2003.

Roebers C. M., McConkey K. M., 'Mental reinstatement of the misinformation context and the misinformation effect in children and adults', 17(4) *Applied Cognitive Psychology* 2003.

Roebers C. M., Moga N., Schneider W., 'The role of accuracy motivation on children's and adults' event recall', 78(4) *Journal of Experimental Child Psychology* 2001.

Roebers C. M., Schneider W., 'Memory for an observed event in the presence of prior misinformation: Developmental patterns of free recall and identification accuracy', 19(4) *British Journal of Developmental Psychology* 2001.

Roebers C. M., Schneider W., 'The impact of misleading questions on eyewitness memory in children and adults. 14 *Applied Cognitive Psychology* 2000.

Roebers C. M., Schneider W., 'The strategic regulation of children's memory performance and suggestibility', 91(1) *Journal of Experimental Child Psycholology* 2005.

Roebers C. M., von der Linden N., Howie, P. 'Favourable and unfavourable conditions for children's confidence judgments', 25(1) *British Journal of Developmental Psychology* 2007.

Saraiva R. B. et al., 'Using metamemory measures and memory tests to estimate eyewitness free recall performance', 28(4) *Memory* 2020.

Sarwar F., Allwood C. M., Innes-Ker Å., 'Effects of communication with non-witnesses on eyewitnesses' recall correctness and meta-cognitive realism', 25 *Applied Cognitive Psychology* 2011.

Schreiber Compo N. et al., 'Witness memory and alcohol: The effects of state-dependent recall', 41(2) *Law & Human Behavior* 2017.

Scoboria A. et al., 'Improving responding to questioning using a brief retrieval training', 2(4) *Journal of Applied Research in Memory and Cognition* 2013.

Scoboria A., Mazzoni G., Kirsch I., '"Don't know" responding to answerable and unanswerable questions during misleading and hypnotic interviews', 14(3) *Journal of Experimental Psychology: Applied* 2008.

Shapiro L. R., Blackford C., Chen C. F., 'Eyewitness memory for a simulated misdemeanor crime: The role of age and temperament in suggestibility', 19 *Applied Cognitive Psychology* 2005.

Sharps M. J. et al. 'Repetition and reconfiguration: Demand-based confabulation in initial eyewitness memory', 9 *Journal of Investigative Psychology and Offender Profiling* 2012.

Sutherland R., Hayne H., 'The effect of postevent information on adults' eyewitness reports', 15 *Applied Cognitive Psychology* 2001.

Tohvelmann M. L., Kask K., 'From Child to Adult Victims and Witnesses: Ways of Improving the Quality of Investigative Interviews', 31 *Juridica International* 2022.

Valentine T., Maras K., 'The effect of cross-examination on the accuracy of adult eyewitness testimony', 25 *Applied Cognitive Psychology* 2011.

Wade K. A., Spearing E. R., 'The effect of cross-examination style questions on adult eyewitness accuracy depends on question type and eyewitness confidence', 31(2) *Memory* 2022.

Wang E., Paterson H., Kemp R., 'The effects of immediate recall on eyewitness accuracy and susceptibility to misinformation', 20(7) *Psychology, Crime & Law* 2014.

Wiggins G. P., *Assessing student performance: Exploring the purpose and limits of testing*, Jossey-Bass/Wiley 1993.

Wright A. M., Alison L., 'Questioning sequences in Canadian police interviews: Constructing and confirming the course of events?', 10 *Psychology, Crime & Law* 2004.

Wysman L. et al., 'The cognitive interview buffers the effects of subsequent repeated questioning in the absence of negative feedback', 32(2) *Behavioral Sciences and the Law* 2014.

Ius, Lex et Res Publica

Studies in Law, Philosophy and Political Cultures

Edited by

Barbara Janusz-Pohl

Vol. 1 Anna Jaron: Socio-Economic Constitutional Rights in Democratisation Processes. An Account of the Constitutional Dialogue Theory. 2012.

Vol. 2 Stanisław Filipowicz: Democracy – The Power of Illusion. 2013.

Vol. 3 Teresa Dukiet-Nagórska (ed.): The Postulates of Restorative Justice and the Continental Model of Criminal Law. As Illustrated by Polish Criminal Law 2014.

Vol. 4 Agnieszka Kupzok: Enforcement of Patents on Geographically Divisible Inventions. An Inquiry into the Standard of Substantive Patent Law Infringement in Cross-Border Constellations. 2015.

Vol. 5 Alicja Jagielska-Burduk / Wojciech Szafrański: Legal Issues in Cultural Heritage Management. A Polish Perspective. 2016.

Vol. 6 Maciej Mataczyński (ed.): The Takeover of Public Companies as a Mode of Exercising EU Treaty Freedoms. 2017.

Vol. 7 Maciej Barczewski (ed.): Value of Information. Intellectual Property, Privacy and Big Data. 2018.

Vol. 8 Pawel Smoleń, Marcin Burzec: Introduction to Polish Tax Law. 2018.

Vol. 9 Łukasz Pohl, Konrad Burdziak: Judicial Interpretation of the 1997 Criminal Code Provisions on Self-Defence. 2019.

Vol. 10 Adam Szot: Judicial Review of Administrative Discretion. The Influence of Court Decisions on Administrative Actions. 2019.

Vol. 11 Michał Peno / Konrad Burdziak (eds.): The Concept of Modern Law. Polish and Central European Tradition. 2019.

Vol. 12 Leszek Leszczyński / Bartosz Liżewski / Adam Szot (eds.): Potential of Precedent in the Statutory Legal Order. 2019.

Vol. 13 Łukasz Bolesta: In Search of a Model for the Legal Protection of a Whistleblower in the Workplace in Poland. A legal and comparative study. 2020.

Vol. 14 Paweł Chmielnicki / Adam Sulikowski (eds.): New Perspectives on Legislation. A Comparative Approach. 2020.

Vol. 15 Marcin Burzec / Beata Kucia-Guściora / Paweł Smoleń: Agricultural Activity in Poland: A Fiscal and Legal Study. 2020.

Vol. 16 Magdalena Półtorak / Ilona Topa (eds.): Women, Children and (Other) Vulnerable Groups. Standards of Protection and Challenges for International Law. 2021.

Vol. 17 Josef Albert Fox: Die polnische Verfassung vom 3. Mai 1791. Hintergründe der Entstehung und der Außerkraftsetzung. Stellung Polens im Zeitalter der Aufklärung. 2021.

Vol. 18 Barbara Janusz-Pohl (ed.): Juvenile Justice Systems: Poland-Brazil-Portugal. 2021.

Vol. 19 Leszek Leszczyński: General Reference Clauses in the Judicial Process. Context of Legislative Intentions Interpretative Discretion. 2021.

Vol. 20 Francisco J. Campos Zamora: Das Problem der Begründung richterlicher Entschei- dungen. Eine Analyse auf der Grundlage der Theorie der juristischen Argumentation. 2021.

Vol. 21 Aneta Skorupa-Wulczyńska: Language Rights of the Citizen of the European Union. 2022.

Vol. 22 Mateusz Osiecki: International Legal Aspects of Aerial Terrorism. Methods of Law Enforcement in Avia-tion. 2022.

Vol. 23 Vladimír Sharp / Gabriela Blahoudková / Jakub Handrlica (eds.): Law, Pandemics and Ownership Restrictions. 2022.

Vol. 24 Piotr Kasprzyk / Anna Konert: Drones – Future of Aviation Law? Interference of Public Law in Private Law. 2023.

Vol. 25 Szymon Pawelec (ed.): Consensual Mechanisms in Criminal Proceedings – Integrative and Comparative Perspective. 2023.

Vol. 26 Dorota Pudzianowska: Statelessness in Public Law. 2023.

Vol. 27 Boguslaw Przywora / Aleksander Wróbel: Formalised Access to Pre-jurisdictional Free Legal Aid. 2023.

Vol. 28 Ewa Dawidziuk / Patricia Panero / Anny Tarwacka (eds.): Family, Law, and Society: from Roman Law to the Present Day. 2024.

Vol. 29 Marian Grzybowsk / Boguslaw Przywora / Aleksandra Syryt (eds.): Free Legal Aid, Theory, Legal Basis and Practice. European Standards. 2024.

Vol. 30 Karolina Gmerek: Trial as a Social Communication Occurrence. 2024.

Vol. 31 Pawel Wiliński (ed.): Effective Legal Remedies in Criminal Justice System. European Perspective. 2024.

Vol. 32 Jakub Hanc / Olga Sitarz / Anna Jaworska-Wieloch: On the (non)existence of the right to religious freedom of persons deprived of liberty. 2024.

Vol. 33 Marian Grzybowsk / Boguslaw Przywora / Aleksandra Syryt (eds.): Free Legal Aid – A Comparative Approach. 2024.

Vol. 34 Dominik Gajewski (ed.): Functioning of Administrative Judiciary in the Context of Economic Changes. 2024.

Vol. 35 Mikołajczyk, Barbara: Older Migrants – Vulnerable and Excluded. 2024.

Vol. 36 Świder, Maciej: The Exercise of the Right to a Fair Trial in the Era of the COVID-19 Pandemic. 2024.

Vol. 37 Tomasz Barankiewicz / Boguslaw Przywora (eds): Public and Civil Service in Poland. 2024.

Vol. 38 Daniele Vicoli (ed.): Effective Justice 1. Effective Justice. International and Comparative Approaches. 2025.

www.peterlang.com

www.ingramcontent.com/pod-product-compliance
Ingram Content Group UK Ltd.
Pitfield, Milton Keynes, MK11 3LW, UK
UKHW021420091026
15624UKWH00010B/286

9 783631 902011